Le sammedi au matin le Roy dan gleterre se parti de la garde robe la royne qui seet en la riole et sen vint a Westmoustier et oyt messe en lesle et tous les seigneurs auecq lui En celle eglise a vne ymaige de nne dame en vne petite chapel le qui sait de beaux et nobles miracles En laquelle ymaise les roys dangleterre xpiens ont eu tousiours grant de uotion et considence le roy sist deuotement ses oroisons deuant cest ymaise et offri et puis monta a cheual et tous les barons aussi qui ento

lui estoient et pouoit estre enuiron heure de tierce le Roy et sa route cheuanche rent toutte la cheuauchee pour entrer en londres Et quant il eut cheuanche vn espace il tourna sur seneste pour passer au dehors et ne sauoit nul de verite ou quil vouloit aller car il prenoit le chemin pour passer au de hors de londres Ce propre iour au matin sestoient ras semblez et cueilliz tous les mauuais de ces paysans desquelz lautre tieulier Ja ques strau et Jehan balle estoient capitaines et leurs parlementer en vne grant

ENGLAND, ARISE

ALSO BY JULIET BARKER

The Brontës: Selected Poems

The Tournament in England 1100–1400

*Tournaments: Jousts, Chivalry and Pageants in
the Middle Ages (with Richard Barber)*

The Brontë Yearbook

The Brontës

The Brontës: A Life in Letters

Charlotte Brontë: Juvenilia 1829–35

Wordsworth: A Life

Wordsworth: A Life in Letters

Agincourt: The King, the Campaign, the Battle

*The Deafening Sound of Silent Tears:
The Story of Caring for Life*

Conquest: The English Kingdom of France 1417–1450

ENGLAND, ARISE

The People, the King
and the Great Revolt of 1381

JULIET BARKER

Little, Brown

LITTLE, BROWN

First published in Great Britain in 2014 by Little, Brown

Copyright © Juliet Barker 2014

The moral right of the author has been asserted.

Maps by John Gilkes

A CIP catalogue record for this book
is available from the British Library.

Hardback ISBN 978-1-4087-0335-9
C format ISBN 978-1-4087-0336-6

Typeset in Sabon by M Rules
Printed and bound in Great Britain
by Clays Ltd, St Ives plc

Papers used by Little, Brown are from well-managed forests
and other responsible sources.

MIX
Paper from
responsible sources
FSC® C104740

Little, Brown
An imprint of
Little, Brown Book Group
100 Victoria Embankment
London EC4Y 0DY

An Hachette UK Company
www.hachette.co.uk

www.littlebrown.co.uk

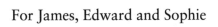
For James, Edward and Sophie

CONTENTS

PREFACE

In the summer of 1381 England erupted in a violent popular uprising that was as unexpected as it was unprecedented. Previous rebellions had always been led by ambitious and discontented noblemen seeking to overthrow the government and seize power for themselves. The so-called 'Peasants' Revolt' was led by commoners – most famously Wat Tyler, Jack Straw and John Balle – whose origins were obscure and whose moment at the forefront of events was brief. Even more unusually, they did not seek personal advancement but a radical political agenda which, if it had been implemented, would fundamentally have transformed English society: the abolition of serfdom and the dues and services owed by tenants to their lord of the manor; freedom from tolls and customs on buying and selling goods throughout the country; the recognition of a man's right to work for whom he chose at the wages he chose; the state's seizure of the Church's wealth and property. Their demands anticipated the French Revolution by four hundred years.

The main events of the rebellion are well known. The people of Essex and Kent were the first to rise, marched to London to confront the fourteen-year-old Richard II, sacked royal palaces and religious houses, and murdered the chief officers of state, including the chancellor and treasurer, who also happened to be two of the most senior clergymen in the kingdom, and the chief justice of the King's Bench. With London in flames around him, Richard was forced to give in to the rebels' demands, only to retrieve the situation after Tyler was murdered in front of him at Smithfield and exact a terrible vengeance on the 'rustics' who had dared to dictate to him. That, at least, is how the revolt is often described: a London-centric orgy of violence luridly characterised as a 'summer of blood' or 'a general riot of destruction and death'.[1]

By and large this was also the view of contemporary chroniclers, who were all clerics and nearly all monks. Almost to a man, therefore, they had neither sympathy nor genuine understanding of the rebels who had attacked their monastic houses and privileges and murdered their leaders. In their eyes rebellion was an unacceptable challenge to divinely appointed authority and the rebels were a bestial mob, ignorant, illiterate, barely capable of cogent language – though that did not stop Thomas Walsingham, the most accomplished storyteller of them all, from putting eloquent, if entirely fictitious, speeches into the mouths of Balle and Straw when it suited him. These chroniclers did not see it as their task to look beyond what they thought were simply wanton and indiscriminate acts of violence to appreciate *why* people and property were being attacked on such a massive scale. The widespread burning of court rolls, charters and administrative and legal records seemed to them an attack by ignorance on the accumulated wisdom of the ages, symbolised most memorably in the example of Margery Starr, who danced round the bonfire of the university of Cambridge's archives, throwing the ashes to the winds and crying, 'Away with the learning of clerks! Away with it!'[2]

To monks whose lives revolved around the scriptorium,

books and chronicling deeds past and present for the education of future generations, such acts had to be portrayed as incomprehensible except, perhaps, as the result of envy, wickedness or the moral corruption imbibed from the preaching of excommunicate heretics and troublemakers like John Balle. The chroniclers' accounts therefore have to be treated with caution because none of them wrote impartially and all of them had a didactic purpose in mind. It is true that many of them had access to important sources of information: Henry Knighton, an Augustinian canon at the abbey of St Mary Pratis, Leicester, and close to members of John of Gaunt's household at Leicester, was able to quote the duke's officials and acquired five of John Balle's letters, which he transcribed into his chronicle; as the official chronicler of his house, St Albans, Thomas Walsingham was able to make use of his abbey's extensive contacts, particularly with the court, was close to events in London and had a ringside seat for both the revolt in St Albans and the subsequent trials of rebels, including Balle, held there; Jean Froissart, the great chivalric historian, had spent seven years in the service of Edward III's wife, Queen Philippa, who was like him a Hainaulter by birth, and retained many contacts within the English court from whom he sought first-hand accounts of the great revolt. Nevertheless, even the best informed of these chroniclers, such as the author of the *Anonimalle*, which was written within a few years of the revolt, probably by a chancery clerk based in York, are riddled with factual errors, but when this is combined with a determination to create martyrs out of unlikely material and to demonise the rebels indiscriminately, the result can be toxic for historical accuracy – particularly when the author writes as persuasively and with as much colour as Walsingham or Froissart.

One might expect greater impartiality from the administrative and judicial records but these too present huge challenges for the unwary. The phrase '*vi et armis*', for instance, is regularly used in the indictments in connection with rebels entering property that did not belong to them; literally it means 'with force and arms', which conjures up images of a baying mob armed to the teeth, storming in and destroying everything in sight. In some instances that is what happened, but the phrase was always used in trespass cases to indicate that force was used, or an injury or damage was caused by force, even if it was accidental: a dentist was thus sued in 1361 for 'imprisoning and extracting' the patient's teeth 'with force and arms'.[3] Many of the incidents where force and arms were used may therefore have been as harmless as opening a closed gate or entering a property without the owner's permission. This must be borne in mind when reading of houses and parks being broken into by force.

The maxim that one man's terrorist is another man's freedom fighter is demonstrated repeatedly in the indictments. Time and again we hear of 'extortions' when money, property or bonds were handed over, allegedly as the result of threats to life and limb, or people being forcibly ejected from their tenements, which were then given to others. In many instances, however, these were not simple criminal acts of the moment, but had a history behind them which is often impossible to disentangle from the judicial charge; it might be an overdue debt, or a bond which had been fulfilled but was being unjustly retained instead of cancelled, or a disputed inheritance withheld or given to someone else by a corrupt escheator or manorial steward. The terminology of the indictment does not allow for the possibility that the accused might consider that their rebel actions were righting wrongs, not committing new ones.

Similarly, there are hundreds of examples in the judicial records of rebels ransacking properties, driving off livestock and taking everything from clothes to kitchen utensils. On the face of it this seems to be blatant theft, but consider the case of John Reve of Sutton, who in December 1380 complained that all his beasts, worth one hundred pounds, had been taken from him by force and arms and he had been compelled to pay one hundred shillings to get them back again. This was theft and robbery to him but the 'thieves' were John White, the sacristan of Ely, and a group of monks who had seized his goods in order to force him to admit that he was the priory's villein.[4] In other words, they were exerting the lord's legal but summary right to distrain a recalcitrant tenant. Since distraint was also commonly used to compel the performance of duties and obtain satisfaction for debts or damages, it is quite possible that the rebels believed that they were using the same process against corrupt officials who had acquired money and goods to which they were not entitled. Geoffrey Cobbe, for instance, supervised a two-day auction of the goods of one such official in Cambridgeshire. This was hardly the action of an impassioned peasant seeking vengeance on his wealthy oppressors: Cobbe was a member of the local gentry and took no further part in the rebellion, which suggests that he believed he was acting within the law.[5]

This brings us to the two main issues to emerge from this book. The first is the fact that this was not a 'peasants' revolt' at all. As with so many neat and enduring labels, including the Black Death, this was a name bestowed by nineteenth-century historians who equated the chroniclers' description of the rebels as *rustici*, meaning rural or country people, with peasants and serfs in particular. The problem with this term is that it is no longer simply a description of agricultural labourers or subsistence farmers, but has acquired a politically charged meaning which elevates the universalities of dogma above the differences of the particular. Marxist historians like Rodney Hilton identified the medieval English peasantry as a monolithic social class, inherently united in its opposition to lordship, which lived off the surplus of its labour. The 'Peasants' Revolt' therefore became understandable in terms of 'a separate peasant self-consciousness' and the 'inevitable antagonism' generated between the peasantry and its oppressors.[6] In other words, the 'Peasants' Revolt' was an unavoidable result of the age-old class struggle.

Recent scholarship has been more nuanced, demonstrating the wide social range of the rebels, from servants and labourers living off wages, through the village elite who served as bailiffs, constables and stewards, to the ranks of the gentry. The fact that such disparate people found a common cause is in itself more interesting but it makes the term 'Peasants' Revolt' redundant. Those in power tended to refer to it afterwards as 'the diabolical insurrection', 'the great insurrection' or, for good measure, 'the great and horrible rumour and insurrection', though the Bermondsey chronicler memorably described it as the year of 'the common people against the nobles of the kingdom of England, which is called "the Hurling"'.[7] Like most modern writers on the subject, I have deliberately avoided 'Peasants' Revolt' and substituted more generalised terms such as 'the great revolt'.

Where I part from most of them, however, is in trying to distinguish between 'real' or politically motivated incidents of rebellion and mere acts of criminality. Every major public disorder unleashes copycat violence and provides the opportunity for settling old scores or helping oneself to other people's property. This does not necessarily mean that such acts did not contribute to the uprising, or were not inspired by it. The activities of the Stathum family in Derbyshire,[8] for example, were part and parcel of their long-running feud with John of Gaunt, but would those particular actions have been taken at that particular time if the revolt had not made them possible?

To dismiss the uprising in York as a 'squalid and obscure municipal quarrel, which had obviously no relation to the general causes of the rebellion'[9] is to suggest that it was irrelevant. Yet the rioters in York were expressing their frustration at ecclesiastical privilege and abuse of civic power just as much as rebels elsewhere who sacked the properties of the Knights Hospitaller, burned the archives of religious houses and executed corrupt officials.

Recent scholarship has done much to widen the focus away from London to reveal the extent of the revolt across the country and its causes. The emphasis remains on the countryside, however; even today it seems we are still trapped by contemporary descriptions of it as a rebellion by *rustici*. While much good work has been done to elucidate the inter-dependence of town and country, the urban revolts have tended to be sidelined as the result of internal petty politics as opposed to the grand causes which inspired the countryside. The urban voice in shaping the rebels' agenda has been neglected, yet the abolition of tolls and customs was every bit as radical a demand as the abolition of villeinage. Men like Thomas atte Raven and John Ferrour, alias Marchall, to pick two examples at random from Rochester, Kent, were leading rebels in their own town but also in the uprising in London. And the root causes of rebellion in the towns were the same as in the countryside: anger and frustration at years of heavy taxation with nothing to show for it, oppressive tolls and customs exacted by landlords such as the abbeys of Bury St Edmunds and St Albans, punitive labour legislation, and corruption and extortion by officialdom. The urban uprisings were just as important and as legitimately part of the revolt as those in the countryside.

Another, perhaps more controversial, theme to this book is my argument that the boy-king sympathised with the grievances of the rebels, willingly granted the letters of manumission and pardon at Mile End and would have stood by them if he had not been overruled by his councillors and eventually by parliament as well. It is ironic that his attitude made a bad situation worse. I will argue that, because he did not revoke and cancel the letters until eighteen days after issuing them, the rebels felt that they had his authority to act as they did, encouraging the spread of the revolt and drawing in many who would not otherwise have become embroiled in what would later be defined as treason. William Grindecobbe and his fellow rebels at St Albans actually had royal letters, granted at Mile End, ordering the abbot to hand over the abbey's charters to the townsmen. Geoffrey Cobbe declared that he was acting on the king's commission when he auctioned off Haseldene's property. It should not be forgotten that these acts did not become 'crimes' or 'treasons' until the king changed his mind, or had it changed for him.

What will surprise most readers is that the three most famous protagonists of the revolt scarcely appear at all in my account. This is as much a source of frustration to me as it will be to them, but it is unavoidable. For despite the fact that John Balle, Wat Tyler and Jack Straw have achieved immortality as the heroic leaders of the revolt, there are remarkably few references to them in contemporary sources. Balle is the one about whom we know most but even he remains elusive in terms of both his character and the role he played in events. Tyler really only emerges from the shadows at the Smithfield meeting where he was assassinated; Straw is glimpsed so fleetingly that it is difficult to explain his continuing hold on the popular imagination. What the absence of these iconic figures does mean, however, is that other local leaders come to the fore. And that, surely, is a vitally important point to grasp. The great revolt was emphatically not inspired and led just by three charismatic men of the people. It was a many-headed hydra. In every locality different local leaders volunteered to take charge of the direction of events – men like John Wrawe, William Grindecobbe, John Hauchach, Thomas Sampson, Geoffrey Lister – and it was their specialised local knowledge which enabled their actions to be so effectively targeted and made them so dangerous. That there were so many of them indicates not only the depth of feeling across the country which caused the revolt in the first place but also the difficulty facing the government in trying to quell the rebellion. It was not simply a question of catching and executing Balle, Tyler and Straw so that the rebels would be leaderless and easily dispersed. There were local leaders in every rebel area, many of whom already held positions of authority, and each of whom had their own particular local grievances to be addressed. It was this multiple leadership which made the great revolt the most serious popular rebellion in England's history.

What I hope emerges from this book is a more comprehensive overview of the revolt than has hitherto been published: one that attempts to answer the questions why, how and who, though sometimes it can only raise them. There is another purpose underpinning this. The great uprising brought into focus the vast majority of people whose lives and concerns were usually beneath the notice of the chroniclers. Even at this critical moment contemporaries dismissed them as 'the commons', or treated them as an amorphous mass, but the records of the revolt provide a rare opportunity to identify individuals and tell their stories. In doing so we gain a far richer insight into what life was like in England in 1381 and, I hope, a more balanced view of medieval society as a whole.

Inevitably, as research continues, more will emerge which will enhance or change some of the conclusions I have reached, but the immense amount of scholarship on which I have drawn should be acknowledged. The bibliography alone attests to that but the work of five scholars in this field deserves special mention. André Réville's compendium of original administrative and judicial documents, *Le Soulèvement des Travailleurs d'Angleterre en 1381* (Paris, 1898), remains the most valuable resource of its kind on the subject. R. B. Dobson's more accessible and chronicle-driven sourcebook, *The Peasants' Revolt of 1381* (Macmillan, 1970), first drew attention to the extent of the revolt outside London and is still the best starting point for any study of the rebellion. The indefatigable work in local manorial records of Christopher Dyer, in particular, has mined a rich seam of social and cultural history which has transformed our understanding of who the rebels were and why they were drawn into revolt. Equally painstaking and revelatory is the analysis of judicial records undertaken by Andrew Prescott, which sheds light not only on the identity of individual rebels, their motives and their organisation, but also on the chronology of the revolt and the many incidents of sometimes startling importance which passed unnoticed by the chroniclers. Finally, Carolyn Fenwick's superb three-volume edition, *The Poll Taxes of 1377, 1379 and 1381* (The British Academy, 2001–5), is a mine of fascinating information and an essential resource for any study of this period.

The internet has long been a poisoned chalice for historians but there are now several sites which offer scholarly information and access to primary sources in a way that transforms the ability to write history. Chief among these are the databases of *The Soldier in Later Medieval England*, *The History of Parliament Online*, *The Oxford Dictionary of National Biography* and the links to original sources provided by *British History Online* and *Medieval Source Material on the Internet*, the last of which is provided by www.medieval genealogy.org.uk.[10] The National Archives also offer a comprehensive and useful online catalogue and an efficient copying service for manuscripts. I would not

have been able to write this book without access to the more traditional library services offered by the University of Leeds and
the Bodleian Library, Oxford, for which I am grateful. I am
indebted to Charles Dent, DL, Ewen Cameron and Sir Evelyn
Webb-Carter for expert advice on the distances achievable by
rebels riding on horseback and to my agent, Andrew Lownie, for
his support as always. I would also like to thank Harvard
University Press's outside readers – Dr Benjamin Thompson of
Somerville College, Oxford, and a second anonymous reader –
who read the first draft of this book, corrected many mistakes
and offered numerous helpful comments; any errors that remain
are entirely my responsibility. I owe especial thanks to my editor,
Tim Whiting, for his constructive criticism and undiminished
enthusiasm for a book which has been difficult to write. There
have been many times when I have joined in Walsingham's
heartfelt lament that 'A confused series of events happening
simultaneously in many places necessitates a disordered way of
writing history: hardly any logical order of composition can be
maintained when so many crimes were committed in so many
different areas at the same time'.[11] Tim has helped to create
order out of chaos and the book now falls naturally into two
parts: the first is a snapshot of life in England in 1381 which
helps to explain how and why the revolt happened; the second
is a description and analysis of the revolt itself. However, the
book must be dedicated to those who have suffered most in its
creation, the three stars in my firmament, James, Edward and
Sophie.

A NOTE TO THE TEXT

References in the text to money are always in pounds (£), shillings (s.), pence (d.) and marks (m.): one pound was worth twenty shillings, a shilling twelve pence and a mark 13s. 4d. For those who like to work out comparisons with contemporary values, according to www.measuringworth.com, using calculations based on the retail price index, £1 in 1381 was worth £620 at the end of 2012.

I have followed standard editorial practice in modernising the spelling of place names so that they can be identified more easily, but I have not done so for personal names, preferring to use the versions most often given in contemporary sources. John Balle is always referred to in that form, so I have adopted that, rather than the modern spelling; there are several variant spellings of Wat Tyler's name, so for consistency I have preferred that to Tegheler or Tiler. I have not attempted to track the changing titles of Edward III's sons, preferring to use John of Gaunt, Thomas of Woodstock and Edmund of Langley as contemporaries did.

Population figures are, at best, intelligent guesswork and vary wildly according to the methods used to assess them. Wherever possible I have taken my figures from the poll-tax returns of 1377. As these exclude children under fourteen and those loosely termed 'genuine beggars', the true figures are likely to be at least double those I have given.

Distances are calculated using the walking calculation on www.maps.google.co.uk.

CHAPTER ONE

The end of an era

On 21 June 1377 King Edward III of England lay on his deathbed at Sheen, a royal manor house on the banks of the Thames at Richmond, just outside London. He was sixty-four years old – a good age for a medieval monarch – and even more remarkably was in the fifty-first year of his reign. But the man who lay dying was no longer the charismatic and commanding figure he had once been. A wooden funeral effigy, created from his death-mask and still preserved in Westminster Abbey, reveals the strong features, prominent forehead and aquiline nose of his Plantagenet ancestry but also the drooping at the corner of his mouth typical of a stroke victim. The impressive muscular physique which had enabled him to excel on the battlefield and in the tournament lists had become wasted and enfeebled. Even more cruelly, the series of strokes which had taken their toll on his health and strength over the previous five years had also destroyed his mind and character. Long gone were the force of personality and political acumen which had transformed England from a kingdom torn apart by internal factional squabbles into one of the greatest military powers in Europe.

Edward had withdrawn from court and government and in his last years had rarely been seen in public, appearing only occasionally when required to preside at state occasions: even then he cut a pitiable figure, having to be propped upright in his chair, unable to speak and looking 'like a statue'. Sometimes he was borne prostrate and hidden from curious eyes on a covered barge along the Thames between the palace of Westminster in the city of London and his beloved country manor houses at Sheen, Rotherhithe and Havering-atte-Bower. These offered him the peace, privacy and comfort not available at court; surrounded by parkland and gardens, they had all been lavishly refurbished in recent years to incorporate the latest modern conveniences such as mechanical clocks and hot water piped into the king's baths.[1]

For a man who throughout his long career had inspired extraordinary personal loyalty it was a particular tragedy that, at the end, he had been deserted by those who had once looked to him for decisive leadership and friendship. He had outlived most of the friends with whose aid his greatest triumphs had been won and many of the next generation, including his own son and heir the Black Prince, had also died before him. Ambitious young men no longer looked to him for advancement but to his sons and the court from which Edward himself was to all intents and purposes exiled by his physical and mental incapacity. The all-powerful monarch before whom the captive kings of France and Scotland had once been forced to bend the knee was now effectively a prisoner in his own household, which was dominated by the malign presence of his mistress, Alice Perrers. Since the death of Queen Philippa in 1369 Alice had openly flaunted her position and influence. She stood at the head of Edward's bed when he received officials, enriched herself and her favourites at his expense and scandalised Londoners in 1374 by appearing at a tournament presided over by the ailing king as 'Lady of the Sun' – her costume being an impertinent reference to their relationship since Edward's personal heraldic badge was a golden sun.[2]

The chronicler Thomas Walsingham, a monk of St Albans who, as we shall see later, did not scruple to bend facts to fit his own particular brand of proselytising history, gives a particularly poignant description of Edward's last hours. Paralysed and robbed of speech by his latest stroke, the helpless king was deserted by his household, who, as it became apparent that he would not survive the night, all slipped away with whatever they could carry, leaving behind only a solitary priest to administer the last rites. Alice, 'that unspeakable whore', sat at the king's bedside until his breath began to fail him – then made off with the rings she had snatched from his fingers. Though almost certainly apocryphal, the story neatly epitomises how contemporaries viewed the king's mistress – and it was undoubtedly true that by the time Edward died Alice had acquired not only jewels worth over three thousand pounds (including a selection which had belonged to the late queen) but also lands in fifteen counties. The dignity denied Edward III in his final years was accorded to him in death by his successor: his tomb, in Edward the Confessor's chapel at the abbey, was adorned with a noble gilt-bronze effigy which bore only a passing resemblance to the more unforgiving and lifelike representation based on the death-mask. Serene and authoritative in expression, with the flowing locks and luxuriant beard of a prophet or sage, the king reposes above a legend proclaiming him 'the glory of the English, the paragon of past kings, the model of future kings, a merciful king, the peace of the peoples ... the unconquered leopard'.[3]

Those who looked back to Edward's reign in the troubled years of his successors would regard it as a golden age. He had presided over one of the longest periods of domestic peace in the history of medieval England. What is more, in an age when such things mattered, his unprecedented success in his military campaigns, particularly in France, had demonstrated that he was the chivalric monarch par excellence: 'famous and fortunate in war; in all his battles, by land and sea, he always won the day and triumphed gloriously'. He had inflicted three major defeats on the French, at Sluys (1340), Crécy (1346) and Poitiers (1356), conquered Calais and its marches (1347), turning them into an English enclave which would endure for two centuries, and laid claim to the crown of France itself. It was no wonder that Froissart, the greatest chivalric historian of the day, lamented his passing by declaring that 'his like had not been seen since the days of King Arthur'.[4]

Yet even as the old warrior king lay dying one of the largest French invasion forces ever yet assembled was gathering across the Channel. The truce with England would come to an end on 24 June and Charles V of France had spent years preparing for this moment. What he envisaged was no less than an all-out assault on England and its dependent territories. He had reformed the royal arsenal at Rouen, begun a huge shipbuilding programme and recruited further naval reinforcements from his Castilian allies. By the beginning of June some fifty or sixty ships were awaiting his orders at Harfleur, including thirty-seven galleys, the most feared of all warships, equipped with cannons capable of firing stones and lead shot and manned by three thousand armed seamen, 3500 crossbowmen and several hundred men-at-arms. For the first time in forty years, the French were about to take the war to England.[5]

The onslaught began barely a week after Edward's death and less than seventy miles from Sheen, where he had died. The

French admiral Jean de Vienne landed his fleet unopposed on the Sussex coast and seized the port of Rye, which he held for several days before reducing it to ashes and carrying off a number of its wealthiest citizens as prisoners, together with a large haul of booty. Over the next few weeks he struck repeatedly and with similar success, raiding as far west as Plymouth in Devon and as far east as Dover in Kent, burning and pillaging some of England's most important Channel ports: Winchelsea, Folkestone, Portsmouth, Weymouth, Poole, Dartmouth, Southampton and Hastings were also attacked and most were put to the torch, as were Yarmouth, Newtown and Newport on the Isle of Wight. The government had received intelligence six months earlier that just such a campaign was in the offing but little had been done to prepare for the onslaught. Plans had indeed been laid for a naval expedition to be led by the king's son, John of Gaunt. Merchant ships had been requisitioned for service and 3940 men had been signed up for the campaign and paid the first instalment of their wages, but the death of Edward III at the critical moment when the truces lapsed threw everything into confusion. No one of any note, least of all Gaunt himself, had any intention of absenting themselves from court at this critical time in the political life of the nation. All preparations for the campaign were therefore suspended, so that when Jean de Vienne led his first wave of attacks on the south coast in June and July there was nothing in place to resist him. Worse still, of the twenty-seven ships in the king's navy in 1369, only five were left in service: against the might of the combined Franco-Castilian fleet they were helpless.[6]

The terrified and despairing inhabitants of the south coast were therefore left to fend for themselves. No English fleet patrolled the Channel to protect the southern coast, vulnerable town walls were non-existent or had fallen into disrepair and aristocrats with castles in the area, including Gaunt, had failed to put them on a war-footing. The French were able to make daring lightning strikes without meeting any serious resistance. Their raiding parties leapt from the Castilian galleys as they swept into port at high tide, fired any ships in the harbour to prevent a pursuit and, in the three hours before they departed on the ebb tide, inflicted as much damage as possible.[7]

In the absence of the local aristocrats who should have taken the lead in defending their estates and the realm, it fell to the other great landowners, local churchmen, to shoulder the burden. The day after the French seized Rye, Abbot Hamo of Battle Abbey became a local hero by donning his hauberk, wielding his crossbow and personally leading the county levies to neighbouring Winchelsea, which stood between Rye and the beached French fleet. Not only did he refuse to discuss terms with the invaders but, when they attacked his forces, success-fully fought them off, compelling them to abandon their occupation of Rye – only for them to sack Hastings instead. Several days later, the prior of St Pancras at Lewes, head of the most important Cluniac house in England, tried to repel the invaders at Rottingdean but the Sussex levies he commanded were slaughtered and he was himself among the prisoners taken back to France; his unfortunate monks not only lost their crops and suffered flooding owing to the destruction of their sea defences but also had to find a crippling ransom of £4666 to obtain his release a year later. The abbot of St Augustine's at Canterbury rallied the local Kent levies and succeeded in driv-ing the invaders out of Folkestone, though not before they had already burned much of the town. Where such spirited leader-ship was missing local people had no choice but to buy their freedom from attack: the Isle of Wight only escaped further destruction after the burning of its three main towns by paying the French one thousand marks simply to go away.[8]

It was not an auspicious start to the new reign but it was a highly significant one. Forty years after the outbreak of what would misleadingly become known as the Hundred Years War, the tide of victory was no longer running in England's favour. The epic battles and successes of the 1340s and 1350s were a distant memory; the war in Spain, where the French and English had continued their struggle by proxy on behalf of the rival contenders for the Castilian throne, had seen a resounding English success at the battle of Nájera in 1367 – but that had been negated by the death of their claimant two years later and his opponent's accession to the throne. The French king, whose defeat and capture at the battle of Poitiers had led to the humiliating Treaty of Brétigny and the concession of great tracts of French territory to his English rival, had died a hostage for his still-unpaid ransom in London in 1364 – but his successor, Charles V, had proved an altogether more able adversary than his father. He had renewed the military and political 'auld alliance' with Scotland, supported the efforts of Owen Lawgoch, a mercenary in his service who claimed lineal descent from the last Welsh princes, to foment rebellion in Wales and forged offensive and defensive agreements with the new king of Castile. More importantly, by 1375, under the leadership of Bertrand du Guesclin, a professional soldier whom he had controversially appointed Constable of France, his armies had recovered almost all the lands that had been ceded to the English at Brétigny.

In the face of these setbacks the English had turned once again to the tried and tested tactic which had formerly brought them such success: the *chevauchée*. Like the French naval raids on the English coast in 1377, though land-based, these were fast-moving military campaigns to spread terror and devastation among the civilian population by killing, burning and pillaging and to draw the enemy out to engage in battle. Under the wise guidance of du Guesclin, however, the French armies refused to take the bait and a series of expeditions launched in 1370, headed by the mercenary captain Robert Knolles, and in 1373 and 1375 under the leadership of Edward III's sons, John of Gaunt and Edmund of Langley respectively, failed to achieve anything. Lack of success in the field was made incomparably worse by the heavy losses which marked these fruitless campaigns: an army bound for English Gascony in 1372 was ambushed at sea off La Rochelle and both the fleet and the expeditionary force it carried were totally destroyed by France's Castilian allies; the following year, after his raid from Calais to the borders of Burgundy, Gaunt lost more than half his men by marching them across France to Bordeaux in the depths of a bitter winter. Perhaps even more frustrating was Edmund of Langley's expedition to Brittany in 1375, which had to be aborted within weeks of its arrival – not by defeat, but by his brother Gaunt's conclusion of a truce with France. An otherwise welcome respite from war was thus soured by the need to abandon an expensive campaign which, unusually, had begun well and promised better.[9]

Where was the great warrior king himself during these years of 'abject and costly failure'?[10] Edward's last personal intervention in the war occurred in 1372 when he decided to avenge the disaster at La Rochelle by raising a large army and leading it himself to Gascony. He never arrived. Contrary winds prevented his fleet leaving English waters (it took three weeks just to sail the fifty-odd miles from Sandwich to Winchelsea) and, after five weeks at sea, he was forced to abandon his plans and return home without even setting foot in the duchy. Whether it was the humiliation of this futile expedition after so many great victories, or simply a growing awareness of his own frailty, Edward now increasingly retreated from his public role. His lack of engagement with his daily duties in his last years created a serious problem for a realm and government which depended on the king as the ultimate source of all authority. More than a decade before his death Edward had declined the king of Cyprus's urgent invitation to join his crusade against the Mamluk Turks on the grounds, he said then, that 'I am too old. I shall leave it to my children'.[11] He might have hoped that his offspring would also help him bear the burden of kingship in his declining years: there were, after all, plenty of them. His queen had borne him at least twelve, including four daughters and five sons who had survived into adulthood, though their third son, Lionel of Antwerp, had died shortly before his thirtieth birthday in 1368.

First and foremost among the royal children was Edward's son and heir, Edward, known since Tudor times as the Black Prince, who for three decades had proved his mettle by leading his troops into victory on the fields of Crécy, Poitiers and Nájera. In addition to the customary titles of earl of Chester, earl of Cornwall and prince of Wales granted to him in childhood, Edward had also been created the first prince of Aquitaine. This was a deeply symbolic act, for Aquitaine, or Gascony as the English preferred to call it, was actually a duchy subject to the French crown which had been inherited by English kings after the marriage of Eleanor of Aquitaine and Henry II. Its status had long been a source of dispute and conflict between the two kingdoms, leading ultimately to the outbreak of the Hundred Years War in 1337. Edward III's military victories since then had forced the Treaty of Brétigny upon the French, compelling them to recognise Gascony as a sovereign state owned by the English crown. Accordingly, in 1362, Edward had granted the 'principality' for life to his eldest son to rule as a 'true prince', owing a nominal ounce of gold annually to his father in recognition of his ultimate authority, but otherwise holding it as a virtually independent

state.[12] The following summer the prince sailed for Bordeaux
with his new bride, Joan of Kent, and for the next nine years
he ruled his new principality with an insensitivity which was
not calculated to endear him to his subjects: virtually his last
act there was to raze the city of Limoges to the ground for its
temerity in surrendering too hastily to the French. Decades of
fighting in foreign fields had taken their toll on his health, however, and at the beginning of 1371 he returned permanently to
England with his wife and their son, four-year-old Richard,
who had been born at Bordeaux.[13]

The return of the heir to the throne should have been an
opportunity to bolster the monarchy but the prince was in no
position to take up the reins of government that were slipping
from Edward III's grasp. He was already sicker than his father.
Though from time to time he would put in an appearance on
state occasions, he rarely travelled more than fifty miles from
London and could no more cope with the minutiae of royal
business than Edward himself. For five more years he lingered
on, his illness as much a mystery to his physicians as it is to historians today, eventually dying, as he had piously wished to do,
on Trinity Sunday 1376. Contemporary chroniclers were lavish
in their praise of this 'second Hector'.

> When he died, all the hopes of the English died with him. As
> long as he survived, they feared no enemy's invasion, and,
> while he was in the field, no shock of war. While he was
> present, the English had never suffered the disgrace of a
> campaign that had been badly fought or abandoned. He
> attacked no nation that he did not conquer. He besieged no
> city that he did not capture.[14]

The criticism of other military leaders implicit in this obituary
was probably justified but the prince's eulogists might have been

less fulsome had he been well enough, or lived long enough, to take an equally active and personal role in England's governance. Impatient and unsubtle by temperament, he had no natural inclination for politics and his diplomatic and administrative record, particularly in Gascony, where he had effectively exercised supreme authority, varied 'from the competent to the disastrous'.[15] Such was the king that England never had, for, by predeceasing his father, Edward never had the chance to tarnish his reputation in that realm by ineffective or divisive government. That distinction would pass instead to his brother and to his son, both of whom shared his autocratic tendencies but not his military skill.

The prince died just a week before his forty-sixth birthday, leaving as heir to the throne his nine-year-old son, Richard. Almost immediately the House of Commons petitioned Edward III that the boy should be recognised as prince of Wales and brought before the parliament then sitting 'so that the lords and commons of the realm could see and honour the said Richard as the true heir apparent of the realm'. The unseemly haste of this intervention, not to mention the pointed reference to the 'true' heir apparent, seems to have been fuelled by fears that Richard's uncle, John of Gaunt, might seize the throne for himself. Whether Gaunt genuinely harboured such ambitions it is now impossible to determine; it seems unlikely but it is telling that such suspicions were already being voiced even before the old king died. There were good reasons for this. A child-king was a prospect dreaded by all medieval societies since it created a vacuum at the heart of government which laid the realm open to faction and abuse of power: a powerful, experienced adult, particularly one of the royal blood, might therefore be an attractive alternative. And there was no one in the entire kingdom more powerful than John of Gaunt. The deaths of his three older brothers had now made him the eldest of Edward

III's legitimate sons but, since the age of twenty-two, he had also been the richest nobleman in the country having inherited, through his wife, the dukedom of Lancaster and earldoms of Derby, Leicester and Lincoln. His gross annual income of around twelve thousand pounds was more than double that of any other English aristocrat.[16]

Gaunt was obviously aware that, once his ailing father died, his young nephew would be all that stood between himself and the throne. He did indeed have his heart set on becoming king – but it was not the crown of England to which he aspired. After the death of his first wife he had married again, this time to Constanza, the elder of the two daughters of Pedro I, king of Castile, on whose behalf the English had fought the battle of Nájera. By this means Gaunt had obtained a claim, by right of his wife, to the throne of Castile, which was currently occupied by his father-in-law's murderer, the pro-French Henry of Trastamara. If Gaunt could gain acceptance of his claim by persuasion or main force he would not only win himself a kingdom but also remove one of France's most important allies, thereby protecting both England and Gascony from the depredations of the much-feared Castilian navy. In 1372, therefore, with the approval of Edward III and his advisers, Gaunt had formally adopted the title 'king of Castile and Léon'; a few months later his younger brother Edmund of Langley married Constanza's sister Isabella to reinforce the link between the two dynasties and prevent anyone else acquiring a claim to Pedro's former throne. However remote, unattainable and even irrelevant Gaunt's ambitions might have seemed to the ordinary man in the street or the field, their repercussions would be felt at every level of society over the next fifteen years. His preoccupation with them would influence, and sometimes dictate, his policies at home and abroad.[17] And throughout the long years of his father's and brother's debilitating illnesses, followed by his nephew's minority, his pre-eminent position meant that his policies were often those of the government.

Not even his brothers were in a position to challenge Gaunt. Edmund of Langley, though only a year younger, lacked the family enthusiasm and aptitude for war. Despite his taking part in numerous military expeditions, his leadership was in name only and he was never entrusted with sole command. Described by Froissart as 'indolent, guileless, and peaceable', Edmund had accepted the choice of bride dictated by his brother's Castilian ambitions even though this deprived him of the opportunity to make a financially advantageous marriage as Gaunt himself had done. Although his father had created him earl of Cambridge and granted him an annuity of one thousand marks in 1362, Edmund never acquired the great estates which would have given him the resources and influence to make him a major player in the affairs of the realm.[18] The same was also true of Edward III's youngest son, Thomas of Woodstock. He was born more than thirteen years after Edmund, and his father had intended to provide for him by marrying him to Eleanor de Bohun, the elder daughter and co-heiress of the earl of Hereford, in 1374. As his bride was then just eight years old Woodstock was given custody of her lands until she came of age and could inherit them in her own right; he was also appointed to her family's hereditary office of constable of England. Any hope of acquiring the entire Bohun inheritance that he might have cherished would be thwarted in 1380 when Gaunt took advantage of his brother's absence on campaign to marry Eleanor's younger sister and co-heiress, Mary, to his own son and heir, Henry, earl of Derby, an act which permanently divided the vast Bohun lands and left Thomas with a festering sense of resentment at the injury done to him. Thomas was the only one of all Edward III's adult sons to whom he did not give an earldom: that honour would have to wait till the eve of his nephew's coronation, when he was created earl of Buckingham and granted an annuity of a thousand pounds – a sum which was entirely dependent on the continuation of war with France since it was derived from the revenues of French-owned priories which were always taken into the king's hands during times of conflict.[19]

Gaunt had no doubt expected that he would be appointed regent for Richard when Edward III died in 1377 but, surprisingly, no plans had been drawn up to anticipate the delicate but inevitable situation of a child inheriting the throne. In the last months of his life Edward had indeed drafted letters patent[20] which entailed the crown on his male heirs and set out the order of succession on his demise: his grandson Richard was first in line but, in the absence of heirs of his body, the crown was to go to John of Gaunt. The legal status of the document is doubtful as it does not appear to have been enrolled or even made public, but the principle that the crown descended to the eldest son, and to his eldest son after him, was already well established in England. Even so it was not necessarily a foregone conclusion that Richard would succeed his grandfather. In 1199 King John had set aside the claims of his elder brother's twelve-year-old son Arthur of Brittany to take the throne himself. It was a precedent that could easily have been repeated in 1377 – and throughout his nephew's minority Gaunt would be haunted by persistent rumours that he intended to seize the crown for himself – but Edward III clearly intended that his grandson should succeed him. He had effectively endorsed him as his heir apparent by creating him prince of Wales in November 1376 and, in his last public act, by dubbing him a knight and admitting him to the Order of the Garter on St George's Day 1377, but he had made no provision for how the boy's reign would work in practice. There was little previous experience to draw on as there had only been one minority since the Norman Conquest. Before

King John died in 1216 he had appointed a council of thirteen
to 'assist' his nine-year-old son – a burden which the council
almost immediately offloaded on their foremost member,
William Marshal, who became 'guardian of our person and of
our realm'.[21] Gaunt was an executor of the old king's will, as he
had been of his brother's, but neither appointed him to a position of authority over Richard's person or realm.[22]

If the idea was ever mooted that Gaunt should become
regent it was quickly abandoned: unlike Marshal, he was not a
man around whom people could rally or unite. In fact he was
widely considered the most unpopular man in the kingdom. He
was blamed not only for the expensive military failures of the
early 1370s but also for his crass and high-handed behaviour
during the last years of his father's reign. Instead, the business
of running the country in King Richard II's name was delegated
to a continual council composed of two earls, two bishops, two
barons, two knights banneret and four knights. Neither Gaunt
nor his brothers had a place on it, though as the king's uncles
their status guaranteed them a role in directing state affairs
which, in Gaunt's case, was further reinforced by the influence
brought him by his unparalleled wealth.[23]

It was not until the middle of August that the council finally
threw off its paralysis and began to organise its response to the
renewal of war. By that time, not only had the south coast of
England been ravaged, but Calais was under siege by land and
sea and Gascony's defences had collapsed in the face of a
French invasion which had captured major towns, as well as the
English seneschal himself, and was now even threatening the
capital, Bordeaux.[24] Disaster and humiliation loomed on every
front.

England in 1381

CHAPTER TWO

The state of the nation

On Thursday 16 July 1377, eleven days after Edward III's solemn interment in Westminster Abbey, his ten-year-old grandson returned to the abbey church and knelt on the cushions before the high altar. There he swore a sacred oath to uphold the laws and customs of his ancestors, to protect the Church and clergy, to do justice to all and to uphold the laws which the people would 'justly and reasonably' choose. He was then anointed with holy oil, handed the three symbols of his authority – the sword to protect the kingdom, the sceptre to chastise wrongdoing and the ring signifying his pastoral responsibilities – and finally crowned. Perhaps in a concession to his age after the long service, he was carried from the church to receive the acclamation of his people on the shoulders of his tutor, Sir Simon Burley, but, in the press of the crowd, he lost one of the slippers of St Edmund which were part of the coronation regalia.[1] On a day of such pageantry and symbolism this was unfortunate but apt: a boy-king would inevitably struggle to fill the shoes of his predecessors.

The kingdom Richard inherited from his grandfather was bounded on three sides by the sea. It stretched across England from the North Sea in the east, across the principality of Wales, which had been annexed to the crown by his great-great-grandfather, Edward I, to the Irish Sea and Atlantic Ocean in the west, and from the Channel coast in the south up to the border with Scotland in the north. Despite English efforts to enforce lordship over Scottish kings, the realm remained fiercely independent and a constant threat to the peace and stability of the border region and also of the wider kingdom. Farther afield, English crown possessions included the Isle of Man in the west and the Channel Islands off the French coast, the latter being all that remained of the English duchy of Normandy lost by King John in 1204. English kings also claimed the lordship of Ireland – a euphemism for an authority over the numerous petty Irish kingdoms which had been asserted since Norman times but was barely enforceable outside a small area around Dublin known as the Pale; the native Irish who lived outside this enclave were regarded as being ungovernable, giving rise to the phrase 'beyond the Pale'. Few English kings ever ventured to set foot in Ireland, Richard himself being a rare exception.

Far more valuable and important in English eyes were the two crown possessions on the continent. The duchy of Gascony extended some 120 miles along the western seaboard of France from the city of Bordeaux (Richard's birthplace) in the north to that of Bayonne in the south but beyond that secure area fluctuated enormously in size according to the fortunes of war. And rapidly acquiring even greater significance was Edward III's conquest just across the English Channel from Dover, the port of Calais and its marches, which spread roughly ten miles in each direction from the town and were guarded by a ring of small fortresses. Both Gascony and Calais were vital to English trading interests. Gascon wine and salt were both highly prized commodities at a time when water was generally unfit to drink and the life of fresh food, particularly meat and fish, could only be prolonged in changeable climates by salting or smoking. The ships that brought these cargoes to England returned with corn, wool, cloth and hides, as well as the salted herrings that were the staple diet of all Christians on the fasting days of Friday and Lent.[2] Calais was both an important garrison and bridgehead into France for military campaigns but also, since 1363, the site of the Staple, or monopoly, on all sales of wool and hides exported from England. The merchants of the Staple company controlled the quality and quantity of goods sold abroad, ensured that the king received his customs duties, and regulated transactions between English and foreign merchants. Their members included the richest and most important merchants in England and, although they were not necessarily resident in Calais, they were nationally influential and significant, not least because they exploited the hugely important cloth markets of the Low Countries on their doorstep and regularly lent money to the crown.[3]

Even at this early period, England was already a seafaring nation. John of Gaunt, in one of Shakespeare's most memorable speeches, would describe the realm as

> This fortress built by Nature for herself
> Against infection and the hand of war ...
> This precious stone set in the silver sea,
> Which serves it in the office of a wall,
> Or as a moat defensive to a house,
> Against the envy of less happier lands.[4]

The sea did indeed serve as a 'moat defensive' but it was also a key factor in England's economy. In a country ranging over fifty thousand square miles of land nowhere was more than seventy-five miles from the coast and a large network of navigable rivers reduced even that distance significantly. As a consequence both personal travel and bulk transportation of goods were often swifter, easier and cheaper than simply using roads, which had to be maintained to be effective, required both bridges strong enough to withstand heavy traffic and an abundant supply of horses and draught animals to cover any distance, and were frequently made impassable by bad weather or difficult terrain. The rivers teemed with boats of every shape and size: coracles, propelled by a single oar and made from basketwork covered with animal hide for the single fisherman or reed-gatherer; larger and sturdier wherries, which were rowed or poled across rivers and marshes to ferry passengers and their horses; shallow clinker-built barges, the workhorses of the river, designed for the bulk transportation of heavy goods such as the iron arrow-heads manufactured in Yorkshire and carried down the Ouse for transportation by sea to the Tower of London. Some of these barges were equipped with a sail and seaworthy: hugging the coastline, they brought a regular supply of coals from Newcastle to feed London's insatiable demand for domestic and industrial fuel. Larger ocean-going vessels, known as cogs, carracks and balingers, usually single-masted with a deeper keel and sometimes with 'castles', or half-decks at the bow and stern, made the longer international journeys to and from the markets of the Baltic and Mediterranean.[5]

If England was first and foremost a trading nation this was because its temperate climate and fertile soils, particularly in the south and east, allowed it to produce a surplus to sell. Unlike in more arid areas of Europe, there was little subsistence farming in the late fourteenth century. In every village or hamlet there were undoubtedly some people who struggled to make ends meet and to feed their families from what they could grow themselves; the northernmost counties on the borders with Scotland also had a higher proportion of people scratching a bare living from land which was less suitable for arable crops and also regularly subject to slash-and-burn raids by the Scots. Generally speaking, however, the majority of those working the land were able to produce more than they could consume, even if it was only a few vegetables, a clutch of eggs or several pats of butter, all of which found ready markets in neighbouring villages and towns.

What is more, farming on a larger scale had become much more common, with entrepreneurial individuals building up substantial estates dedicated to animal husbandry, which was less labour-intensive than growing crops to eat and produced meat, hides and the all-important wool upon which so much of the nation's wealth depended. It was no coincidence that the fourteenth century saw a transformation in the diet of the English lower classes from one composed mainly of cheap cereals, beans and pulses, with coarse black bread (made from rye or barley) and the occasional flitch of bacon to one with a high proportion of meat, particularly beef and mutton, and bread made from wheat. Though domestically brewed small beer with its low alcohol content remained a household staple, the demand for professionally brewed strong ale also increased: manorial officials at one Sussex manor in 1354 had to buy in ale to replace the cider normally offered to its reapers because the reeve in charge 'would not drink anything but ale in the whole of the harvest time'.[6]

That workers were able to imitate their superiors by demanding – and receiving – better-quality food and drink was in no small measure due to the greatest natural catastrophe to befall the Middle Ages. The first outbreak of the great plague now referred to as the Black Death occurred in England in the summer of 1348. The disease arrived from the continent, by August it had reached London and by the following summer it had spread throughout the country. Precisely what it was or how it was transmitted is still debated, though recent analysis of skeletons found in plague pits seems to confirm that it was caused by an early variant of the *Yersinia pestis* bacterium, which causes bubonic and pneumonic plague. The symptoms, as described by contemporaries, certainly point that way: the sudden appearance of egg-shaped swellings in the groin, neck and armpits and the equally sudden haemorrhaging and vomiting of blood, which both presaged immediate death. The shocking nature of the disease was compounded by its indiscriminate choice of victim: rich and poor, young and old, town and country dwellers, laymen and churchmen all succumbed; there was no cure, no palliative, and people who had appeared fit and healthy one day were struck down and died a few days later. Whole families, sometimes whole communities, were wiped out. In the city and suburbs of Rochester, Kent, fifty per cent of the priory's tenants died; it was the same story in the Cambridgeshire manor of Cottenham, the Norfolk manor of Hakeford Hall in Coltishall and, in the north of England, on the estates of Durham priory, where the death rates on some manors reached as high as seventy-eight per cent.

Parish priests who visited the sick and dying were particularly at risk from infection and in 1349 more than eight hundred died in the diocese of Norwich alone. St Mary's Abbey at Malling, Kent, lost three abbesses in the space of three weeks and was reduced to just four nuns and four novices, while the brothers in the small Augustinian houses of Alnesbourne and Chipley in Suffolk were wiped out completely; even the hugely wealthy and privileged abbey of Bury St Edmunds, Suffolk, one of the greatest Benedictine houses in the country, lost forty per cent of its monks. 'So great a multitude was not swept away, it was believed, even by the flood that happened in the days of Noah', wrote one monastic chronicler. It was a catastrophe on an apocalyptic scale which was explicable only to a medieval society familiar with the biblical stories of Noah's flood and of the ten plagues inflicted on the Egyptians (which included boils, blood and death of the first-born) as God's punishment for sin. The survivors therefore flocked to their churches to do penance and seek forgiveness: the golden shrine of one of England's most popular saints, Thomas Becket, at Canterbury Cathedral cannot have been the only object of pilgrimage to receive a massive boost to its funds as a direct result of penitential alms-giving in the wake of the first onset of the plague.[7]

As a result of the pandemic the population of England, which had probably peaked at around five million in the first half of the fourteenth century, suddenly plummeted by between a third and a half. What is more, further outbreaks in 1361–2, 1369 and 1374–5, though not as severe in their mortality, pre-vented any recovery in population levels, which remained stagnant at between two and three million from the mid-fourteenth century until the end of the fifteenth.[8] The second plague, in particular, which was colloquially known as the 'mortality of the children', wiped out large numbers of the next generation, and had a knock-on effect on the replacement birth rate in the future. High infant mortality, possibly combined with lower fertility rates, combined to ensure that in London and most major provincial towns, where the records exist, seventy-five per cent of families failed to produce a male heir for even three successive generations.

Statistics tell us that life expectancy may have been reduced to around thirty-five years but the figures are warped by the fact that infant mortality rates were so high. Even before the advent of the plague at least thirty per cent of babies and children died

before their seventh birthday and the wealthiest and most privileged could not escape unscathed: Edward I, for example, lost
seven of his sixteen children before the age of seven. In fact,
however, even after the advent of the plague, anyone who survived their first five years stood a good chance of living much
longer. Though few could hope to attain the three-score years
and ten which the Bible taught was the natural span of human
life, men who reached the age of twenty could expect to live
into their fifties whether they were wealthy London merchants
or agricultural labourers in the Midlands or south-east of
England. Despite the dangers of childbirth, life expectancy
among women appears to have been similar. Aristocratic
women, however, had a disconcerting tendency in this period to
live much longer than their male counterparts, not least because
so many of the latter became casualties of war: over twenty per
cent of the nobility born between 1351 and 1375 met violent
ends.[9]

Horrific and tragic though the high levels of mortality were
for victims of the plague and their families, the financial
circumstances of many of those who survived improved dra-
matically. As we shall see, shortage of manpower created
opportunities for the ambitious and able to demand higher
wages both in cash and in kind, to negotiate improved terms of
employment (including better food), to exploit gaps in the
market and to acquire more land. Greater availability of land
and fewer mouths to feed also removed the pressure to grow
crops in marginal land and encouraged its conversion from
arable to pasture. Living conditions also improved. If there was
ever any truth in the popular image of several generations of
medieval peasant families living cheek by jowl with their animals in the cramped and squalid conditions of dark,
windowless, smoke-filled and filthy hovels, it was no longer per-
tinent by Richard's reign. Longhouses, where livestock occupied

a byre built under the same roof as the family home, were already a rarity in most regions by 1350, though for pragmatic reasons they survived in the harsher climates of northern England. Even the smallest landholdings usually consisted of a single-storey house of up to three bays (a hall and two chambers) with a separate barn, and many, if not most, had at least one or two additional buildings for food processing and agricultural use clustered round a yard where the animals were kept. The main edifices were generally professionally constructed from timber and stone or, where the latter was not available, cob, which was made from a mixture of compressed clay, straw, sand and water; they were either thatched with straw or reeds or roofed with tiles or slates. Buildings like these were valuable assets and landlords were quick to punish tenants who allowed them to become dilapidated and to enforce their repair or even rebuilding. Although more than one family might share a holding, they lived in separate quarters and the evidence of the 1377 poll-tax returns suggests that by then most households were composed of small conjugal units consisting of just over two people above the age of fourteen (younger children did not appear in the returns). Single dependent relatives, or elderly people who had given up their landholding or urban tenement to others in return for bed and board for the remainder of their lives, usually occupied specifically designated private rooms or even a cottage on site, rather than sharing in the communal domestic arrangements.[10]

The face of England was changing in other ways. Rural industries were flourishing in an increasingly cash-based economy. Open-cast tin-mining in Cornwall, famous since at least Roman times, was now said to consume more than three hundred acres annually; similarly, ancient open-cast mining for lead in Derbyshire and for coal in the shallow seams along the banks of the river Tyne in north-eastern England had thrived under the impetus of urban building and the demands of war. The ten per cent of the country that was still covered by woodland was carefully managed by coppicing to provide charcoal, a vital fuel for many industries, mature timber for the construction of buildings and ships and cover for game, which the aristocracy alone was privileged to hunt. A significant new rural industry was also emerging in the years after 1360. It was now more profitable to sell finished cloth rather than raw wool, particularly for the domestic market, so weavers, dyers and finishers multiplied in villages and towns with access to the necessary supplies of wool and flowing water – the latter just as necessary as the raw material, since plentiful supplies were needed to wash both wool and cloth and to drive the mechanical fulling machines.[11]

Although England remained primarily an agrarian society, some twenty per cent of the population now lived in towns where specialist trades, crafts and markets could flourish more easily than in the countryside. As we shall see, these ranged from the suppliers of daily essentials such as the tailors, smiths, butchers and grocers to be found in every small town to the more exotic and unusual parchment-makers, embroiderers and goldsmiths plying their skills in the shadows of, and for the benefit of, great cathedrals and monasteries. The influence of the Church permeated society and daily life. It was the Church calendar, rather than simply the weather, which dictated and marked the passing of the seasons. The very hours of the day were marked out for both labourers in the field and townsmen going about their business by the bells which called monks and canons to their prayers.

Church buildings literally dominated town and country in both their scale and magnificence. Nothing, not even a royal castle or palace, could compare with the exquisite tracery and soaring pinnacles of a remote Cistercian abbey in Yorkshire or an urban cathedral like Salisbury or Gloucester. For the weary traveller these were landmarks which would be seen hours before they could be reached by road: signposts not only to God's kingdom but also to the baser pleasures of rest and refreshment. Parish churches too were enjoying a building renaissance in the wake of the plague as grateful survivors sought to extend and beautify their local places of worship by adding porches and steeples and to memorialise themselves and their families by paying for tomb effigies, stained-glass windows and chantry chapels where a priest or priests sang masses continually for the souls of the dead. Even those who could not afford such ostentatious alms-giving were legally obliged to give their tithe to the Church, a tenth of their annual income, which was claimed from every adult in the kingdom, whether it was in cash from wages or rents or in kind in the form of grain, wool or livestock. The Church claimed other 'gifts' or payments too, on feast days, for churching ceremonies to purify women after childbirth and, most notoriously, as a mortuary fine on the death of a parishioner.

All these funds were necessary to support a church hierarchy which ranged from bishops and abbots, some of whom lived like princes and were just as involved in the country's administration as their secular peers, to simple anchorites like the mystic Julian of Norwich who had voluntarily immured herself in a cell adjoining the church of St Julian in 1373 and remained there till her death in 1414, surviving on donations of food and drink from local well-wishers and the pilgrims who sought her out. In towns like Norwich it must have been virtually impossible to stir abroad without encountering a cleric of some sort: monks conducting their abbey's estate business, friars sermonising to the crowds from the preaching crosses erected in most churchyards, canons hurrying to take their places in the cathedral, parish priests paying duty calls to the bishop, perhaps even a Knight Hospitaller riding to visit his order's local preceptory; not to mention the host of unordained clergymen, such as the lawyers, clerks and even pardoners who sold papal indulgences granting remission of sins and, like Chaucer's charlatan, false relics of varying degrees of ingenuity (the pigs' bones alleged to be those of saints, the pillowcase said to be the Virgin Mary's veil, even a piece of sail from the boat from which Christ called St Peter) to the unwary and credulous. Something like one in thirty men in England in 1377 was either a member of a religious order or a fully ordained clergyman. An unquantifiable number, probably far in excess of that, were members of the minor orders who were tonsured, wore ecclesiastical vestments and enjoyed benefit of clergy, which meant that they could not be executed for certain crimes by secular courts so long as they could read or recite the 'neck-verse', the first verse of the Fifty-First Psalm (literacy being regarded as proof of a clerical vocation); as they were not fully ordained they were therefore free to marry and live and work in secular society. It was these men who were the backbone of English government and administration: the clerks working in the royal chancery, in the sheriffs' and bailiffs' courts and in the localities, where they wrote wills and charters and kept accounts for the lord of the manor.[12]

The higher echelons of the Church were also deeply embedded in the government of the realm. Those who had served the king well could expect promotion not only within his various departments of state but also within the ecclesiastical hierarchy: parishes, prebendaries, canonries, archdeaconries, even bishoprics, were often the reward of loyal service to the crown, with many of the offices being held at the same time by a single individual who could not, therefore, perform his sacred duties in person. Bishops always served as members of the king's council and regularly held the highest offices in the land: in 1381 the chancellor was none other than Simon Sudbury, archbishop of Canterbury and head of the Church in England and Wales, while the treasurer was Sir Robert Hales, prior of the Knights Hospitaller and head of this international military order of monks in England, Wales and Scotland. The Church owned vast swaths of land, putting bishops and abbots on a par with the secular aristocracy: even the poorest see, Rochester, was worth four hundred pounds a year, while the wealthiest, Winchester, brought its incumbents an annual income of over ten times that amount. The same people who advised the king and played a large part in determining the course of national and even international politics were therefore among the greatest landlords in the country, whose exercise of secular lordship affected the daily lives of a large proportion of the population.[13]

This identification of Church and state fuelled anticlericalism in a society which was still deeply religious. The wealth of the Church, contrasting so sharply with the simple life of Christ himself, had been a source of contention almost since its foundation. Every reforming movement, including the Cistercians, the friars and, most recently, the Carthusians, attempted to strip the Church back to its fundamental concept of apostolic poverty. The pride, greed, sloth, ignorance and sexual misconduct of the clergy were frequently attacked by churchmen themselves, though the convention was that this was done in Latin and reserved for an audience of clergy, monks and scholars. Sermons for the laity were preached in the vernacular but were supposed to abstain from criticism of the Church and concentrate instead on admonishing the vices of laymen, encouraging reformation of character and giving instruction on the prayers, creed and Ten Commandments that were the building blocks of the liturgy. Yet because parish priests were only required to preach four times a year, and many of them had neither the talent nor the inclination to do so, an army of itinerant preachers had grown up to feed the huge popular appetite for sermons. Though some preachers complained that their congregations fell asleep, 'for in these days men like a short sermon, or no sermon at all, when in church, and long drinking in the ale-house', the demand since the mid-century had literally changed the face of churches, leading to the introduction of pulpits and huge naves where the congregation could gather to hear a sermon.[14]

Many churches, including most famously St Paul's in London, also had preaching crosses in their churchyards, enabling travelling preachers to address vast crowds of people without entering the building itself. This facility was particularly used by the friars, whose obvious personal commitment to evangelical poverty and highly emotional rhetoric played deeply into contemporary notions of individual responsibility for sin and hopes of salvation. They were unsparing in their criticism of the Church and its hierarchy, feeding the anti-clericalism of the age, which was so at odds with its genuine piety. Just like the renegade and rebel John Balle, they were accused of denigrating the clergy and discouraging the payment of ecclesiastical dues. Balle's instruction to withhold tithes from priests who were richer or less moral than their parishioners finds echoes in the preaching of his contemporary, the Franciscan friar Thomas Richmond, who told vast crowds gathered to hear him on the outskirts of York that 'A priest fallen into mortal sin is not a priest. Again I say that he is not a priest; and thirdly I say that before God he is no priest'; he even argued that secular judges should cleanse the Church of immorality by jailing offenders. Another contemporary Franciscan, John Gorry, was the subject of a royal writ ordering his house in Dorchester, Dorset, to silence and punish him for encouraging the tenants of the abbot of Milton to rebel against the abbey and to violate the Statute of Labourers. And it was two Augustinian friars who, in 1371, submitted a set of learned articles to parliament arguing that the Church's property should be impounded by the king and used for the service and defence of the realm.[15]

Such attacks on the Church by its own members blurred the distinction between what was acceptable criticism within the bounds of reformist zeal and what was actually heresy and therefore contrary to orthodox teaching. The last quarter of the fourteenth century was one in which the Church's wealth and its moral standing were being questioned at every level of society. Even the papacy itself was under attack. Its authority had already been compromised and challenged by its relocation from Rome to Avignon in 1305. Subsequent popes were, of necessity, Francophile, and therefore unable to act as the independent arbiter and mediator of Europe at the very time when such intervention was most required to halt the Hundred Years War. The papacy reached its lowest point in 1378 when rival popes were elected, Urban VI in Rome and Clement VII in Avignon, beginning the Great Schism which would divide the loyalties of Christendom until 1417. As the two popes struggled indecorously for supremacy and the Church throughout Europe fractured along national lines, it was no wonder that there was growing disillusionment with God's representatives on earth.

There were plenty of people in England, even around the young king, including his mother and his uncle Gaunt, who were prepared to protect and sanction those who argued that the Church had lost its way and should therefore be stripped of its worldly wealth. Whether they did this for purely pragmatic reasons, so that they could force the Church to contribute to the cost of the war against France, or because they were genuinely persuaded of the need for a root and branch reformation of a corrupt institution, court patronage of dissident preachers was bound to endorse and encourage the spread of their message. Gaunt's most famous protégé was John Wyclif, an Oxford doctor of philosophy and former master of Balliol, whose ideas were even more radical than John Balle's. His treatises denied the pope and the Church the right to exercise not only temporal lordship, but also spiritual authority, rejected the central role of the priest in man's relationship with God by elevating preaching above the sacraments as the means by which salvation could be found, and considered the words of the Bible itself, not anyone else's interpretation of it, to be the true foundation of all authority and law in Church and state.[16]

Such ideas were doubly dangerous in the changing world of the late fourteenth century because literacy was no longer the sole preserve of the clergy. The aristocracy had long educated its children by means of private tutors, often the household chaplain, who taught their sons and occasionally their daughters to read and write in Latin, the language of diplomacy, administrative and legal record, and French, the written and spoken language of the court, polite society and chivalric literature. Monasteries and convents too had always educated their novices in preparation for entering the religious life and sometimes opened their doors to local children, whom it was hoped would also join them: one of the reasons why the abbot of St Albans was so vindictive in his treatment of William Grindecobbe, who had forced him to concede freedoms to the abbey's tenants and townsmen during the great revolt, was the fact that he had been educated and brought up in the abbey's school.[17]

Many religious houses sponsored or ran grammar schools for the laity where university graduates taught Latin to fee-paying students from dawn to dusk. Some were boarding schools and some admitted able pupils free of charge, depending on whether the school had a foundation which could cover the cost of a schoolmaster; William Wykeham, bishop of Winchester, who owed his own spectacular rise from relatively humble beginnings to his education, founded Winchester College in 1382 to support seventy free scholars who were destined for his other foundation, New College, Oxford, and a career in the Church. Smaller and less exalted institutions existed throughout the country, usually in towns. Where there was no dedicated room or building available, classes were held in the local church: in 1373 the bishop of Norwich prohibited this practice in the schools of King's Lynn on the grounds that the cries of beaten children interrupted services and distracted worshippers.[18]

But side by side with these ecclesiastical schools which aimed to produce a new generation of clergy were independent schools and teachers, which had flourished in towns for at least two hundred years: Boston, Bristol, Coventry and Nottingham, for example, boasted such schools by the end of the fourteenth century. Many of these owed their foundation to the generosity of individuals, particularly wealthy merchants, but also to the enterprise of individual teachers, who were not always university graduates but who were educated enough to earn a living by teaching. And though the impression we get from both modern historians and contemporary books of advice on how to bring up girls (which were inevitably written by men) is that the female sex was destined solely for a domestic role and to make their husbands happy, the extent of their education has been consistently underestimated. As early as the beginning of the fourteenth century it was acknowledged that 'mother teacheth child on book' and since the most common books available in the days before printing were primers, or first books, containing the prayers of the liturgy and of the hours, these implied at least a basic knowledge of Latin. Significantly too one of the most popular subjects for depiction in manuscripts, wall paintings and stained-glass windows at this time was St Anne teaching her daughter the Virgin Mary to read. By

1335 we even have our first documented example of a professional female schoolteacher, Margaret Skolmaystres, who ran an establishment in Oxford.[19]

Education, as Wykeham's career demonstrated, was the key to social mobility. Though clerics liked to consider that they had the monopoly on learning, they, and consequently later generations, greatly underestimated the levels of literacy among the laity at this period. The ability to understand, read and write both letters and numbers was a daily necessity for a significant part of the population, from the bailiff producing his records in the manorial court to the merchant putting his signature to a contract or casting his accounts. What is more, the supremacy of Latin was being challenged by a burgeoning confidence in the native language as an effective means of communication outside and beyond the simple verbal exchanges of ordinary people in the normal course of their everyday lives. It is no coincidence that Richard's reign would see an extraordinary flowering of English literature, from Chaucer to Langland, Gower and the anonymous author of *Sir Gawain and the Green Knight*. English was not just the new language of choice among poets. The ability to read and write in the vernacular had percolated down through society. In the year of the revolt, William Smith, an artisan from Leicester who had taught himself to read and write, embarked on a project which eventually led to his being forced to hand over 'weighty books which he had written in the mother tongue, from the Gospels and from the epistles and bishops and doctors of the Church, and which (he confessed) he had worked studiously at writing for eight years'.[20]

Smith was exceptional but not unique. One of the most striking and unusual features of the great revolt would be its emphasis on the written word. The rebels set out to destroy the records which restricted their freedoms but also to replace them with new documents enshrining in perpetuity their newly won liberties; they communicated by letter and written proclamation; and, perhaps most significant of all, at least six letters, purportedly written by John Balle, were in circulation at the time of the revolt and preserved by contemporary chroniclers as examples of the sort of revolutionary rhetoric which had inflamed the people to rebel. If Balle's letters were a call to arms they are pretty opaque: they include no practical information such as the date, place or time to begin the revolution and are, in fact, simply a patchwork of enigmatic quotations from well-known phrases, proverbs and verses which also occur in fourteenth-century mendicant preaching manuals, sermons and sermon notes. Their author could just as easily have been a perfectly orthodox member of the Church inveighing against the sins of the age, rather than an incendiary preacher intent on raising rebellion. It was their timing that made them so dangerous – at least in contemporary eyes – combined with the fact that Balle had chosen to write, as he preached, in English. Whatever his message was, he wanted it to reach the widest audience possible.[21] And, as we have seen, there was a growing audience for such material. What is more, that audience was increasingly well informed and interconnected. The idea that medieval men and women rarely stirred off their native manors, let alone outside their villages or shires, is wide of the mark. Aristocrats were continually on the move, visiting their various homes, attending the royal court and parliament, employed on diplomatic or military business in various parts of the realm and even overseas. They did not travel alone, but literally took their households (and often their household contents) with them: not just their immediate family and personal servants but their esquires, chaplains, surgeons and physicians; further down the social scale their kitchen staff, including cooks, clerks of the table linen and scullery boys; their minstrels and entertainers, grooms and stableboys, even their falconers and masters of the hounds.

It was not just those in the service of medieval noblemen who could expect to travel. Merchants were also continually on the move, purchasing wool or corn in the English countryside, travelling overseas to bargain for wine, spices or the essential dyes and chemicals needed for the burgeoning English cloth industry, taking up residence in Calais to supervise the Staple. Churchmen too were frequently to be found on the road, going to London to present their petitions to the king, to Rome to seek preferment from the pope or employment in the papal curia, acting as diplomats or envoys on behalf of Church and state. Friars were peripatetic by the very nature of their order, wandering from town to town preaching and begging as they went. Minstrels, messengers and pedlars were similarly itinerant and, like friars, could travel great distances, both on horseback and on foot. Even those living on rural manors travelled regularly, if only within a relatively small radius of their homes, to visit markets to buy and sell, but their children would often find employment in nearby towns as servants or apprentices, returning for the harvest. The humblest carter on a great monastic estate could find himself driving two-wheeled carts or the more cumbersome four-wheeled wagons pulled by a team of draught animals to the coast to collect barrels of fish or wine, or to one of the great towns to pick up spices and incense.

Freemen were required to travel regularly to the hundred courts and shire courts to act as jurors, transact business and pursue or defend legal action; male villeins over the age of twelve were also obliged to make one or two annual trips to the hundred courts to prove that they were enrolled in a tithing, the basic administrative unit for enforcing justice. And every able-bodied Englishman, whatever his social status or place of residence, was required by law to be prepared to fight in

defence of the realm, which, in practice, meant regular attendance at certain designated places within each county to be
arrayed and demonstrate that he had the appropriate weapons
in good working order. From these commissions of array were
chosen the local levies, who would turn out to resist invasions
by the Scots and French, including those of 1377. Edward III's
law of 1363 requiring every able-bodied man between the ages
of sixteen and sixty to practise at the archery butts every
Sunday and feast day fulfilled its intended purpose of ensuring
that the kingdom had a ready supply of trained and well-
equipped soldiers standing by; the unintended consequence was
that half the population was legally armed with at least longbow, sword and dagger, and knew how to use them. This
undoubtedly contributed to general levels of violence in society
but in periods of civil unrest, particularly the great revolt, it had
the potential to create serious problems for the government.

There was one other facet of medieval society which contributed to its mobility and that was its piety. This was not
expressed solely by attendance at the nearest church but by visiting shrines and holy places in England and overseas. The
travails, dangers and expense of the journey were regarded as
expiation for sin; indeed some pilgrimages were imposed by
ecclesiastical and secular authorities as punishment for moral
failings and even criminal acts. Other pilgrims voluntarily took
up the scallop shells and staff that symbolised their status in
order to find a cure for failing health, as an act of thanksgiving
for recovery from sickness or, like Chaucer's knight, for a safe
return from campaign, or even, as two veterans of Agincourt
would do, in fulfilment of vows they had made on the battlefield. From Beverley in Yorkshire to Walsingham in Norfolk,
the country was liberally provided with shrines for the pious to
visit, buy their leaden pilgrim's badge to add to their collection
and make their sacrificial offering. Many of the great abbeys,

such as Bury St Edmunds and St Albans, had grown up around such shrines and owed their own prosperity to the miracles attributed to their patrons. The most popular English shrine of all was that of St Thomas Becket at Canterbury, where some two hundred thousand pilgrims were said to make their way annually, from both home and abroad, making donations valued at almost a thousand pounds a year.[22]

The importance of pilgrimage as a means of obtaining and spreading information should not be forgotten. Chaucer's pilgrims to Canterbury, who were an authentic representation of the genuine article, were a disparate lot drawn from Church and laity, country and town, and from every rank of society below that of the nobility, thrown together in close proximity in a way which would not have occurred in any other aspect of life. First and foremost were the two real characters, the author himself and 'oure Hoste' Harry Bailly, organiser of the story-telling, who was a genuine innkeeper of Southwark and not only appears in the 1381 poll-tax returns paying twelve pence each for himself and his wife Christiana but also acted as the controller, or chief accounting officer, for the collection of the tax in the borough. The fictional characters included a prioress with her accompanying retinue of a nun and three priests, a monk, friar, Oxford clerk, physician, poor country parson and pardoner standing for the Church; a knight, squire, franklin (wealthy farmer), yeoman, reeve (manorial official), miller and ploughman exemplifying rural life. The more complex nature of urban society was reflected in its representatives: a merchant, a shipman from Dartmouth, Devon, who knew every harbour from Gotland in Sweden to Finisterre in Spain, the much-married Wife of Bath, a haberdasher, carpenter, weaver, dyer, tapestry-maker and cook, together with a small but important legal sub-group consisting of a sergeant-at-law or barrister at the peak of his profession, a summoner who identified wrong-

doers and brought indictments against them in the courts, and
a manciple of the Temple, who acted as quartermaster for the
Inns of Court.[23]

Chaucer was not being fanciful in the range of his fictional
pilgrims – even the Wife of Bath, who had already been on pilgrimage to Rome, Santiago de Compostela, Boulogne, Cologne
and three times to Jerusalem, had a real-life contemporary
counterpart in Margery Kempe, the wife of a burgess of King's
Lynn, whose outbursts of noisy weeping as she contemplated
the passion of Christ irritated preachers and her fellow pilgrims
the length and breadth of England and as far afield as the Holy
Land, Assisi, Rome and Santiago. Pilgrims would play a small
but significant role in the great revolt, not least because they
travelled the same route between London and Canterbury as so
many of the rebels. Well aware of these travellers' potential
value in spreading the revolt, the rebels deliberately blocked
every pilgrimage route to Canterbury and compelled them all to
swear allegiance to 'the king and his true commons', to enlist
their neighbours in the cause and to join the rebels when summoned to do so. In this way the pilgrims carried first-hand news
of what was happening back to their home towns, just as they
had always done. Several months after the great revolt, it was
pilgrims to Canterbury from northern England who sparked a
fresh uprising in Kent by bringing rumours that John of Gaunt
had freed the villeins on all his estates.[24]

The England that the boy-king inherited from his grandfather was in the process of significant change. Post-plague, its
population had begun to find its feet again. There was a sense
of opportunity, of dynamism in the air. The old, more rigid
structures of society, particularly those at the lowest levels, had
been challenged and subverted. Earlier medieval churchmen
had preached that humankind was divided into three simple
groups (three being the mystical number representing the

Trinity): those who fought, those who prayed and those who worked; the body politic was similarly divided into three, with those who governed in Church and state as its head, their officials as the body and those who were governed as the feet. That remarkable preacher and fearless critic of abuse of power Thomas Brinton, bishop of Rochester since 1373, could now offer a more nuanced view:

> the head are kings, princes, and prelates; the eyes are wise judges and true counsellors; the ears are clerics; the tongue, good learned men; the right hand, soldiers ready to mount a defence; the left hand, merchants and faithful artisans; the heart, citizens and burghers placed as if in the centre; the feet are farmers and labourers as if firmly supporting the entire body.[25]

Among those merchants, artisans, burgesses and farmers who had at last had their role in society not only recognised but put at the heart of the state, as well as providing the base upon which it stood, there was a new feeling, perhaps of individualism, certainly of confidence, fostered by the growth of personal wealth, literacy and numeracy. Increasing physical and social mobility in a more market-driven economy added impetus to the exchange of ideas – and grievances. A new middle class had been created which was aspirational, questioning and articulate but had little or no voice in the way the realm was run. And the forces of reaction were mustering and closing in as both government and landowners sought to exploit the new-found wealth being created by their subordinates and yet, at the same time, to turn back the clock and reassert their authority over them. A clash was inevitable.

CHAPTER THREE

Landlords and tenants

The village of Fobbing in Essex whose inhabitants began the great revolt was not an obvious place to find a nest of insurgents. Some thirty miles from London, it sat on a spur of higher land above the tidal marshes which separated it from the Thames estuary. With an adult tax-paying population of 225 in 1377, it was the second largest of about a dozen small settlements established round the northern edge of the salt marshes which would all produce rebels in 1381. The marshes were then an archipelago of small islands separated by creeks, some of them large enough to be permanently filled with water and navigable by boat, others simply natural channels which drained the surface of the marshes but were liable to flood at high tide. Since at least Roman times they had provided valuable grazing for livestock and by the time Fobbing, with its Saxon church, was mentioned in Domesday Book there were already hundreds of sheep pastured on and around the manor. The proximity of London, which was easily accessible by both river and road, meant that there was a ready market for the flocks farmed on these south Essex marshes and by the thirteenth century the great ecclesiastical landowners were enthusiastically buying land and attempting to reclaim more. The Cathedral Priory of Christ Church in Canterbury was one of these early investors but, despite heavy spending on maintaining its sea defences, in 1327 it 'lost beyond recovery' 240 acres of salt marsh, providing pasture for 120 sheep, when the embankments were breached; this did not deter the monks who continued their programme of reclamation on Canvey Island into the fifteenth century. Between 1350 and 1365, Westminster Abbey also built up its estates around South Benfleet, purchasing a dwelling house and its appurtenances, sixty acres of land and 240 acres of marsh.[1]

More significantly, for our purposes, however, in 1208 the lord of the manor of Fobbing, Sir Thomas Canville, made a gift of land there to Barking Abbey, a Benedictine nunnery founded in the seventh century, some twenty miles away on the outskirts of London. Barking had long enjoyed royal patronage and was one of the wealthiest and most prestigious convents in the country. John of Gaunt secured places there in 1377 for Margaret Swynford, the daughter of his mistress by her first marriage, and in 1381 for her cousin, Elizabeth Chaucer, daughter of the poet, whose admission cost him £51 8s. 2d. in expenses and gifts. Thomas of Woodstock's widow may also have taken the veil there in her final years, while Sybil, daughter of Sir Thomas Felton, the seneschal of Gascony captured in the French invasion of 1377, was not only a nun at Barking but rose to become its abbess in 1394. (Her widowed sister, by contrast, seems to have been an unwilling postulant because in 1385 she absconded from the convent of the Minories in Aldgate, London, and was declared an apostate and vagabond nun.)[2] The abbess of Barking enjoyed not only extensive rights to fell and take wood for fuel and building work but also to hunt hare and foxes in the forest of Essex and to free warren on her demesne, providing her with rabbits which were then the preserve of 'gentlefolk'. Church law prohibited members of monastic houses from hunting and hawking, though many did so. Abbot William Clowne of Leicester, who died in 1378, was such a skilled hunter of hare that Edward III and the Black Prince were among the many magnates who sought to join him in the field. (He justified his sport by claiming that he hunted not for pleasure but to facilitate the abbey's business with important men.)[3] As we shall see, such monopolies on hunting, which also involved enclosing forests, woodland and parkland to prevent poaching, were to be vocally challenged by the rebels in 1381.

Perhaps because of its prestigious clientele, in 1279 Barking Abbey had been criticised for its laxness: the nuns were ordered to celebrate the divine offices in full and at the proper hours, to observe their rule of silence and, in particular, there was to be no more chattering in the parlour after sunset, they were not to go outside the convent except in the gravest necessity, such as a parent dying, and no men were ever to be admitted to their rooms except, again, in exceptional circumstances. By 1291 the abbey had acquired substantial landholdings throughout south Essex, including estates worth over thirty pounds a year at Ingatestone, twelve miles north of Fobbing, to which were later added eight churches, including those of Mucking and Horndon-on-the-Hill, and the advowsons to six rectories, including that of Ingatestone: men from all these places took part in the assault on the poll-tax enforcers at Brentwood on 30 May 1381 which began the revolt and they would play a major role in the events that followed. It seems likely that the reason for this was that in recent years the abbey had become a more exacting landlord. In 1377 it had suffered a major disaster when flooding swamped many of its Thames-side estates, leading to a loss in annual income of four hundred marks; despite receiving royal permission to impress labourers to repair their sea defences and spending over two thousand pounds in their efforts to reclaim the land, their marshes at Barking and Dagenham still appear to have been largely under water more than a century later. The man charged with administering the abbey's estates and maximising its income was its steward, John Bampton, JP and enforcer of the Essex poll-tax collection. Clearly, then, he, and his methods, would have been well known to the men of Fobbing when he demanded their presence at Brentwood and tried to bully them into making a further contribution to the poll-tax.[4]

In 1381 almost a third of the manors in Essex were held by ecclesiastical landlords. In addition to the great houses outside the county, such as Christ Church in Canterbury and Westminster Abbey and St Paul's in London, whose property extended into most counties in the south-east, there were many local foundations. The most influential were those closest to London, Barking Abbey and the Augustinian abbey of Waltham Holy Cross, the wealthiest house in Essex, which had been re-founded by Henry II and had particularly close links to the crown. Richard II had spent some time living there as a young prince and rewarded the abbot by granting him extensive hunting rights in the forests of Essex in 1378 and 1379 and permission to increase his parks by enclosure in 1380. Waltham's properties would also be attacked in the revolt and it too had a link with Fobbing, owning the rectory or advowson of the chapel of St Nicholas in the nearby village of Stanford-le-Hope, which had joined its neighbours in resisting Bampton's demands at Brentwood.[5]

In addition to these larger foundations, whose tentacles reached into almost every corner of the county, there were many smaller houses whose impact on their locality could be

Curiously, two other powerful widows held large estates in Essex: the king's mother Joan, countess of Kent, widow of the Black Prince, and Margaret of Brotherton, a granddaughter of Edward I. Both had been touched by scandal. At a time when the Church accepted a simple exchange of vows in front of two witnesses as a valid contract of marriage, Joan, aged twelve, had clandestinely married a twenty-five-year-old landless knight, Sir Thomas Holland, only to make a better match the following year while her husband was away on crusade by marrying the son and heir of the earl of Salisbury. Only after eight years, during which time her first husband served as his successor's steward, did they admit the bigamy and secure papal annulment of the second marriage. Less than a year after Holland's death, Joan required papal dispensation again, this time to marry her cousin Edward, the Black Prince. Margaret of Brotherton's life was no less colourful. Married off at fifteen to Lord Segrave, she endured fifteen years of marriage before setting out in person for Rome to secure a divorce, only to be arrested for travelling abroad without the king's licence. When her husband died in 1353 she promptly married Sir Walter Mauny, and was imprisoned again, this time for marrying without the king's permission. After Mauny's death in 1372 she remained a widow for twenty-seven years, acquiring a vast portfolio of lands and wealth through her marriages and a series of inheritances which she managed with ruthless efficiency: demanding royal commissions of oyer and terminer to defend her property, declining to pay the annuities charged on lands she held in wardship and leaving it to her executors – in 1400 – to pay compensation for the oppressions that she and her officers had caused. Her forceful character even persuaded the crown to accept her self-bestowed titles, Countess Marshal and countess of Norfolk, even though her father's hereditary office of Earl Marshal had been granted to others and neither of her husbands had adopted his title to the earldom. It will come as no surprise to learn that this formidable woman's estates in Essex, and elsewhere, were at the heart of the revolt and suffered substantial losses. Or that, after the revolt, she personally obtained a royal order to the sheriffs of Essex, Norfolk and Suffolk to compel her tenants to return to their former status and duties and a special royal commission to inquire into the depredations committed by the rebels on her lands so that she could obtain exemplary punishments.[9]

The crown itself held lands in Essex, including the manor of Havering-atte-Bower, where there had been a royal house since at least the eleventh century. A favoured royal residence because of its woodland setting, just seventeen miles north-east of London, it usually formed part of the queen's dower. Its tenants, like those of all lands held directly in the king's hands, enjoyed numerous privileges denied to those who lived outside the royal demesne, including the extremely valuable right to exemption from paying tolls throughout the kingdom, which Richard confirmed in 1383. The fact that there is no record of any offences being committed at Havering-atte-Bower during the revolt suggests that the king's tenants here, at least, were not unhappy with their lot: the two who did join the revolt, John Hermare and Nicholas Gromond, were arrested in Guildford, Surrey, and were apparently engaged in a personal vendetta, despite almost certainly being falsely indicted on charges of having boasted that they were the first in Essex to rebel and that they had participated in the attack on John of Gaunt's Savoy Palace in London.[10]

By contrast, other royal properties in the county did suffer: Aubrey de Vere, a member of the king's council between 1378 and 1380 and, since January 1381, chamberlain of the king's household, had been granted the constableship of Hadleigh Castle in 1378, the keepership of three royal parks at Hadleigh,

Thunderly and Rayleigh, in 1379 and the keeping of Rochford hundred in January 1381. Just a few months later Rochford hundred was to be one of the worst afflicted areas of Essex during the revolt and both Hadleigh and Rayleigh, where Geoffrey Dersham was their unpopular steward, would suffer attacks on property and the burning of official documents. Men from both places, together with Dersham's former servant William atte Stable, would go to Dersham's own manor of Bernehall, several miles away at Downham, where they demolished buildings and made off with five oxen, three bulls, 160 sheep and 120 capons as well as household goods and chattels which together were worth over twenty-five pounds. Dersham had obviously done well out of his stewardship: in 1369 he had been disqualified from acting as coroner for Essex because he did not have sufficient economic standing but by 1380 he was rich enough to be counted a member of the gentry and was appointed a justice of the peace. No doubt the turnaround in his personal fortune was connected to his stewarding methods and explains his being targeted by those whom he managed.[11]

Just under a half of Essex manors were in the hands of men like Geoffrey Dersham whom we might loosely term the gentry: knights, esquires, prosperous farmers, even successful London merchants and lawyers who had invested their profits in country estates. Unlike the magnates, whose lives were largely spent in a constant round of travelling, shuttling between their London houses and their various provincial castles and following the king and court as they moved around the realm, the gentry were much more likely to be resident on their manors and were therefore the backbone of the county administration. They served the king as coroners, escheators, sheriffs and justices of the peace, but also the magnates as stewards and administrators and their own peers as members of parliament. They therefore exercised multiple layers of lordship on behalf of others – and, of course, in their own right as lords of their own particular manor or manors.[12]

However large the great estates, whether they belonged to the king directly, or to the Church or secular magnates, they were not the monolithic blocks of countryside we associate with more modern aristocrats but a collection of manors spread piecemeal across the county and beyond, whose acquisition was dictated principally by accidents of inheritance rather than a deliberate policy of purchase. Of course families looked to extend and consolidate their landholdings by judiciously marrying off their sons and daughters to the children of their neighbours: it made financial and administrative sense to do so. What they could not control, however, was the permanency of those arrangements. A failure to produce a male heir in the direct line or his early death, the division of lands between female co-heirs, like the Bohun sisters, the requirement to provide a widow with a third of the estate for her lifetime, a decision to give property to the Church or a conviction for felony or treason, could all diminish or even wipe out an ancestral landholding. Although a number of manors might be concentrated under one lordship in certain areas, therefore, the more usual pattern was for them to be scattered across different parishes and intermingled with other lordships. The same was also true of individual manors: some were so large that they extended into several parishes and the various component pieces of land might be as much as fifteen miles apart; others consisted of little more than a single house and garden. Most Essex parishes had at least two manors within their boundaries and sometimes many more, each held by a different lord. Most had some free tenants who paid rent for their land; some had villeins or bond tenants, who were personally tied to the manor and obliged to perform customary dues and services. It was the exercise of lordship over these tenants, specifically through the lord's private court, that was the defining quality of a manor and made it distinct from a simple landholding no matter how large or small.[13]

What the entire landholding system had in common, regardless of the social or financial status of the owner, was that there was no such thing as freehold tenure as we understand it today. The concept that one might own one's own property outright was alien to medieval society. In theory only the crown could claim ownership and the whole structure of English society since the Norman Conquest was based on the premise that all land belonged to the king and ultimately was held of him. Certain estates, as we have seen, remained in his hands and were one of the sources of income from which he maintained his household and funded the administration of the realm; the only area of government which did not have to be paid for out of his own pocket was war, the defence of the kingdom being considered a shared responsibility to which his subjects ought to contribute. Virtually all magnates, including the bishops and abbots of great monastic houses, held their lands directly from the king as tenants-in-chief. They acknowledged this relationship by doing homage to him in each generation whenever an heir came of age, or forfeited lands were granted to a new tenant, or a new bishop or abbot was appointed. This was a public ceremony in which the new tenant knelt down, placed his hands between those of the king and swore an oath of personal loyalty 'for the tenements I claim to hold of you'.

Only after the ceremony had taken place was the new incumbent formally vested with his lands and allowed to enjoy his income. By the fourteenth century the old obligations of having to serve with the king in his wars and provide a certain number of knights for his campaigns and for castle guard had been commuted into cash payments but the legal fiction that the lands were only held of the crown for life endured. When a tenant-in-chief died, therefore, his eldest son had to pay a 'relief', or entry fee, to succeed to his father's estates, the rate for which had been fixed by Magna Carta at one hundred shillings for a knight's fee and one hundred pounds for a barony. If the heir was under age he became the king's ward and his lands remained in royal hands until he was twenty-one, allowing the crown to exploit the revenues to the benefit of the royal purse. If the heir was a daughter (or daughters), then the king could sell off her marriage to the highest bidder, though not against her will. The same was true for widows. The king could also claim financial aid from his tenants-in-chief to pay his ransom if he was captured (as Richard I had been in 1192), for the knighting of his eldest son and for the marriage of his eldest daughter. In return for these benefits, the crown incurred the obligations to protect its tenants-in-chief from attack by force or by legal process and to consult with them on issues affecting the realm. The greater tenants-in-chief, including some sixty lay peers, were personally and individually summoned to attend parliament by the king's writ; there they formed the House of Lords, which acted as a form of high court, as well as offering advice to the king. By the beginning of Richard's reign their titles had become hereditary and the summons to parliament of this elite group was therefore a matter of course.[14]

The relationship between the crown and those who held land directly from it was therefore mutual and personal. It was upheld by the sacred nature of the oath sworn at homage, breach of which (in theory at least) dissolved the bond, allowing the king to take back his lands and the tenant-in-chief to withdraw his services. In practice, however, both rights and duties were defined and limited by custom and by the common law which protected rights of tenure and inheritance. An eldest son expected to inherit his father's lands, whatever the king's wishes, as Richard II would discover to his cost: it was his arbitrary decision to seize John of Gaunt's lands on his death in 1399, thus disinheriting the latter's rightful heir, Henry Bolingbroke, that led to his own deposition. Greater freedom in disposing of land according to the holder's personal wishes had also been assisted by the development of sophisticated legal devices, such as entails in tail male, which preserved the inheritance as a whole by excluding heiresses, and enfeoffment to use, which circumvented royal occupation and wardship by putting the land into the hands of trustees. Considerable latitude in choosing a marriage partner, for instance, could also usually be obtained simply by purchasing the king's licence.[15]

The same sort of relationship was replicated further down the social scale by those lords of the manor who held from the tenants-in-chief and, yet again, a step further down, by the tenants who held from the lords of the manor. There was, of course, a world of difference between tenants-in-chief such as Thomas of Woodstock, Edmund Mortimer and the abbot of Westminster Abbey, whose incomes of over five pounds a day were more than three hundred times the average daily wage of an ordinary labourer, and the many smaller landlords who could expect to receive anything between ten and one hundred pounds per annum from their estates. What they all had in common, however, as lord of many manors or just one (or even part of one), was the right to exact certain dues and services from their own tenants in return for the land the latter held from them. Theoretically there were only two types of manorial tenants: the free and the unfree. To a casual observer the distinction was not always entirely clear-cut: free tenants were able to dispose of their land to whomsoever they wished and were at liberty to leave the manor whenever they wished, but they still paid annual rents and were obliged to perform (or pay someone else to perform) certain services, such as a specified number of days' harvesting on the lord's personal holding or demesne each year; they were also subject to the manorial court, though they could appeal against its judgments to the royal courts over the head of the lord. Unfree tenants, otherwise known as villeins, bondsmen, or serfs, were legally the property of their lord, together with their families and their chattels, and they were tied to the land they held of him: they could not leave it for longer than a day without his permission; they could not sell it or bequeath it; in addition to paying rent they were also required to give several days a week of their labour to the lord; they could be taxed by the lord at his discretion; they were obliged to attend his court every three weeks, where they were entirely subject to his authority and could be punished for alleged misdemeanours at his will; and when they died the lord had the right to have the best beast or chattel they owned in a tax known as the heriot. In practice, however, the arbitrary rights of lordship were limited and restrained by the power of custom. Just as it did with the secular tenants-in-chief, custom demanded that the eldest son of a villein could take on his deceased father's tenancy so long as he paid his lord an entry fine. Similarly, since villein status was hereditary, his daughters were not allowed to marry without the lord's approval, which again meant paying for the privilege, in this case a cash payment known as a merchet. By the fourteenth century the heriot too was more commonly levied as the value of the best beast or chattel, rather than the physical object itself. Permission to leave the manor temporarily or permanently could be purchased by paying the chevage. Any villein who ignored or attempted to get round these, or any other limitations on his freedom of action imposed by his caste, was liable to punitive fines in the manorial court – from which he had no right of appeal.[16]

That, at least, was the theory, though there was no single or

absolute definition of villeinage in the Middle Ages and its practical application differed from manor to manor according to
local custom. Thus, for instance, though it was usually the case
that a villein owed three days' labour each week to his lord, on
some manors it was much more: the bishop of Ely's villeins in
his Norfolk manor of Walpole, for example, were even said to
have had to work an improbable six days a week for him, leaving them no time to tend their own land. There were even
differing practices on manors within the same county and lordship: Canterbury Cathedral Priory, for instance, was still
claiming labour services from its Essex manor of Lawling in the
late 1380s even though it had entirely commuted them to cash
at Bocking by 1369. Indeed, the lord's own manorial court
sometimes struggled to decide whether a tenant was a villein or
not, though usually it accepted that past performance of regular week works and payment of heriot and merchet were the
qualifiers. Though such decisions were taken by the steward or
bailiff sitting as judge in the court, he had to rely on the evidence presented to him by the tenantry, acting as jurors, who
were not always willing to denounce their neighbours. In 1378,
for example, two villeins from Great Leighs, Essex, who 'could
not deny' that they had conspired to present false evidence that
Joan Lyon was free and therefore should not be fined for having
married without licence, were themselves fined exemplary payments of 13s. 4d. and twenty shillings.[17] On the other hand, as
Nicholas Est discovered in 1377, villeins on the manor of
Heston, Middlesex, who begrudged his holding three acres of
bond land without having to perform any services, maliciously
indicted him before the manorial court as a villein, even though
he and his ancestors had been free from time immemorial. Est
was obliged to petition the king through parliament to obtain
confirmation of his free status and avoid being compelled to
carry out the services. Though he was successful, his resentful

neighbours did not forget their feud and, under cover of the great revolt, exacted their revenge by robbing his house, beating him up and holding him to ransom.[18]

In fact the whole question of freedom and villeinage was much more nuanced than a bare recital of duties and obligations suggests. Many landlords had been forced to make concessions to secure tenants in the labour crisis caused by the great mortality of the first outbreak of the plague in 1348–9. Some villages had to be abandoned altogether, such as Tusmore and Tilgarsley in Oxfordshire and Hale in Northamptonshire, but these were exceptional cases and most landlords were able to find new tenants, albeit by excusing entry fines, relaxing services and leasing out holdings for a term of years. Nearly half the holdings at the Hertfordshire manor of Park, which belonged to the abbey of St Albans, thus changed hands between 1348 and 1350, all but four being taken on by relations of the original tenants. A third of the heirs were under age, however, and when many of them died in the second plague of 1361–2, their places had to be taken by remoter relatives or passed out of a family's hands altogether; four tenancies remained vacant in the abbot's hands until 1374.[19] The landlord's fear of losing his income if he could not find the labour he needed to prevent his estates going to waste was an opportunity for the ambitious and able, whether free or unfree, to increase the size of their holdings and exploit the tenurial concessions on offer. Landlords naturally regarded these arrangements as temporary and for the term of the lease only, but they also wanted the security of enduring tenancies, so, initially at least, they were often prepared to turn a blind eye to their more successful tenants building up substantial holdings in return for an assured income from the rents they paid. The more often the lease was renewed and the longer these supposedly interim measures continued, however, the more difficult it became to reassert the original status of the land in question. Landlords therefore had to look to new arrangements in order to obtain an alternative secure supply of labour, such as employing freemen to work for wages as tied labourers: in 1364 John Dryvere of Foxearth, Essex, was granted a cottage, its curtilage and an acre of land for life, at an annual rent of five shillings, 'on condition that the same John will serve the lord of this manor for the whole of his life ... as a common labourer'. In 1377 Thomas Whetelee was similarly granted five acres at Birdbrook, Essex, 'as long as he remains in the service of the lord' and the following year Roger Wiseman was granted a holding in Suffolk in return for serving the lord 'as his labourer, taking for his wage what is just'.[20]

Long before the Black Death challenged the dynamic between landlord and tenant, labour dues on many manors had already been commuted into cash payments, reserving only the seasonal reaping and mowing when as many hands as could be found – free or unfree – were needed to bring the precious crops safely into store. Distinctions between the free and unfree were further blurred by the fact that there was a difference between personal status and the status of the land itself: at the bottom of this social pile were the '*nativi*', or 'serfs by blood', whose obligations were both personal and tenurial; at the top were the freemen, who had charters which set out the terms of their tenure, ensuring that these remained fixed and enduring. In between, however, and by far the largest group in Essex and East Anglia, were those who held some lands which were freehold and some which were customary tenure (owing villein services). The majority of these mixed holdings were acquired through purchase or exchange, though they could result from a serf by blood being formally set free by his lord or from the marriage of a free man with a bond woman. Manumission of an ancestor should have made his descendants free for ever – though in 1373 Margaret of Brotherton found a way of extorting punishingly high merchet fines of 13s. 4d. each from the two daughters of a man whom her father had freed by declaring void the late earl's charter of manumission (which the women produced in court) on the legally spurious grounds that the earl, who had died in 1338, could only alienate land for the term of his life, rather than in perpetuity.[21]

Strictly speaking, villeins were not allowed to acquire freehold land or hold land by charter, but in practice they had been doing so for over a century. When the abbey of Peterborough, Cambridgeshire, carried out an investigation in the 1330s, the monks discovered that their villeins had been purchasing land, much of it freehold, since as long ago as Edward I's reign. What is more, they had recorded its conveyance to themselves 'and their heirs' in charters even though the common law held that villeins could not have heirs or devise land by charter. The abbey therefore confiscated both the charters and the land: the unfortunate purchasers were only able to regain the latter if they agreed to hold it in future by customary tenure and at increased rents. The abbey of St Albans, Hertfordshire, had similarly cracked down hard on such illegal acquisitions since at least the beginning of the fourteenth century and would only recognise the legal title of even its free tenants to their land if the charter conveying it was copied into the abbey's own manorial court rolls. Though they had to pay the abbey for the privilege of having it enrolled, this provided security for those who did have legal charters since the abbey seized the land of any of its villeins who could not find their transaction recorded in the abbey's court rolls and confiscated their charters as spurious. Simon Sudbury, acting as bishop of London just before he was elevated to the see of Canterbury in 1374, similarly ordered the seizure of William Joyberd, together with his family, lands, goods and chattels in the Essex manor of Crondon, because he had acquired a messuage and nine acres of free land in a neighbouring village and 'never gave to the lord an increment of rent, nor rendered the said lands to the lord as serfs ought'. Margaret of Brotherton, too, was a vigorous enforcer of this policy, seizing around fifty acres and ten and a half messuages between 1358 and 1376 in her Norfolk manor of Forncett alone, downgrading them from freehold to customary tenure and imposing heavier taxes and rents.[22]

Such manifestly unfair tactics were not calculated to improve relations between landlords and tenants and they were criticised by contemporaries. Chaucer's shining example of a country parson, for instance, citing St Augustine's *De Civitate* as his authority, roundly condemned the practice: 'certainly these lordships do wrong that take away from their bondsmen things that they never gave them'. It therefore comes as no surprise to learn that some of the rebels in 1381 had been penalised in this way. William Grindecobbe, who had an acre of land transferred to him by charter confiscated by the abbey of St Albans in 1377, would lead the revolt in his town against the abbey; when James atte Ford of Takeley rebelled he was still paying off a huge fine of almost two shillings an acre so that he could recover eighteen and three-quarter acres of customary land seized into his lord's hand because he had bought it without permission the previous year.[23]

Why, then, did landlords continue to pursue such an unpopular policy? The first and most important reason was to avoid losing their tied tenants and tenancies: holding by charter was recognised as a mark of freedom and no landlord wished to lose their much more profitable villeins and customary land by a covert process of creeping emancipation. The second was the desire to establish a permanent written record which could then be produced as proof whenever disputes arose in future: proving that a person was a villein was much more difficult than proving that a tenement was held by customary tenure. And the documentary evidence of the manorial court rolls was much harder to challenge or subvert than the collective memory and oral witness of the tenantry. The third reason, however, was that landlords were looking to increase their profits by any way or means possible. Rents and services from freehold land were fixed but they could be varied for customary tenements, providing a useful source of income when revenues from other sources were under pressure. It therefore mattered whether a tenancy was free or customary and the 1370s and 1380–1 consequently saw a number of great estates tightening up their administration, making enquiries into the status of their tenants' holdings to discover if any had been 'usurped' by unofficial transfers and drawing up new rentals. These inquisitions sometimes turned up long-concealed or simply long-enduring offences, such as the unlicensed marriage of a widow in 1366 which was not uncovered by her manorial court until 1378; but their primary purposes were financial – to obtain payment of punitive fines known as amercements, as distinct from the usual fines, which might be regarded as permission fees – and to record acknowledgement of error so that future transgressions could also be punished. In Eleanor de Bohun's Essex manors of Great Waltham and High Easter, heavy amercements were imposed on twenty out of forty-six villeins who had married without the lord's permission between 1350 and 1389, compared with only seven out of fifty-one between 1327 and 1349. It would appear that it was not the incidence of illicit marriages taking place that had changed, but rather the lord's determination to enforce his rights. Merchets were also being imposed more frequently in the 1370s on Westminster Abbey's Essex manor of Birdbrook than they had been in previous decades.[24]

At the same time many landlords were also ratcheting up the pressures on their tenants by stricter enforcement of other customary dues. The abbey of Bury St Edmunds doubled the payments it demanded of all new tenants taking up customary holdings from 3s. 4d. in the 1340s to 6s. 8d. in the 1370s and demanded a heriot of a cow worth 6s. 4d. from a widow whose husband had held only a single acre of customary land; her co-heirs found the abbey's levies so onerous that, after fifteen years, they eventually gave up the effort and in 1386 abandoned the holding altogether. It was no doubt in an attempt to avoid such arbitrary impositions that in 1378 the villein tenants of Barking Abbey at the Essex manor of Ingatestone offered to pay forty shillings just to have their rents and services made 'certain'. The abbey of St Albans had also become noticeably more vigilant after the first outbreak of the Black Death, imposing amercements on those who cut down trees on their holdings without the abbot's licence, allowed their beasts to trespass on his demesne or poached in his woods, parks and waters: all issues which, as we shall see, were grievances for which the local rebels in 1381 specifically sought redress.[25]

Few tenants could escape fines of one sort or another imposed by the manorial court – either for obtaining the lord's permission to do something or as punishment for failing to do so – or even, in some cases, for protesting against a verdict. Edmund Patyl was amerced 3s. 4d. in 1380 for contempt and for abusing the jurors who had revealed his illicit purchase of nine acres of customary land which the court had therefore just seized into the lord's hands. William Morkyn was similarly amerced twelve pence in February 1381 because his wife refused to accept a judgment against her and 'spoke badly' of those who had given the evidence which convicted her. New offences were constantly being created. Allowing buildings on customary holdings to fall into disrepair was rarely subject to punitive fine before 1349 but became commonplace in the 1360s and 1370s as lords asserted their right to the ownership of the property of their villein tenants. Similarly, in an extension of the lord's right to chevage, the mother, brother and uncle of a villein, William Phelipp, who 'received and entertained' him after he had absconded from the Essex manor of Thorrington were found guilty of trespass against their lord and had *their* goods seized into his hands: unsurprisingly, a few weeks later, mother and brother joined the rebels in burning the Thorrington court rolls.[26]

It was the arbitrary and discriminatory nature of so many of these judgments that grated with tenants. Two families in the same village with adjacent holdings of the same size and comparable productivity might find themselves paying vastly different amounts in rent, services and customary dues simply because one was free and the other unfree: the same might even be true of a single tenant who held one holding by charter and the other by customary tenure. Wealthier tenants, in particular, often found themselves in the position of paying regularly, and above the odds, for alleged infringements of manorial by-laws. Robert Wryghte of Foxearth, Essex, for instance, had three horses, two cows and six pigs and year after year was constantly amerced unusually high amounts for allowing his animals to trespass on the lord's demesne, paying out the considerable sum of 4s. 8d. in 1378 alone; the following year his wife, the chief brewer in their village, was also subjected to a very high fine of ten shillings for breaking the minimum standards of quality and quantity nominally regulated by the assize of bread and ale. Geoffrey Rook, a tenant of the abbey of St Albans' manor of Park, Hertfordshire, was also regularly amerced for allowing his cows and pigs to forage in the abbot's grain, peas and pastures and was the most persistent offender in the manorial court for breaking the assize of bread and ale, incurring fines on eighteen separate occasions, and being succeeded in this dubious distinction by his widow. Both Wryghte and Rook would become rebels, the latter venting his frustrations by plundering the house of Richard Scryveyn, whose name suggests that he may have been one of the court clerks responsible for recording his offences.[27] Imposing and paying a regular punitive fine or amercement for offences, particularly those against the assize of bread and ale, was regarded by both parties as an incidental expense more akin to acquiring a licence than an acknowledgement of guilt for producing allegedly substandard goods. In effect the lord was using his manorial court to take a regular cut from, or tax on, the success of men like Wryghte and Rook and there was little or nothing his tenants could do to prevent it. Chaucer's country parson voiced the frustration of many when he complained that greedy landlords demanded 'more taxes, customs and tolls than duty or reason requires' and that they took fines from their bondsmen that 'might more reasonably be called extortions than amercements'.[28]

The most effective way of resisting such 'extortions' was to withhold customs and services, especially when the tenantry of a manor acted in concert. In the first parliament of Richard's reign, which met in October 1377, the House of Commons expressed fears that the country was now on the brink of civil war because so many villeins and tenants were withholding customs and services from their landlords, who were unable to act against the disobedient 'through fear of death which might arise from their rebellion and resistance'. Tenants were not only banding together to offer communal defiance to their landlords' demands but also contributing to a common pot to pay for lawyers to challenge their legal status in the king's courts as well as in their local manorial court. What they were trying to prove was that their manor had once belonged to the crown and could therefore be classified as 'ancient demesne'. Tenants of ancient demesne, like the crown's current tenants, had access to the royal courts, did not have to attend the hundred courts or county courts, were not liable to pay taxes to anyone except the king and, most important of all, their rents and services were fixed and could not be increased.[29]

The key to demonstrating this privileged status was Domesday Book, William the Conqueror's great survey of 1086, which was the land registry of its day: a written record of which of his tenants-in-chief owned what, and where, in England 'on the day that King Edward was alive and dead' in 1066 and again in 1086. If a manor was recorded in Domesday Book as belonging to the crown its tenants could claim that it was ancient demesne despite the fact that it had subsequently changed hands. To obtain this information required both legal knowledge and money to pay for a certified copy of the relevant entry, known as an exemplification from Domesday Book, which was purchased in the form of letters patent from the royal chancery, hence, as the parliamentary petition had noted, the formation of 'leagues and conspiracies', the employment of lawyers and the communal funds set up by dissident tenants.[30]

There had been regular appeals to Domesday Book since at least the reign of Edward I, when written verification of tenurial status began to be more important than the oral memory of local juries, but the outcome was not necessarily predictable. In 1320, for example, Roger Hervy, acting on behalf of a group of tenants at Mildenhall, Suffolk, brought an action against their landlord, the abbot of Bury St Edmunds; Domesday Book revealed that Mildenhall had belonged to Edward the Confessor, so the manor was indeed part of the ancient demesne. It was a hollow victory, however, as the abbot argued that, as a villein, Hervy had no right to bring a case against his lord, and the abbey continued to exact all the additional customs and services which Hervy had disputed. On the other hand, in 1364 Edward III intervened on behalf of the tenants of the manor of Crondall,

Hampshire, and prohibited the priory of St Swithun at Winchester from imposing 'other services than those which their ancestors used to do at the time when the manor was in the hands of our forebears': this despite the fact that Domesday Book actually showed that Crondall, which had been given to the priory by King Edgar in 972, had 'always belonged to the Church'. Clearly, Domesday Book was not quite the ultimate arbiter whose 'decisions, like those of the Last Judgement, are unalterable'.[31]

What caused parliament such alarm in 1377 was a sudden and exponential rise in the number of appeals to Domesday Book. Between October 1376 and August 1377 just under forty manors applied for exemplifications. Most of them lay in Wiltshire, Hampshire and Surrey, and all but one were held by ecclesiastical landlords. This was an extraordinary number of appeals in such a short space of time and the fact that the manors were situated within a relatively small geographical area (some even within the same parish) suggests that this was either a concerted campaign of action or that news of it spread quickly, inspiring others to follow suit. Certain landlords seem to have been specifically targeted: four Surrey manors of the abbot of Chertsey applied for the writ, as did eight of the abbess of Shaftesbury in Wiltshire and Dorset.[32] Some of the appellants were repeat offenders: despite winning its claim in 1364, Crondall reapplied in 1377, presumably because St Swithun's Priory had succeeded in overturning the king's orders or had simply reimposed the additional services. The villein tenants of Badbury, Wiltshire, had failed to qualify as ancient demesne in a previous application made in 1348 but appealed again in 1377. Quite why they thought they could obtain a different result is unclear, especially as their earlier attempt bore all the sophisticated organisational hallmarks of the later mass of applications which so alarmed parliament. According to their landlord, St Mary's Abbey at Glastonbury, they had formed a conspiracy, contributed to a common fund according to their means, ranging from six pence to five shillings each, and even appointed their former reeve as its assessor and collector. We do not know how they organised their second application but, like their first, it failed to produce the result they wanted.[33]

But what did those who appealed to Domesday Book really hope to gain? The desire to escape the burden of arbitrary fines and dues and replace it with fixed rents and services was clearly an important motivation – and it would be at the heart of the rebels' demands in 1381. But there is a clear implication (at least on the part of the landlords) that those who sought exemplification believed that they were also gaining personal freedom. The warden and college of St Mary Ottery, Devon, alleged that its tenants relied on their exemplification to declare that they were exempt from rents and services; the Commons petition similarly stated that the applicants used the process to claim 'that they are entirely released from all manner of service as well of their bodies as for their aforesaid holdings'. The abbot of Chertsey went even further, complaining that the villeins and tenants of villein holdings on four of his Surrey manors had performed all their rents, customs and services without interruption until their recent purchase of their exemplification 'by which they really imagine that they are free and of free condition'.[34]

If the allegation is true, then it suggests a misunderstanding about the nature of ancient demesne, since personal freedom, unlike fixed rents and services, was not a privilege of crown tenants. We might suspect the landlords of deliberate exaggeration to gain their point, but there were other misconceptions about the whole process which originated with the appellants. For example, they seem to have believed that the act of purchasing the exemplification was in itself a form of licence to withhold services rather than simply evidence of former manorial status. Only three out of the forty manors which applied for exemplifications in 1376–7 actually had legally justified claims to ancient demesne status, yet the rest still relied on their purchase to refuse their dues. They also seem to have thought that any land which had ever belonged to the king, even long before the Conquest, qualified as ancient demesne. Very many of those who applied for writs were actually looking back to the tenth century, and some as far back as the seventh, as the period when their manors had been in possession of the king, who had then donated them to the Church. The fact remains, however, that the legal definition of ancient demesne did not extend any further into the past than the day that Edward the Confessor died.[35]

This unprecedented spate of appeals to Domesday Book is clearly relevant to the great revolt which would erupt just a few years later. It is true that nearly all the manors where most of the appeals originated appear not to have been involved in the revolt, perhaps suggesting that they preferred to put their faith in the legal process which so many of them had evoked before, and would evoke again, as part of a long tradition of resistance to their landlords' demands. It is also true that the king's council responded so promptly and forcefully to the parliamentary petition that it effectively ended the practice, declaring that the exemplifications 'could not and should not have value or force in respect of the [appellants'] personal freedom, nor change the condition of their tenure and customs due of old' and allowing aggrieved lords to have letters patent confirming this. Special commissions were to be available to indict, imprison and fine those tenants who refused to perform their accustomed dues and services; as for 'their counsellors, procurers, maintainers, and abettors', their more serious offence required that they were to be imprisoned and not released until they had paid a fine to the king and compensation to the lords they had aggrieved.[36]

Despite this, the 'great rumour', as modern historians have christened this episode, anticipates many of the themes which would emerge so forcefully in the great revolt: the desire to end arbitrary exactions by landlords, to have rents and services 'fixed and certain' and to win personal and tenurial freedom; the belief in the power of the written word; the idea that royal lordship was fairer and less onerous and therefore preferable to any other. At another level, it gives us a valuable insight into the ability of rural inhabitants to organise themselves both within the manor and as part of a group: half of the writs issued were on behalf of tenants of one or more manors in the same lordship, bearing out their landlords' accusations of 'conspiracy' and 'confederation', emotive words which would also be used against the rebels of 1381. We even have an example of the disaffected tenants at Farnham, Surrey, making their alliance against the bishop of Winchester more solemn by swearing an oath to resist him and his officials, just as their later counterparts (including men from Farnham) would do on so many occasions.[37]

In the light of what happened in 1381, it may be significant that seventeen out of the twenty-two applications made during the 'great rumour' were registered between 7 March and 10 August 1377. This coincides with the imposition of the first poll-tax, the collectors of which were appointed on 4 March.[38] Did the necessity of paying this new burden add to the grievances of those who were seeking a reduction in their manorial liabilities and give impetus to their campaign? Clearly it did not provoke revolt, or even resistance, as it would in 1381, but the government's abrupt blocking of the only legal avenue for obtaining the abolition of manorial dues can only have added weight to popular frustration and encouraged violence. When the abbot of Chertsey tried to enforce his rights in his Surrey manors of Chobham, Frimley, Thorpe and Egham, his officials were attacked 'with arrows, cudgels, halberds and other weapons' by the tenants, who seized back their distrained goods and allegedly threatened to burn down the abbey with all the monks in it; they subsequently defied a writ of distraint from the sheriff and 'openly threatened that if they did not get their own way, a thousand men in this country would die'.[39] The tenants of the priory of Harmondsworth, Middlesex, had claimed ancient demesne status as long ago as 1233; when they appealed to Domesday Book in 1276, and lost again, they still refused the disputed services, 'saying they would rather die than render them'; they too forcibly recovered goods seized by distraint and 'openly threatened' to burn down the priory. Royal intervention restored order but a century later a low-level campaign of disobedience had begun which built up into something akin to organised resistance: tenants refused to take part in the lord's haymaking and harvesting or obey the bailiff's summons; they were trespassing in the abbot's woods, poaching in his waters and in 1379 one of them opened the sluices so that his hay field was flooded. Tensions were running so high that the man elected as reeve in the manorial court of 1379 paid 13s. 4d. rather than take up office; the following year, in a worsening situation, the price for escaping the onerous role had risen to £1 6s. 8d. – but it was still paid since none of the tenants were prepared to act as the prior's enforcer. It was not until the revolt of 1381 that the priory's tenants exchanged passive resistance for physical violence but then they made a concerted effort to ensure that their disputed services could never be demanded again. As the prior claimed in an emotional plea to the king, large numbers of them had come to him

> threatening to cut off his head and burn his houses, and they entered his chamber, and commanded him to open his coffer, and when it was open they took from it everything

that was inside, including all the foundation charters of the house and the custumal, registers, rentals, court rolls and account rolls, letters of quittance and all the other muniments relating to the house and they burnt them all to powder.

When they discovered that he kept other letters at Westminster they ordered him to have those sent over, on pain of death, and then burned them to ashes too. Among those who were later punished for their involvement in this wholesale destruction of the priory's archives were those whose names had featured frequently as defaulters and delinquents in the manorial court records in the years leading up to the revolt.[40]

Increasing levels of discontent among the tenantry in the years leading up to 1381 are observable in the court records of many places which would participate in the great revolt. The manor of Brandon, Suffolk, which belonged to the bishop of Ely, is a case in point. In the 1370s, despite his attempts to impose punitive fines on offenders, the bishop's control over the manorial court was demonstrably slipping: in 1372 the chief pledges were fined forty shillings for not presenting their evidence and thus hiding poaching offences, concealment of rent arrears was endemic (one man had not paid his for twenty-two years) and it proved more financially viable to allow tenants to buy licences to absent themselves legitimately from court than repeatedly to fine defaulters.[41] At the abbey of Bury St Edmunds' manor of Lakenheath, Suffolk, which would play a pivotal role in the revolt, there had been a decade of hostility and violence: in 1370 the constables of Blything and Hoxne hundreds were charged with corruption and extortion; a year later Simon, vicar of Lakenheath, led twenty-six named people 'and others' in an attack on the abbot's officials who were trying to take goods in lieu of the parish tax which the villagers had refused to pay, breaking one's wand of office and threatening them so that they were forced to flee empty-handed; and in 1379 the two constables of Lakenheath (who had both taken part in the assault in 1371) were indicted before the King's Bench for refusing 'to answer for certain articles', probably concerning the Statute of Labourers, resulting in a common fine which the villagers refused to pay.[42]

Concerted action, even in the form of passive resistance to the lord's demands, was not always an option and many individuals preferred to take the easier course of simply running away. The evidence suggests that many places saw a marked increase in flight of bond tenants after the Black Death. At the Bohun manors of Great Waltham and High Easter the court rolls record only eight instances of villeins paying chevage to leave or having left illegally without payment between 1327 and 1349; in the period 1350 to 1389 this increased to sixty-two, the vast majority of them being orders for illegal absentees to return. This was not an isolated phenomenon and though in part it reflects an increased determination on the part of landlords to record offences, prevent the loss of tied labour and increase income from fines, it also seems to represent a heightened desire on the part of the villeins themselves to escape and better their condition. A man like John Hamond, for instance, who had the intelligence (and the means) to conceal from Margaret of Brotherton the fact that he had acquired a free tenement and enjoyed its profits for ten years by using the sophisticated legal device of putting it into the hands of feoffees, was clearly capable of achieving much more than the limitations imposed on him by his status and her repressive regime. Two of her other Suffolk villeins similarly demonstrated their entrepreneurial skills by setting themselves up as leading townsmen in Manningtree, Essex, one of them acquiring sixty-three and a half acres of freehold land, the other twenty-one acres and eleven messuages, shops and cottages, all without the knowledge of her manorial officials.[43]

If enterprise was effectively punished by rural landlords, it was more likely to be rewarded in towns, where it was said that if a villein could live undetected for a year and a day he would earn the right to his freedom. Their former lords naturally took an entirely different view: Richard Gregory, who abandoned his holding at the abbey of St Albans' manor of Park in 1354 and fled to London, was recorded as a fugitive at almost every single court for the next fifty years, only disappearing off the list after 1396, presumably because he was either dead or deemed irrecoverable. William Colyn, a leather worker who fled the same manor in 1356, was known to be living and working right under the abbot's nose in the town of St Albans itself; though he was not brought back to Park he clearly bore a grudge since, like Geoffrey Rook, he joined in the attack on the house of Richard Scryveyn during the revolt of 1381, and he remained on the manorial list of fugitives for an impressive fifty-nine years.[44] For the most part there was little that landlords could do to enforce the return of their recalcitrant villeins. As a matter of course the latter's holdings and any goods they left behind them were seized into the lord's hands. Sometimes their relatives were also punished: Robert atte Chirche of Drinkstone, Suffolk, was fined twenty shillings because he failed to produce his two runaway sons before the court (and flatly refused to do so) and we have already seen how William Phelipp's mother, uncle and brother were fined for receiving him after he had absconded from Thorrington.[45]

The most notable case for our purposes, however, was that of Robert Bellyng – not just because he was pursued and arrested but because his plight was alleged to have sparked the revolt in Kent. According to the *Anonimalle* chronicle, the only one which tells this story, Sir Simon Burley came to Gravesend on 3 June 1381 with two royal sergeants-at-arms, accused Bellyng of being his villein and, when the townsmen intervened on Bellyng's behalf and tried to negotiate a settlement between them, demanded no less than three hundred pounds in silver, 'a sum which would have ruined the said man'. Deaf to all pleas for mercy, he ordered Bellyng to be seized, bound and thrown into Rochester Castle for safe-keeping. 'Great evil and mischief derived from this action; and after [Burley's] departure, the commons began to rise, welcoming within their ranks the men of many Kentish townships': three days later they laid siege to Rochester Castle and set Bellyng free.[46]

There are several problems with this account, not least the fact that Burley, the young king's tutor and trusted confidant, had already left England on 15 May to negotiate Richard's marriage to Anne of Bohemia, so he clearly did not visit Gravesend in person or act as described; until October 1379, however, he had personally been constable of Rochester Castle and had then sanctioned his successor's appointment, so he had strong connections with the place.[47] Secondly, the county of Kent was unique in England in that its peculiar forms of land tenure meant that villeinage did not exist there; Bellyng therefore cannot have been a Kentishman. While it is possible that the men of Kent were acting entirely altruistically in taking to arms on behalf of a single escaped villein from another county – and it should not be forgotten that they were as ardent in their demands for the abolition of serfdom as the men from Essex – it seems extremely unlikely that this was the sole, or even the main, reason for their rebellion. Yet the story cannot be dismissed out of hand. Among the indictments lodged against Robert Cave, otherwise known as Robert Baker of Dartford and Otford (Kent), was that, aided by unidentified rebels from Kent and Essex, he had broken into Rochester Castle on 6 June and carried away Robert Bellyng, a prisoner detained there.[48]

Dartford was just seven miles from Gravesend so it is likely that the two men knew one another if both were, as the evidence suggests, substantial citizens in their towns. The particular significance of Gravesend was that it lies on the south bank of the Thames at the point where the river begins to narrow and become shallower: and on the opposite shore, a short boat distance away, lay Essex. Was Bellyng an Essex man? That remains speculation but the town had links with its neighbour across the Thames, including the fact that the endowment of its chapel, chantry and hospital at Milton was almost entirely based on lands in the Essex hundreds of Barstable and Rochford. Its geographical position enabled Gravesend to secure a royal charter confirming its right to ferry passengers to London by river in 1401, thus avoiding the difficult and dangerous road over Blackheath, and, as the first riverside borough and market on either side of the Thames on the approach to the capital, it benefited from the shipment of goods upstream from the easternmost parts of both Kent and Essex.[49] Gravesend was therefore an ideal place for a runaway Essex villein to build a new life and, since the town had been a borough with its own mayor since 1268, the reaction of its townspeople to Burley's attempt to recapture him becomes more understandable: it was not just the principle of serfdom and personal freedom at stake but the borough's own liberties and independence, which were being infringed by the arrest of one of its own. That was a cause for which many proud burgesses throughout the kingdom were prepared to fight and even die.

CHAPTER FOUR

Urban society

For the upwardly mobile, including escaped villeins, town life had many attractions. Unlike life in the countryside it was not dependent on the seasons and therefore offered the opportunity of less cyclical work. There were also more openings for engaging in different kinds of unskilled employment, ranging from domestic service in a merchant or artisan household to working as a groom or ostler in an inn. The more ambitious might have hoped to acquire a craft or a trade, though apprenticeship schemes were hard to come by without contacts, as was the substantial sum demanded as down-payment by the employing master.

Urban living in the late fourteenth century had far more in common with rural life than it does today, even in the largest towns and cities. Indeed, the two were inseparably linked, since the towns relied on their surrounding countryside for a regular supply of fresh produce such as eggs, butter and cheese as well as less perishable but equally essential consumables like

firewood. There was a constant two-way traffic between them.
Country people brought in the surplus yield from their fields
but also reared livestock and made goods specifically for the
market: they had to pay tolls to obtain a licence to sell and
might have to engage an intermediary who held a market stall
or shop, but the sales brought in cash which was vital in what
had become a predominantly money-based economy, not just
to purchase essentials such as tools, cooking pots and shoes,
but also to pay rents, tolls and taxes. Townsmen too would go
out into the countryside to help with the harvest in August and
to seek suppliers of raw materials either for their own trades or
acting as factors on behalf of larger concerns such as magnate
households, university colleges and even great monastic houses
which made their own contracts direct with rural producers of
grain and meat. East Anglian grain and wool were regularly
shipped through its ports, not only to London but as far afield
as the Low Countries and the Baltic, so corn-mongers, wool-
mongers and clothiers from the towns travelled the countryside
buying up local produce for bulk selling to longer-distance
markets. Walter Sibil, for instance, one of the elite band of
wealthy London merchants and aldermen of the city, was at
Great Yarmouth in 1375 when a band of men armed with
swords assaulted him and carried off 160 quarters of his
wheat, worth one hundred pounds, which prevented him selling it in the market. Such people were familiar figures in the
shires – so much so that when John Seynt-Pere set out in 1381
to recruit rebels in the Northamptonshire villages of Church
Brampton and Harlestone to avoid detection by the authorities
he passed himself off as another great London merchant and
financier, Sir John Philipot, on a wool-purchasing mission.[1]

London was far and away the largest city in the kingdom –
and the only one comparable in size and population to its commercial competitors in the Low Countries and Italy. Exchequer

records from 1377 reveal 23,314 tax-payers over the age of fourteen living within the city limits, though this figure does not take account of the hundreds, if not thousands, who had their principal homes outside the capital, nor the vast numbers of clergy who lived or worked there but were taxed separately, nor indeed the large numbers living in the adjacent suburbs, nor those who were exempt from paying tax. Taking these omissions into account, London's total population was probably at least double that figure and possibly around fifty thousand. London was more than three times the size of the largest provincial cities, York and Bristol, which had comparable tax-paying populations of 7248 and 6345 respectively.[2]

As the rebels of 1381 were well aware, London was also the political capital of the realm. Kings, who in the past had been itinerant, were now increasingly in residence there, holding court in the Tower or at Westminster Palace, a couple of miles upriver, beyond the city walls. The expansion of government and its administration, which had always centred on the person of the king, had made a more permanent home necessary for the various departments of state. The courts of law, the exchequer and the chancery had therefore all settled into Westminster Hall, carrying out their different functions in elbow-jostling proximity. The vast number of documents they generated could not all be stored there, so repositories were to be found all around Westminster and in London itself: the chancery rolls, for instance, were stored in the House of the Jewish Converts in Chancery Lane from the 1370s.[3] Anyone wishing to transact legal or financial business, whether a soldier about to go abroad and seeking a royal protection for his property in his absence, a plaintiff demanding a royal writ in a dispute with his neighbours, or a sheriff coming to present his accounts, had to go to Westminster Hall. All around Westminster, and in the Temple and Chancery Lane, he would find lawyers and clerks with the necessary expertise to draw up his petitions and charters, so there was a constant influx of people from the country in need of the services that only the capital could provide. Parliament, too, met more frequently at Westminster in the later fourteenth century, drawing to it not only those lay and secular aristocrats, shire gentry and borough representatives who sat in its sessions, but also a horde of petitioners seeking remedies for their problems.

Even without the constant ingress of visitors from the rest of the realm, London was already a cosmopolitan city. It was home to merchants from the Low Countries, the Baltic and the Mediterranean, who brought in wine, spices and luxury goods, including silks, fine linens and armour, as well as bulk raw materials such as the alum and dyes which were vital for English cloth manufacture. Merchants based in the capital were responsible for exporting between thirty and forty per cent of English wool and forty-five per cent of the country's cloth. The city was therefore a major centre of international trade but it was also a distribution hub for the rest of the country. Great magnates of Church and state, in particular, relied on London for their supplies of hard-to-find merchandise which could then be transferred to their homes in the provinces: wax, exotic imports of dried fruit and nuts, home-produced pewter-ware and the intricately chased, enamelled and gem-studded gold-ware and silverware for which English goldsmiths were justly renowned. Bishop Arundel of Ely even spent eight pounds in 1381 on having a heavy carriage made in London, presumably so that it could be used to cart his purchases on the long seventy-mile journey back to Cambridgeshire. Twenty-five years later, bishop Mitford of Salisbury was buying forty-one per cent of his supplies from London – slightly more than he did from the much nearer ports and markets of Bristol, Southampton and Salisbury combined – and he still managed to save a halfpenny on every pound of liquorice by buying directly in bulk from the importing merchant in the capital instead of in Southampton.[4]

Commerce had changed the face of the city in subtle ways. It still retained its Roman walls, enclosing a square mile within which most of the population lived; seven gates controlled access to the landward side and two, Billingsgate and Dowgate, remained on either side of London Bridge, even though the Thames-side wall itself had long gone to make room for quays, wharves and jetties where merchandise could be loaded and unloaded. Ludgate and Newgate also served as prisons, the former for debtors, the latter, notorious for the corruption of its regime, for criminals referred from the provinces. The other gates were mainly occupied by city officials, including the poet Geoffrey Chaucer, who, in 1374, had been appointed Controller of Customs and granted a lifelong lease on 'the whole dwelling above the gate of Aldgate'. Since this was the city gate nearest the Tower he must have had a prime vantage point for viewing the rebels as they surged through the streets of London; in his only recorded comment on the revolt he would note that 'surely Jack Straw and his band never made shouts as shrill when they wanted to kill the Flemings' as the crowds pursuing the fox which had taken Chanticleer the cockerel.[5] We might have expected more than this passing reference from the greatest poet of the age, particularly given Chaucer's close connections to the royal court, and even closer personal relationship to John of Gaunt, but his discreet silence is symptomatic of the careful course this consummate diplomat steered through all the political travails of Richard's reign.

Within the city walls the greatest building, in every sense, was the twelfth-century St Paul's Cathedral, which was destroyed in the Great Fire of 1666: six hundred feet long, with a rose window forty feet in diameter at its east end, and a spire soaring five hundred feet above the city, it was 'one of the most

magnificent Gothic buildings in Christendom'.[6] Some 114
parish churches were constantly being rebuilt and enlarged by
prosperous Londoners anxious to earn salvation by endowing
chantries where daily prayers and masses would be said or sung
for their souls. Outside the walls the city was ringed by a series
of great religious houses, churches and hospitals, from the
Carmelite convent of the White Friars on Fleet Street in the
west, round to St Katherine's church and hospital for the poor
next to the Tower in the east. Slightly farther out, but still
within a quarter of a mile of the walls, lay three more important
buildings: the Temple, once the monastery of the Knights
Templar, but now owned by the Knights Hospitaller and leased
out by them since the beginning of Edward III's reign to the
justices, lawyers and clerks who formed the embryonic inns
of court; the Hospitallers' own great preceptory, head of the
order in England, lay a short distance away to the north-east at
Clerkenwell; and, close to that, the Charterhouse, a new
Carthusian monastery founded by Sir Walter Mauny in 1371
on the site of the chapel serving the cemetery he had dedicated
for plague victims.[7] The position of all these major buildings
outside the city walls and on London's periphery made them
vulnerable to attack and all, except the Charterhouse, would
suffer incursions by the rebels in 1381.

In addition to the great religious foundations, there were
some fifty town houses, or inns, belonging to Church prelates,
which they used as a base for attendance at court or parliament.
Both archbishops, all nineteen bishops and most abbots and
priors owned one, ranging from the relatively modest quarters
of the abbot of Waltham, just outside Billingsgate, which had a
chapel, dormitory, great hall, kitchen, gatehouse, stable, courtyard and other domestic offices, to the palatial residence of the
bishop of Ely in Holborn, which was set in large private gardens with an orchard and fourteen acres of pasture beyond.

Most of these ecclesiastical inns were in the favoured suburbs of Holborn and the Strand, lying between the crowded walled city and Westminster, which was then a separate community under the jurisdiction of the abbot, but three were on the south side of the river: the bishop of Winchester's inn was at Southwark, which lay in his own diocese and conveniently close to London Bridge, while the archbishop of Canterbury and the bishop of Rochester both had their establishments in Lambeth, a short boat ride across the Thames from Westminster. Virtually all lay aristocrats also had their London inns, chiefly in Southwark, Holborn and the Strand. The most sumptuous of these was the Savoy Palace on the Strand, which had been rebuilt at a cost of thirty-five thousand pounds by Henry, duke of Lancaster, out of his profits from the Hundred Years War; the most eminent prisoner of those wars, King John of France, had lived and died in his custody at the Savoy. Now it belonged to Lancaster's son-in-law, John of Gaunt, and its fabulous buildings, combined with its dominant position on the Strand, with gardens, orchards and fishponds running down to the Thames waterfront, made it a potent symbol of his power.[8]

Access to the river was highly prized since the Thames was a larger and faster thoroughfare than any of the city's roads. The medieval Thames would have borne a strong resemblance to the modern Grand Canal and Canal Basin in Venice, its waters indiscriminately crammed with merchant vessels and fishing boats vying for space with aristocratic barges and hundreds of small boats rowed by the watermen (and women) ferrying their passengers up, down and across the river. London Bridge, too, was a longer and shabbier version of the Rialto: built of stone in the twelfth century to replace an earlier wooden one, it had nineteen arches, with towers and drawbridges at each end, and a chapel dedicated to St Thomas Becket in the middle. Altogether there were 139 shops lining the bridge: many of them were several storeys high and encroached on the road, so that it was scarcely wide enough to allow carts and carriages to pass. The throng of pedestrian traffic was swelled, at times, by the many pilgrims who, traditionally but inconveniently, began their pilgrimage to Canterbury at St Thomas's chapel. (The bridge and chapel had been built as an act of penance by Henry II for the murder of his archbishop, so the chapel was a natural starting point for a pilgrimage to the place of Becket's martyrdom.) The bridge's considerable upkeep was the responsibility of the city but delegated to two bridge-masters elected annually to maintain it from the income raised by tolls from those passing over or under it, charitable dona-tions and property rental.[9] London Bridge was the only crossing over the Thames in the city – indeed it was the only river cross-ing between London and the North Sea and there was no other bridge farther inland for some twenty miles. This gave it an importance out of all proportion to its size: possession of the bridge effectively controlled access not only to the heart of London itself but also to the north bank by those on the south. Anyone intending to enter the city in any number – as the Kent rebels wished to do – would first have to gain the bridge. That they were able to do so with such ease would naturally raise suspicions of treachery and, after the revolt, Alderman Walter Sibil, who was responsible for Bridge ward, would have to stand trial on charges of criminal conspiracy with the rebels.[10]

In addition to the bridge itself, the city corporation also owned the waterfront on either side, stretching from Queenhithe in the west to Billingsgate in the east, and it was here that ships were loaded and unloaded on the quays, wharves and jetties, wholesale markets were held and Londoners bought their coal, salt, corn and oysters. A new customs house had been built below the bridge at the end of Edward III's reign, reflecting a shift in commercial focus downstream owing to the increasing size of ships, which made it more difficult and dangerous for them to negotiate the narrow arches of the bridge. Other than the goods sold at the landing places, most were taken for sale to various market-places throughout the city, each having its own dedicated areas: fish, for instance, in New Fysshestrete, meat in Eastcheap and corn outside St Benet Gracechurch – though gardeners selling their produce close to St Paul's church-yard had been moved on because their cries were disrupting mass. The livestock markets, particularly for larger animals such as horses and cattle, were held at Smithfield, a large open area just outside the city walls, which was also the site of the annual St Bartholomew Fair and a favourite venue for tournaments and public gatherings: it was here, well away from the crowded streets of the city, that Richard would summon the rebels to meet him for the dramatic denouement of the revolt in London.[11]

Despite the pressure on space within the city walls, a sixteen-foot-wide band of land immediately inside their circuit was kept free of development for defensive and maintenance purposes. This, together with the area between the walls and the outer ditch that surrounded them, was given over to gardens which could be leased from the city authorities. All the great houses, and many of the smaller ones too, had their own private gardens where they grew vines, herbs and vegetables, and kept poultry, goats and even pigs. These would generally be for home consumption but on some large estates, like that surrounding the bishop of Ely's palace, gardeners were employed to produce onions, garlic, turnips, leeks, parsley, herbs and beans for the market. Many of the merchants, the financial elite of the city, lived in grand houses modelled on those of the aristocracy: they imported Caen stone from Normandy to build vaulted cellars and arched gateways leading to a courtyard, with a great hall on one side and subsidiary chambers, kitchens, outhouses and a private chapel completing the quadrangle, and walled gardens, yards and orchards beyond. Richard Lyons, the notorious financier who was murdered in the great revolt, might not have been an aristocrat but he lived like one; his hall was hung with tapestries from Arras, leopard skins and ermine decorated his chamber, and his bed curtains, fashioned from the finest red and blue worsted cloth, were embroidered with lions (a playful allusion to his name). He even had a pavilion or tent to put round his bathtub to keep out the draughts as he bathed.[12]

Most inhabitants of London could only aspire to such luxury. The poorest families lived and worked in a single room within a tenement in an alleyway which they rented for a few shillings a year. Small shopkeepers were at least able to separate their living and working spaces, though the majority probably only had one room behind or above a shop which itself might only be five or six feet by ten; even the larger shops, purpose-built in identical rows, often had a street frontage only ten or twelve feet wide, though they extended twenty feet back and might have a garden of equal size to carry out the noisier or smellier aspects of their craft (the manufacture of leather-work and armour was particularly noxious). The ground floor of such buildings would be dedicated to the shop, with a store-room and perhaps a counting house behind, the first floor would house the living quarters and the second floor the bed-chamber in which the whole family might sleep. Ever since the great fire of 1212, which began in Southwark and destroyed the church of St Mary Overy before spreading across London Bridge into the city, building regulations had been imposed which decreed that all party walls were to be three feet wide, sixteen feet high and made of stone. Though difficulties in obtaining stone meant that this was not always followed, most houses were built over stone cellars and with stone chimneys, only the superstructure being of wood, and tiles of clay, stone or lead, rather than thatch, were used to cover the roof. Windows, even in quite ordinary houses, were shuttered for warmth and security but usually glazed as well.[13]

As the existence of building regulations and glazing suggests, urban life at this period was much more sophisticated than popular legend would have us believe. Accounts of the city being overrun with rats, pigs wandering out of control through streets awash with animal and human excrement, where households flung their waste and butchers the entrails of slaughtered animals, are a huge exaggeration. Since they are drawn chiefly from complaints to the city authorities and prosecutions of offenders they reflect not common practice but the opposite – public intolerance of such things being allowed to take place. Rats, of course, were as endemic then as they are now but breeding pigs within the city was forbidden and carried a hundred-pound fine; butchers were obliged to carry out their trade in appointed areas – though that did not stop a myriad of complaints from neighbours about the nauseous smells and filth emanating from the Shambles. (The problem was not solved until 1392–3 when the butchers were ordered to cut up their offal on a special pier in the Thames, take it out by boat to the centre of the river and dump it there at ebb tide so that it could be carried away without polluting the river banks.)

It was already recognised that insanitary conditions bred disease and the city tried hard to enforce cleanliness in private homes and public areas. Larger houses had their own cesspits which had to be properly lined and drained or the owners could be fined for causing a nuisance to their neighbours; those living in upper tenements or small houses had access to shared privies which would have to be regularly emptied unless, like the householders along Walbrook, they were able to pay an annual fine of twelve pence for a licence to have their latrines built over the running waters of the stream. There were even public latrines available in many wards, some of them provided and maintained by charitable donation or bequest: as early as the twelfth century the wife of Henry I had built a 'necessary house' at Queenhithe 'for the common use of the citizens' and London Bridge had its own set which emptied directly into the Thames.[14]

In each of the twenty-four wards of the city scavengers were employed to oversee the work of publicly funded rakers, who travelled round with a horse and cart, cleaning and clearing the streets and lanes, and carting away the rubbish to specially designated sites outside the walls; dung boats were also in operation, some of them privately chartered to carry valuable horse dung from the city's many stables out to manure the fields in the surrounding countryside. Illicit dumping into the rivers and the city ditch was an incurable problem but the perpetrators were fined heavily if caught. Where there was a recurrent problem, caused by the transaction of legitimate business, such as the cattle market at Smithfield or the quays between the Bridge and the Tower, tolls were levied on the sale of beasts and merchandise specifically to fund regular cleansing of the area.

In 1372 the penalties for causing nuisance were increased: householders who left rubbish outside their houses, threw kitchen slops or the contents of chamber pots out of their windows or had excrement inside or outside their houses were to be fined two shillings, rising to four for anyone who committed such offences outside someone else's house. It was permitted to carry 'dirty water' (including urine) to empty into the open drains which ran down each side, or along the middle, of the street but faecal matter was strictly prohibited: an ingenious woman who put a latrine in her solar and connected it to the street sewer by a wooden pipe was ordered to remove it immediately.[15] The city even had its own municipal water supply, which, from the mid-thirteenth century, was piped from the Tyburn via a conduit to storage cisterns in Cheapside; at times of exceptional public rejoicing, such as Henry V's return from his victory at Agincourt, they could be converted to carry wine. Water was also available to purchase from commercial water carriers but most people relied on rainwater, collected from their roofs in cisterns or butts and sometimes carried by gutters directly to their kitchens; the wealthiest were able to sink their own wells, though at the risk of contamination by leakage from neighbouring cesspits.[16]

Though furniture remained simple, even in the grandest houses, with trestle tables for dining, chests for storing clothes, documents and silverware, and canopied beds serving a dual purpose as couches, Flemish and German influences were beginning to be felt by the end of the fourteenth century: chairs, folding tables, clothes presses and carved bedsteads 'of beyond sea making' were all introduced. Soft furnishings added considerably to comfort and warmth. Wall tapestries and bed curtains served not only to keep out draughts but also as opportunities to boast of one's ancestry by displaying family heraldry or insignia and of one's cultivation by depicting hunting scenes or stories from the chivalric romances. Linen sheets, tablecloths and napkins were obligatory in polite households, as were linen towels.

The idea that medieval people rarely washed is a nineteenth-century fallacy. Every courtesy book stressed the need to wash one's hands and face daily and it was also customary to wash the hands before eating: guests might be offered water scented with garden herbs or flowers or even, in the wealthiest households, with perfume imported from the east. Bathing was a regular ritual for those with servants to fetch and carry hot water from the fire to the portable bathtubs which look like half-barrels in the manuscripts where they are portrayed. Those fortunate enough to possess a dedicated bathroom could enjoy the luxury of piped hot water and tiled floors: Richard II upgraded his grandfather's facilities by adding new bath-houses at his favourite manor houses and purchasing two thousand painted tiles to pave the floor of the one at Sheen. (The fastidious Richard, incidentally, is also credited with the invention of the pocket handkerchief and normalising the use of spoons instead of hands at dinner.) Such luxuries were only available to a very few but even those who did not have access to a bathtub at home could utilise the public bath-houses which had been a feature of urban life since Roman times. They were popularly known as 'stews', deriving their name from the stoves which were used to heat the rooms and water. Although there were 'honest stews', which women were not permitted to enter, stews in general had a deservedly unsavoury reputation because, like massage parlours today, they were frequently a cover for running a brothel. In Richard's reign there were eighteen of them in the London ward of Southwark alone and so many were sited along the waterfront that it was known as Stewsbank.[17]

Richer merchant households possessed a substantial amount of silverware, not just for use and ornament, but because it was readily pawned as security for loans or cashed in to pay debts. It was in this portable wealth that canny merchants preferred to invest, together with their merchandise, shipping, money-lending and property in London: only a few, having made their fortune, invested in land outside the capital. Richard Lyons was an exception, as was the draper John Hende, a collector of the third poll-tax in London, whose manors and other properties in Kent and Essex brought in annual revenues of some eighty-two pounds, compared with an annual income of almost fifty-five pounds from his London properties. This was insignificant in terms of Hende's overall worth, however, for when his investments in money-lending and merchandise were also taken into account, this amounted to four to five thousand pounds: trading was where fortunes were to be made – and lost – not building up a portfolio of landholdings in the countryside.[18]

Men like Lyons and Hende belonged to an elite group of super-rich merchants from whose ranks the mayor and aldermen of the city were elected; only nine of the 260 aldermen serving in the fourteenth century were not merchants, and one of those, a corn-monger, had to resign for lack of means. In 1381 the mayor of London was William Walworth, who was serving his second term of office; since 1369 he had also been mayor of the Westminster Staple, but he had also served as sheriff of the city in 1370 and as its MP in 1371, 1376 and 1377. Friend, adviser and money-lender to many royal courtiers and to the crown itself, Walworth's glittering career and fabulous wealth belied his origins. For, like the better-known Richard Whittington of pantomime fame, and indeed, like many others in London's highly mobile society, he had come to London from the provinces (in his case from a family manor just outside Darlington, County Durham) and risen by a combination of luck and ability. He had served an apprenticeship with John Lovekyn, a wealthy fish-monger and wool merchant who had himself served four times as mayor of London, and, when Lovekyn died in 1368, stepped into his shoes both in business and in politics.[19]

Walworth had lived the dream even before he achieved the ultimate accolade of knighthood as a reward for his loyalty during the great revolt and, more especially, for his decisive action in striking down Wat Tyler at Smithfield. Like Lovekyn before him and Whittington after him, however, Walworth died childless, so his enormous wealth was not handed down to the next generation but instead dedicated mostly to charitable causes: not content with merely adding a new choir and chapel to the London church in which he chose to be buried, he also endowed it with a college of chantry chaplains to sing masses for his soul. He also bequeathed twenty pounds to each of his two apprentices, one of whom, William Askham, would then step into his shoes just as he had stepped into Lovekyn's: Askham would take over the house Walworth had acquired from Lovekyn, become sheriff, mayor of the Staple and city, and serve several times as a member of parliament for London.[20]

As the Lovekyn–Walworth–Askham example demonstrates, apprenticeship was the key to making a fortune and the prospect of doing so drew young men from all over the country, a high proportion of them from the north of England. They came from every social background between the two extremes of pauperhood and aristocracy: many were younger sons of either the gentry or provincial merchants, but the majority were sons of artisans, yeomen and husbandmen – the aspirant middle class. They had to pay for the privilege: apprenticeship to a goldsmith, for instance, was for a period of at least seven years and cost the young man's parents anything between £6 13s. 4d. and one hundred pounds, usually in the form of an interest-free loan. The only pre-condition was free status but, in practice, London's liberties allowed a villein who served a year and a day unchallenged to claim his freedom. This was a sore point with landlords, who, in 1376, complained in parliament about the difficulty of retrieving their absconded villeins from the city, but it perhaps made Londoners more sympathetic to the rebel demand for the abolition of serfdom.[21]

Completion of an apprenticeship opened the doors to membership of the guild which regulated that particular craft and to citizenship which entitled the holder to a voice, and even a role, in the governance of the city, as well as to enjoy the commercial privileges and legal protections of the royal charter of liberties. Even though the older, more powerful, guilds, such as the mercers, drapers, grocers, fish-mongers, goldsmiths, skinners and vintners, embraced a wide range of men (and sometimes women), from the great merchants who had fingers in many pies to independent artisans with a single shop and even those working for wages, the majority of those living in London were not citizens. Known as 'foreigners', even if they had been born in the city, they were unenfranchised and excluded from many commercial activities, such as buying for resale or keeping a retail shop, but the opportunity to succeed remained open to them. Indeed, it was actually encouraged. In 1381, the very year of the great revolt, the Common Council of the city decided to make it easier to obtain the freedom of the city because houses were standing vacant and the number of citizens had fallen.[22] It was no wonder that London attracted so many immigrants dreaming of a freedom and wealth denied them in more rigidly structured parts of the country.

No other city in the kingdom could come even close to London in terms of size, wealth or political influence. The next largest towns, York, Bristol, Coventry and Norwich, with tax-paying populations in 1377 ranging from 7248 to 4817, shared similarities in appearance, structure and governance but could not compare in scale. Yet even these towns must have seemed huge metropolises to ordinary urban dwellers, most of whom lived in small market towns which were little more than glorified villages. A typical example was Chelmsford, Essex, where around 240 tax-payers were recorded in 1377. The town consisted of little more than a quarter of a mile of high street, topped and tailed by its church and its bridge over the river Can; by 1381 a 'new street' had begun to develop, together with an area to the north where a particularly entrepreneurial family lived. The houses were much the same as those found in rural villages and hamlets, consisting mainly of single-storey cottages and hall houses built with thatched roofs, timber frames and walls made with a mixture of clay and straw or wattle and daub (a weave of thin wooden lathes or twigs plastered over with mud or clay). Just as they did in the countryside, more prosperous families would have added extra chambers, wings or even a second storey to their hall, creating private space for the owners to sleep or withdraw from the communal life of the hall, but also to provide separate accommodation for servants; in towns, however, one of these additional chambers might have been built to create a shop or workshop with a door or window on to the street allowing customers to come and go without impinging on the domestic life of the inhabitants. Unlike modern towns, each house was surrounded by its own gardens and orchards capable of producing staple dietary items such as garlic, onions, cabbage, peas, beans, herbs, apples, pears, plums and walnuts, as well as the more exotic items favoured by urban gardeners, including cucumbers, parsnips and celery, and even flax and hemp for spinning. Additionally, each house would have its own yard, where the privy would be sited – its contents, one assumes, being one of the reasons why urban gardens were so productive – and usually an oven or bakehouse built of stone or brick and separate from the main house to limit the risks created by cooking over open fires.[23]

In appearance, then, a small town would have had little to distinguish it from a rural village. In the case of Chelmsford the distinction was blurred even further since the town was situated within the manor of the same name which belonged to the bishop of London. Just like any other ecclesiastical manor it was administered by the bishop's steward, who visited regularly to hold manorial courts, and, in the intervals between his visits, by the bailiff. Indeed it might be argued that the only reason that it should be classified as a town at all was that its inhabitants pursued non-agricultural occupations: the tax-payers of Chelmsford in 1381, for example, were mainly smiths, chandlers, bakers, maltsters, skinners, tanners, shoemakers, ostlers and servants, with a mercer, fuller, roper, chaloner and wool-monger thrown in for good measure. Yet rustic appearances could be deceptive, for Chelmsford was a medieval 'new town', founded by the bishop of London in 1199 to take advantage of a focal position at the junction of routes to all four points of the compass: it therefore had a thriving weekly market but, more importantly, it was also the place from which royal administrative, financial and judicial business was carried out in Essex. That is why, after the rebels had raided the houses of the sheriff and escheator and collected up all their records, they did not destroy them immediately but instead made the symbolic gesture of carrying them off to Chelmsford, where they made a bonfire of them in the middle of the high street.[24]

The significance of small towns like Chelmsford is that they were particularly prevalent in the counties most severely affected by the great revolt – and those counties were the ones with the highest population density. By the late fourteenth century East Anglia had more than sixteen people for every two and a half square miles, compared with less than three and a half in the northern marches of England, where the lack of both good-quality arable land and access to markets, as well as regular raids by the Scots, all combined to keep population levels low. The average number of markets across the country was 3.7 per hundred square miles, but again East Anglia had a much higher proportion and in Suffolk it rose to almost ten, the highest density in England. Suffolk, like Hertfordshire and Kent, which were also at the forefront of the revolt, was a county of small market towns and the practical consequence of this was that an ambitious and hard-working small farmer or craftsman might have four or five local markets, all held on different days, within a few miles of his home. He or his wife, or his children, could therefore travel there and back within daylight hours to sell his goods. And of course those who lived and worked in the market towns had the advantage of not having to travel to sell their own products but also a weekly influx of potential customers coming to buy from them.[25]

The importance of the market economy in Suffolk is indicated by the fact that eighty per cent of its poll-tax-payers in 1381 were recorded as non-agricultural workers – a proportion which was much higher than in many other places in England, though broadly equivalent to that of Essex and Norfolk. Though this figure included labourers and servants, it clearly demonstrates that only a small minority of people were able to live solely off the land, despite this being one of the most fertile and productive areas of the country. The practice of dividing up holdings between children, rather than allowing the eldest to inherit, had increased pressure on the availability of land and created many small holdings which could not support a family: only three per cent of Suffolk tenants held more than thirty acres of land, hence the diversification into the market economy, particularly into the burgeoning cloth industry.[26]

Even those who were employed in agriculture were often obliged to seek other sources of income to supplement the seasonal nature of their work: records of offences against the Statute of Labourers reveal that a ploughman might also have worked as a carter and a labourer, threshers and mowers as carpenters, or, in the case of one versatile Norfolk man in the 1370s, as a plasterer, mower and thatcher. Conversely, those in domestic service, even in towns, were sometimes required to return to their homes to assist with the harvest, an obligation which was not as onerous as it might seem, since a month's harvesting might double a female servant's usual wage.[27]

A large number of urban residents were actually temporary emigrants from the countryside. Servants, in particular, were far more common in towns than in rural areas: less than a sixth of households in rural Rutland employed servants, compared with over a third in most towns. In the wealthiest parts of a town or city the proportion was much higher: in Coney Street, York, over sixty-five per cent of households had servants and over forty-five per cent of those living there were in service; in Bailey Lane, Coventry, a remarkable eighty-four per cent of households employed servants. The reason why such high numbers of servants were employed in places like these was that their duties extended beyond the purely domestic into the commercial activities of their employers. Female servants were most often to be found in the households of victuallers and merchants, where they would be involved in baking, brewing, preparing food, needlework and dealing in the market-place or shop; male servants tended to work in more physically demanding trades such as metal- and leather-work as well as weaving, which was then predominantly a male occupation.[28]

Almost all servants were young, unmarried and lived with their employers. Unless they were apprentices, in which case they were legally bound to serve their masters for a term of years, they rarely stayed more than one or two years in the same situation, moving on at the traditional hiring time of Michaelmas at the end of September. Many of them came from the countryside in search of payment for labour which they might otherwise have to give to their families free of charge or find in seasonal tasks: service in towns offered year-round security of employment and frequently better wages than could be found back at home, but it was not usually a long-term career choice. Most servants in Essex, for example, left their rural homes in their early teens and returned in their twenties; very few of them travelled more than ten or fifteen miles to find employment. They regarded their time in service as a short-term opportunity to earn a nest egg which could then be used to purchase land or the tools to establish a craft or trade; frequently it also laid the financial foundations which enabled a marriage to take place. Crucially, however, most of them kept up their connections with the place of their birth, returning seasonally to help with the harvest and then permanently as soon as they were ready or able to do so. For them there was no sharp distinction between being a country dweller or a townsman; they had a stake in both places.[29]

Servants, together with craftsmen, artisans and tradesmen, formed the eighty per cent of poll-tax-payers in East Anglia who followed non-agricultural occupations. This meant that four-fifths of the adult population in this region depended on wages to earn a living – wages which, as we shall see, would be specifically targeted both by the Statute of Labourers and by the poll-taxes. It was no wonder, then, that so many of those living and working in market towns felt aggrieved enough to rebel in 1381, or that East Anglia, with its unusually high number of such places, should have been at the heart of the revolt.

If small market towns were primarily centres of local trade, larger ones tended to be regional centres for more specialist trades. Colchester, Essex, was a prime example of a failing ancient borough which had been revitalised and found a new identity as a centre of cloth manufacture in the years after the Black Death. Colchester russets were a byword for mid-market, good-quality cloth. Unlike the finer cloths produced for the aristocracy, they were scoured and thickened mechanically by water-powered fulling mills and, despite their name, they were mainly shades of grey, which required less and cheaper dye than the vivid colours of more expensive fabrics. Of better quality than home-produced cloths, they enjoyed a niche market among the religious orders, who made them into habits and cloaks, but were also bought for garment-making by the better-off among the labouring, farming and artisan classes. From the moment that the raw wool was brought into the moot-hall cellars, every part of the cloth-making process was carried out in the town: from the washing, carding and combing to the spinning, weaving and finishing. The river Colne was vital to the trade: it supplied water power to the fulling mills, some of which had been converted from grain because of the demand, and it provided direct access to the sea via the neighbouring quays at Hythe, which had been developed specifically so that cloth could be carried inexpensively to its principal markets in London, Gascony, Prussia and the Baltic. It was a mark of the town's commercial success that it not only had a thriving market but also, twice a year in June and July, it held a two-day annual cloth fair which, in 1374, was extended to three days; this attracted sellers from the wider region but more importantly merchant buyers, particularly from London.[30]

The 1370s saw Colchester at the peak of its prosperity, with 2995 inhabitants over the age of fourteen according to the returns for the first poll-tax. Confined as the town was within the bounds of its crumbling Roman walls, which were about to be repaired at vast expense, pressure for building space meant that two-storey shops and houses with cellars below now filled the high street on both sides and houses and tenements were frequently subdivided. As in many other larger towns, certain streets had become home to specialist trades: 'the bakery', Cook Row and the butchers' shambles vied for space with the fish market, corn market and Cordwainers' Row, where the shoemakers plied their wares. There were ten churches within or just outside the walls, as well as a decaying royal castle, which was mainly used as a prison. Just across the fields lay the fast-developing quays and warehouses of the Hythe, where demand for a street frontage meant that many new buildings were narrower than their older counterparts. Nevertheless, despite the crowded streets, most houses retained their gardens and court-yards and there was still open space within the town.[31]

Colchester enjoyed borough status, which granted it the highly prized privilege of self-government. Some boroughs had existed since before the Conquest but the vast majority had been created by royal or seigneurial charter in the twelfth and thirteenth centuries. In return for paying an annual fee farm, or rental, a borough received in perpetuity the right to exercise civil and sometimes criminal judicial power over its own towns-men and to administer justice according to its own customs; since the reign of Henry III such boroughs could even be sum-moned to send two elected representatives to parliament. By the fourteenth century they were recognised in law as corporate bodies, governed by a mayor and aldermen, who were nomi-nally elected by the burgesses but in practice were self-selected by a small group of the wealthiest families. Simply living in a borough did not qualify a resident to be a burgess: this role could only be acquired by inheritance, by purchase or by com-pleting an apprenticeship to a craft. Townsmen who were burgesses enjoyed the privilege of being able to sell directly to the public without paying any tolls; they could also, in theory, have a say in the borough's government, hold office and be members of a craft guild, but they were liable to taxes which were not levied on 'foreigners', the residents who did not share their elite status.[32]

Unusually, Colchester had avoided many of the internal con-flicts which, as we shall see, contributed to the revolt of 1381 in similar towns, despite an influx of emigrants from the coun-tryside and also from the Low Countries. Colchester had encouraged such immigration since the Black Death, admitting an average of twenty-two new burgesses each year in the 1350s, including, uncommonly, a number of women. In 1372 its con-stitution had been reformed so that the two bailiffs had to provide annual accounts for scrutiny by auditors and were to share responsibility for governing the town with a newly instituted council of twenty-four leading townsmen, most of whom were merchants. This opening up of civic office to the newly wealthy seems to have forestalled the struggles for power between old and new money which broke out in other urban centres, such as York, particularly as lesser tradesmen were given a role in electing officials which also included them in the process of government. The complete absence of craft guilds in Colchester may have contributed to its commercial success, since there were none of the restrictive regulations and practices which frustrated the efforts of new entrepreneurs to establish themselves in business elsewhere. The bailiffs and their councillors had even managed to protect the town's inhabitants from prosecution under the Statute of Labourers by failing to present any offenders to the justices.[33]

Colchester, then, might be regarded as a model town full of happy citizens, who had little motivation to join the revolt in 1381. Yet this did not mean that it escaped unscathed. The town was a gathering point for rebels from Tendring hundred who were preparing to march to London, and men from Colchester were present at Mile End on 14 June when their demands were put to the king. After their return, on 16 June, they invaded the moot-hall and carried off some of the borough records, preventing any courts being held for the next five weeks; the same day they attacked St Cross Chapel in Crouch Street and St John's Abbey, which lay just outside the town walls, carrying off and burning both muniments and court rolls. The town clerk and custodian of the borough court rolls later wrote that he had been 'in very great fear both for himself and for his friends' but neither he nor any other borough official appears to have been targeted personally or harmed in any way. Indeed it seems that at least some of the rebels came from the

outlying villages and their anger was directed solely against the
abbey: two men from Brightlingsea were involved in the attack
there and the court rolls of Greenstead and West Donyland
were destroyed – all three places being manors in the abbey's
hands. Men from the town were responsible for the most serious acts of violence, however, which resulted in the only
fatalities in Colchester. The victims were the usual casualties of
English mob violence – the Flemings who had settled there to
pursue their craft of weaving. Who or how many they were we
do not know. Indeed their fate would have passed unnoticed
had not one of their murderers, Adam Michel of Colchester,
received the king's pardon for his involvement four years later.
What his motives were we can only speculate, though the fact
that he employed three servants suggests that he might have
been their competitor.[34]

More significant than any of these events, which were
repeated in almost every place involved in the revolt, is that
Colchester appears to have produced not one, but two, of the
most famous rebel leaders. Wat Tyler, despite being 'a captain,
leader and chief ... of the county of Kent', was identified by
Kentish jurors, at the beginning of July 1381, as being 'of Essex'
and, even more specifically, as 'of Colchester'.[35] John Balle, the
revolutionary priest, in one of the letters circulating in his name
during the revolt, refers to himself as 'now of colchestre'. For at
least seventeen years, and probably much longer, Balle had been
a vagabond, wandering from place to place throughout Essex
and 'preaching articles contrary to the faith of the church to the
peril of his soul and the souls of others, especially of laymen'.[36]
Monastic chroniclers would be quick to blame him for stirring
up the great revolt by his heretical and seditious preaching but,
if this were so, the seeds he had planted had taken many years
to grow and had been scattered far beyond East Anglia.

For the evidence suggests that tensions were rising in many

other towns too on the eve of the great revolt. Just eleven months before its outbreak, there was a riot in Winchester, Hampshire, when some three hundred townsmen attacked the prior of Southwick, who was meeting his fellow commissioners of array in the city. The reason for the assault is not clear but it was not a random riot: the mob was led by the bailiff of the commons, William Wygge, a member of one of the borough's most important families, whose father or uncle had served three times as mayor and four times as an MP, and who would himself become the future leader of the revolt in Winchester in the summer of 1381.[37] Not long afterwards, on 2 September 1380, and less than twenty-five miles away, John Haukewode was alleged to have come to Salisbury, Fisherton Anger and elsewhere in Wiltshire, with a band of Salisbury men armed with swords, shields, bows and arrows. In each of these places he denied the king's statutes and laws and proclaimed in the market-place that anyone who contradicted him or denied him his will would be beheaded. The reference to 'statutes' as well as laws suggests that this was possibly a protest against the Statute of Labourers, but the indicting jury had no hesitation in declaring Haukewode 'a common rebel', agitator and inciter of rebellion. Haukewode was found not guilty when he was tried for this offence in April 1384; a couple of weeks later he obtained a pardon at Queen Anne's request 'for taking part in the revolt'. Whether his pardon was a precautionary purchase after his acquittal to protect him against further accusations of wrongdoing, or whether he had genuinely joined the great revolt as well, is unclear.[38]

Shrewsbury, Shropshire, also witnessed violent upheavals over the winter of 1380. The mayor and 'worthy men' of the town petitioned the king in the November parliament, complaining that 'men of lesser sufficiency' in the town had banded together and chosen two bailiffs ahead of the appointed time, who had removed money from the town coffers, 'risen against their betters and assaulted and imprisoned one of them, Reginald Scryveyn, refusing to obey the king's writ for his release, so that his three sons died of grief'. The bailiffs counterclaimed that Scryveyn had rescued an outlaw indicted for murder and assaulted the bailiff who had arrested the alleged murderer. When the customary time came round for the election of bailiffs, a mob of people who had no lands or tenements in the town (and were therefore not qualified to vote) assembled and by their menaces and threats prevented the elections taking place. On 26 March the king intervened, appointing seventeen men from the locality as commissioners to restore order, supervise the election and imprison all who disturbed the new bailiffs or made unlawful assemblies and would not give security for their good behaviour. Three days later, under the auspices of their lord, the earl of Arundel, the bailiffs and commonalty reached an agreement that twelve men elected from their number should govern the town for the next two years, but they had to render an account of their receipts at the end of each year to six auditors also elected from the commonalty.[39] This suggests that the financial probity of the bailiffs was at the heart of the dispute, an issue that was of major concern in many urban areas owing to the increasing exactions made on the community by the king.

Similar reasons lay behind the serious uprising in York which had taken place a couple of months after the Salisbury riots. On 26 November 1380, 'various malefactors among the commons of the city' forcibly ejected their mayor, John Gisburn, from York. They then commandeered the guildhall, which they had stormed by breaking down the doors and windows with axes and other weapons, and there compelled the leading citizens to swear an oath of loyalty to Simon Quixley, whom they had chosen as their new mayor. They went on to issue a new ordinance that whenever the bells on the bridge were rung 'aukeward', meaning backwards or in reverse order, 'all the commons of the said city should rise together and have proclaimed various ordinances newly composed by them'. The significance of this was that the bridge was where the council chamber was situated and, in normal circumstances, the bells were rung in the proper way to assemble the inhabitants for the reading of public proclamations. Both Quixley, and those who had sworn to be loyal to him, later claimed that they had acted under duress and against their will but the whole episode smacks of a coup organised by his party against Gisburn and his supporters. That was certainly the interpretation put upon it by the king and parliament, who acted immediately to order the arrest and imprisonment without bail of twenty-four of the 'most notorious leaders and abettors of the said rioters and malefactors' and summoned Quixley to resign his post and answer for his actions before the king and council. Gisburn was to be restored and remain in office for the rest of his term and a royal proclamation was to be made in York commanding the populace to obey him 'as the person who represents the state of our lord the king in the said city'.[40]

These words must have had a hollow ring to those who had engineered Gisburn's overthrow, for no one was more identified with the abuse of royal authority. This was one of the main reasons for the coup against him. Gisburn was one of the richest and most powerful men in the city. His wealth was built on the export of wool and cloth and he was mayor of the York Staple from 1358 until its closure in 1363, then one of the twenty-four aldermen chosen to govern the town of Calais and the new national Staple which had been established there. As an elite member of both the Staple and York's civic government he was instrumental in securing huge corporate loans to the crown and in building ships to serve in the king's wars; he had also made his own personal contributions as a royal creditor and supplier of ships. And he reaped his rewards by being appointed to royal offices which gave him further opportunities to extend his influence and to enrich himself, often at his fellow citizens' expense. He was a regular collector of royal taxes, including the 1379 poll-tax, a justice of the peace for York every year from 1377 and represented the city in parliament, where he was appointed to royal advisory committees. He even had influence over the royal mint in York, where, it was later alleged, he profiteered from the conversion of ten thousand pounds of English money into the lighter Scottish coin of the same face value. None of these things was calculated to make him popular in a city which, throughout the 1370s, had found itself increasingly burdened by the crown's financial demands to support the war in France. The issue of building ships at the city's cost to serve in the royal navy was a particularly sensitive one since Gisburn and his cronies benefited from using them when they were not in the king's service to carry their wool and cloth abroad, so that York's citizens were effectively subsidising Gisburn's private business interests. Yet he had still succeeded in being re-elected as mayor four times between 1371 and 1380, despite a city ordinance which prohibited re-election until eight others had occupied the post – a measure which, ironically, had been brought in after Gisburn himself was elected in two successive years.[41]

Simon Quixley, on the other hand, despite being a wealthy merchant in his own right, was one of only four aldermen not to have served as mayor by the time Gisburn received his third term of office and obviously resented the fact that he had been excluded from his turn at the post. That Quixley enjoyed so much support right across different interest groups is telling evidence of the levels of discontent in the city. This was not a purely factional struggle for power among York's oligarchy, even though Quixley's main supporters were the butchers, who had complained long and vociferously about the penny a week toll they had to pay for selling meat from their stalls and the extortions and heavy-handed tactics of the city bailiffs. The leading rebels were all freemen of the city and included a mercer, shipman, carpenter, sheather, two tailors, four weavers and three drapers, as well as six butchers. Only one of them had ever held high civic office, which suggests that this uprising was an attempt to obtain more say in the way the civic administration was run, not least by obtaining a mayor who had been chosen and installed by those excluded from the self-selecting elite which controlled the city. With their own mayor at the helm, the rebels could, and did, become involved in actual decision-making, rather than simply endorsing decisions already taken by the oligarchy. They immediately began issuing ordinances, including one imposing a new tax, the collection of which was prohibited by royal writ on 5 December as part of the measures to overturn the uprising in York.[42]

Gisburn may have prevailed upon his royal connections to have himself re-installed as mayor, but he was unable to prevent his being legitimately replaced by Quixley in the elections held in February 1381. Their rivalry had now reached such a pitch that the two men began issuing liveries of different-coloured hoods to their supporters, a move which inevitably exacerbated tensions and escalated acts of violence, since tribal loyalties were paraded publicly and provocatively. Quixley continued to cultivate popular support to shore up his position but the uprising had made both men more aware of the dangers in destabilising the city. This perhaps explains the concerted efforts made by the collectors of the third poll-tax to ensure that the burden was as light as possible. Not only did the wealthy subsidise their poorer neighbours, as they were required to do, but the poorest parishes were excluded entirely from the assessment, resulting in a drop in taxable population from 7248 in 1377 to just 3810. A reassessment carried out by local officials only added a further 205 to the total.[43] Since collection of the poll-tax spanned the change in mayoralty from Gisburn to Quixley it can be assumed that both men sanctioned this deliberate evasion of the city's common liability. If so, it was a brief moment of consensual politics in a period of increasing division and volatility which, a few months later, would erupt into a second uprising even more violent in character than the first.

York was a long way, physically and metaphorically, from the village of Fobbing whose inhabitants began the great revolt at the end of May 1381. Yet the men and women of the second city in the kingdom shared a deep and abiding sense of grievance with those from the fen-edge village in rural Essex. Indeed, the sense of grievance was almost nationwide. Town and country might have different causes for dissatisfaction, and there were specific local issues which roused strong feelings, but there was a groundswell of opinion that was united in its resentment of what contemporaries would call 'bad governance'. The reek of corruption was everywhere: whether it was civic officials lining their pockets at the community's expense or religious houses abusing archaic rights to extort the maximum amount of money and labour from their tenants; sheriffs and escheators who accepted bribes to give a favourable judgment; justices of the peace who enforced the Statute of Labourers against others but happily breached its terms themselves to obtain the labour they needed; royal justices who were in the pocket of lay and ecclesiastical aristocrats and used their knowledge to benefit these private clients at the expense of less well-connected litigants.

There was, of course, nothing new in any of this, hence the popularity of the aphorism quoted in one of John Balle's letters:

'no man may come to truth but he sing *"si dedero"'*, in other words pay a bribe.[44] From time to time popular frustration had boiled over into violence, and even concerted action by a community, against the perpetrators of perceived injustice. These had always been local incidents, however, which did not have the resonance to chime with discontent elsewhere. The difference in 1381 was that there was a common cause to unite all the disaffected: bad governance at the heart of the realm. The convention had always been to blame the king's advisers, rather than the king himself, since to criticise the monarch risked the charge of treason. But because Richard II was a boy, albeit one whom parliament had as recently as 1380 judged old enough to rule in person, he really could be excused responsibility for the failures of his reign. The disastrous conduct of the war against France, with its ineffectual campaigns abroad and its inability to protect English coastlines and shipping from attack, could be placed squarely at the feet of the king's uncles, especially John of Gaunt. So could the crippling financial burden which this military incompetence placed upon the realm, though it was the chancellor, archbishop Sudbury, and the treasurer, Sir Robert Hales, who would have to bear ultimate responsibility for the way in which this had been imposed and, in particular, for the crass attempts to reassess and enforce collection of the third poll-tax, which sparked the great revolt.

CHAPTER FIVE

Wars and taxes

War and taxation were inextricably linked in the medieval period. They were cause and effect in a way that is no longer applicable in an age when defence spending is only a twelfth of the total UK budget and three times as much is spent on healthcare.[1] Medieval English monarchs could not legitimately demand direct taxes from their subjects except in extraordinary circumstances, which, in practice, meant only when the security of the realm was under threat. This might be interpreted fluidly to include embarking on aggressive wars abroad but the fundamental principle remained that direct taxation could only be required for military purposes. In the eyes of the tax-payer, therefore, there was a simple correlation between paying taxes and successful warfare; if that was broken by failed campaigns or, worse still, as in 1377, by enemy invasion, then the tax-payer did not blame the fortunes of war as soldiers were accustomed to do, but the incompetence and corruption of those in government who had misspent the taxes granted to them.

Equally fundamental was the principle, established during the early years of Edward III's campaigns in France, that taxation could only be imposed with the consent of the king's subjects represented in parliament. This gave the House of Commons, in particular, the leverage to hold the king to account and to demand reforms which the crown might find unpalatable but was compelled to accept if it was to receive the money it needed to prosecute its wars. John of Gaunt, for instance, presiding over the radical 'Good Parliament' of 1376 as 'lieutenant of the king', had been forced to receive the largest number of petitions ever sent by the House of Commons to a medieval monarch and to listen to outspoken criticism about royal maladministration. Worse still, because he needed the Commons to grant a new tax to pay for another expedition to France once the truce expired, he had been compelled to concede not only that a new council, named in parliament and from which he was himself excluded, should be appointed to advise his ailing father but also that the king's mistress, chamberlain, household steward and a coterie of rich London merchants should be tried and sentenced by the lords in parliament on charges of financial corruption and illegal profiteering at the king's expense. This innovation, later known as impeachment, meant that royal councillors and servants were no longer accountable solely to the king but were also legally answerable to his subjects represented in the public forum of parliament. These were bitter pills for a man of Gaunt's autocratic tendencies to swallow and, to add to his humiliation, it was this same parliament which petitioned for Richard, the 'true heir apparent', to be brought before it and then, despite all Gaunt's concessions, refused to grant him the tax he had requested – the first such refusal since 1325.[2]

Since the late twelfth century the usual way of implementing a direct tax had been to charge a fraction (usually a tenth in the towns and a fifteenth in the countryside) of the value of an individual's movable goods. Until Edward III's reign that value had been reassessed with each new imposition but the need to speed up and simplify the process had prompted the adoption of a new method of assessment in 1334: the king's commissioners negotiated and collected a block payment from each town and village, based on its size and estimated wealth, but left the actual assessment of individuals and the collection of the tax to each community. The advantage of this system was that the crown knew in advance that each subsidy was worth approximately thirty-seven to thirty-eight thousand pounds and could plan its finances accordingly: in times of extreme emergency it could ask for (and sometimes receive) one and a half subsidies or even a double subsidy. The great disadvantage was that the level of the assessment had remained unchanged since 1334 and therefore did not reflect changes in demography, local economies or personal wealth.[3]

There was a general perception both in government and among landowners and employers that a large and increasing class of people was becoming wealthier but not shouldering its fair share of the tax burden. The 1370s would therefore see experiments in new forms of taxation intended to tap into these hidden reserves. The first of these was the parish tax of 1371, which was levied at the rate of 22s. 3d. on every parish in the kingdom, including those which were traditionally exempt from direct taxation because they were at the forefront of the war with France and Scotland, such as the Cinque Ports and Cumberland, or because they enjoyed privileged status, such as the county palatines of Chester and Durham. Nevertheless, it swiftly became clear that parliament had made a major error in its basic calculations: there were not forty-five thousand parishes in England and Wales, as originally estimated, but just over 8600, so the levy on each one had to be increased to 116s. The parish tax impacted most severely on areas like East Anglia which had the densest populations: by comparison with assessments for a normal subsidy Norfolk saw its contribution increase by thirty-four per cent, Essex by eighty-three per cent and Suffolk by a staggering 103 per cent. Not surprisingly there was a backlash: in Norfolk there were so many refusals to pay that £4674 16s. (the equivalent of 806 parishes) was still owing in January 1373 and local officials were told in no uncertain terms that if they did not cooperate with royal agents and collect the money due immediately 'the king will be wroth with them as with men who rebel against him'. At Lakenheath, Suffolk, attempts to force reluctant villagers to pay by seizing their goods and chattels provoked a riot in which the collectors were physically attacked and driven empty-handed from the village; the role of the future chief justice Sir John Cavendish in punishing the rioters would not be forgotten a decade later when Lakenheath was once again a centre of revolt.[4]

Though the parish tax of 1371 had raised more money in a shorter time than a conventional subsidy it had provoked such universal hostility that the experiment would not be repeated. Nevertheless it had effectively proved that there was untapped wealth in the kingdom, particularly among those who earned wages, and that a more efficient means of taxing it was possible. The House of Commons therefore drew on its example in setting its next experiment, the first poll-tax, of January 1377. Like the parish tax, this was to be levied regardless of status, the only exemptions being for children under the age of fourteen and genuine beggars. Everyone else, male and female, from highest to lowest in the land, was to pay four pence per head. This was not a huge sum at a time when skilled workmen could expect a daily income of around five pence and even a simple labourer could earn three pence a day for 'digging and collecting stones'. In the context of purchasing power, four pence could buy two and a half gallons of ale, or two hens, or a dozen eggs.[5]

The new tax was therefore deliberately set at a low rate and at an established level which the tax-paying population would have recognised.[6] The differences were that now every adult, rather than only wealthier households, would have to pay and that, instead of being able to spread the payment over two instalments which were usually a year apart, the entire sum was due in cash at the exchequer on 6 April 1377. Parliament obviously felt that, with the threat of a renewal of open war with France looming, a simple poll-tax would be easier and quicker to assess and collect than a conventional subsidy.[7]

In financial terms the first poll-tax was a success, raising around £22,580 from the laity alone, which was considerably more than the £18,500–19,000 from a comparable half-subsidy. It is clear even from the fragmentary evidence of the collectors' records that the exchequer had also succeeded in drawing within its grasp thousands of people who had previously escaped its clutches. In Colchester, Essex, for example, many households included not only a husband, wife and adult children but also servants: Richard and Alicia Baker employed three male and four female domestics, while John Reek and his wife had eleven unnamed employees working for them, probably in their master's workshops rather than on domestic tasks.[8]

The clergy were also liable to the poll-tax, though their consent had to be obtained from convocation, their formal representative assembly. In practice, convocation usually authorised the collection of tax from the clergy in conjunction with parliamentary grants, but this time there was strong resistance led by William Courtenay, bishop of London, who was himself of royal descent and had no fear of John of Gaunt. This culminated in a public clash between the two men when Courtenay presided over the meeting in convocation to which John Wyclif had been summoned to answer charges of seditious preaching. An Oxford scholar and former royal envoy, Wyclif had argued that secular government had the right to use Church property in time of need – a view so convenient for royal policy that Gaunt had brought him to London in the autumn of 1376 specifically to stir up popular anti-clericalism and put pressure on the clergy to be more generous in their financial dealings with the crown. Gaunt had no intention of allowing his protégé to be censured and therefore, together with his ally Henry, lord Percy, whom he had just appointed marshal of England, accompanied Wyclif to the hearing. Percy, in an act of calculated offensiveness, had his staff of office carried before him, which implied that Wyclif was under his protection and that the court was subject to his own authority. This attempt to intimidate the proceedings was no more successful than Gaunt's subsequent angry threat to pull the bishop from his chair by the hair: in the end Gaunt simply stormed out of the building. The London mob reacted with fury at this insult to their popular bishop and, the next day, when rumours spread that Gaunt also intended to extend Percy's powers as marshal over the city, threatening its powers of self-governance, full-scale riots broke out. Not content with simply attacking the obvious symbol of Gaunt's wealth and prestige, his fabulous Savoy Palace, the mob sought out Gaunt himself. They found him dining with Percy at the house of one of Gaunt's retainers and the pair narrowly escaped with their lives by fleeing across the Thames in a boat and taking refuge with the princess of Wales in her manor house at Kennington.[9]

In the circumstances it might not have been surprising if convocation had refused to cooperate in making a grant but the clergy had too much to lose to further antagonise the most powerful man in the land. Nor could they ignore the imminent threat of the renewal of war with France. Perhaps with Wyclif's preaching in the forefront of their minds, the clergy offered a more generous tax than that provided by the laity. Instead of imposing a flat-rate poll-tax, however, they attempted a fairer solution. The wealthier clergy, including all holders of a benefice and all members of religious orders, without exception, were to pay twelve pence; every other cleric above the age of fourteen was to pay four pence, with the exception of the mendicant friars, who were the religious equivalent of 'genuine beggars' and therefore altogether exempt.[10]

As we have already seen,[11] the untimely death of Edward III threw all the government's military preparations into chaos and it was not until 1 November 1377 that an English fleet finally took to the seas – by which time the campaigning season was virtually over. The French had abandoned their siege of Calais but much of Gascony remained in their hands and the Franco-Castilian fleet, which had wreaked such havoc on the south coast, was moored just across the Channel at Sluys in Flanders. The king's uncle, Thomas of Woodstock, had almost a hundred ships under his command, manned by some 3600 sailors and four thousand men-at-arms and archers, but his fleet was scattered by storms before he could attack the Castilians. All that this mighty force succeeded in doing was lifting the siege of the English garrison at Brest in Brittany and capturing eight enemy merchant ships.[12]

Even before Woodstock launched his expedition, the first parliament of the new reign had already met to respond to the invasion crisis. Not daring to risk further taxation experiments in such a grave situation, parliament had fallen back on the old tried and tested system, making a generous grant of a double subsidy of two-fifteenths and two-tenths which was to be paid into the exchequer by 2 February 1378. This was a huge amount of money, particularly following so closely on the heels of the poll-tax earlier in the year, and it was also to be collected in an unusually short period of time. The House of Commons therefore insisted that war treasurers should be appointed to receive and account for its expenditure 'to the end that such money might be wholly devoted to the costs of the war, and not put to any other use' – though more than fifteen thousand pounds in debts owed by the crown from the last expedition at sea were also to be paid from its revenues. The two members of parliament chosen as war treasurers, John Philipot and William Walworth, were both wealthy London merchants and highly experienced financiers. Though they had links to the court (not least as moneylenders to the crown) they had also been leading opponents of Gaunt's attempts to ride roughshod over the city's privileges and liberties. They could therefore be relied upon to resist any diversion of funds from the war effort.[13]

Money poured into the war chest from the subsidies but many cities and towns throughout the kingdom found themselves effectively taxed again as they were peremptorily ordered to build, at their own cost, thirty-one balingers, seagoing ships powered by between forty and fifty oars, which were to form the basis of a new royal navy 'knowing assuredly that if by their lukewarmness the voyage be hindered or delayed the king will deservedly punish them'. Though the writs specifically commanded that the cost should fall on 'the best, the most able and richest men of the city only, not charging other middling people of lower estate', the governing elites within cities such as York, Norwich and London ensured that the financial burden of building, equipping and maintaining the vessels was spread as widely as possible. This was to become an issue of simmering discontent within urban communities, not least because, when the ships were not in royal service, they were returned to the

place which funded them so that they could be used as trading
vessels but, as we have seen, only a handful of the most powerful merchants engaged in overseas trade enjoyed the benefits
of this concession. York, for instance, which in a fit of enthusiasm had volunteered a third ship in addition to the two
demanded of it, soon found that the costs of maintaining them
were such a drain on the city's finances and so divisive a factor
in civic politics that two of the balingers were sold off to private
owners.[14]

The rebuilding of the royal navy over the winter of 1377–8
should have meant that the government did not have to rely as
heavily on seizing merchant ships and forcibly pressing them
and their reluctant crews into service; significantly, at least one
squadron in Woodstock's expedition, under the command of
lord Fitzwalter, had mutinied after being compelled to put to
sea again in December. Nevertheless, though Gaunt himself was
to lead the new campaign planned for 1378, lack of shipping
again proved a stumbling block in mobilising the English
armies. The earls of Arundel and Salisbury set sail with part of
the expedition at the beginning of April but their attempt to
land in Normandy was thwarted by local levies and they were
worsted in an engagement at sea which resulted in the capture
of Sir Peter Courtenay and his men. Delayed by the need to
impress more ships and mariners, and by the desertion of many
of his men who got tired of waiting to embark, Gaunt himself
did not depart with the rest of the expedition until July.
Following a similar course to the earls, he too tried and failed
to land in Normandy, then made for Brittany, where he set siege
to St Malo, on the Atlantic seaboard, only to abandon it five
months later when he was unable to breach its defences. And
while he was preoccupied in Brittany, the Franco-Castilian fleet
took advantage of his absence to launch a series of raids on
Cornwall which resulted in the burning and destruction of

Fowey and other coastal towns, as well as many of the ships and boats upon which the locals' livelihood depended, while many other places were forced to buy off their attackers by paying ransoms.[15]

The failure of Gaunt's expedition was particularly unfortunate because it represented a change in tactical policy since the old king's death which had genuine potential to alter the course of the war. Instead of employing only the aggressive old-style *chevauchée*, which, even in its heyday, could only achieve temporary success, the English had developed a new approach which might be called 'fortress England'. Since its annexation by Edward III in 1347 Calais had helped to secure control of the English Channel and provided a bridgehead into France. The campaigns of 1378 (and possibly that of 1377) were designed to establish a series of similar English strongholds along the coast of northern France and Brittany: the fact that they did not do so was due to a failure in execution, not to the intrinsic value of the plan. Ironically, the only success was achieved through diplomacy with the installation of English garrisons in Brest and Cherbourg, both of which were formally leased to the English crown in 1378 by Charles of Navarre. Had Gaunt managed to take St Malo – and his persistence in besieging the place for five months is a clear indication that he appreciated its importance as part of the general strategy – then England would have controlled four of the most significant fortified ports on the northern seaboard of France. As Sir Richard Scrope, the steward of the royal household would try to explain to parliament, together with Gascony these overseas strongholds 'are and ought to be like barbicans to the kingdom of England, and if the barbicans are well guarded, and the sea safeguarded, the kingdom shall find itself well enough secure; otherwise we shall never have tranquillity or peace from our enemies'.[16]

When parliament met again at the end of October 1378,

however, it was in no mood to appreciate the niceties of a new long-term military strategy, particularly one which had signally failed to protect the realm against French attack. Complaints flooded in from all sides. Cornwall was not the only place to have suffered: the Isle of Wight had been raided again and declared itself surrounded by enemy ships committing arson and robbery; the commons of Kent petitioned that the great lords of their county did nothing towards its defence and left its castles and fortresses in disrepair, unprovisioned and lacking garrisons, putting them all at risk of French invasion; East Anglia complained that Norman balingers lying off the coast north of the Thames prevented fishermen, victuallers and merchants plying their trade; Cumberland added its voice to the litany by deploring the fact that the Scottish allies of France had committed such devastation that there were no English settlements left between Carlisle and the borders, and that Carlisle Castle, the last bastion protecting the kingdom, lacked both repairs and a keeper.[17] All were seeking funds from the war chest to improve their defences. When told by the chancellor that it was empty and that the king needed a further grant of taxation to fill it again, the Commons flatly refused to believe him: 'it seemed to them and was clearly the case that our lord the king was not in so great a need as he would have them believe'. They had only granted the double subsidy the previous year, they said, because they had been promised that they would not be taxed again 'for a long time after' and it was simply not possible that all the money had already been spent. They insisted on scrutinising the accounts of the two war treasurers, Philipot and Walworth, only to discover that some forty-six thousand pounds had been taken for maintaining the defences of Calais, Ireland and Gascony, together with the new garrisons in Brest and Cherbourg, 'which were not the responsibility of the commons'. It had always been the case that the day-to-day expense of maintaining the kingdom's defences came from the normal revenues of the crown, not direct taxation, and therefore the Commons indignantly refused to grant another subsidy. Their sole concession, which was perhaps an acknowledgement of the additional burden on the royal purse imposed by Brest and Cherbourg, was to increase export taxes on wool and allow a sixpence in every pound import and export tax on other merchandise, but even this was for one year only.[18]

The suspicion that Gaunt had been fiddling the figures was yet another blow to his reputation. Indeed, popular feeling against him was now running at such a level that the parliament had actually been held in Gloucester, rather than risk riots and confrontations in London. The failure of his most recent military expedition had not helped matters but it was the violation of the sanctuary at Westminster Abbey by his men which had provoked outrage in both Church and city. Gaunt had imprisoned two soldiers who had refused to surrender to him their hostage for a very valuable Aragonese ransom; in August 1378 they had escaped from the Tower and taken refuge in the abbey sanctuary, where they were pursued and one of them killed on the steps of the high altar during mass, together with a sacristan who had attempted to intervene on their behalf. Bishop Courtenay of London immediately excommunicated all those who had taken part in the murders but the response of the government was to claim that there was no right to sanctuary in cases of debt. When the abbot stood before the House of Lords to refute this, it was Gaunt's controversial protégé, John Wyclif, who was once again brought forward to argue his patron's corner, allegedly repeating for good measure his contention that in times of war the king had the right to confiscate Church property to pay for the realm's defence.[19] Though Gaunt was not personally responsible for the sanctuary affair, he was blamed for it, further poisoning his already fraught relationship with Londoners, the Church and bishop Courtenay in particular.

The refusal of parliament to grant any more direct taxation severely limited the options available to the government for the military campaigns of the forthcoming year. Again, this was unfortunate, as new opportunities opened up in December 1378 with Charles V's decision to annex the independent duchy of Brittany. This threw the Bretons back into the arms of their exiled duke, who had been living in England since 1372. If an English army could help restore him and establish a cross-Channel alliance, the activities of the Franco-Castilian fleet could be severely curtailed. Since there was nothing left in the war treasury, the king's ministers were forced to pawn the king's jewels to secure loans from individuals and towns. They succeeded in raising almost fourteen thousand pounds, which was enough to finance a fleet to defend the sea and coasts, but not sufficient to fund a military expedition.

As Scrope, now elevated to the role of chancellor, admitted, the government had no option left but to go back cap in hand to parliament. In April 1379, just five months after the dissolution of the previous one, a new parliament gathered at Westminster. An emollient Scrope volunteered the receipts and expenses of the war treasurers for public scrutiny and asked the Commons to discuss diligently how the kingdom's defence might best be funded 'with the least harm, injury and burden being inflicted on you and [the king's] good people'.[20] He got his money but not without making concessions. In return for the abolition of the export taxes granted in October and the appointment of a committee with power to investigate the expenditure of the royal household, the parliament of April 1379 voted not for a subsidy, but for a second poll-tax. Like the previous clerical poll-tax, this was not to be levied at a flat rate but according to rank or profession. Thirty-three separate categories were listed in the detailed and highly complex schedule drawn up and approved by parliament, beginning with the dukes of Lancaster and Brittany, who were each to pay £6 13s. 4d., followed by the justices of the King's Bench and Common Pleas and the chief baron of the exchequer at five pounds, and earls, their widows and the mayor of London at four pounds each. Landowners, merchants (including foreigners) and lawyers of every degree were carefully assessed and rated, as were the franklins, pardoners and innkeepers familiar from Chaucer's *Canterbury Tales*. Anyone, male or female, who did not fall into one of the defined ranks was to pay the lowest rate of four pence and genuine beggars were once again exempted. The collectors were to deliver the payments in cash at the exchequer on 24 June and 1 August 1379. Convocation granted a similarly graduated poll-tax for the clergy, rising through fifteen categories from the four pence due from the humblest clerks to the £6 13s. 4d. payable by the two archbishops.[21]

Though this second poll-tax has rightly been hailed by historians as a progressive and more equitable attempt to distribute the tax burden across the social classes, it should not be forgotten that, in most cases, it also substantially increased the amount payable by each individual. Apart from those aged between fourteen and sixteen, who were now excluded altogether, and married couples in the lowest category liable, whose contribution was halved, everyone else, including some of those at the lower end of the social scale, saw their assessment increase. Chaplains reliant on wages, rather than a benefice, for instance, saw their poll-tax liability multiply sixfold, from four pence in 1377 to two shillings in 1379, while innkeepers could end up paying ten times more than they had done in 1377. The sliding scale was also something of a blunt instrument since it relied more on status than actual income. Though some categories allowed for varying degrees of wealth by offering alternative assessments, such as 'a sergeant or franklin of the country', who was to be charged either forty or eighty pence 'according to his estate', this qualifier left plenty of room for manoeuvre by both tax-payer and tax-collector.[22]

Whether it was the complexity of the second poll-tax or, as the government suspected, widespread under-payment and evasion, its results were disappointing. Only about twenty-two thousand pounds was delivered to the exchequer from both laity and clergy alike – less than half the amount expected and considerably less than half the amount it would cost to finance a full-scale military expedition to Brittany. Having promised to send an army of two thousand men-at-arms and two thousand archers, whose wages would have cost at least fifty thousand pounds, all the government could now afford was a mere thirteen hundred men, only half of whom were men-at-arms.[23] Like its predecessors, this expedition too was cursed by bad luck and mismanagement. Delayed first by the need for the proceeds of the poll-tax to arrive at the exchequer, it was then unable to sail owing to unfavourable winds which kept the ships pinned in their ports. For several weeks, therefore, the soldiers were forced to kick their heels in Hampshire, where they camped wherever they pleased, helped themselves to the goods and chattels of the local people and, if Walsingham's diatribe is to be believed, to the local women too. It was not until the first week in December that the expedition was finally able to sail and by then it was too late in the season. Just as in 1377, it was hit by winter storms which scattered the fleet, wrecking nineteen ships carrying horses in Mount Bay, Cornwall, and the rest off the Irish coast. The admiral, Sir John Arundel, was drowned, together with most of his men, and not a single ship reached its destination.[24]

Monastic chroniclers, like Walsingham, saw the disaster as God's punishment for the sinful behaviour of the army before it set sail, but public opinion was equally convinced that it was all the fault of government mismanagement and corruption. Over a quarter of a million pounds had now been spent on the war in the two and a half years since Richard's accession – yet there was virtually nothing to show for it. Parliament, and the House of Commons in particular, was determined to hold the government to account. The writs summoning a new parliament were issued less than five months after the dissolution of the previous one and before Arundel's expedition set sail; by the time it met at Westminster in January 1380 the full extent of the debacle was clear. Significantly, after the customary first petition from the Commons that the liberties of the Church and state should be confirmed, the next was from the people living near the coasts of Hampshire, as well as those of Norfolk, Suffolk, Kent, Sussex, Dorset, Devon and Cornwall, complaining of the robberies and destruction committed by soldiers on their way overseas and demanding that the leaders of such expeditions should be forced to pay damages. There were also petitions from the towns and boroughs which had not yet received a penny in repayment of their loans to the king the previous year, and from ship-owners protesting about the damage and dilapidation caused to their vessels 'on account of numerous and lengthy seizures' for various expeditions 'without any payment received from the king'.[25]

When Chancellor Scrope repeated his now tediously familiar statement that the treasury was empty and urged the need for more money to finance the war, he met with a barrage of outspoken criticism. Through their Speaker, Sir John Gildesburgh, the Commons insisted that the thirteen-year-old Richard II was now of age to rule for himself. They therefore demanded the abolition of his entire royal council and its replacement by the usual five principal officers of state, who should be appointed in parliament and remain in office until its next meeting. Another commission was also to be appointed to audit all the king's accounts since his accession, both personal and state, and remedy any faults or negligence discovered there. When all these terms were met, including the replacement of Scrope as chancellor by Simon Sudbury, archbishop of Canterbury, the Commons reluctantly granted a further one and a half subsidies to be collected by 23 April. Though generous, this concession was subject to extraordinary conditions: the half-subsidy was not an outright grant, only a loan; no parliament was to be held again for at least eighteen months so that there could be no further direct taxation in that time; and the receipts of the subsidy were to be spent solely on financing a new expedition to Brittany. Though the Speaker was clearly articulating the concerns and demands of the Commons, and a new expedition to Brittany remained the top military priority, Gildesburgh's advocacy was not entirely transparent. Unusually for a Speaker, he was sitting for the first time as a member of parliament and, though his military career dated as far back as the Crécy campaign, he had not been knighted until 1378 while serving in Thomas of Woodstock's retinue during a previous unsuccessful Breton campaign. Woodstock had already been chosen as the leader of the new expedition and Gildesburgh, the earl's tenant and retainer, therefore had a vested interest in ensuring that it was properly financed and organised: he was even appointed one of the receivers of the subsidy.[26]

What this suggests is that the abolition of the royal council and the change in government personnel also paved the way for a reversal of recent military policy. Instead of crossing the Channel from Devon to Brittany, as originally planned, Woodstock's army of 5200 men would now sail from Dover to Calais at the end of July. The earl would then lead an old-fashioned *chevauchée* which would take him south to Troyes then in a loop skirting south of Paris before travelling west to meet the duke of Brittany at Rennes. Shortage of shipping alone cannot explain this change of plan: though ferrying batches of men and horses across from ports in Hampshire or Devon to Cherbourg would have taken longer than doing the same from Dover to Calais, it would have saved the army over three hundred miles and some two months of overland travel through hostile territory. The only explanation would seem to be that Woodstock hankered after the glory days of his father's reign and sought to replicate their success by re-adopting their methods. The fact that he was accompanied by Sir Robert Knolles and Sir Hugh Calveley, two professional soldiers and brothers-in-arms, who had spent several decades fighting in France and Brittany, is also telling. The route of Woodstock's *chevauchée* was almost identical to that taken by Knolles in his expedition of 1370, and the result was similar: a French army shadowed him most of the way but refused to give battle, denying Woodstock his chance of glory. By late September, when he finally arrived in Brittany, his presence was an embarrassment to the duke: Charles V of France had died on 16 September, opening up the possibility of concluding peace with his successor, Charles VI. Rather than send the English army home, or to overwinter in Gascony, the duke hedged his bets by directing them to lay siege to Nantes in the south-west corner of the duchy: far enough away to avoid antagonising the French but close enough at hand to be recalled should his negotiations fail. Woodstock had envisaged spending the winter overseas – his contract of service was for one year – but Nantes was well fortified and any siege was likely to be long and expensive, particularly as Woodstock had no ships to blockade its port and needed reinforcements. More money would be required from England's empty war coffers if his siege was not to fail.[27]

In fact, only a month into his campaign, it had already become clear to the government that the receipts from the subsidy would not fully fund Woodstock's expedition. More-over, an escalation in cross-border hostilities between the Percy and Douglas families threatened to end the Anglo-Scottish truce which had been in place since 1369. In October 1380 John of Gaunt therefore led a large army to the northern bor-ders which, if negotiations failed, was to invade Scotland. This, too, cost money which the exchequer and war treasury simply did not possess. The king's ministers therefore had no option but to renege on their promise of a tax-free eighteen months. Less than six months after the previous parliament had ended, the writs were issued summoning a new one to meet at the beginning of November. Perhaps anticipating trouble in London, but also to enable Gaunt to attend, it was held in the Midlands, at Northampton. Archbishop Sudbury, as chancel-lor, pleaded the pressing financial need: the king was contractually obliged to pay Woodstock's army for the next six months; he could not afford to redeem the jewels he had pledged to fund Gaunt's expedition to Scotland; the wages of soldiers at Calais, Brest and Cherbourg were more than nine months in arrears; investment had to be made for the safe-guarding of the sea coasts before the enemy's galleys descended once again. 'For the love of God', Sudbury urged the Commons, 'avoid all extraneous topics which might provoke rancour or conflict, and deal effectively with this'.[28]

Sir John Gildesburgh, reprising his role as Speaker, responded by urging the government not to demand more than was absolutely necessary, adding that the common people 'were now too poor and in too weak a state to shoulder any greater burden'. When Sudbury informed the Commons that the gov-ernment needed £160,000 – the equivalent of four and a quarter subsidies – Gildesburgh replied that this was 'quite out-rageous, and altogether beyond them'. Eventually, however, a compromise was reached in which the Commons reluctantly offered one hundred thousand pounds on condition that two-thirds of this sum was to be paid by the laity and one-third by the clergy. How to obtain such enormous sums was another matter. The Commons sought the advice of the lords in parliament, who suggested three alternatives: another subsidy, but this was not recommended because it weighed heaviest on the poor and would take too long to collect; a new excise duty on buying and selling merchandise within the kingdom, though no one could predict its likely yield so its potential could not be estimated; or, as the lords themselves concluded, 'the best and the easiest course' would be to levy another flat-rate poll-tax. The Commons were clearly unhappy but could see no other solution. So they granted the notorious third poll-tax, which turned out to be the spark that would ignite the greatest popular revolt in English history.

The third poll-tax was to be levied on every man and woman in the kingdom over the age of fifteen, including those living within traditionally exempt areas, the only exception being 'genuine beggars'. The terms of the grant hint at some of the problems encountered with its predecessors, whose records the collectors were specifically prohibited from re-using in making their assessments. As before, the tax was to be levied from individuals only where they were resident, but now it was specifically stated that all craftsmen, labourers, servants and other laymen living in the households of lay or ecclesiastical employers were liable; even royal household servants could not escape on the grounds that their permanent homes were elsewhere or that they enjoyed privileged status. Another clause, stating that, unlike previous poll-taxes, 'it should be charged only on persons who are now living', suggests one of the more ingenious ways that corrupt collectors had increased their takings in the past. In another lesson learned from the second poll-tax, complex graduated tax bands were dropped in favour of a universal rate, as the lords had suggested, though their advice that it should be levied at a crippling sixteen or even twenty pence a head was rejected in favour of twelve pence per person. This was still a great deal of money but, more importantly, it represented a major shift in the fiscal burden away from the wealthiest and on to the shoulders of the poorest in society: every single person who had been wealthy enough to fall within one of the defined categories of the 1379 poll-tax would now pay less, while those who had been too poor to qualify for the higher rates then would now see their individual assessments triple and, in the case of married couples, rise sixfold. The hardship was increased by the speed with which the tax was to be paid: two-thirds of the money was to be collected by 27 January 1381, the remaining third by 2 June 1381. These timings could not have been more insensitive, especially for those who earned their living from the land, since they coincided with the straitened months of winter and early spring, when food stores were running low and seasonal labour for wages was not available. Taxation was normally collected at the end of September, after the harvest had been gathered in, and even previous poll-taxes had been levied between May and September, when work in the fields was most needed and best rewarded. The new poll-tax was to be paid in the wake of a particularly bad harvest and during one of the worst winters in living memory: its timing was therefore particularly onerous.[29]

In the light of the rebellion which followed its imposition, contemporaries and historians have been quick to blame the royal ministers and parliament for setting such an iniquitous tax. Yet the Commons did not really intend that everyone should pay the same universal rate. The figure of twelve pence a head had been adopted simply because it was three times the rate levied in 1377, which had produced around £22,580: it could therefore be expected to raise the £66,666 13s. 4d. that the Commons had now offered the crown. The other advantage of the twelve pence figure was that it also represented a shilling, making it mathematically quicker and easier for collectors and auditors to check that the correct amount had been brought in: a town like Colchester, Essex, for example, which declared 1609 inhabitants over the age of fifteen should have paid a straight 1609s. (£80 9s.), without any of the awkward odd pennies which made accounting for earlier poll-taxes so complicated. As the wording of the 1380 grant makes clear, however, this was to be a poll-tax in name only: following the same principle as the subsidy, each town or village was to be assessed to pay a total sum, based in this instance on the size of its population, and then 'each lay person will be charged in accordance with his means ... those of adequate means helping those of lesser means as far as they are able'. The problem was that no instructions were given as to what the boundaries for requiring or giving assistance were to be, or how, if necessary, richer men were to be coerced into paying more than their personal liability to help their poorer neighbours. The only guidance was that no one was to pay more than twenty shillings (one pound), or less than four pence for himself and his wife. So once again, in a worthy attempt to mitigate the effects on the poorest, the Commons had introduced an element of variability into the equation which unscrupulous tax-payers and tax-collectors could both exploit.[30]

Throughout all the parliamentary proceedings in November 1380, no one had mentioned the government's breach of its promise to have an eighteen-month tax amnesty (at least as far as the formal record was concerned), but the Commons clearly felt implicated in the crown's bad faith. In a remarkable condition attached to their grant they distanced themselves from its implementation by insisting that 'the knights, citizens, and burgesses who have come to this present parliament are by no means to be made collectors or controllers of the aforesaid sums'. Since they were precisely the sort of people who would normally have taken on such a role, and indeed many members of parliament had served as collectors and controllers for previous poll-taxes, this was a significant abdication of responsibility for implementing the levy that they had granted and suggests, at the very least, an awareness that the new tax was likely to be extremely unpopular.[31]

One of the reasons for this, apart from the financial hardship it would cause, was the entirely justified suspicion that John of Gaunt had designs on its proceeds. The government could demonstrate that it needed around £110,000 to meet its defence commitments, including the further expenses of Woodstock's campaign, yet archbishop Sudbury had requested £160,000. He made no reference as to why the additional fifty thousand pounds was needed, but it would appear to have been earmarked to fulfil a treaty commitment, made just a few months earlier, for military aid to Portugal. This was part of Gaunt's grand scheme to further his personal ambitions in Spain and he was already planning to lead an expedition there in person. By hiding its costs within the general demand placed before the Commons, Gaunt could avoid having to make a separate plea to fund it. His presence at the parliament, albeit only in its later stages, might thus be seen as an attempt to intimidate its members; likewise, the Commons' refusal to grant any more than a hundred thousand pounds, and their pointed insistence that it should be spent only on Woodstock's campaign, the defence of the realm and safeguarding the seas, might be regarded as a deliberate refusal to finance Gaunt's expedition. The members of the Commons, many of whom were merchants and financiers themselves, were clearly financially astute enough to recognise that Sudbury's claim that the king had received 'nothing' from the export taxes on wool was untrue;

the outbreak of civil war in Flanders in 1379 had indeed impacted on the wool trade but it had only reduced sales by about a third, not wiped them out completely, as the request for, and grant of, another extension to the export taxes demonstrates. There is therefore no reason to assume that the Commons were unable to see through Sudbury's financial sleight of hand on behalf of the duke, particularly as they put on record the fact that 'they feel greatly aggrieved ... by the multitude of wars resulting in unsustainable costs' and petitioned the king to remedy this, 'since the commons are unable to sustain further such burdens'.[32] If this was intended as a warning shot across Gaunt's bows, it passed unheeded.

The government was in such a hurry to get the money in that it issued the writs commissioning the assessors and collectors of the new poll-tax for each county or large urban area on 7 December 1380, the day after parliament ended, only then to be obliged to rescind eighty-three inappropriate appointments, including one of a man who turned out to be a prisoner in Winchelsea jail. Separate commissions were also issued at the same time to smaller groups of men who were to 'survey and control' the assessments. The actual door-to-door job of assessing and collecting the money owed was given to sub-collectors who were men with local knowledge – the constable and two men of each township and the mayor, bailiffs and two other men of each city or borough. All the information they gathered between them, including the names of each individual tax-payer and the amount levied from him or her, was to be recorded in indentures, one copy of which was to be kept by the collection commissioners, the other to be presented at the exchequer in the palace of Westminster. The government's determination that there should be no evasion or fraud was further demonstrated by the appointment on 2 January 1381 of commissions of inquiry, headed by the most senior royal officials in each county,

the sheriff and escheator, who were to draw up their own separate records of all the eligible taxpayers in their area and send
them to the exchequer: to prevent collusion, they were expressly
forbidden from communicating 'in any way' with either the collectors or controllers of the poll-tax. Perhaps because they did
take this short cut, a month later many of the sheriffs were fined
for making false returns.[33]

Two-thirds of the poll-tax revenue was due at the exchequer
by 27 January yet, despite all the government's efforts to ensure
transparency, speed and accuracy, the results were significantly
less than had been anticipated and certainly not enough to
finance the preparations for sending reinforcements to
Woodstock in Brittany. On 20 February, therefore, the very day
that new contracts were being signed for the expedition, the
king's ministers brought forward the date for the payment of
the final third of the poll-tax from 2 June to 21 April. Even
though the government was aware of the shortfall, and of its
public commitment to spend the money only on the Breton
campaign, by the end of February it was also pressing ahead
with payments for Gaunt's expedition to Portugal, the leadership of which he had now delegated to his youngest brother,
Edmund of Langley.[34] Yet the incontrovertible evidence from
the returns to the exchequer was that the number of eligible
tax-payers had fallen significantly in the four years since the first
poll-tax: in Essex they had reduced from 47,962 to 30,533; in
Kent from 56,557 to 43,838; in Norfolk from 88,797 to
58,714; in Suffolk from 58,610 to 31,734.[35] Even though the
exchequer normally excluded 'paupers' from tax liability, as
well as the 'genuine beggars' specified by parliament, this dramatic drop in numbers could not be explained away simply as
the result of so many of the rural population falling into desti-
tution because of the bad harvest and severe winter. Nor could
it be blamed on unusually high death rates, since there was no

outbreak of plague or other natural disaster, nor even on the rise in minimum age for eligibility from fourteen to fifteen. The obvious conclusion, which the government was able to reach because it had the records of the previous poll-taxes readily available for comparison in the exchequer, was that there had been widespread fraud and evasion on a massive scale.

The problem was that local communities had no incentive to submit to an accurate census: it was cheaper and simpler to pretend that the poor did not exist, rather than to admit their presence, which then forced everyone else to shoulder the extra burden of paying all or part of their poll-tax for them. An improbably high number of dependent relatives, particularly females, were therefore simply omitted from the record. This deception must have been countenanced by the local assessors and collectors, who, as members of the local parish, village or town themselves, had to live with their irate neighbours, and answer to them, on a daily basis. And it was not just a few isolated examples of passive resistance but a nationwide act of defiance, with the poorest areas of the country revealing the steepest falls in recorded numbers of eligible taxpayers: fifty-four per cent allegedly vanished between 1377 and 1381 in both the North Riding of Yorkshire and Devon, for instance, and as many as sixty-five per cent in Cumberland and Cornwall. Even in the wealthy south-east, where there was a thriving market economy to compensate for agricultural dependency, around a third of the taxable population apparently disappeared.[36]

The government could have responded to this unprecedented act of mass resistance by accepting that the poll-tax was a failure and scaling back its military plans. There were actually very good reasons to do so. The Scottish threat had evaporated even before parliament had granted the third poll-tax, John of Gaunt having successfully negotiated a peaceful resolution in November 1380 and renewed the truce until

1 June 1381. More significantly, before the first tranche of the tax was due at the exchequer, Thomas of Woodstock's campaign in Brittany was also over. On 6 January 1381 he had been obliged to abandon his siege of Nantes, having lost a fifth of his men and almost all his horses. Nine days later, the duke of Brittany made his peace with Charles VI of France, promising to get rid of his English allies who had supported him for so many years and to 'damage them in every way possible'. This unexpected act of treachery made redundant not only Woodstock and his army but also the poll-tax which had been granted specifically to fund their campaign. A furious Woodstock accepted the inevitable with bad grace and by early March agreed to leave Brittany in return for a payment from the duke of £8333, just over half of it in cash, and decamped to Brest to await shipment home. Yet despite the finality of these arrangements, the government in England inexplicably pressed ahead with its plans as if nothing had changed. In February two thousand reinforcements for the army that was now disbanding were recruited to serve under Sir Thomas Felton, paid their advance wages and ordered to muster at Plymouth and Dartmouth ready for embarkation; on 15 March a royal official was sent to Brest with a new war chest, filled with the proceeds of the poll-tax, and orders to use it to persuade those English soldiers still left in the duchy to stay on until June. It was all wasted money and effort. Many of the men had already deserted, including Hugh Calveley's company, which had left the previous month, and no one, including Woodstock himself, could see any purpose in remaining any longer than was absolutely necessary to secure shipping home. Woodstock was among the last to leave, taking ship from Brest on 30 April and arriving at Falmouth on 2 May with nothing to show for his expensive campaign except disaffected troops and huge personal debts which were still unpaid in 1388.

In a further ludicrous twist to an absurd story of military, political and financial incompetence, he returned to find the new recruits for his abandoned campaign, now leaderless since Felton's death on 26 April, still waiting for transport in Devon and expecting to join him in Brittany. Even now the government was unwilling to cut its losses and send them home: perhaps thinking that it might divert them to Gascony, or even join them to the three thousand troops already mustering in Dartmouth for John of Gaunt's Portuguese expedition, it left them unemployed and increasingly fractious until June, when orders were finally given that they should disband.[37]

Since the military situation no longer demanded the levels of expenditure originally anticipated, the king's council could justifiably have abandoned its attempt to enforce further collection of the poll-tax. Yet it did nothing of the sort. Instead, oblivious to the groundswell of popular resentment, it decided to turn the screw. Since it held the local collectors responsible, openly accusing them of omitting or concealing large numbers of taxpayers, 'some deliberately, some through negligence and others through favour', the council decided to institute a countrywide investigation, led by new commissioners, to rectify the problem and enforce proper collection. On 16 March, therefore, it began by issuing nine commissions addressed to the sheriffs of Norfolk, Suffolk, Cambridgeshire, Huntingdonshire, Essex, Hertfordshire, Somerset, Northamptonshire and Gloucestershire. These were followed on 3 May by further commissions for Kent, Nottinghamshire, Derbyshire, Devon, Cornwall, the West Riding of Yorkshire and finally, on 20 May, for the city of Canterbury. Each sheriff was assigned several named local gentry, who were often also justices of the peace, to act with him, a royal clerk from the exchequer or chancery to record their findings and a sergeant-at-arms from the royal household to enforce their decisions. They were given detailed instructions on what they should do, including travelling in person from place to place throughout the county to inspect all the existing assessments, make their own inquiries to verify who should have paid the tax and draw up written lists of those who had evaded payment. Perhaps in an attempt to give greater clarity to the vague exchequer term 'poor', and to avoid subjective judgements as to who should be placed in the exempt category, the description of those who did not have to pay was expanded from 'genuine beggars' to include 'and those who survive solely by alms'. It was no longer sufficient to be scraping together a pittance: one had to be totally dependent on the generosity of others for the necessities of life to avoid paying the tax. 'In this way', the commission stated emphatically, 'no lay person in the county shall be omitted at all'. Anyone who resisted paying, or hindered the reassessment in any way, was to be arrested and imprisoned.[38]

The appointment of the reassessment commissions would make the third poll-tax the most personally intrusive of all medieval taxes. The specific injunction that old records, such as those for the subsidy or previous poll-taxes, were not to be used had already meant that local assessors were supposed to start from scratch with their door-to-door enquiries. These had been followed up by the independent shrieval investigations, which had provided the exchequer with a second set of records, and now, for the third time, royal officials were to come into the localities and draw up their own lists of individuals who were liable to be taxed. Such scrutiny was unprecedented and unwelcome, not least because it produced a written record of the names, status and occupations of all adults and identified where they lived – a written record that was to be preserved outside the local community and could be used for future oppression. In the past the king's financial demands had been met by community agreement and based on peer assessment of household wealth: now not even the humblest cottage could escape visitation and the officials counting the number of inhabitants and deciding whether they were eligible to pay were increasingly strangers. The enormous resentment caused by their power is typified by the story of John Legge, a royal sergeant-at-arms from the king's court in London appointed to the Kent commission, who is alleged to have taken his diligence in determining the age of young people to extraordinary and prurient lengths: 'horrible to relate, [he] shamelessly lifted the young girls to test whether they had enjoyed intercourse with men'. Of course our monastic chronicler reveals his naivety in assuming that sexual activity could be determined by such actions, but it is possible that Legge used pubic hair as the test for females being over the age of fifteen. (For boys less invasive methods were available since they had been registered in their local tithing from the age of twelve.) Whether the story is true or not, Legge's notoriety was such that he would be specifically targeted and executed by the rebels in the days to come.[39]

As the commissioners made their returns to the exchequer the scale of the under-assessment by local collectors became clear. In almost every case where the comparative figures survive, the reassessors located substantially more tax-payers – though still nothing like the numbers who had paid their dues in 1377. The Norfolk commissioners pulled in an extra 8005 people and therefore an additional £400 5s. in cash; in Suffolk they discovered 12,901 hitherto hidden taxable persons and increased the take by £1173 19s. What also emerged from the commissioners' findings was that the people missing from the original assessments were, by and large, the poorest in their areas – though not poor enough to qualify as living entirely on charity. In Gloucestershire, for example, the reassessment identified a further 5663 tax-payers beyond the 22,194 originally listed: where the detailed records survive they reveal that every one of the new entries, without exception, was assessed at the full twelve-pence rating, even though all were described as labourers and servants and many of them as 'impoverished' for good measure. That this may have been intended as punishment for evading the original payment is suggested by the figures for the little town of Lechlade. One hundred and fourteen people in the town had previously paid the third poll-tax, of whom nineteen had contributed over the odds, the largest sum, twenty pence, being paid by the boat-owner Geoffrey Cook; seventy-four people had paid their standard twelve pence but twenty-one, most of whom were also labourers or servants, had paid less than their official dues. Twenty-four 'impoverished labourers and servants' were now added to the taxable population by the reassessors; thirteen were male, eleven female, all were apparently single and at least four of them were identified as children of previously taxed couples. With no wealthier townsmen to share their burden, the unfortunate newly 'found' twenty-four had to pay their tax in full, even though the servant of Richard and Margery Mulleward therefore ended up paying two pence more than either of his employers.[40]

Lechlade was by no means an isolated case and there must have been many thousands of people up and down the country who shared their sense of grievance, perhaps even more so when they had made their payments in good faith and then discovered that their neighbours had been let off more lightly. In Suffolk, for instance, all the sixty-four eligible artisans, labourers and servants living in Chevington had to pay twelve pence each, yet just five miles away, in Brockley, a village of some seventy people, twenty-two individuals of the same status paid between four and ten pence.[41] The reason for this discrepancy was that Chevington had only one person, an unmarried farmer, who was capable of paying more than his due (two shillings), whereas Brockley had eight married couples who

1. Richard II (1367–1400), who became king of England on the death of his grandfather Edward III in 1377. Fourteenth-century portraits are exceptionally rare and this full length, larger than life size portrait is unique. Painted in oils on a wooden panel, probably in the 1390s, it hangs in Westminster Abbey. Richard was highly conscious of his regal dignity and more images of him survive than of any other monarch before Henry VIII.

2. Edward III (1312–77). This wooden funeral effigy is a more realistic portrayal of the king than his idealised tomb effigy because it was taken from his death mask: the droop at the corner of his mouth was caused by one of the strokes that eventually killed him. The effigy, dressed in royal robes, was displayed on his hearse at his funeral and then preserved at Westminster Abbey, where it is the earliest surviving example of its kind.

3. John of Gaunt (1340–99), Richard's uncle, whose properties and servants were targeted during the great revolt. The heraldry of this Renaissance copy of a contemporary portrait demonstrates not only Gaunt's own royal lineage but also his adopted title of king of Castile and Léon, which he claimed through his wife Blanche. Her father's arms, the castle and lions of Castile, appear on Gaunt's surcoat and are also overlaid on the royal coat of arms within the Order of the Garter at the top left hand side of the portrait.

4. A panorama of London in 1616 by the Dutch engraver, map-maker and publisher Claes Jansz Visscher (1587–1652). Southwark is in the foreground, with the church of St Mary Overy and the High Street leading to London Bridge by which the rebels from Kent entered the city. Note the customary display of traitors' heads on poles above the gatehouse at the entrance to the bridge: this was where the rebels exhibited the heads of the chancellor and treasurer, the former with his archiepiscopal mitre nailed to it.

5. A country household in winter is the illustration for the month of February in a richly illuminated manuscript Book of Hours commissioned in the fifteenth century by the duke of Berry. English land-holdings similarly consisted of a house, with a separate stone-built bake-house to minimise the risk of fire, agricultural buildings for the stock and food processing, and an enclosed yard. Note the hay-stack behind the barn and the four bee-skeps against the far wall.

6. Bath-tubs were a feature of every moderately wealthy home where there were servants to fetch the water: the rich even had dedicated bathrooms with tiled floors and piped hot water. This painting of a man bathing is contained within an initial letter in the four-volume manuscript of *Omne Bonum*, the first encyclopaedia of universal knowledge to be arranged in alphabetical order, compiled by James le Palmer, an exchequer clerk, probably in 1375.

7. A woman feeding her chickens, a marginal illumination from the Luttrell Psalter commissioned by Sir Geoffrey Luttrell between 1320 and 1340. Note that the hen is tethered to prevent it flying away and that the woman is carrying her distaff and spindle so that she can spin wool or flax into thread for weaving.

8. A team of oxen ploughing a field in preparation for sowing crops. Ploughing was a skilled occupation commanding high wages. A marginal illumination from the Luttrell Psalter (see plate 7).

9. A horse pulls a harrow to break up the clods created by ploughing and to cover the seed planted in the tilled earth. A boy follows, armed with a sling and stones to scare away the birds and prevent them eating the precious seed. A marginal illumination from the Luttrell Psalter (see plate 7).

10. Sowing the seed, a task which had to be carried out by hand. Note the bird helping itself to the grain in the sack. A marginal illumination from the Luttrell Psalter (see plate 7).

11. Reaping the harvest. It was vitally important to gather in the harvest while the weather was fine so that the crops did not rot. Everyone had to lend a hand, young and old, men and women; many servants working in towns also returned to their villages to help with the harvest. Here the women are cutting the crop with sickles while a man follows behind to bind it into stooks ready for threshing the grain. A marginal illumination from the Luttrell Psalter (see plate 7).

12. After the ears of grain have been removed for threshing, the stooks are gathered up and piled into stacks to provide fodder and bedding for animals throughout the winter months. A marginal illumination from the Luttrell Psalter (see plate 7).

13. The sacks of grain are brought to the local windmill for grinding into flour. Many landlords made a substantial income by insisting that their tenants should use the manorial mill and charging them to do so. In a bitterly resented exercise of its power, the abbey of St Albans prohibited its tenants from owning or using hand-mills so that they could not grind corn even for their own personal use. A marginal illumination from the Luttrell Psalter (see plate 7).

jointly contributed sums ranging from 2s. 4d. to six shillings. The artisans, labourers and servants of Chevington therefore had every reason to be angry that they had been forced to pay more than their luckier neighbours in Brockley. The sense of injustice worked both ways, however, for the eight married couples at Brockley had been obliged to bear the additional burden of paying part of the tax for a third of their fellow villagers. This might not have mattered so much for the gentry, William and Elizabeth de Walsham and John and Beatrix de Somerton, who paid six shillings and 5s. 6d. respectively, but for the 'squeezed middle', such as the farmers John Shortnekke, Thomas Alston and Geoffrey Alisander, who were liable for 2s. 6d. for themselves and their wives, and the smith Simon Smyth and the labourer Geoffrey Soneman, who paid 2s. 4d. for themselves and their wives, finding those extra pennies might have caused considerable hardship, as well as a sense of resentment, which might help to explain why so many of those who took up arms in the following weeks were from just this class of people: not the poorest members of society but those who, through their own efforts or those of their families, had managed to build up a larger than average landholding or a modestly successful business.

For the ordinary men and women labouring in the fields, plying their trade in the towns or working in the service of others, there can have been little connection between the money they were being forced to pay in taxes and the prosecution of a remote war against France. For those who lived in the southern and eastern coastal counties and therefore suffered from the Franco-Castilian raids, attacks on their shipping and the equally disruptive passage of English troops through their regions, the war was more real but the disconnect even greater. The disastrous military campaigns of the decade had failed in their primary purposes of protecting the realm or advancing the war

against France. It must have seemed to many of those struggling
to earn their livings and feed their families that their hard-
earned money was being seized only to finance the personal
ambitions of powerful princes. And it should not be forgotten
how much and how often they had had to pay. At least one
direct tax, and sometimes two, had now been collected in every
single year since Richard II's accession in 1377. This was
unprecedented. What made it even more onerous was the fact
that between 1357 and 1371 the country had enjoyed fourteen
years without any direct taxation at all being levied on the laity.
The next five years had seen the imposition of the parish tax in
1371 and the grant of a double subsidy in 1373, but annual
taxation was a phenomenon only introduced with the new
reign. Three and a half subsidies and three poll-taxes had been
levied in five years to pay for the defence of the realm. Of all
medieval monarchs only Henry V would be able to sustain similar levels of taxation, receiving eight and a third subsidies in the
five years between 1414 and 1419 – but he had Agincourt and
the conquest of Normandy to justify such extraordinary impositions on his subjects.[42] Richard II had nothing. His subjects
did not blame the boy-king personally but they were about to
hold his advisers and his officials to account in the most brutal
way possible.

CHAPTER SIX

Resistance

The first indication that there was going to be active resistance to the poll-tax came as the deadline approached for paying the third and final part into the exchequer and the government increased the pressure on its officials to enforce its collection. On 8 April 1381 the sheriffs of all the counties were strictly enjoined 'by all manner of ways and means' to compel the collectors to pay all the dues and arrears at Westminster by 21 April 'without delay or dispute'. When the collectors and controllers for the city and suburbs of London duly appeared at the exchequer the following day, they declared that they were unable to supply the names, rank and condition of every person, as required, without causing 'dangerous agitation' among the tax-payers. House-to-house enquiries to find evaders had been instituted in March but only £1019 17s. from 20,397 people had been collected – despite around forty thousand having been eligible for the first poll-tax in 1377. Perhaps because the London populace was so notoriously volatile, the exchequer officials accepted that the risks of pursuing the missing tax-payers outweighed the benefit of their contribution and allowed the collectors to submit their accounts, as they had done in the past for subsidies, solely on the basis of the number of eligible tax-payers in their district.[1]

The first recorded act of violence – an attack on a poll-tax collector – occurred shortly before this. There were two surprising elements: first, it took place in Oxfordshire, which was not a county at the forefront of the revolt, and secondly, its victim, the aptly named William Payable, was collecting not from the laity but from the clergy. He had been sent by the dean of Bicester to levy the money due from the vicars and rectors of four villages between Bicester and Woodstock when he was set upon by a group of unidentified assailants: they allegedly tortured him, beat him to within an inch of his life and cut off the ears and tail of his horse, which they fixed to the pillory for public derision. He had not even reached his first destination, so robbery is unlikely to have been the motive, but many of the clergy were as aggrieved as the laity at the imposition of the poll-tax. For them the burden was even greater, since all beneficed clergymen were expected to pay 6s. 8d. and the unbeneficed, including nuns and monks below the rank of prior, 3s. 4d. Whether it was the clergy expecting a visit from Payable who were responsible for ordering the attack, or simply a random criminal act, on 20 April 1381 the bishop excommunicated the unknown perpetrators and ordered that the sentence against them was to be read each Sunday and feast day in every church in the archdeaconry of Oxford until further notice.[2]

There must have been other poll-tax collectors up and down the country who were subjected to violence but there was one incident, at Brentwood, Essex, on 30 May, which at least two contemporary chroniclers[3] would identify as the start of the great revolt. Its significance was due to the fact that it was not relatively humble individual collectors who were assaulted but the powerful judicial commissioners appointed to investigate and reassess the poll-tax: what is more, the victims were actually holding court when they were attacked.[4] That it should happen in Essex was unsurprising. One of the greatest land-owners in the county, through his wife Eleanor de Bohun, was Thomas of Woodstock, on behalf of whose Breton campaign the poll-tax had been levied. What is more, his personal retinue had made up almost half of his army in Brittany, many of them were from Essex and by May they were returning home to regale their family and friends with personal tales of how the campaign had been mismanaged and the tax revenue wasted. The people of Essex therefore had good reason to know that the poll-tax was no longer needed for its avowed purpose – and yet the reassessment and enforcement of its collection were still being pursued actively in the county.

The seven members of the Essex reassessment commission were typical of those teams working in every shire. They were led by the sheriff, John Sewale, of Coggeshall, whose office dated back to Saxon times. The sheriff was the king's personal representative in the thirty-nine counties of England and in the two cities, London and Bristol, which also enjoyed county status. He was entrusted with a wide range of military, judicial and financial duties: he alone could raise the *posse comitatus* (the direct ancestor of the sheriff's posse in the American west) by summoning all the able-bodied men of the shire to arms so that they could assist him in arresting felons and dealing with breaches of the peace, including invasion and rebellion; he presided over a monthly county court which dealt mainly with small personal actions of trespass and debt and received indictments for serious crimes, such as murder, wounding, arson, rape and robbery, which were then forwarded to the higher courts for judgment; he was personally responsible for executing the king's writs and collecting debts to the crown and he enforced justice by levying fines, proclaiming outlaws and arresting and executing convicted criminals. Though officially appointed by the king's council, local magnates often exerted their influence to secure candidates favourable to themselves, and many sheriffs were actually retained by them, either for life or by annuity, receiving fees which obliged them to act in their lord's interest, rather than with the impartiality the office should have required.

There were also plenty of opportunities for self-advancement. The sheriff, in common with other royal officials, paid a farm to the crown for all the royal revenues derived from the shire: this was a fixed sum, payable annually and agreed in advance, but set at a level below the expected return, allowing the sheriff to collect the difference personally in lieu of wages. The more efficient, extortionate or corrupt the sheriff, the more he could collect for himself. Bribery was ubiquitous and sheriffs were notorious for assisting or impeding plaintiffs in their cases, procuring indictments simply to increase the fines they received for bailing the indicted and fixing the selection of jurors to secure favourable verdicts. The popular perception was that the shrievalty was oppressive and dishonest – it is no coincidence that the sheriff was one of the principal villains in medieval ballads about Robin Hood. This was a view shared by the rebels in 1381, who made sheriffs a prime target of their violence, and also by the House of Commons, which had tried to limit their powers by obtaining statutes restricting their tenure of office to one year and, as recently as 1377, prohibiting their reappointment within three years. Yet the system would not have worked if it had been totally venal; the influence of one local magnate might prevail for a period but this was in no one else's interest and others would intervene to undermine or overthrow such dominance. And the administrative burden borne by the sheriff outweighed for some the benefits that might accrue from office.

John Sewale had actually paid for a licence excusing him from holding any public office in 1380, only to find himself in post as sheriff of Essex and Hertfordshire (the two counties were often linked together for administrative purposes) when the revolt took place. Nothing in his record suggests that he particularly merited the hatred of the rebels: it was what he represented, rather than what he was, which made him one of the revolt's first victims.[5]

There were two other royal officials directly employed by the crown on the commission. John de Asshewell was a royal sergeant-at-arms, a professional soldier who was a member of the king's household and employed by him to carry out his commands whenever something more than simple message-carrying was required, such as carrying writs requiring enforcement by arrest or seizure of goods. Asshewell may have had links with the Hertfordshire town of that name but not all medieval surnames were necessarily an indication of place of origin or occupation. Thomas de Wilford, the king's clerk, was employed in the royal chancery, which issued the king's orders in the form of writs and enrolled copies of them which were preserved at its base in the palace of Westminster. Like many medieval clergymen he held several offices simultaneously, being not only a chancery clerk but also parson of Ardingly, Sussex, and a prebendary of Chichester Cathedral. Ironically, given his current employment, Wilford had been excused his own contribution to the first poll-tax because, like the prior of Lewes, he had been captured while fighting the French invaders at Rottingdean, Sussex, and forced to pay a crippling ransom to obtain his release. Both Asshewell and Wilford acted in a supervisory role and had a number of deputies who assisted them in completing their business.[6]

The local gentry appointed to assist the royal officers were all powerful and influential men in their own right. Thomas

Bataill had been escheator of Essex and Hertfordshire in 1377, a position which, though inferior to that of sheriff, was only open to those with more than twenty pounds in annual landed income. Escheators were responsible for the old feudal revenues of the crown. When one of the king's tenants died, his lands would be taken into royal hands, valued and administered by the escheator until a local jury, empanelled by him, confirmed the identity of the heir and anyone else, such as the widow, who might have a claim upon the estate; where the heir was a minor the lands would remain under royal control until he or she reached the age of twenty-one. It was therefore in the escheator's power to determine the value of an estate and effectively to decide disputed inheritances. He was also empowered to forfeit into the king's hands the property and goods of convicted felons, value them and sell them. Like the sheriff, he was required to keep detailed records of all these transactions and make regular submissions of his proceeds to the exchequer. It was a role which naturally offered the escheator opportunities for exercising undue influence and feathering his own nest, but it also aroused considerable hostility from those who felt themselves to have been unfairly or wrongly treated even when there had been no maladministration. As recently as the November parliament of 1380, a Commons petition had complained that escheators procured biased inquests by which 'your people are frequently and fraudulently disinherited, and suddenly ousted from their lands and tenements'; they were then prevented from recovering them by cunning, the exercise of undue influence or legal chicanery. A request for a remedy was rejected and escheators, like sheriffs, were to become a primary target of the rebels.[7]

The other reassessors had all served regularly on royal commissions in the county, often acting in conjunction with Thomas of Woodstock, the sheriff and each other. Sir William de

Wauton had been a commissioner of array, responsible for mustering and inspecting the armed levies when they were called up to defend the shire, a commissioner for examining and putting into good repair the sea defences of the county and, most significantly, as we shall see, a justice of the peace.[8] Another commissioner of array was Sir Richard Waldegrave, whose name appears to have been added to the Essex poll-tax reassessment commission by mistake. He was actually a knight of the king's household and a major Suffolk landowner who sat as MP for that county in every parliament between 1376 and 1390 and would be elected Speaker of the Commons in the first parliament after the great revolt.[9] Perhaps because his links were primarily with Suffolk, he seems to have been replaced by John Bampton, who was not an original member of the commission but may have been co-opted to serve as one of the 'loyal and faithful men in the county'. Bampton was a justice of the peace and commissioner of array who first appears in the records as bailiff of Ongar hundred, one of the nineteen jurisdictional subdivisions of Essex dating back to Saxon times. Though some hundreds (known as wapentakes in the north of England) belonged to the crown and the bailiff was therefore directly answerable to the sheriff, more than half, including Ongar, were in private hands, so Bampton, in this instance, was responsible to the earl of Stafford, though he also worked closely with the sheriff. His duties were primarily judicial and financial, including holding a court every three weeks for which he empanelled a jury of twelve freemen to hear all the cases which could not be dealt with further down the system in the manorial courts and to indict those whose cases would be referred to the higher courts of the sheriff and, ultimately, for the most serious felonies, to the judges of the King's Bench. As bailiff Bampton had been notorious for repeatedly imprisoning those accused of breaking the labour laws and only releasing them when they paid him fines, which he kept personally. Blatantly accepting bribes had not hindered his career: he had served as sheriff of Essex in 1372 and by 1381 he was steward of the estates not only for the nuns of Barking Abbey but also for the royal manor of Havering-atte-Bower.[10]

The final member of the reassessment commission was the current MP for Essex, none other than Sir John Gildesburgh, the Speaker of the Commons which had granted the third poll-tax. Like many of those MPs who had obtained the exemption from serving as a collector or controller of the third poll-tax, he apparently had no qualms about acting as its enforcer. The combination of his close involvement with the tax and his being a well-known retainer and councillor of Thomas of Woodstock made him hugely unpopular – and a provocative figure to have appointed to the commission. He too had served as a commissioner of array, most recently in September 1380, when he had been appointed 'to take order for the defence of the coast of Essex against the enemy's galleys and other vessels now there, to assemble and array all men of that county able to defend it and lead them to the sea coast or to the Thames to resist invasion'. Like his gentry colleagues he was also a justice of the peace.[11]

The presence of so many justices of the peace on the Essex commission, as on those for every other county, was an indication of how influential they had become. They permeated, indeed dominated, the entire county administration. Yet this was a relatively recent development. Local knights and gentry had been appointed occasionally to assist the sheriff in enforcing law and order since at least the end of the twelfth century. From 1287 they had acquired a more formal role as keepers of the peace: between two and six landowners in each county were thereafter regularly commissioned to act as supervisors and enforcers of the Statute of Winchester (1285), which had set out a community-based framework for the maintenance of the peace and defence of the realm. The provisions of the statute included curfews and night-watches for towns, the clearance of trees and undergrowth from two hundred feet either side of roads to remove hiding places for robbers and community penalties for any vill (the smallest administrative unit of the medieval hundred, similar to the later civil parish) which failed to bring robbers and felons to justice. The statute also pre-scribed that every man aged between fifteen and sixty, on his personal oath, should have in his possession the appropriate arms for his status, which was assessed on the value of his lands and chattels: these ranged from the hauberk, open helmet, sword, dagger and horse required of those with lands worth fif-teen pounds and goods worth forty marks down to the bows, arrows, crossbows and bolts of 'everyone else that can'. Two constables from each hundred were to carry out biennial inspec-tions and present defaults and defaulters to the sheriff or to the keepers of the peace.[12]

Edward III's reign had seen an exponential expansion in the role of these keepers of the peace, not least because the gentry, sitting in parliament as members of the Commons, had demanded it. Royal justice, in the form of professional judges sent out on circuit from the central courts in London, was in great demand because it was open to all free men and deemed more impartial than private manorial courts, giving all litigants a chance of winning, even against their social superiors. Paradoxically, this also caused problems because it could spring nasty surprises by riding roughshod over local custom. The Statute of Treasons (1352), for instance, which identified the crimes that were treasonable and therefore punishable by death and forfeiture to the crown, was the direct result of a Commons complaint that the king's judges were condemning people as traitors 'for various reasons unknown to the commonalty as treason'.[13] Reliance on a small group of professional judges also meant that the administration of justice was extremely slow and, as central government became increasingly interventionist in social and economic affairs at local level, particularly after the Black Death, it was in the crown's interest to rely more heavily on the gentry in the shires to act on its behalf. By 1361 they were no longer merely keepers of the peace but had officially become justices of the peace, with powers to pursue, arrest, imprison and punish malefactors, to hold trials and decide cases involving felonies and trespasses, to take securities for good behaviour and to enforce legislation concerning weights and measures. The justices were appointed in a commission for the peace which was issued by the crown for each county, led nominally by a magnate, with 'three or four of the most worthy in the county, together with some who are experts in the law': in practice it was usually sufficient for two or three of the 'worthies' to act together and magnates rarely attended the regular quarterly sessions. The Statute of Westminster (1361), which formalised these powers and used the term 'justices' for the first time, was not a radical departure from previous practice, but by gathering the various strands together and placing them explicitly within the jurisdiction of the justices of the peace it gave their role greater emphasis and authority. The following year they were also given authority to enforce one of the most unpopular of all pieces of medieval legislation, the Statute of Labourers (1351).[14]

This statute had been introduced in the panic engendered by the first outbreak of plague in England. The personal suffering was unimaginable but such high levels of mortality also seriously affected the economy. Agriculture was particularly badly hit because it was so labour-intensive: there were tales of ripe corn being left to rot in the fields because there was no one to reap it and of beasts and cattle straying everywhere because there was no one to tend them. 'There was such a dearth of servants and labourers', wrote Henry Knighton, 'that men were quite bewildered as to what they should do about it'.[15] With no access to any form of census and only anecdotal evidence to rely on as to the scale of the disaster, the first instinct of landowners was to blame the idleness and greed of survivors for rocketing prices and shortage of labour. In June 1349, with the plague at its height, the government therefore responded to the crisis by issuing the Ordinance of Labourers, which attempted to set the clock back by compulsory enforcement of wages and prices at pre-plague levels. Underpinning the legislation was the principle that all able-bodied men and women under the age of sixty were to be compelled to work unless they were demonstrably self-sufficient, earning a living by carrying out a trade or craft or cultivating their own land. The act of giving alms to able-bodied beggars was made illegal and punishable by imprisonment 'so that thus they may be compelled to labour for the necessities of life'. No one was to ask for, or pay, wages which were higher than those paid in the five or six years preceding 1347, on pain of fines double the amounts involved for both employee and employer; sellers of foodstuffs were similarly penalised for charging more than a 'reasonable' profit; 'craftsmen' ranging from carpenters and tilers to boatmen and carters were to be imprisoned for charging more than they had done in 1347, as were servants who left before their agreed term of service had ended.[16]

None of this was particularly radical in itself: similar measures had been enforced in local manorial courts for at least sixty years. What was new was that the ordinance was nationally imposed and took no account of differences in local customs or rates of pay. What was also new, and even more iniquitous, was that it lumped together all tenants in one category, regardless of their personal or tenurial status, thereby extending the powers landlords already possessed over their villeins, who were bound by customary law to perform certain dues and services for their tenancies, to their free tenants who were under no such obligations. Landlords were also given first call on the labour of their own tenants, so that a cottager or smallholder, who supplemented his income by working for wages in the fields of his richer neighbours, on or off the manor on which he resided, was obliged to give priority to his lord, even if he could earn more working for others. The ordinance was, of course, intended to prevent exactly this scenario: demand for agricultural labour services at peak times, such as reaping or mowing, had meant that free tenants could offer their services to the highest bidder. The fixing of wages and the legal prioritising of the lord of the manor's rights to that labour were intended to reinforce the latter's control over his own tenantry and ensure that the short window of opportunity available for such time- and weather-critical events like harvesting would always be open to him before anyone else. The crops of his neighbours or his wealthier tenants, who had too much land to cultivate without assistance, would have to wait until his own were safely taken in.[17]

Early in 1351, the first parliament to meet after the outbreak of the plague confirmed and reinforced the provisions of the ordinance by issuing the Statute of Labourers. This set out in great detail the wages allowed for a range of activities from a penny per day for weeding and haymaking to five pence per day or per acre for mowing meadows. The most important variation was that enforcement was no longer the prerogative of the local manorial court but of specially appointed royal justices who were given the power to investigate and punish all offences against the statute. (These were the same justices whose jurisdiction would later be absorbed into that of the justices of the peace.) All agricultural workers were now to appear twice a year in front of local officials to swear to abide by the terms of the statute, and those same local officials, stewards, bailiffs and constables had themselves to take an oath before the justices to seek out and certify the names of 'rebels'. Craftsmen too had to swear before the new justices that they would practise their crafts as they had done in 1347. Breach of any of these oaths made the perpetrator liable to fine and imprisonment and further infringements could result in outlawry. As an inducement to prosecute offenders who were likely to be neighbours, the statute allowed that any fines collected before 1351 could be offset against the local contribution to the final part of the subsidy due for payment that year. The new justices, most of whom were landowners themselves, set to work with such alacrity that in the first year the statute was in force, in Essex alone over 7500 labourers – a sixth of the adult population of the county – were prosecuted for labour offences. A further amendment in 1361 extended punishments from fines to imprisonment without bail and allowed labourers who absconded to be branded on the forehead with the letter 'F' for 'falsehood'.[18]

As a response to a specific crisis it might have been expected that the labour legislation would become redundant as the emergency faded. This was not the case for two reasons. First, renewed outbreaks of plague in 1361–2, 1369 and 1374–5 meant that the population would not quickly recover to pre-1348 levels: it remained static at around two to three million (from a pre-plague height of perhaps five million) and would not even begin to rise again until the end of the fifteenth century. The shortage of labour would therefore continue.[19] Secondly, it was in the interests of landowners, both secular and ecclesiastical, to enforce the legislation so that they could continue to enjoy a reliable and relatively cheap supply of labour. As late as the October parliament of 1378 MPs were still petitioning for stricter implementation by the justices and demanding the arrest and punishment of those servants and labourers who 'refuse now to work, serve, or labour, and take themselves off to the towns, boroughs and cities, both old and young, some of whom become artificers, and others mariners, or clerks, so that husbandry cannot be maintained, nor the lands of the realm cultivated, to the great injury of the kingdom'.[20]

Not unnaturally, the rigorous enforcement of the labour legislation caused huge resentment. It was seen as self-interested and corrupt because the same people who benefited as landowners and employers also sat as justices to decide offences and were allowed to keep a proportion of the fines they imposed as their wages (one-sixth in 1378); nor were they above competing for labour by offering their own workers higher wages and extra payments in kind while using the statute to prevent others from doing so.[21] Some landlords were able to apply the law to the letter without causing unrest or dissent among their tenants. The bishop of Durham, for instance, who owned one of the largest estates in England at around thirty-seven thousand acres, over half of it as villein tenements, actually enrolled a copy of the statute in his chancery roll – the only statute to appear there – and employed a commission to implement it: yet this repressive lordship apparently did not cause protest or revolt. The same was also true of the duchy of Cornwall.[22] These were unusual cases, however, where a single lord not only dominated the landownership but also enjoyed extensive judicial rights over his tenantry.

In many more areas of the country, however, there were multiple lordships, or large numbers of substantial landowners who were not lords of the manor and therefore relied on hired servants and labourers to farm their lands. With only a diminished pool of available labour to draw on, the statute was as much an impediment to them as it was to those seeking better payment for their work. And the people who were expected to enforce the legislation at local level, the constables, bailiffs and jurors, were the wealthier, more 'respectable' members of their communities, who were precisely those who had taken advantage of the increased availability and cheapness of land since the plague, to build up their own holdings to a size where they also needed to hire labour at peak periods. Trying to freeze wages to the levels of 1346–7 was therefore unrealistic, particularly as the years rolled by. By the 1360s even great estates belonging to bishops, earls and Oxford colleges routinely hired labourers at double the wages prescribed by the statute, concealing these illicit payments in their accounts as cash bonuses and grants of food, clothing and even allotments of demesne land. There is perhaps no more illuminating example of the way that the statute was routinely ignored than the fact that the carpenter who made the stocks to imprison those labourers who refused to take the oath at Knightsbridge, Gloucestershire, was himself paid 5½d. per day – instead of the two or three pence he was supposed to receive depending on whether he was an ordinary or master carpenter. And, despite the statute, the reality was that wages for both agricultural and craft workers would increase by thirty per cent between 1350 and 1380.[23]

Nevertheless, whenever the justices of the peace held their quarterly sessions, it could be guaranteed that much of their business would be concerned with the labour legislation. More than half the indictments before the Norfolk justices in 1375–9 were concerned with its breaches, as were some two hundred of the two hundred and eighty extant cases dealt with in Essex in 1377–9. Often they were brought by aggrieved employers who had lost their servants to others despite paying over the statutory limits themselves: one man who lost his two servants had been paying them two pence a day, plus their food, an extra seven shillings a year and a quarter of corn every ten weeks;

their new employer had offered them twelve pence a day.[24] A typical Essex indictment included the accusation that Richard Blake, a reaper, was paid '3d. per day and food and 6d. for an acre', in contravention of the statutory two or three pence daily rate 'without food or other favours being demanded, given or taken'. More interestingly, we also see examples of passive resistance, a common tactic in manorial disputes but more perilous where royal justice was involved. Gilbert Rougge, from Sturmer, Essex, was indicted as 'a rebel against the constables' because he was 'unwilling to swear or justify himself', in other words take the oath to the statute. His refusal to cooperate, even at this level, is understandable since he was one of the poorest labourers in the village and would pay only twelve pence jointly for himself and his wife in the poll-tax of 1381: clearly he actually needed better wages if he could get them. In another area of the county it was the constables themselves who were mutinous: the Essex justices were told that 'no constable of Dunmow hundred has done his duty of making labourers swear to serve and take wages according to the statute'. In the royal borough of Colchester the bailiff was responsible for collecting the fines imposed by the justices: in 1352 he and his sub-collectors were imprisoned for refusing to surrender the £84 7s. 7d. they had collected, presumably because they feared it would not be offset against the town's subsidy payment as the statute had then allowed. The justices also found it equally difficult to enforce the statute within the town in later years when no such concessions were available: in 1377–9, for example, no breaches of the labour laws are recorded at all, which is highly unlikely given the thriving economy of Colchester.[25]

The Statute of Labourers was deeply unpopular because it represented repressive lordship at its worst and one of the main political objectives of the rebels would be its abolition, enunciated in their demand to the king that 'no one should serve any man except at his own will and by means of regular covenant'.[26] Those who enforced the labour legislation were hated for the same reason, even by those who did not personally fall foul of it. Justices of the peace who combined that role with being commissioners appointed to enforce the equally hated poll-tax were to find themselves prime targets of the rebels' wrath. When the Essex commissioners, led by John Bampton and Sir John Gildesburgh, arrived at Brentwood at the end of May 1381 it may have been unclear, even to those gathered there, whether they were acting in their familiar capacity as justices of the peace or as new-fangled poll-tax commissioners. The quarter sessions were due to be held in the first week of June, as was the annual view of frankpledge, and, as far as the people of Essex were concerned, they had paid their poll-tax as demanded and there was nothing more to be said or done about the matter.[27]

When, therefore, Bampton displayed his royal commission and announced to the assembled constables, bailiffs and other 'sound and law-worthy' representatives of the county administration whom he had summoned to meet him at Brentwood that he had come to inquire into how the poll-tax had been levied and ensure that the shortfall was made good, he was greeted with anger and disbelief. The general view was that they were being asked to pay a new tax: no doubt they even suspected that Bampton himself, rather than the royal treasury, would be the beneficiary, as he had been of the 'fines' he levied for offences against the Statute of Labourers. Thomas Baker from Fobbing, a small village at the southernmost edge of the county, spoke for them all when he protested that they would not pay a single penny more because they had already paid the tax and indeed had a receipt from Bampton himself for their contribution. They therefore regarded themselves as fully discharged of any further obligation. The commissioners responded, as they were entitled to do, by threatening to arrest them but the representatives of Fobbing, having consulted with their fellows from the other villages, decided to stand firm. Around a hundred of them were then alleged to have confronted Bampton, refusing either to give him any more money or have any further dealings with him. When the commissioners ordered their sergeant-at-arms to arrest them and put them in prison, Baker and his fellow representatives drew their bows and arrows and forced them to flee, possibly even, as the indictments later alleged, 'pursuing them to kill them', though this may have been an exaggeration to ensure conviction because all the supposed victims escaped with their lives and, apparently, without injury.[28]

The incident at Brentwood was by no means an unprecedented act of violence: royal officials were often attacked in the course of their duties. We have already seen how attempts to enforce the collection of the parish tax in 1371 led to the villagers of Lakenheath, Suffolk, assaulting the collectors and how, only the previous year, 1380, up to three hundred citizens of Winchester had physically attacked the prior of Southwick when he led a commission of array in their town.[29] The incident at Brentwood, however, was significant because it was a concerted act of defiance by respected and responsible delegates from sixteen different villages: most of them came from within a twelve-mile radius of Brentwood, and from the two adjacent southernmost hundreds, or administrative districts, of Barstable and Chafford, so they probably knew one another and had worked together in the past. But there were also representatives from Benington, more than thirty miles away in Hertfordshire, and from Bocking, twenty-three miles north-east of Brentwood in Hinckford hundred, the northernmost administrative district of Essex. Whether they consulted together before they decided to act is unclear, though it seems likely. What is beyond doubt is that, having attacked royal officers as they attempted to carry out their official duties, they knew that they had crossed a threshold and would be held to account. Rather than submit to royal justice, or rather to royal justiciars,[30] from whom they could not expect a sympathetic hearing, they decided to raise the standard of revolt.

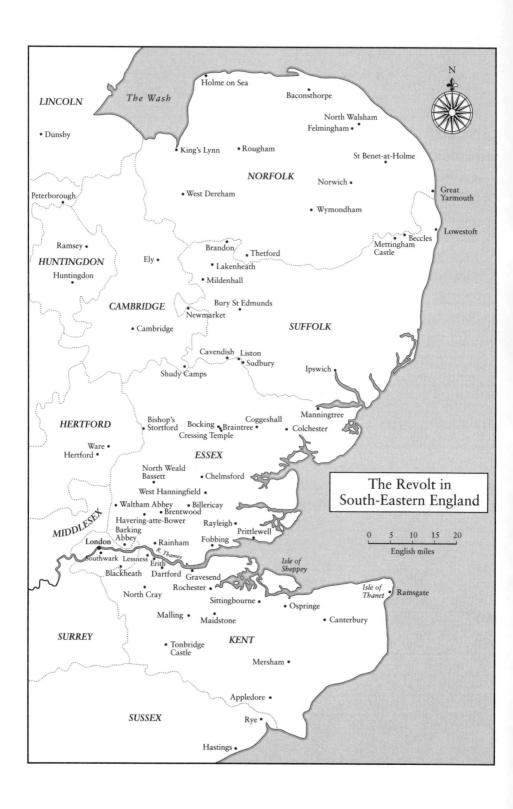

The Revolt in
South-Eastern England

N

0   5   10   15   20
English miles

LINCOLN

• Dunsby

The Wash

Holme on Sea

Baconsthorpe

North Walsham
Felmingham •

King's Lynn • • Rougham

St Benet-at-Holme

NORFOLK

• West Dereham

Norwich •

Great
Yarmouth

• Wymondham

Lowestoft

Peterborough

HUNTINGDON

Ramsey •

Brandon

Thetford

• Beccles
Mettingham
Castle

Ely •

• Lakenheath

Huntingdon

• Mildenhall

CAMBRIDGE

Bury St Edmunds
Newmarket

SUFFOLK

• Cambridge

Cavendish   Liston
• • Sudbury

Shudy Camps

Ipswich •

HERTFORD

Bishop's
Stortford

Coggeshall

Manningtree

Bocking •Braintree •
Cressing Temple

• Colchester

Ware •
Hertford •

ESSEX

North Weald
Bassett

• Chelmsford

West Hanningfield •

• Waltham Abbey   • Billericay
• Brentwood

MIDDLESEX

Havering-atte-Bower
Barking
Abbey

Rayleigh •

Prittlewell

London
Southwark Lessness

• Rainham

Fobbing

R. Thames

*Isle of
Sheppey*

Erith
Blackheath   Dartford Gravesend •

*Isle of
Thanet* • Ramsgate

North Cray

Rochester •

Sittingbourne •

• Ospringe

Malling •
Maidstone

• Canterbury

SURREY

KENT

• Tonbridge
Castle

Mersham •

SUSSEX

Appledore •

Rye •

Hastings •

CHAPTER SEVEN

Essex and Kent arise

Having made their stand at Brentwood the newly fledged rebels appear to have dispersed back to their homes to organise the uprising in their own localities. Thomas Baker and William Gildeborne, for instance, returned to Fobbing, accompanied by almost half of the village's adult males who had gone with them to Brentwood. They appear to have been the biggest group: around half of just over a hundred names on one of the indictments prepared at Chelmsford on 3 July to prosecute Gildesburgh's and Bampton's attackers were from Fobbing itself, while at least twenty more came from their neighbouring villages of Corringham, Stanford-le-Hope, Mucking and Hornden.[1] At some point soon after their return, Baker and Gildeborne contacted Robert Berdon of Orsett, who had not been at Brentwood (or is not mentioned in any of the relevant indictments) and commissioned him to proclaim the uprising in at least six places throughout Rochford hundred and as far north as Witham. Berdon was the most active of all the agitators in Essex, covering distances of between twenty and thirty miles from Orsett over the course of the following week and he was still at his task on 7 June when he made his proclamation at Rayleigh.[2] Whether he proclaimed an oral message or read out letters addressed to the people of each place is another of the frustrating questions to which we have no answer, though he seems to have passed the torch on to others: John Hurt of Shoebury, for instance, came from one of the places visited by Berdon and, at the behest of John Syrat of Shoebury, went to Prittlewell to cause that town to rise.[3]

While the Fobbing contingent was raising the south-east of the county, other representatives at the Brentwood meeting were spreading the word elsewhere. William Roger of South Ockendon, for example, went home and joined forces with John Smyth of neighbouring Rainham; both then rode throughout Chafford hundred, giving the signal to rebel and allegedly forcibly compelling the local men to join them in 'conspiratorial meetings and assemblies'.[4] Only one of the indictments gives us an insight into what went on at such meetings. On 2 June there was a major gathering of men from north Essex at Bocking. Presumably it was called by Robert Cardemaker, who had been involved in the Brentwood assault on 30 May and would play a very active role in the revolt. A maker of cards for combing wool, he was one of only twenty people out of 216 in Bocking who had already been forced to contribute more than twelve pence for his poll-tax in 1381, paying 2s. 6d. for himself and his wife Agnes.[5] Perhaps this explains his willingness to join the Brentwood representatives in refusing to accept any further demands from the reassessment commissioners: the level of his payment certainly suggests that he was not a wealthy man, even if, like many other rebel leaders, he was one of the better-off inhabitants. Most of those who attended the Bocking meeting were from six villages in Hinckford hundred, including Bocking itself, but they were also drawn from Great Coggeshall and Dedham in Lexden hundred, Little Coggeshall in Witham hundred and Dunmow in Dunmow hundred.[6] All lay within a twenty-five-mile radius of Bocking, the area where the rebellion in Essex would assume its most serious dimension. Significantly, this same region was the heartland of John Balle's influence.

We first hear of the man whose preaching was blamed for inciting the great revolt in a royal writ of 25 February 1364 which declared that 'John Balle, chaplain' had petitioned and received from the king a special protection because 'he feared bodily injury from some of his enemies in the prosecution of his business'. The king now withdrew that protection because he had learned that Balle was 'not prosecuting any business but wanders from country to country [sic] preaching articles contrary to the faith of the church to the peril of his soul and the souls of others, especially of laymen'.[7] Eight months later Simon Sudbury, who was then bishop of London, notified the secular authorities that he had excommunicated Balle, whom he described as having been 'staying for a considerable length of time in our diocese'. Sudbury's intervention arose not because Balle had found his way to the capital, as some commentators have believed, but because the London diocese then included much of the county of Essex: Balle was therefore subject to the bishop's authority and answerable to him for his preaching activities in that county. Two years later, in 1366, when Sudbury's superior, archbishop Langham, cited Balle to appear before him to be interrogated 'for the safety of his soul', the recalcitrant chaplain must still have been in Essex because the order was sent to the dean of Bocking – the very place where the rebels of 1381 gathered to plan and launch their revolt.[8]

Sudbury became archbishop of Canterbury in 1375 and in December of the following year stepped up his actions against Balle, certifying him as excommunicate at Canterbury and, on

13 December 1376, obtaining a royal writ which ordered the parsons of Panfield and Little Tey, together with Thomas Joye and John Blyton, both of Colchester, and John Flecham of Shalford, to seize 'John Balle, chaplain' and deliver him to the sheriff of Essex so that he could be brought to justice as an unrepentant excommunicate. Since Panfield, Little Tey and Shalford all lay less than twenty miles from Colchester, Sudbury clearly believed Balle was still in that area twelve years after their first confrontation.[9]

It is surely highly significant that Sudbury's final efforts to bring Balle to account took place just weeks before the outbreak of the great revolt. On 29 April 1381, the archbishop wrote again to the secular authorities, reissuing the excommunication and ordering the arrest of 'the said vagabond John Balle, on account of the errors and divisions he has sown'. In the strongest terms he had yet used, Sudbury accused Balle of being a false prophet who spread his poison by preaching sermons that 'reeked of heretical depravity', holding forth not just in churches and cemeteries, but also in public markets and other secular places. What is more, the archbishop alleged, he had falsely denigrated the Church authorities, attacked the pope and bishops and even slandered Sudbury himself by spreading 'scandals about our person'. It is a measure of how personal their quarrel had become that Sudbury reserved to himself alone the right to sit in judgment on Balle, who, at this point in his long career, had succeeded in attracting condemnations from four successive archbishops of Canterbury as well as bishop Bateman of Norwich, bishop Buckingham of Lincoln and bishops Northburgh and Courtenay of London. On this occasion Balle was quickly arrested and incarcerated in the episcopal prison at Bishop's Stortford, Essex.[10]

The fact that Balle had been able to elude the authorities for so many years, despite his activities being confined largely to one county, suggests that his radical preaching had won him friends and sympathisers among the inhabitants of Essex. Not only had they sheltered him from the authorities but now, at Bocking, they would seem to have turned his beliefs into a political agenda which they were prepared to risk their lives to implement. One indictment tells us that the men who met at Bocking 'swore an oath that they would be of one accord in seeking to destroy divers subjects of the lord king and his common laws and even all lordship of divers lords'; another states that 'they would be of one accord in killing and destroying divers subjects of the lord king, saying and pledging that they did not wish to have any other law in England excepting only certain laws that they themselves put forward to be ordained'.[11] These objectives chime well with what we know the rebels sought from the king at Mile End and Smithfield: the execution of 'traitors' among the king's ministers, no law except for the law of Winchester and the abolition of all lordship except that of the king. The natural conclusion to be drawn from this is that the men of Bocking had a radical agenda even before the revolt began in earnest and that it was one they carried with them to London.[12] There are a couple of caveats that need to be entered here, however: we cannot entirely trust the wording of the indictments since the specific details could well have been beefed up by clerks anxious to secure conviction; and, even if the pledge to destroy 'all lordship' is true, even in the indictment it was limited to 'all lordship *of divers lords*', which is a rather different thing. Even if we interpret the abolition of 'lordship' as only getting rid of villeinage and villein tenure, rather than the dismantling of all private jurisdictions, there is no denying the revolutionary nature of the programme the Bocking rebels pledged themselves to carry out.

We do not know whether all the other 'conspiratorial meetings and assemblies' taking place at this time adopted the same set of principles as their plan for action, but this seems likely given that rebels in Essex and indeed throughout the whole of that part of England affected by the revolt, pursued remarkably similar targets. The swearing of an oath to bind themselves together and to carry out their objectives was also a feature of rebel gatherings from Surrey to Yorkshire.[13] Its value should not be underestimated because it was never taken lightly. The oath underpinned the fundamental workings of medieval society: it bound tenants and manorial officials to their lords and local men when they joined their tithings or served on juries; it was even taken by the king's subjects on a regular basis to ensure that they obeyed the Statute of Labourers and the Statute of Winchester, both of which had a daily impact on their lives. An oath was a personal and sacred obligation upheld by state and Church: to a deeply religious society, breaching an oath was punishable in this world and the next. So when the rebels pledged themselves to be of 'one accord' in what they set out to do they were committing themselves as seriously as if they had signed a legally binding contract – with the added twist that their eternal salvation depended on them being true to what they had sworn to do.

There was also a religious significance to the date on which the Bocking meeting was held: 2 June 1381 was not just a Sunday but Whitsunday, a festival of huge importance in the Church calendar. Much has been made of the fact that the rebels entered London on the feast of Corpus Christi, but the importance of the religious festivals preceding the revolt, which provided the opportunity for it to be planned and organised, has not been fully recognised.[14] Whitsunday marked the end of the Easter cycle, with its highly emotional sequence of events, from the self-denial of forty days' fasting in Lent (Shrovetide) through the desolation of the crucifixion of Christ on Good Friday to the joy of His resurrection on Easter Day, His ascent into heaven at

Ascension and the descent of the Holy Spirit on the apostles on Whitsunday (Pentecost). For almost fourteen weeks, therefore, parish life had been dominated by Church ritual and a mixture of public humiliation and celebration. Shrove Tuesday, when all meat, eggs and cheese had to be eaten up in preparation for the fasting through Lent, was an opportunity for licensed gluttony, drunkenness and sports such as football and cock-fighting. The following forty days of fasting were marked by an absence of festivity and the exclusion of notorious sinners from church, where the images and altar were veiled. Palm Sunday brought blessings on foliage, processions through the churchyard to church, the readmission of excluded sinners and the unveiling of the altars. Maundy Thursday brought the socially awkward ceremony of washing the feet of the poor, which not only royalty but all the upper hierarchy of the Church, including abbots and priors, were supposed to carry out. On Easter Eve all the lights in church were extinguished and a new, single Paschal candle was lit in preparation for Easter Day, which ushered in three days of feasting and merry-making second only to Christmas, since Lent had ended and the Church had decreed that not even villeins by blood could be made to work. Throughout the weeks between Easter Day and Ascension Day most parishes held boundary walks and Rogation processions, led by their priest, with banners carried, bell-ringing and communal feasting. According to a fourteenth-century commentary on Holy Days, attendance was compulsory: absence from the Rogation processions was regarded as a sin on a par with not attending church since their purpose was to seek God's protection on the growing crops. On Ascension Day itself, the Paschal candle was extinguished for the last time and church bells were rung. Ten days later Whitsunday brought more processions and celebrations, including the holding of church-ales, where communal feasting and merry-making were held to raise funds for the parish church.[15] As the feast celebrating the gift of the Holy Spirit to the apostles, enabling them to go out and preach the Gospel to the whole world, it was a peculiarly appropriate day for the Bocking rebels to hold their meeting in preparation for sending out messengers to raise the revolt throughout the rest of the county.

No doubt the Eastertide message also fanned the flames of the prevailing sense of injustice: every clergyman in every church and at every preaching cross would be proclaiming that Christ died for all men, not just for the privileged few. Or, as John Balle put it, 'the king's son of heaven shall pay for all'.[16] Ascension Day, in particular, was one of the high points in the preaching calendar, when public sermons would be preached in English, often by mendicant friars and other travelling preachers. Even after the great revolt they could still be inflammatory: Nicholas Hereford, a follower of Wyclif at Oxford University, preached a public sermon in English in St Frideswide's churchyard on 15 May 1382 in which he called on all faithful Christians to put their hands to the wheel, seize the property of the friars, monks and canons who lived off the labour of others, and set them all to manual work. If this were done, he argued, there would be no need to tax the poor commons.[17] Sentiments like these, if uttered just a year previously, could well have tipped popular anger over into a desire for action. Perhaps, in this context, it is significant that archbishop Sudbury's order for the arrest of John Balle was issued on 29 April 1381, in the period between Easter Day and Ascension Day: the specific condemnation of Balle's sowing 'errors and divisions' and of his attacks on the Church hierarchy suggest that he may have made the most of the season to spread his views and so incite revolt.[18]

The Church calendar observed thirty-nine holy days in the year, with an additional four days each for Eastertide and

Whitsuntide. That was two periods, in mid-April and the beginning of June, of four consecutive days in which no one had to report for work or perform labour services.[19] The week after Whitsunday, with its processions, merry-making and church-ales, was also traditionally the period for the annual view of frankpledge, when the courts of each hundred checked that every adult male was enrolled in a tithing, the small group of around ten men which formed the basic unit of judicial administration and was collectively held responsible for the good behaviour of its members. This provided a valid excuse for large numbers of men to travel outside their manors and meet together to exchange information. In the weeks and days leading up to the revolt, therefore, there were an unusually large number of legitimate opportunities for people to gather together for communal activities in every parish and in every hundred in the country. There could have been no more convenient time of year to organise resistance to the commissioners enforcing collection of the third poll-tax and to plan for rebellion.

This perhaps explains why Whitsunday was also the day on which the first act of the revolt took place in Kent. Abel Ker of Erith, near Dartford, confessed after the revolt that he and his fellow villagers John Eylward and John Young, and Richard atte Frythe from the adjoining village of Lessness, who had served as one of the local 'worthy men' levying the first poll-tax there, had gathered together sworn assemblies of malefactors and entered Lesnes Abbey, where they compelled the abbot to swear 'that he would be of their company'. This phrase could be interpreted in different ways, to mean being forced to agree with their objectives, to accompany them, or to give them varying degrees of assistance, but the monk of Westminster tells us that the rebels forced 'everybody they met who was not of their fellowship into sworn association with themselves in the defence of King Richard, since they held themselves out as champions of the king and the welfare of the kingdom against those who were betraying them'. The next day the same four individuals with three others from Erith and Ralph Erliche of Bexley, banded together under oath and sailed across the Thames to Essex. Once there they set about raising a sworn company of more than a hundred men whose names Ker professed not to know. The following day, 4 June, they sailed their Essex recruits back across the Thames to Dartford, where they incited the men of the town to join their rebellion.[20] The remarkable fact that a band of Kentish rebels thought fit to cross the Thames twice in order to bring back sympathisers from a different county to instigate rebellion in their own neighbourhood raises obvious questions. Could they not find enough support locally to carry out their aims? Were they aware of the Bocking assembly and its stated aims? Were they already in touch with dissidents in Essex before they acted? How did they ship such a large company across the Thames without attracting hostile notice?

The likely answer to all these questions lies in the abbey of Lesnes, a house of Augustinian canons with a poor reputation for both religious discipline and management of its affairs. What it did have, however, was extensive property in Essex, including the churches of Elmdon, Ramsden Bellhouse and Rainham, so that there must have been regular contact between these places and Lesnes Abbey before the revolt. Rainham lay just across the Thames from the abbey and the nearby town of Dartford; a ferry already operated between Erith and Coldharbour Point, just outside Rainham, so it was the obvious place to land and to gather recruits for the return journey. We can speculate that the abbot was forced either to provide shipping for the rebels or to lend his authority to recruit in the towns where he held property. The Kentish rebels were concerned to obtain such validation for their actions: Ker's men were alleged to have compelled John Chaundeler of Prittlewell, on the eastern Essex coast, to go with a message to Sir William Berland and John Prittlewell senior commanding them to rise and come to Rainham to join the rebel recruits.[21] This suggests that Ker expected a sympathetic response, though it is not immediately obvious why: Berland was a justice of the peace with extensive lands in Prittlewell, Rayleigh, Rawreth and Goldhanger, all places which would be involved in the revolt; Prittlewell had served as an assessor of the second poll-tax in 1379. The two men were neighbours in Prittlewell, had served on the same commissions and the latter would witness the former's will in 1383. We know more about Berland than Prittlewell but there is little to mark him out as different from the Essex gentry who would be targeted by the revolt. He had the military distinction of having captured the French hero and 'flower of chivalry', Bertrand du Guesclin, at the battle of Nájera in 1367, which earned him a ransom of £1427 14s. 6d.; and, more relevantly, having made conventional provision in his will for his two daughters and co-heiresses, and for alms for the souls of himself and his family, he left the remainder of his estate 'to aid the poor of his lineage, to mend public bridges and highways where shall be most in need in the towns where his said lands are, especially in the hundred of Rochford, and to aid his tenants who are poor or distressed'.[22] This was an unusual and generous provision, especially as Berland had ordered all but one of his lands to be sold after his death, so the estate was likely to be considerable. If he was as charitable in his life as he intended to be after his death, this might explain why the Kentish rebels thought he would come to Rainham and join their cause.

Ker seems to have stolen a march on his Essex allies, for while they spent the week after Whitsunday sending out messengers to rally support and gathering their forces, he landed his recruits in Dartford on 4 June and immediately set about gathering reinforcements in the town. The townsmen were in receptive mood, not just because of simmering discontent about being subjected to a reassessment of their contributions to the poll-tax but also because Robert Bealknapp, chief justice of the Common Bench, had held assizes in Dartford the day before. It is possible that among the cases he heard was that of Robert Bellyng of Gravesend, who was still in Rochester Castle as a result of failing to purchase his freedom from Sir Simon Burley.[23] Feelings were already running high on this subject and the coincidence of the timing of the chief justice's arrival is suggestive, particularly as Dartford erupted in riots the day after the assize ended there.[24]

An equally intriguing possibility is that John Legge, the king's notorious sergeant-at-arms, was also in Dartford or its vicinity, carrying 'with him a great number of indictments against the people of that area, to make the king rich'. Legge may have brought indictments to Bealknapp at the assizes; he may even have been one of the sergeants-at-arms sent to arrest Bellyng as a runaway villein; but what we do know for certain is that he had good reason to be in Kent at this time because on 3 May he had been appointed as the sergeant-at-arms to the poll-tax reassessment commission for that county.[25] Whether or not he did use the inappropriate method of determining if teenage girls were old enough to be eligible for the poll-tax attributed to him,[26] Legge's very presence on the commission was enough to make him a hated figure. His name alone, out of all the Kent commission, appears on the list of royal councillors whose heads the rebels sought from the king at their first encounter at Rotherhithe on 13 June and he was one of the handful to be summarily executed the following day. The other commissioners, as we shall see, did not escape popular vengeance but the attacks on them were limited to their property and did not endanger their lives.

Legge was clearly in a different category, perhaps because he was not a local man and, as the sole 'courtier' on the commission, was held personally responsible for its work. The chronicler Knighton even went so far as to assert that Legge had suggested the commission to the king in the first place and had 'contracted to give the lord king a large sum of money for his assent'. This was probably not true but Legge had benefited substantially from his court associations in the past. In 1370, for instance, he had agreed to pay the crown £9 6s. 8d. annually for the right to collect in Surrey and Sussex the subsidy on cloth granted by parliament, a grant which was initially made for three years but renewed on the same terms for five years in 1377; he got to keep anything raised above the fee he paid to the crown and also any forfeitures, making it a highly lucrative business venture. He had even served as a knight of the shire for Surrey and Sussex in the parliament of 1378, despite not being of knightly rank.[27] All this suggests that Legge was capable of driving a hard bargain and lining his own pockets at the expense of the hard-pressed Kentish tax-payers, which may have contributed to the loathing he inspired.

The activities of the reassessment commission in Kent were the final ingredient in an already toxic situation and anyone involved in collecting the third poll-tax was likely to be a victim of the rebels' anger. On 5 June, the day after the arrival of Ker and his Essex contingent, there were 'uprisings and assemblies' in Dartford, culminating in an attack on the house of Nicholas Heryng in which goods and chattels worth a hundred pounds were carried off. This was not a random act of violence. Heryng was just the sort of local official who would feel the full weight of the rebels' anger. A former escheator of Kent, he was a justice of the peace and steward of the king's lands in the county: to cap it all, he was a member of the reassessment commission. The rebels may have been searching his Dartford house for poll-tax records to destroy but they were also determined to inflict as much damage as they could. Three days later they attacked his manors of North Cray and Foots Cray, which were less than six miles from Dartford, destroying his records there, demolishing the buildings and taking property worth a thousand marks. The following day they broke into his house at Rochester. His estates on the Isle of Sheppey were also plundered and two oxen, twenty-seven sheep and 482 fleeces were stolen, together with twenty-four pounds' worth of movable goods. Not finding him in residence in any of his houses, they were so determined to capture him that they even broke into Tonbridge Castle, fourteen miles from Maidstone, thinking that he and John Bampton were hiding there and hoping to kill them both. Heryng was fortunate to escape with his life – though not for long, as he was murdered a year later.[28]

During the disturbances in Dartford two notable rebel captains emerged to join forces with Abel Ker and his band of Essex men, both of whom were accused of causing uprisings and holding assemblies on 5 June. Thomas atte Raven is described as being of both Rochester and Southwark; he was an important and influential figure in Rochester and had represented the town in the House of Commons in 1378, where Legge would have been one of his fellow MPs. He was involved in most of the early violence in Kent, including the attacks on Heryng's manors at North Cray and Foots Cray, and, as we shall see, he was one of those who joined the march to London, where he also played a major role in the events unfurling there.[29] The other leader to emerge at this time was Robert Cave, or Baker, of Dartford, who also owned a dwelling house with a garden and four acres of land eleven miles away at Otford, where the archbishop of Canterbury had one of his Kentish palaces. Although he was acquitted by a trial jury of involvement in the revolt and his pardon stated that the charges against him had been made by his enemies, he did not secure his release from prison or his pardon until 1392, which must raise some doubt as to his innocence. He is named in a number of indictments and in Abel Ker's confession as actively participating in every stage of the early days of the Kentish rebellion, though there is no suggestion that he went with the rebels to London. What is particularly interesting about Cave's alleged role is that he alone was indicted for having led the band of men from Essex and Kent that rescued Robert Bellyng from prison in Rochester Castle on 6 or 7 June, which implies that this was a personal mission on behalf of a friend.[30]

The *Anonimalle* tells us that Cave's band 'laid strong siege to the castle and although the constable defended it vigorously for half a day he at last handed the castle over for fear of the great multitude of people'. When one looks at the impressive ruins of the castle today it defies belief that it should fall to rebels armed only with hand weapons of the most basic kind, even if there were several hundred of them. It is possible that their leader was a man of professional military experience, if he was the same Robert Cave who had served as a man-at-arms in Arundel's naval expedition of 1378, but this would not have been sufficient to enable him to lead such ill-armed troops to victory in a siege against one of the kingdom's most renowned strongholds. This was a castle which had withstood a two-month siege by the armies of King John in 1215: it had suffered considerable damage to its domestic offices from artillery fire during another major siege in 1264 but since the renewal of the war with France thousands of pounds had been poured into repairing its curtain walls and building new towers, including, most recently, one overlooking the bridge over the river Medway. The ancient stone bridge itself had been badly damaged on 2 February when a sudden thaw, after a winter so severe that the river had frozen above Rochester, sent a huge flood of water and ice downstream which carried away 'the great part of the bridge'. Since it was one of the most important river crossings in Kent repairs were carried out immediately but it was still in a ruinous state at the time of the revolt and indeed for over a decade until a new bridge was completed in 1392.[31] Only a skeleton garrison would have been in residence but, even so, had those guarding the castle simply pulled up the drawbridge the rebels could not have breached its defences. Either the constable and his garrison were taken by surprise and were therefore remiss in their duty, or they must have actively colluded with the rebels.

Froissart's answer to the conundrum of Rochester's capture echoes the *Anonimalle*'s: the constable, Sir John Newenton, surrendered his castle and his person when the rebels threatened to kill him unless he joined them. Newenton had only been in post since October 1379, paying the king a yearly rent of twelve pounds for the city and thirty-eight for the castle and its wards, while collecting any surplus revenues for himself. Even so, he must have been aware of the serious consequences he would incur for failing to defend the castle properly, including prosecution for treason under the law of arms for 'negligence, carelessness or feeble resistance'.[32] No such action appears to have been taken against him and there is no evidence of his seeking or receiving a pardon for colluding with the rebels, even though, as Froissart tells us, he was forced to accompany them to London and act as their messenger to the king. The key to Newenton's behaviour, including his holding out for half a day before suddenly surrendering the castle, was that the rebels captured his children and held them hostage, threatening to kill them if he did not do their will. We learn this only from Froissart, who cannot always be trusted: he was not a witness of the events he described and his accuracy is often compromised by his love of flowery speeches and all things chivalric, not to mention an abysmal knowledge of English geography. In this instance, however, at least two of his close friends and fellow Hainaulters, Jean, lord of Gommegnies, 'whom I had known at the English court when he and I were both young', and Robert, count of Namur, the patron at whose request he wrote his *Chronicles*, were present when Newenton delivered his message from the rebels to the king and told them that, unless he returned to his captors, his children would be killed. And, as we shall see, the vital role he played as intermediary would more than compensate for his failure to hold Rochester Castle.[33]

While Cave and his company sprang Bellyng from jail, Raven and Ker made for Maidstone with their combined forces. Maidstone was the last navigable town on the Medway, making it an important commercial centre for the cheap transportation of grain and wood to London and its famous local stone to Canterbury; its thriving markets served as a hub for the exchange of pastoral and arable products throughout the Weald and into north Kent and they were regularly frequented by London merchants. It was dominated by the presence at its centre, on a loop in the river, of a palace belonging to the archbishop of Canterbury, who was lord of the manor of Maidstone. Like the palace at Otford it was intended to serve as a resting place for the archbishop on his journeys between London and Canterbury, but it was also a potent symbol of his lordship over the town.[34]

The rebels' objective was not the palace, however, but the house of William Topclyve, a local justice of the peace who had been sitting with Bealknapp at the assizes in Dartford but was also steward of the archbishop's liberty in Kent. Neither occupation was calculated to make him popular. The rebels burned down his house on the outskirts of the town and stole goods and chattels worth a thousand marks (Robert Glover of Strood even made off with a hauberk, shield, lance, bow and two quivers of arrows); what is more, they made a bonfire of all his 'evidences', the legal documents upon which his stewardship depended.[35] A year later he exacted his revenge by obtaining a royal commission to compel all the archbishop's tenants to draw up new rent and custumal rolls to replace those they had burned and destroyed; he also obtained a licence from the king, at the new archbishop's special request, to add battlements and fortify his 'small place called "Shoford" in the parish of Maidstone' which had been 'levelled' by the insurgents: this was not so much to make the place more defensible but rather a defiant public gesture to reaffirm his status and authority in the face of those who had tried to destroy him.[36]

It was at Maidstone on 7 June that the first recorded fatality of the Kentish revolt occurred: John Stonhelde of Maidstone was killed there, allegedly by his fellow townsman John Webbe and William Brown of Bexley, though Cave's and Raven's companies were also implicated. Stonhelde is likely to have been a local official, since he was one of the 'worthy men' appointed to levy the first poll-tax in 1377, but no reasons for his murder are given in the indictments. His alleged murderers were also accused of going three days later to Borden, ten miles from Maidstone, where, with others, they murdered John Godwot, demolished his house and burned 'certain evidences' kept there.[37] How Godwot had offended the rebels is unclear but he was probably a lawyer and evidently a close colleague of several of the revolt's most prominent Kentish victims; only a few weeks before the revolt, on 6 April, for example, he had been in Dartford to have a document witnessed which granted the reversion of rents and services in various parts of Kent jointly to himself, Nicholas Heryng, Elias Reyner and Thomas Holt, which suggests that they had business interests together.[38]

Elias Reyner had been attacked the day before Godwot at his home in Strood, on the north bank of the Medway, just across the bridge from Rochester. Reyner was the escheator for Kent and steward of the king's hundred of Milton, in north-eastern Kent, which included the village of Borden and the Isle of Sheppey. He and Nicholas Heryng had been appointed royal commissioners of inquiry on 10 January 1380 on behalf of five London merchants whose chartered Flemish vessel had foundered in a storm off the Isle: the merchants claimed it was not actually wrecked, but the islanders had treated it as such, broken up the ship, carried off the tackle and goods and were now refusing to pay for them. We can guess the result of the inquiry given that Heryng's extensive estates on Sheppey were plundered during the revolt.[39] Despite his having served by virtue of his office as one of the Kent commissioners to reassess and enforce the collection of the third poll-tax, Reyner's house and property were spared, possibly because he took the judicious decision to offer no resistance to the rebels but simply handed over all the records of his escheatorship and stewardship, which the rebels took to Rochester, where they were ceremoniously and publicly burned in the market-place on Trinity Sunday, 9 June. The same thing happened to his colleague Thomas Shardelowe, the chief coroner of Kent, whose house in Dartford was plundered and all his documentation stolen and publicly burned in the town's market-place.[40]

John Glovere, however, did not escape so lightly: his house was demolished during the disturbances in Rochester on Trinity Sunday and he himself was murdered by John Boox of East Malling, a village five miles from Maidstone. It is unclear whether this was a private quarrel or, as the demolition of his house suggests, a targeted action against a local official who was probably a lawyer, possibly steward of a local estate or perhaps an under-collector of the poll-tax. A similar target was John Charlet of Chatham, on the outskirts of Rochester. He was beheaded the same day by William atte Broke of Chatham, who had also been involved in razing Glovere's home, though not, apparently, in his murder; Charlet's house in Clerkenwell, London, would also be broken into by another Chatham man, William Drew, on 14 June.[41]

Over the course of the next few days the rebels sought out three former MPs who had all served as sheriffs of Kent and on numerous commissions of array and inquiry. Thomas Cobham, of Allington Castle, near Maidstone, was a substantial land-holder in Kent and London; John Freningham and James Peckham were both justices of the peace and on 3 May had been appointed commissioners to reassess and enforce the poll-tax collection in Kent. All three would be captured, threatened with death and held prisoner until they swore the oath to become members of the rebel associations or assemblies. Before he was released, Peckham, who had been sheriff in 1379–80, was also compelled to surrender to William Skele and Nicholas Hakbourne eighty acres of meadowland which he had acquired by an assize of novel disseisin before Chief Justice Bealknapp; this was presumably an example of abuse of power and process by a sheriff who had bribed a jury to swear that he was the rightful owner.[42]

Trinity Sunday marked a noticeable escalation in the level of violence as the revolt, having taken hold throughout north-western Kent, began to spread into the east of the county. This coincides with what appears to have been changes in leadership. Although Robert Cave would later be accused of taking part in the burning of the Savoy Palace, the Hospitallers' preceptory at Clerkenwell and John Butterwick's manor at Knightsbridge, his activities as recorded in the local indictments appear to have been limited in time to Whitsuntide and geographically to Dartford, Maidstone and Rochester. The later accusations, plac-ing him in London at events which excluded him from the general pardon and made him liable to the death penalty, are no doubt the false and malicious charges brought by his enemies that delayed his release for over a decade. It seems, rather, that, like many other unlikely rebels provoked into action, he dropped out of the picture because he had achieved his limited local objectives.[43] Both Abel Ker and Thomas Raven remained involved but their names are now associated with other leaders in the indictments, such as John Hales and William de Appledore of East Malling, a village five miles north-west of Maidstone, where, on 8 June, Sir Thomas Trevet had been abducted and imprisoned until he took an oath to support the rebels. Trevet's capture was a major coup as he was a professional soldier who had spent a lifetime in loyal service to the Black Prince and his son: most recently he had been a captain in Arundel's disastrous naval expedition of 1379 and Thomas of Woodstock's campaign in Brittany, where he had served on the earl's inner council during the siege of Nantes. On his return earlier in 1381 he had been made a commissioner of array and charged with the defence of the Kentish coast.[44] His seizure removed one of the people most likely to take up arms against the rebels, leaving the way clear for them to head east under the leadership of the most famous of all the rebels, Wat Tyler.

Although his name is synonymous with the rebellion we know next to nothing about Tyler: not his background, not his motives, not even what he looked like.[45] He emerges from complete obscurity to the attention of the chroniclers only after the rescue of Bellyng from Rochester Castle and the disturbances in Maidstone on 7 June. The *Anonimalle* tells us that it was at this point that the people of Maidstone 'made their chief one Watt Teghler of Maidstone, to maintain and advise them'. The timing is confirmed by the indicting jury from Maidstone, which described the events of 7–9 June and then put Tyler at the top of its list of 'first malefactors and maintainers of the malefactors and perturbers of the peace'.[46] It is tempting to think that he was chosen to lead because he had displayed military skills: the choice of Canterbury as the rebels' next objective suggests some appreciation of tactics, particularly if the decision to go to London had already been taken. Canterbury was the seat of England's premier archbishop but it was also the centre of royal administration in the county. If the rebels anticipated that any action might be taken against them by the authorities, it was most likely to have come from the sheriff of Kent, who was based in the city; it would not have been sensible, therefore, to leave his power-base in his hands behind them while they marched west to London. And of course the sheriff himself, William Septvans, personified everything that the rebels were seeking to destroy: he was second only to the king in the administration of the county and he headed the commission which had sought to reassess and enforce collection of the third poll-tax. It is only surprising that he had not been the first target of the revolt, as his counterpart in Essex would be.[47]

The attack on Canterbury was carried out with such speed and efficiency that the authorities were caught by surprise. Riding good horses and travelling at around eight miles an hour, it would have taken the rebels just over four hours to get from Rochester to Canterbury.[48] They were unencumbered by the baggage and ordnance which slowed down conventional armies and had the advantage of being able to use Watling Street, the old Roman road that ran straight between the two places, but all along their route they had sparked further uprisings: the theft of 'charters, writings and muniments' from Thomas Bedemanton at Gillingham, who was so traumatised by the threats made against him that he fled and did not dare return home even after the revolt was over; the murder of John Godwot at Borden; disturbances and assaults at Sittingbourne, Faversham and Ospringe; the demolition of a house and a violent attack on the constable at Boughton, who, presumably, had tried to intervene to stop the disorder.[49] In each case it was people from the locality who committed the offences, not members of the rebel band on their rapid march to Canterbury. The popular image of Tyler at the head of a growing army of angry rebels, armed with pitchforks and staves, marching on foot and swelling their ranks with new recruits in every place through which they passed, is therefore wide of the mark.

Much the same was to happen when Tyler's forces arrived at their destination. Canterbury, like so many other English towns, especially those with a powerful ecclesiastical presence, had a long history of internal conflict between the townsmen and the cathedral priory dating back to the 1320s. The 1370s, however, had brought a change of focus, pitching the town increasingly against the crown and its insatiable demand for money. Almost every year of the decade inflicted new commissions on the city and its wider area, enforcing improvements in the coastal defences and repairs to Canterbury's walls, towers, gates and dykes, which were in such a poor state that the Westgate was completely demolished in 1380 so that it could be rebuilt from scratch. All these repairs were funded from murage, a tax on rents in the city and on market tolls, which added to the financial burden of the townsmen and their suppliers from the surrounding countryside.

Additionally, because of the renewed threat from France, every able-bodied man between the ages of sixteen and sixty was regularly arrayed almost annually throughout the decade, the latest such commission being issued on 14 May 1381. This too necessitated financial outlay in order to keep equipment and weapons in good order. Added to these burdens was the repeated imposition of poll-taxes and, for Canterbury, the unwelcome distinction of being the only city in the country to merit a commission to reassess and enforce collection of the third poll-tax. A fifth of its tax-paying population of 2574 had

disappeared off the record since the first poll-tax of 1377 and
a commission of three local men, not including the sheriff or
escheator, was appointed on 20 May in the last of its kind to be
issued.[50]

Canterbury had a large and volatile population of tradesmen, craftsmen and their servants working to supply food and
drink to the many pilgrims visiting the shrine of St Thomas
Becket as well as manufacturing leather goods, cloth and tex-
tiles. The urban rent rolls reveal a very high turnover in
tenancies, which usually lasted no longer than three or four
years, though a substantial number survived for only one. Such
was the demand from hopeful entrepreneurs migrating in from
the surrounding villages, however, that tenancies were rarely left
vacant for more than three weeks, even after the plague of
1374–5, which had a significant impact on the population of
the city and its monastic houses. At the other extreme, there
was a small but extremely wealthy group of merchant tradesmen who had significant business connections with London and
regularly traded as far afield as the Low Countries and Italy: as
in most urban governments, they dominated the administration
and it was from their elite that the two annually elected bailiffs
and six aldermen representing each ward in the city were
chosen.[51]

The latter part of the 1370s had seen regular clashes
between city officers and middle-ranking townsmen, many of
whom were excluded from the franchise. In 1376 the bailiffs
and commons were ordered, under pain of forfeiture of life and
limb and loss of the liberties of the city, to desist altogether from
dissensions and brawls and in July 1378 a royal commission
was appointed to inquire into 'certain malefactors and dis-
turbers of the peace, citizens and other inhabitants of the city
and suburbs, [who] have assembled in great numbers and
stirred up strife, debates and contentions therein, sowing great

discord amongst the citizens, and so obstinately holding together that they will not in any way submit to justice, but combine by insurrection to resist the king's ministers in the execution of their office'. On 8 April 1380 the king sent a strongly worded mandate ordering the bailiffs to arrest, imprison and certify the names of those 'citizens and other inhabitants thereof [who] have recently assembled in large numbers and daily cause great disturbances therein, refusing to submit to justice, and resisting the king's ministers in the execution of their office'.[52] Even this did not have the desired effect: the troubles continued and, when Tyler's rebel force appeared at the city's gates on 10 June, it was assured of a sympathetic reception.

No doubt it was this local knowledge that allowed the rebels to target their action so effectively. Their main objective was Canterbury Castle, which, since its foundation by William the Conqueror, had been eclipsed by Rochester and Dover as a fortification and had become the county prison. It was there that, by luck or acting on information, the rebels surprised the sheriff of Kent, William Septvans: Wat Tyler, Abel Ker, John Hales and many others surrounded him and forced him, under threat of death, to swear an oath to them that he would deliver up all the rolls and writs in his custody. They then frog-marched him to his manor house at Milton, on the outskirts of the city, where he kept all his records. There he was compelled to hand over the fifty rolls of the pleas of the county and the crown and all the royal writs in his possession to Tyler, who took them back to Canterbury and publicly burned them. In a further grand gesture, the rebels broke open the prison and released all the fettered and manacled prisoners, who turned out to be a rather pathetic bunch of just four people: an informer, John Burgh, a convicted cleric, Richard Derby, and two women, Agnes Jenkyn and Joan Hampcok, whose crimes are not specified.[53] Septvans apparently escaped without injury because he cooperated with the rebels: he would continue in office and serve on the commission to suppress the rebellion but there is an interesting coda to his story which suggests that his experience affected him deeply and permanently. Before he died in 1407 he made an unusual provision in his will that, in return for their good services to him, all his servants, even those who were villeins by blood, were to be set at liberty and each of them was to be given a deed of manumission under his seal in testimony of his will.[54]

The rebels' next target was William Medmenham, the county coroner, steward of the lands of St Augustine's Abbey, Canterbury, and officer of the crown, whose house was broken into by a mob which 'trampled upon' and carried away ten pounds' worth of goods and chattels. They evidently didn't find what they were looking for – the estreat rolls recording outstanding fines and amercements, also known as the rolls of the green wax because they bore the exchequer's distinctive seal – because three days later a proclamation 'by commission of John Rakestraw and Watte Tegheler' was made by, among others, the chaplain, clerk and sacristan of the churches of St John, Ramsgate and St Lawrence, just outside Margate, that the county levies of the Isle of Thanet were to be called out to search Medmenham's house there and destroy any records they found. This is, incidentally, the first recorded reference to Jack Straw[55] and the coupling of his name with that of Tyler is significant because he too was from Essex, where he is alleged to have been one of the leaders of the revolt in that county.

The clerical status of those making the proclamation suggests that it was read out loud, rather than a verbal message, which has implications for our interpretation of how agitators elsewhere raised the revolt by proclamation. The fact that the rebels hijacked the official forms and usages for raising the county levies, rather than simply urging everyone to rebel, also reveals a degree of sophistication in the organisation of the revolt which implies either that someone at its heart was famil-iar enough with the workings of the system to draw up the appropriate documentation or, perhaps, that Septvans or one of the other royal officials captured by the rebels was compelled to do so. At least one of those who attacked Medmenham's house in Canterbury, John Reade, came from Thanet, so he could well have carried the proclamation back to the Isle. It was a pun-ishable offence not to obey the summons, so some two hundred men were said to have answered the call, broken open Medmenham's gates, doors, chambers and chests of his house at Manston, taken away his rolls of the crown and estreat rolls and burned them. Though it is possible that the 'commission to raise the county levies' was invented afterwards to provide an excuse for those who had taken part in the rebellion on the Isle, two other indictments name the same group of Church officials and laymen and state that they raised a proclamation or cry in the churches compelling everyone, on pain of death and forfei-ture of goods and chattels, to demolish Medmenham's house, destroy his muniments and kill him if he could be found.[56]

Further evidence that the rebels were using official ad-ministrative systems to attack their targets comes from the raids carried out against Medmenham's fellow coroner John Colbrand, a former MP and associate of Simon Burley. His muniment rooms at both Wye, where he stored his books and papers, and Boughton-under-Blean, where he kept his estreat rolls, were broken into on Tuesday 11 June and everything was taken away and burned; his wife, who evidently tried to intervene, was assaulted and badly beaten. Both places were within eleven miles of Canterbury, which suggests that orders for the destruction of his records were issued there. The attack at Wye, in which Joan Colbrand was injured, was led by Thomas Steyhame, constable of the neighbouring hundred of

Longbridge and therefore leader of the local levies there. The following day, a local esquire and tenant-in-chief of the king, Bertram de Wilmington, led a group of rebels to plunder and burn the documents held by two of his landowning neighbours, John Laycestre and Thomas Kempe, at Wye. On Thursday 13 June, Wilmington was accused of having called out the local levies by ordering John Gerkyn to make a 'proclamation that all of the foresaid hundred should assemble and prepare themselves with divers arms'. Wilmington received a pardon in April 1382 but Kempe successfully brought a civil suit against him and was awarded substantial damages for the destruction of his records.[57] After destroying Colbrand's estreat rolls at Boughton, some of those involved made their way fifteen miles south to Mersham, where, the same day and with the assistance of willing locals, they broke into the manor of John Brode, Elias Reyner's predecessor as escheator of Kent and also an assessor of the third poll-tax; they destroyed not only his escheat roll but also his poll-tax records. The death of John Hemyngherst, killed by rebels at Mersham, may have been linked to the attack on Brode's records.[58]

Back in Canterbury on Monday 10 June, the rebels were systematically destroying all the records and disabling all the machinery of royal and civic government. They broke into the town hall and set free all the prisoners held there. Septvan's under-sheriff, Thomas Holt, had his house outside the walls at Westgate attacked and goods worth forty pounds stolen. Holt was a highly successful professional lawyer with a client base stretching throughout Kent into London who, over the previous decade, had built up a huge personal property portfolio in Canterbury and Thanet; his neighbours in Westgate were among those who attacked his house but, significantly, he was also personally threatened and told that he should no longer carry out his duties as under-sheriff.[59] Thomas Oteryngton had been one of the bailiffs in 1376 when the trouble between them and the commons first broke out and two years later was one of the royal commissioners appointed to inquire into the dissensions; it was not just his lack of impartiality in this ongoing confrontation, nor even his being the rent collector in the city for the cathedral priory, which led to his house being sacked, but rather the fact that he was one of the hated reassessment and enforcement commissioners of the third poll-tax. Oteryngton himself was seized during the attack on his house, carried outside, threatened and assaulted so that, in the words of the indictment, 'he despaired of his life'.[60]

Both his fellow poll-tax commissioners, John Taunton and John Tece, seem to have escaped unharmed, perhaps because they were absent from the city at the critical moment, but Tece's reprieve was short-lived. On 15 June, after Richard agreed the rebels' demands at Mile End, Henry Bongay the armourer had it proclaimed through the city that Tece was a traitor who should be killed and he was therefore dragged from his horse and murdered in a mob attack. Bongay had been a thorn in the flesh of the Canterbury authorities for at least six years before the revolt began (though he had paid his poll-taxes) and had previously clashed with Tece, who had arrested and imprisoned him for helping a prisoner escape from the town jail and find sanctuary in a local church. He undoubtedly played a leading role in the Canterbury revolt, just as he had in earlier dissensions within the city and although his name was not on the list of rebels excluded from pardon in November 1381, this was probably because he had already been executed for treason and felony: property he owned in Norfolk, including a cottage at Great Yarmouth and thirty-three acres of land and 2s. 6d. rent in Mundham, are recorded as being confiscated to the crown.[61]

John Tebbe was another member of the city elite who had been involved in the long-running dissensions in the city: he had been appointed to the commission with Oteryngton in 1378 to inquire into the discords between officers and people, was closely associated with the cathedral priory for which he acted as a rent collector and had served as MP for Canterbury in 1373, 1376 and 1380. Since the parliament of 1380 was the one which granted the third poll-tax it is particularly ironic that he managed to avoid paying the tax himself and was only caught during the sheriff's reassessment. Perhaps this had become public knowledge, for he was murdered on Monday 10 June by a local mob and his house in St George's parish was plundered and burned; his widow was unable to produce her title-deeds at the assizes two years later because they had been destroyed in the fire.[62] Thomas Garwynton, who had served regularly on royal commissions, had both his houses, inside and outside the city, ransacked;[63] Sir Thomas Fogg, a retainer of John of Gaunt with many years' service in France, MP for Kent in 1376, 1378 and 1380, and regular commissioner of array for the county, suffered extensive damage to his house in Canterbury and to his manor house at nearby Tonford, where the rebels took a fancy to his wife's wardrobe, purloining a white ermine fur for a gown, a length of scarlet cloth, fine linen, rings and brooches;[64] William Watership, one of two brothers who had served as civic officials and collectors and assessors of the poll-tax, was forced to pay a ransom and threatened with having his house burned down unless he handed over the keys to a shop near St Andrew's church; Nicholas atte Crouch, a sheriff of Kent in 1376 and a commissioner of array in Thanet who had also been given powers in February 1380 to compel the islanders to repair their neglected sea defences and the boats they were supposed to maintain to carry people and animals, was physically assaulted at his house in Ospringe on Saturday 15 June and compelled to pay one hundred shillings.[65]

The list of Canterbury victims reads like a roll-call of royal officials; many more were attacked in the days following the arrival of the rebel forces under Tyler and Hales on 10 June. The riots in the city continued for the rest of the month and spread out across the surrounding countryside, where so many of the Canterbury elite had second homes. Although most of those involved, rebels and victims, had played leading roles in the city's turmoils since 1376, it had required Tyler's arrival to turn that unrest into a coordinated assault on officialdom which wiped out the administrative records and machinery of city and county, leaving both in a state of complete paralysis. Having passed the torch of rebellion into willing hands, Tyler and his cohorts were able to leave Canterbury, retrace their steps across Kent and head for London.

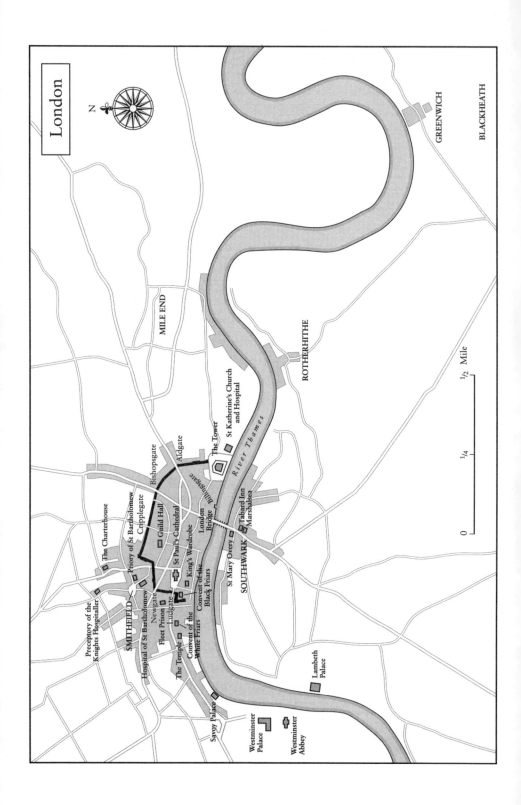

CHAPTER EIGHT

To London

On the same day that the Kentish rebels launched their attack on their sheriff and the workings of royal government in Canterbury, the Essex rebels began a similar all-out assault in their county. Men from more than forty parishes throughout Essex had gathered at Bocking, where the meeting had been held on 2 June and the oath taken to be of one accord in their rebellion. Since then, messengers and agitators had ridden the length and breadth of the county preparing the way so that, when Monday 10 June dawned, a sizeable army of rebels from every corner of Essex was gathered there. All the men who had been involved in the initial assault on Gildesburgh and Bampton on 30 May were alleged to have been present, including Thomas Baker and William Gildeborne from Fobbing, Robert Cardemaker from Bocking itself and one of the more unusual rebels, John Flemyng, a Flemish weaver who represented the parish of Benington, just over the border in Hertfordshire. They were joined by John Geffrey, a serf from

Suffolk, whose administrative talents had allowed him to rise in the service of the earls of Pembroke to the point where he became bailiff of the earl's Essex estates at East Hanningfield: there he had bought a smallholding, purchased the reversion of a further fifteen acres and was about to build himself a new house. Yet, when the revolt came, he used his personal authority to call out all the men from East, West and South Hanningfield and then personally led them seventeen miles north to take part in the rebel gathering.[1]

Their first objective, surprisingly, was not the sheriff but Cressing Temple, a preceptory of the Knights Hospitaller just four miles south-east of Bocking: it had originally belonged to the Templars and passed into the hands of the Hospitallers only when the Templar order was suppressed in 1312. It was one of their most valuable possessions in England, comprising the two manors of Cressing and Witham and the half-hundred of Witham, over fifteen hundred acres of prime agricultural land, five mills, a weekly market at Witham and two annual fairs. An inventory drawn up for the Grand Master in 1338 recorded its annual profits as £133 12s. 4d. Just two Hospitallers lived on the estate, John Luterell, the warden, and his assistant, but within the household they employed a steward, baker, cook, gate-keeper (literally 'a keeper of the keys'), two grooms and two pages, all of whom were laymen, and three chaplains to pray for the souls of their benefactors in the chapel at Cressing. What the inventory does not record are the labourers who would have been essential to maintain the home farm, nor the value of the tithes collected from its parishioners. How important these were is still obvious today in the sheer size of the two great aisled barns which are now all that remain of the medieval buildings. Tree-ring dating on the locally felled oak which was used to create their framework suggests that the barley barn was erected in 1205–36, and the wheat barn in 1257–90; using techniques employed in building cathedrals, almost five hundred oaks were shaped in the green for each barn then allowed to season in situ so that they could support the massive weight of the huge roofs, which were each covered with forty-five thousand tiles.[2]

Cressing Temple was targeted either because of local issues over its lordship (one of its most profitable sources of income was the proceeds of its courts) or the fact that it belonged to the Hospitallers, whose prior, Sir Robert Hales, had been an extremely active royal councillor and, as treasurer of England since 1 February 1381, was responsible for the appointment of the reassessment commissions which had sparked the revolt in the first place. Either way, the rebels broke into the preceptory buildings, stole armour, vestments, gold, silver and other goods and chattels worth twenty pounds, and burned 'books', presumably manorial records, valued at twenty marks. They also allegedly looted and razed the buildings – one man, for instance, was accused of stealing lead worth eight shillings from the buildings – but the survival of the two great barns is a clear indication that the destruction was not as wholesale as is usually claimed.[3]

From Cressing it was just a few miles to Coggeshall where the sheriff and escheator of Essex and Hertfordshire were both in residence. The rebels found the sheriff John Sewale[4] at home, forced their way in, abused him, tore his clothing and did such 'insult' to him and Robert de Segynton, an exchequer clerk, that they had despaired of their lives. They stole a thousand marks in cash (presumably the proceeds of the poll-tax reassessment), all his writs, rolls and summonses from the exchequer, as well as his personal goods and chattels worth ten pounds. More to the point, they pursued John Ewell, the county escheator, who was responsible by virtue of his office for surveying and controlling the assessment of the poll-tax, cornered him in front of the sheriff's house, beheaded him and placed his head on a lance; two of his clerks and Nicholas Davenant, an 'auditor' of the chief chamberlain and royal favourite Aubrey de Vere, were similarly murdered at Brentwood.[5] Some of the rebels then went to Ewell's house, two miles away at Feering, where they broke in and removed all 'the writs and muniments pertaining to his office'. These records, together with all those seized from Sewale, were carried off to Chelmsford, where they were ceremonially burned in a public bonfire the following day, just as the Kentish rebels had burned the shrieval records in Canterbury on 10 June. These defiant public acts were a symbolic rejection of abuse of process by royal offices but they must also have inspired others to take matters into their own hands and do the same.[6] Sewale, like his counterpart in Kent, was apparently so traumatised by his experience that he sued for his immediate release from office and was replaced as sheriff on 25 June. The fact that he would later bring charges against 193 named individuals is an indication of the numbers involved in the attack on him, since there must have been many more unnamed rebels drawn from the poorest ranks of society who were not worth his pursuing through the courts for compensation. That those he was able to name came from sixty-seven different places in Essex is also telling evidence of how effectively the original group of rebels had managed to spread and organise the insurrection.[7]

The rebels also targeted Sewale's fellow poll-tax reassessment commissioner Sir John Gildesburgh, whose house in Coggeshall was robbed and demolished; two days earlier, in what must have been one of the first such attacks in Essex, goods had been stolen from his manor at Wennington on the outskirts of Rainham, probably by men from that place who had been involved in the attack on Gildesburgh and Bampton at Brentwood on 30 May. Before the rebels left Coggeshall they also invaded the precincts of the local Cistercian abbey and carried away 'divers goods, charters, writings and other muniments' to destroy them.[8]

Most of the rebels then seem to have made their way to Chelmsford to watch the burning of the sheriff's and escheator's rolls on Tuesday 11 June before splitting up into various groups which were despatched to carry out raids against royal officials farther afield, just as had happened after the Kentish rebels swept through Canterbury. Robert Rikedon, an Essex justice of the peace and lawyer employed by both Woodstock and his mother-in-law, Joan, countess of Hereford, was attacked in his house at Witham on 11 June by a band of men led by John Frost from Chipping Ongar, over twenty miles away; they forced Rikedon to ride back to Chelmsford with them and to swear to join their conspiracy to 'destroy divers lieges of the lord king'.[9] The same day William Pampelon went to Rivenhall, some thirteen miles north-east of Chelmsford, and there used 'hangs and hooks' to demolish the houses of Robert Leynham, another lawyer and colleague of many other victims of the Essex rebels; his unscrupulous behaviour was characterised by his concealing rents he owed in Rivenhall, worth 19s. 3d., from the heir when his landlord died.[10] Also on 11 June there was a concerted attack on John Gildesburgh's property: his manor house at High Easter, ten miles north of Chelmsford, and a house at Fambridge, on the river Crouch, fifteen miles south-east of the county town, were both broken into, his charters and muniments burned and his servants driven away; his manor at Wennington was also attacked for a second time in the same way. The fact that the rebels were able to organise a coordinated assault on three of Gildesburgh's far-flung properties on the same day says much for their focus and for the sophistication of their planning and logistical skills, particularly as property on the southern bank of the river Crouch at Canewdon belonging to Gildesburgh's colleague, the hated John Bampton, was also given similar treatment.[11]

In addition to Rikedon, Gildesburgh and Bampton, almost all their fellow justices of the peace who had been appointed to the bench with them the previous year were singled out for some act of violence against their persons or, more usually, their property; some, like Sir Walter Fitzwalter, had all their records burned; others, like Geoffrey Dersham, had their manors ransacked and everything of any value stolen, from their oxen and sheep right down to the brass pots and pans from their kitchens.[12] A more unusual victim was Edmund de la Mare, whose house at Peldon on the northern shore of the Blackwater estuary was broken into by a company of rebels led by Ralph atte Wode of Bradwell. There they 'despoiled him of all his goods and chattels' but also carried off 'a writ patent of the King with all the muniments touching the office of Admiral upon the sea'. Instead of burning the writ, however, they stuck it on a pitchfork and allegedly had it carried before them all the way to London for the meeting with the king at Mile End, and then back to Peldon again. This was clearly a symbolic action, perhaps intended to show that Ralph atte Wode had claimed the office of admiral from de la Mare. In fact, there were two Bradwells in Essex. Atte Wode is likely to have come from Bradwell near Coggeshall, since he had been involved in the attacks on Cressing Temple and at Coggeshall, but it is possible he came from Bradwell-on-Sea, a maritime village on the opposite shore to Peldon, which makes it more likely that he had clashed with de la Mare, possibly over the seizure of his boats or their cargo, or because he had been prevented from carrying out his trade by the French ships which plagued the south-east coast. Whether his reasons were personal or political, he received a pardon on 20 April

1382, but when he produced it before the court to secure his release he was recommitted to prison while consideration was given as to whether his action in assuming royal office to himself put him outside the scope of the general amnesty.[13]

As the rebellion spread, two other notable figures found themselves the object of the rebels' loathing. Henry English was sheriff of Cambridgeshire and Huntingdonshire at the time and had served as MP for Cambridgeshire in 1373 and 1377; although the bulk of his property and interests lay in that county and Suffolk, he also owned estates at Birdbrook, twenty-six miles north of Chelmsford, which he had acquired through his wife. He had been a justice of the peace for Essex, as well as Cambridge, in the decade before the revolt, and had served regularly on crown commissions and as an administrator for the East Anglian estates of Edmund Mortimer, earl of March. Described as a franklin in the third poll-tax records, he paid just five shillings, jointly for himself and his wife, which seems a serious underestimate for a man of his means and standing. English was therefore the archetypal lawyer and royal official but his shrieval office, albeit for an adjacent county, probably made him the rebels' quarry. His manor at Birdbrook was invaded on 12 June and goods and chattels stolen. Interestingly, one of the main agitators for the revolt in Cambridgeshire and Suffolk, Henry Wroo, came from Woodditton, where English's principal residence lay, and he had already been at work for several days preparing the groundwork for the revolt in those counties.[14]

Again the pinpointing of specific victims and the coordinated nature of the revolt is evident in the fact that two of the leading rebels who had taken the oath at Bocking, Robert Cardemaker (who had also been at Brentwood) and Robert Chapman of Dunmow, led the attack on English's property at Birdbrook. More importantly, earlier in the day, they had also led their band to the village of Liston, twelve miles away, on the river Stour which formed the border between Essex and Suffolk. It was here that Richard Lyons, one of the most notorious figures of the late fourteenth century, had a manor. Lyons was a merchant and financier, probably of Flemish origins, who had made his fortune as a vintner and ship-owner. By 1363 he was already so rich that, when he divorced (in itself an extremely unusual and expensive process), his London revenues alone were valued at £2443 and his wife claimed £3333 6s. 8d. as her share of his wealth. In 1376 he had been impeached in the Good Parliament on charges of corruption, including abuse of his monopoly on the sale of sweet wine in London, by-passing the Calais Staple to export his wool, acquiring customs duties and subsidies without the sanction of parliament and profiteering in his loans to the crown. Though John of Gaunt had secured his pardon and restoration of his lands and properties, Lyons was never re-elected to office in London; the corporation's refusal to readmit him even to the franchise would add to the tensions between the city and Gaunt. Denied his former status in London, Lyons turned instead to establishing himself as a country gentleman with a property portfolio across several counties. He achieved recognition of this in 1380 when he was elected MP for Essex, only to sit in the parliament which granted the third poll-tax. This alone was enough to make him a marked man but his previous record as a corrupt royal official and the perception that he had escaped his due punishment through Gaunt's influence would seal his fate. Lyons was not at his manor of Overhall at Liston when the rebels came to call but two days later he would be beheaded in Cheapside by the Londoners who were only too glad to seize this opportunity to avenge themselves on a man universally loathed.[15]

The significance of the attack on Overhall was not just that the place was deliberately wrecked – doors, windows and walls demolished, even the tiles stripped from the roofs of the buildings and smashed – but that this was a combined operation by Cardemaker, Chapman and their band of Essex rebels and a newly formed group of insurgents from just over the border in Suffolk. The latter were led by John Wrawe,[16] who, despite turning approver and giving a lengthy and detailed confession, John remains something of a mystery figure. The list of people excluded from being able to apply for the general pardon, published in parliament in November 1381, includes two men of his name: the first, who heads the list of Suffolk rebels, is simply described as 'John Wrawe, chaplain'; the second, who is tenth on the same list, as 'John Wrawe, late parson of the church of Ringsfield'. The former was the ringleader of the revolt in Suffolk; he is called 'of Sudbury' in his confession and all his alleged and admitted offences were committed in the west of the county, culminating in his inciting the rebellion in Bury St Edmunds and the events of 15 June.[17]

The name John Wrawe does not appear among the parsons of Ringsfield but the crimes for which the 'late parson' was indicted were all committed within three and a half miles of that village, between Beccles and Bungay in the north-easternmost corner of Suffolk on its border with Norfolk. He was accused of having led 'an estimated five hundred men' in an attack on Mettingham Castle, a fortified manor house belonging to William Ufford, earl of Suffolk. The raid netted gold and silver to the value of forty pounds, jewels and armour worth over a thousand pounds and all the court rolls and other manorial records. The next day, 19 June, Geoffrey de Southgate was dragged from his house in Beccles, even though he was clutching a royal protection in his hand, and brought before Wrawe, who appears to have sentenced him to death because Southgate was then taken to the east end of the town and there beheaded by Edmund Barbour, whose name is the eleventh on the list of Suffolk rebels excluded from grace. Southgate had been investigated by a royal commission as long ago as 1363 after allegations that he and his fellow constable of Beccles had repeatedly abused their powers to collect 'much corn and other victuals as well as divers sums of money beyond those at which the commonalty of the town was assessed ... and detained the same to their own use, and [they] have done and do many trespasses and oppressions in the town by colour of their office'. That he had felt the need to obtain a royal protection and his brutal execution on 19 June both suggest that he had continued to milk his fellow townsmen over the years.[18]

It is possible that the two John Wrawes were one and the same man, who had returned to his former haunts to seek revenge for old injuries after completing his more serious business in west Suffolk; how or why he had been demoted from parson to a mere chaplain might provide the answer to his doing so. Nevertheless, it seems odd that he should not have included his offences committed in and around Beccles in his confession. Neither the clerks drawing up the indictments, nor those compiling the parliamentary list from them, made any connection between the Wrawe there and Wrawe of Sudbury, but that does not mean it can be ruled out altogether: John Bettes of Wymondham appeared twice on the parliamentary roll because the clerks did not realise he was also known as John Creyk.[19] Beccles, as well as most of the local churches (though not Ringsfield), fell within the all-powerful lordship of the abbey of Bury St Edmunds. If Wrawe had lost his position because the abbey had intervened in some way, or if Southgate was an employee of the abbey, then we might have a reason for Wrawe's actions in Bury St Edmunds.[20]

The sacking of the manors of Henry English at Birdbrook and Richard Lyons at Liston on 12 June by the joint forces of

Essex and Suffolk marked the end of the politically motivated phase of the revolt in Essex and the passing of the torch to the rebels of Suffolk and Cambridgeshire. This did not mean that the Essex rebels had ended their uprising: far from it; but having joined together systematically to destroy the records of a corrupt administration and vented their wrath against those who had been involved in it, most rebels now returned to their homes and, if they had not done so already, turned their attention to their local landlords. Just as they had burned the records emanating from central government, they would also seek out and destroy the manorial court records, the rent rolls and custumals which shaped their daily lives. The rebels believed that, if there were no written evidence of services, rents or dues exacted in the past, then their lord's administrators would not be able to enforce them in future: in a perceived return to a golden age, the bailiffs and stewards would have to rely completely on the oral testimony of village memory which the rebels believed would be less arbitrary, more sympathetic and more nuanced than the black-and-white proofs afforded by memoranda written by the landlord's own clerks. Throughout the whole of Essex, tenants seized the opportunity to destroy their manorial records: documents were burned in at least seventy-seven places and eighty-two more were affected by unrest of some kind, usually the destruction or seizure of disputed property. Many acts of violence were an attempt to right a perceived wrong: in December 1384, for instance, Robert Palmer was accused of having incited the murder of John Ewell so that he could enter the manor of Langdon Hills, some four miles from Fobbing, which the escheator was then holding on the grounds that its rightful ownership was unclear; Palmer had occupied it and enjoyed its revenues for three and a half years before an investigation was launched into how he had acquired it.[21]

Although no corner of the county was spared, the destruction was neither random nor wholesale: the targets, once again, were carefully chosen. Joan, countess of Hereford, and the king's mother, Joan of Kent, each had at least five manors attacked and their archives burned; the great religious houses, including the cathedral priories of Canterbury and St Paul's, London, similarly suffered heavily, as did local houses such as Coggeshall Abbey and individuals like the bishop of London. But not every manor belonging to a particular landlord joined the uprising, presumably because customs varied from place to place and local officials were not uniformly oppressive. Adjoining manors did not necessarily suffer the same fate: while Henry English's manor at Birdbrook was attacked and property stolen, the manor of Birdbrook Hall apparently remained untouched. Even at Childerditch, where the lord of the manor was Coggeshall Abbey, the tenants reclaimed as common land a croft which the monks had enclosed as part of their demesne and allegedly caused all the abbey's servants 'to depart from their offices and duties against their wills', but they did not burn the court rolls where their offences were duly recorded.[22]

Some 954 individual Essex rebels have been identified from the various records still extant, more than from any other county except Norfolk, which had 1214. Yet the mass actions taken privately by John of Gaunt and John Butterwick, under-sheriff of Middlesex, to obtain punishment for, and compensation from, those who had destroyed their properties in London, which together list about twelve hundred people, name only around 170 rebels from Essex.[23] The two Essex figures are not entirely comparable and neither is an exhaustive record, yet they support the broad conclusion that the majority of the rebels appear to have chosen to remain at home rather than take their grievances to London to share them with the king himself. What is surprising is that the former group includes most, if not all, of those who had assumed early leadership of the revolt: Thomas Baker and William Gildeborne of Fobbing, Robert Cardemaker of Bocking and Robert Chapman of Dunmow. The only member of that first group who can be identified as being involved in events in London was William Roger of South Ockendon, who had also been one of the first agitators sent round the Essex villages to raise the rebellion in the first week of June.[24] Even more surprising is the fact that, unlike Wat Tyler in Kent, no single captain seems to have stepped forward to take their place. Neither chroniclers nor judicial records give any hint as to who led the Essex rebels to London. The nearest we get is the accusation that on 13 June Henry Baker, bailiff of Tendring hundred, William Cundewayn, constable of Manningtree, and Richard Beve ordered the men of Manningtree to prepare themselves and go to join the rebels at Colchester on pain of having all their goods confiscated if they refused. Since this evidence of organisation and compulsion comes from a confession by John Glasene and John Webbe of Manningtree, who were seeking a royal pardon for their involvement in the revolt, it is not necessarily trustworthy, though Glasene admitted having been present at Mile End and killing a Fleming (again under orders) on his return.[25]

Three groups of Essex rebels appear to have made their way to London. The smallest, a band of just nineteen, came from in and around North Weald Bassett, twenty miles from the city. It was here that John Bampton had first held public office as bailiff of the hundred and the king's mother later prosecuted 110 people for burning her manorial records. The ruthless nature of royal lordship exercised there was epitomised by the Black Prince's orders to the sheriff of Essex in November 1374 to impress carpenters and other workmen to enclose a park and make his charcoal within its bounds: although he undertook to pay their costs and wages, none of them had the luxury of refusing to do his will since the sheriff had powers to arrest and imprison 'all who are contrariant or rebellious'. The enclosure of woodland was a serious loss to tenants who relied on it for firewood and forage for their pigs. In their circumstances, nothing short of an appeal to the king in person could improve their lot, though their proximity to the capital also made it an obvious objective.[26]

The second and largest group was an amalgamation of rebels from Thaxted, some forty-six miles from the capital, and men who joined them along their route, but particularly at the halfway point as they passed through Ware, Hertfordshire. Since the original party must also have gone through Bishop's Stortford on their way to Ware, it is possible that they were responsible for storming the bishop of London's prison there and releasing 'the traitor John Balle' and the Carmelite friar Brother Andrew, but it seems more likely that this was carried out in a separate raid coordinated from Chelmsford after the burning of the sheriffs' and escheator's records.[27] The arrival of the rebels from Thaxted sparked off a major uprising in Ware, which had a long and bitter commercial rivalry with its neighbour three miles upstream, the town of Hertford, which claimed the monopoly on river traffic and the right to levy tolls on freight passing through Ware. Men from Ware had repeatedly broken the weirs at Hertford, held illicit markets when theirs was suppressed in favour of Hertford's and, despite having their bridge torn down several times, eventually won the battle for the more convenient river crossing on the profitable Cambridge to London road. Hertford had responded with frequent litigation, most recently using the Statute of Labourers to accuse Ware's dyers and tanners of charging and receiving exorbitant rates. The fact that the lord of the manor of Hertford was John of Gaunt made his castle there an obvious target: the rebels from Ware stormed it, ripped the lead off the roof, battlements and Gaunt's own chambers – causing considerable damage which would necessitate major repairs over the next couple of years – and carried off goods worth a thousand pounds. Some fifty men from Ware would also join the Essex rebels on their journey to London, including Nicholas Blake, who owned a manor just outside the town, and Philip of Hertford who, confusingly, was vicar of Ware. Not surprisingly, they chose to repeat their assault on Gaunt's property by attacking his Savoy Palace, forming the largest group of rebels from outside London whom Gaunt would prosecute for its destruction.[28]

The third group to make their way to London, consisting of forty-two Essex rebels, included those who had also travelled the furthest, sixty-six miles, from Manningtree, via Colchester and Chelmsford. They were therefore drawn from the most active area of the revolt in Essex and, if the indictment against them is to be believed, they were involved in all the most brutal incidents of the rebellion there, including the chasing down and beheading of John Ewell at Coggeshall and the executions of two of his clerks and Nicholas Davenant at Brentwood. In their own home town, much of their anger had been directed at Thomas Hardyng, lord of the manors of Manningtree and Mistley and 'a common extortionist [who] had been a plague to his neighbours for twenty years'. Hardyng had manipulated food prices in Manningtree, avoided paying customs duty on wool and, in the weeks leading up to the revolt, used his position as 'the steward of the king to inquire into royal revenues in Essex' to extort money and goods from his neighbours. He was also just the sort of person who brought the law into disrepute, bringing malicious and vexatious prosecutions against those who crossed him until he met his match in Sir Richard and Sir John Sutton, whom he had accused of conspiring to defraud the crown over the manor of Bradwell, Essex: the case was appealed to parliament in 1391 which found that Hardyng had acted 'wholly out of malice' and sentenced him to remain at the king's will in the Fleet prison. Hardyng's property was the first to be attacked in Manningtree and some of the leading figures who joined the group travelling to London were among those who had suffered at his hands. Naturally he brought private prosecutions against them and against all those he alleged had damaged his property during the revolt, unscrupulously persuading them that he would drop his action if they entered a bond with him, only to start new actions against the same people on slightly different terms so that he could extract more bonds from them. He actually earned more money from his actions against them than he had lost as a result of the attacks on his property during the revolt. Several of those whom he vindictively pursued through the courts in this way for years were described as 'rich', including John Sumner, who had extensive lands and owned goods worth four hundred marks in Manningtree alone; at least three others were able to pay Hardyng ten pounds each in compensation.[29] These men, again, were unlikely rebels, yet years of provocation and persecution at Hardyng's hands tipped them over the edge. And since they could not obtain satisfaction against him through the normal processes, they joined in the destruction of county administration which had failed to protect them and took their grievance against his royal servant to the king himself.

As the various rebel groups from Essex converged on the northern fringes of London on the eve of 12 June, their fellow insurgents from Kent were also gathering on the opposite side of the Thames on the great open heathland above Greenwich known as Blackheath. This suggests that there must have been a plan of joint action in place before the trip to Canterbury. It would therefore have been possible for the Kentish rebels to make their way to London for the appointed time, just as the Essex rebels did, either travelling in independent bands or joining Tyler as he made his way back from Canterbury. The evidence of the private prosecutions brought by Gaunt and Butterwick suggests that most of the Kentish rebels came from places closest to London: only forty-one came from more than fifteen miles outside the capital and most of them were from either Rochester or Maidstone. One of the largest groups, for instance, came from Eltham, which lay on Tyler's direct route to Blackheath, and it says something for the universal appeal of the revolt that they were led by William Spalding, keeper of the king's manor there. The approach of the rebel army proved a magnet for further willing recruits from Surrey villages slightly farther afield, places like Tooting and Wandsworth, whose inhabitants would play a major role in the sacking of Gaunt's Savoy Palace.[30]

How many rebels there were we do not know. The chroniclers predictably claim that between one and two hundred thousand were eventually gathered in London but, even when joined by the Londoners themselves, the reality is likely to have been less than ten thousand. Only 456 Kentish rebels have been identified from the records and the majority of them did not go to London.[31] Just as in Essex, some of the earliest rebels appear to have remained in their localities. There is no suggestion that either Abel Ker of Erith or Robert Cave of Dartford, for example, took part in this stage of the revolt, though Thomas atte Raven of Rochester, who had been a prominent figure in the uprising from the beginning, not only went to London but played a significant role in the events there too.[32]

Wat Tyler was also at the forefront of the Kentish rebel hordes, though it is unlikely that John Balle was with him. Although historians have always believed that Balle was rescued by the rebels from Maidstone prison in Kent, the only chronicle source for this information is Knighton, who specifically states that Balle was in the archbishop of Canterbury's prison in the archbishop's town of Maidstone and was released by the rebels because they proposed to make him archbishop of Canterbury. Two pieces of judicial evidence lend weight to this: the writ ordering his arrest was issued to the sheriff of Kent (though it may have been duplicated to others) and two indictments confirm that rebels broke open Maidstone prison and freed all the prisoners on 11 June. Given that Wat Tyler may also have been living in Maidstone at the time, it seems obvious that he would have made a point of rescuing his fellow denizen of Colchester when he became involved in the revolt.[33]

Why, therefore, should there be any doubt? The problem is that an Essex indictment reveals that the same day, 11 June, John Bowyers of Pleshey 'broke open the prison of the bishop of London at Bishop's Stortford and treacherously carried off a certain Friar Andrew of the Carmelite order and John Balle the traitor incarcerated in that same castle having been convicted of divers felonies'. This indictment has been dismissed as 'difficult to reconcile with the other evidence, and probably mistaken' by the scholar who discovered it.[34] Yet there are compelling reasons for believing it to be true. All Balle's known activities over almost two decades had been located within the bishop of London's diocese and Essex in particular. His only identifiable link with Kent was that Sudbury, the former bishop with whom he had tangled for so long, was now archbishop of Canterbury. What is more, since at least the 1330s the prison at Bishop's Stortford had housed mainly convicted clerics, particularly apostates and heretics. Where more natural for Balle to have been incarcerated than in his own diocesan prison? Conditions were harsh, with prisoners kept shackled and fettered on a daily allowance of ¼d. each for food, and there were high mortality rates. Perhaps because it was not in the keep but in buildings near the gatehouse, the prison had a large number of escapees, including mass break-outs of sixteen in 1392, eighteen in 1393 and ten in 1401, all of them being 'convicted clerks'.[35] The escape of Balle and Friar Andrew was comparatively small scale.

By contrast, none of the Kentish indictments mention any of the released prisoners by name, let alone one as notorious as Balle. What they do say is that Julia Pouchere, wife of Richard, 'came to meet with the men of Canterbury and the county of Essex' and persuaded them to attack the warden of Maidstone jail Alan Doghere and his servant John Grage, 'with the result that the ... evil-doers tore down the above-mentioned jail and destroyed it, similarly threatening to tear down and destroy the house of the same Alan ... and Julia was a party to this and encouraged it'.[36] Aside from the fascinating glimpse this gives us of a woman inciting rebels to act, this sounds like a wife seeking revenge for her husband's imprisonment and provides a more likely local scenario for the attack than a desire to rescue an excommunicate chaplain from Essex. The problem with accepting that Balle was sprung from prison in Bishop's Stortford, rather than Maidstone, is that it makes it virtually impossible for him to have given his famous sermon at Blackheath on the eve of the feast of Corpus Christi. He could not have made his way across London in time to preach to the Kentish rebels on the other side of the city and the Thames the following day. Indeed, why would he do so, since he could more easily have preached to the Essex rebels who had released him and were assembling on the northern side of city? In fact, not a single source authoritatively places Balle in London during the revolt: his name is mentioned with those of Tyler and Straw in general references to the rebels' activities in the city but no individual sighting of him is recorded. He disappears from view from the moment of his release on 11 June until his appearance before the chief justice on 13 July.[37]

Despite this, the Blackheath sermon has been a cornerstone of every account of the great revolt. It is seductive because it gives us an insight into the character of this evidently charismatic leader and it articulates powerfully the sense of injustice that drove so many otherwise respectable people to rebel. It also seems entirely credible that the rebel leaders would have wanted to fire up the morale of their disparate troops as they prepared to unite for their biggest challenge yet by giving a platform to their very own rabble-rouser and firebrand. This is Walsingham's account of that celebrated speech:

> ... to corrupt more people with his doctrine, at Blackheath, where two hundred thousand of the commons were gathered together, he began a sermon in this fashion:

> When Adam delved, and Eve span,
>   Who was then a gentleman?

> And continuing his sermon, he tried to prove by the words of the proverb that he had taken for his text, that from the beginning all men were created equal by nature, and that servitude had been introduced by the unjust and evil oppression of men, against the will of God, who, if it had pleased Him to create serfs, surely in the beginning of the world would have appointed who should be a serf and who a lord. Let them consider, therefore, that He had now appointed the time wherein, laying aside the yoke of long servitude, they might, if they wished, enjoy their liberty so long desired. Wherefore they must be prudent, hastening to act after the manner of a good husbandman, tilling his field, and uprooting the tares that are accustomed to destroy the grain; first killing the great lords of the realm, then slaying the lawyers, justices and jurors, and finally rooting out

everyone whom they knew to be harmful to the community in future. So at last they would obtain peace and security, if, when the great ones had been removed, they maintained among themselves equality of liberty and nobility, as well as of dignity and power.

This speech might not sound completely unreasonable, even if the call to violence is unpalatable to modern sensibilities, but Walsingham himself had no hesitation in condemning it as 'perverse ... insane ... ravings'.[38]

Walsingham is the only contemporary source to place Balle at Blackheath. It is true that Froissart also 'quotes' an example of Balle's preaching (which he describes merely as 'reckless'). Froissart's version is far more elegant, eloquent, passionate and reasoned than Walsingham's, which suggests to the modern reader that the author is himself sympathetic to the plight of the 'poor commons'. In fact, to his intended audience, the literate 'gentlefolk' who loved their aristocratic tales of knightly deeds and chivalry, it merely enunciated, powerfully and alarmingly, the politics of envy which threatened to destroy them.

> ... things cannot go right in England and never will, until goods are held in common and there are no more villeins and gentlefolk, but we are all one and the same. In what way are those whom we call lords greater masters than ourselves? How have they deserved it? Why do they hold us in bondage? If we all spring from a single father and mother, Adam and Eve, how can they claim or prove that they are lords more than us, except by making us produce and grow the wealth which they spend? They are clad in velvet and camlet lined with squirrel and ermine, while we go dressed in coarse cloth. They have the wines, the spices and the good bread: we have the rye, the husks and the straw, and

we drink water ... Let us go to the King – he is young – and show him how we are oppressed, and tell him that we want things to be changed, or else we will change them ourselves ... when the King sees and hears us, he will remedy the evil, either willingly or otherwise.[39]

It is telling that Froissart has Balle propose that redress for the people's wrongs should be sought from the king, rather than in the universal bloodbath of Walsingham's version, because this points to the fatal flaw in both accounts. Despite their persuasiveness and air of what we assume to be authenticity, they were written not just by hostile witnesses but by men who were not present at Blackheath and had never heard Balle preach. They are not first-hand accounts, therefore, even though they claim to 'quote' Balle's words. Both chroniclers used hindsight to extrapolate his alleged ideas from the actions of the rebels during the course of the revolt. They were also familiar with the sort of language that was the common vocabulary of all critics of the Church. There was, for instance, nothing radical or new about Balle's alleged preaching that in the beginning God had created all men equal and that serfdom was thus unlawful and should be abolished. The counter-argument (also drawn from the Biblical Book of Genesis), that serfdom, like slavery, had been imposed on mankind as punishment for sin, officially prevailed in both Church and state.[40]

Although Froissart's sample of Balle's preaching has elements in common with Walsingham's, he does not suggest that it relates to Blackheath or even to a single grand-standing sermon. He even admits that it is a generic representation rather than a verbatim record of a particular sermon, introducing it by stating that Balle 'had a habit' of preaching in the churchyards on Sundays to the people as they were leaving church and reiterating at the end that 'These were the kind of things which

John Balle usually preached in the villages on Sundays when the congregations came out from mass'.[41]

We therefore come back to the fact that the only evidence for the great revolutionary sermon delivered at Blackheath comes from Walsingham. And Walsingham had form where the fabrication of speeches was concerned. Just a few pages earlier in his chronicle he had described how Jack Straw, 'the most important of [the rebel] leaders after Walter Tylere', had been captured and sentenced to death by William Walworth, mayor of London. At the place of execution, and in response to Walworth's offer to have three years' worth of masses celebrated for his soul, Straw was persuaded to make his public confession to the assembled crowds, which 'proved' how the rebels had planned to destroy the realm. Walsingham gives the confession in full, as if reporting it verbatim, and it is a suitably long and horrific catalogue of murder and arson. Yet we know from a parliamentary petition of 1383–4 that Jack Straw was one of four rebel captains who were summarily executed during the revolt without due process of law, making it impossible for him to have been tried and condemned to death in London by Walworth.[42]

Reluctantly, therefore, we shall have to accept that the Blackheath sermon was the invention of a partisan historian determined to blame the corruption of heresy, embodied in Balle, for causing the revolt. By putting his speech into Balle's mouth at Blackheath, making him address the assembled rebels who were about to invade London and murder the head of the Church in England, he placed the excommunicate chaplain at the spiritual and physical heart of a rebellion which threatened to overthrow the establishment in both Church and state.

With or without John Balle, the Kentish rebels gathered on the heights at Blackheath had a spectacular panorama of London lying before them. The marshy south bank of the river Thames was a semi-rural patchwork of fields and woods, with the palaces, gardens and parks of royal and episcopal manors fronting the river, culminating in the archbishop's palace at Lambeth to the west. Immediately below them lay the royal manor of Greenwich on a peninsula in one of the many loops in the river Thames as it wound its way lazily past the city on the opposite bank. From their vantage point the rebels would have been able to see right across the city: rising above the mass of lowlier buildings, the solid mass of the White Tower of the Tower of London some five miles away; the soaring spire of St Paul's beyond it within the city walls; and, farther west, round a further bend in the river, the distinctive twin towers of Westminster Abbey. They would also have seen that there was only one bridge by which their forces could make their entrance into the city and that Watling Street, the old Roman road and pilgrimage route which they had followed from Canterbury and across Blackheath, would lead them straight there.

That same evening, a contingent of rebels rode on a further seven or so miles down the road to Southwark, a small town set on a tongue of land in the low-lying marshes of the south bank of the Thames, which stood at the entrance to the bridge.[43] Though Londoners liked to consider Southwark a suburb of the city, it was actually an independent borough composed of five different lordships (each with their own courts, liberties and privileges), five separate parishes and just 1750 inhabitants, many of whom had moved there to take advantage of the lack of a single over-arching authority: entrepreneurs escaping the restrictive commercial practices and regulations of the city, fugitives from justice slipping through the cracks between the jurisdictions, foreigners seeking refuge from the xenophobia of more tightly knit communities. Its distinctive, slightly raffish air

was enhanced by the constant influx of travellers, especially pilgrims, from all over the country for Southwark was, above all
else, the gatehouse and guesthouse for London.

As the rebels rode into the borough they could have counted
twenty-five inns along the High Street alone, including the
famous Tabard, where Harry Bailly presided in fact and fiction
as the host of Chaucer's Canterbury pilgrims. The inns,
displaying at the front their painted signs or carved representations of their names – the Boar's Head, the Bell, the Cardinal's
Hat – were several storeys high, with gables overhanging the
street and courtyards behind; chambers and beds were rarely
private but shared between travellers of the same sex; ostlers
and grooms looked after the horses, took them out to graze in
the neighbouring fields or offered those belonging to the establishment for hire.

Alongside the inns jostled a host of small shops offering their
wares to the passing trade. There were victuallers of every kind,
including 'pyebakers' and brewers, as well as the saddlers,
carters, hackneymen, porters and boatmen who facilitated the
travellers' onward journey. Towards the bottom of the street,
near its junction with the old Roman road to Chichester,
Sussex, was the twelfth-century priory of St Mary Overy, with
its massive cruciform church. Had they been interested in
poetry, the rebels could even have called in on Chaucer's friend
the poet John Gower, who was then living within the priory
precincts and would later express his gratitude by choosing its
church for his burial-place and founding a chantry chapel there.
They might not have received a sympathetic hearing, for though
Gower had bewailed the corruption which permeated every
level of society in a poem of 1376–9, he had also warned the
nobility to guard against 'the folly of the common people',
which he compared to a nettle 'which is too violent in its
nature' and has been allowed to grow unchecked:

He who observes the present time
Is likely to fear that soon,
If God does not provide his help,
This impatient nettle
Will very suddenly sting us,
Before it can be brought to justice.[44]

To the east of the priory, on the other side of High Street, the rebels would have seen St Thomas' Hospital, originally the canons' own infirmary but refounded and expanded in the early thirteenth century to care for the poor and sick of the parish. On the priory's other side stood the sumptuous palace of the bishops of Winchester which had a double quadrangle, gardens, fish-ponds and a park as well as its own private wharf and landing-place on the banks of the Thames. The bishop held one of the five lordships in Southwark and in the grounds of his palace stood what now claims to be the country's oldest prison, the infamous and eponymous the Clink, which housed both men and women (in separate accommodation) who had transgressed the laws of his liberty.

To modern minds it seems odd that these prisoners did not include the prostitutes who plied their trade alongside the boatmen on the river-bank and even odder that they actually enjoyed the bishop's protection. The Church had an ambivalent attitude towards prostitution, condemning the sin but in practice being prepared to look the other way 'withholding censure, lest perhaps something worse result from it'. It was considered acceptable to take tithes from prostitutes (as from actors and minstrels, who were held to be equally immoral) but only after they had repented and given up their life of sin. The state, by contrast, saw no reason not to tax prostitutes and their pimps and brothel-keepers, whatever the state of their immortal souls. It is a curious fact that the stew-mongers of Southwark paid some of the highest rates recorded in the borough's 1381 poll-tax returns, ranging from 4s. 6d. to a massive 6s. 8d. As a result of the bishop's leniency, however, there were so many brothels in the Bankside area of his lordship that it was colloquially known as 'The Stews'.[45]

The rebels who rode down High Street, however, were not interested in any of the services Southwark had to offer. Under the leadership of Thomas atte Raven, the former MP for Rochester, who was himself a Southwark man, they had one objective in mind: to break open the prisons and free the prisoners, just as they had already done in Kent and Essex. In addition to the Clink, there were two royal prisons in Southwark, that of the King's Bench and the Marshalsea. The attack on the latter was particularly significant because the Marshalsea housed many of the king's prisoners, especially debtors and indicted felons sent from the shires, such as Roger Forster, otherwise known as Roger Underwode, from Billericay, Essex, who escaped when the prison was stormed. It was also a major source of contention between the crown and the city of London. The marshal of the royal household had always had jurisdiction over the king's servants and his court dealt with debt, contract and covenant cases between them and with trespass offences involving any one of them committed within twelve miles of the king's person. This had been designed to suit a travelling royal household but the increased residency of the king in London in the fourteenth century, coupled with a more elastic view of the court's jurisdiction, had led to clashes with the city corporation, which saw its own jurisdiction being threatened and undermined. The tensions were manifest in the building of a new courtroom on Southwark High Street to hear the growing volume of pleas in 1373, repeated parliamentary petitions to the crown to observe the city's privileges in 1376–7 and the riots that followed rumours

that John of Gaunt was planning to extend the marshal's jurisdiction over the city in 1377.[46]

Thomas atte Raven, whose pardon describes him as 'the
principal and chief malefactor and maintainer [of malefac-
tors]', may have had personal experience of the Marshalsea,
perhaps through his business dealings: not only is he described
as being 'of Southwark' as well as 'of Rochester', but his wife,
Alice, was the daughter and co-heiress of Thomas Skynner,
a London goldsmith. Clearly he knew his way around
Southwark for he led the rebels on an orgy of targeted but
wholesale destruction that demolished not just the prison
buildings but also the houses of the jurors and professional
informers involved in the court and the personal property of its
warden. Richard Imworth had profited so much from his office
that he had had to pay six shillings for himself and his wife
Margery, as well as a further twelve pence for his daughter
Margaret, in the recent poll-tax.[47] Imworth was well aware of
the hatred that he and his office inspired and took the precaution of fleeing into sanctuary at Westminster Abbey. Two days
later, in one of the more horrific incidents of the London uprising, Richard Mugge of Westminster and a clerk named William
Pecche barged into the abbey church at the head of a band of
rebels, entered the sanctuary where Imworth was lying prostrate at his prayers before the tomb of St Edward, prised him
from the pillars of the shrine to which he was clinging and
dragged him outside to kill him. This was a serious offence –
a flagrant breach of the sacred and legal protection which the
Church afforded to those who sought sanctuary – but it was
compounded by the allegation that it was done 'in the presence
of the king himself', which would have been an act of lèse-
majesty. Though Richard did attend a service at the abbey the
following morning, it seems unlikely that he was present when
Imworth was murdered since Pecche received a pardon on 12

January 1382; three months later another cleric, Richard de Uttokcestre, parson of Lyminge, five miles from Folkestone, Kent, was acquitted of the charge that he had bribed Mugge to commit the murder.[48]

As Raven led the destruction of the Marshalsea and its associated buildings another group of Kentish rebels crossed to the other side of the Southwark peninsula and made a concerted attack on the archbishop of Canterbury's manor at Lambeth Palace. Forewarned of the rebels' approach, Simon Sudbury, together with the king and his court, had already moved earlier in the day from Westminster Palace to the greater security of the Tower of London; it was there that Sudbury, realising that his position was no longer tenable, resigned as chancellor of England and handed over the Great Seal to the king.[49] The archbishop was therefore absent when the rebels sacked his twelfth-century manor house, burning all the books, registers and chancery rolls they could find, together with vestments and his personal possessions; they broke open his casks of wine, pouring away what they could not drink, and they even shattered his kitchen utensils by smashing them together. All the while, according to a monk sitting across the river at Westminster, they shouted 'A revel! A revel!', as if they were taking part in some midsummer festival.[50]

Just as had happened elsewhere, the Kentish rebels' arrival encouraged the local people to rise up, join in and spread the disturbances. John Trentedeus, an innkeeper of Southwark who had just paid double the per capita poll-tax rate for himself and his wife, was later prosecuted by William Latymer for the loss from his inn of chests worth forty marks and the muniments they contained and by Robert Grey for the disappearance of fifty-four pounds: they held him responsible whether he stole them personally or was simply negligent in preventing their theft. On 14 June three men from Lambeth, Richard Lorchon,

Ralph atte Croste and Simon Gerard, were also inspired to lead a group of men from the vicinity in an attack on the king's manor of Kennington, just a mile outside Lambeth, burning the custumal and other muniments kept there; all the king's demesne tenants on the manor implicated in this action were later arrested and held without bail.[51]

With the south bank of the Thames now firmly in their hands, or those of their sympathisers, the rebels could turn their attention to their principal objective: obtaining a personal interview with the king.

CHAPTER NINE

Mile End

At some point on Wednesday 12 June messengers had begun passing between the city and the rebels at Blackheath. Two infamous inquisitions held before the sheriffs of London in November 1382 recount how the mayor William Walworth and his council had appointed three aldermen, John Horn, Adam Karlille and John Fresshe, to go to Tyler's forces and tell them not to come any closer to the city. The rebels 'had been on the point of returning to their homes' but Horn 'exceeded his instructions' and persuaded them 'with sweet words ... that the whole of the city of London felt as they did and that they would be received in the city with the friendship that a father offers his son or a lover his loved one'. As a result, the indictments claim, the rebels immediately advanced towards London and sacked the Marshalsea. Horn entertained some of the rebel leaders at his home overnight and then the next day, pretending to have mayoral authority, he took a standard of the royal arms and, contradicting a royal envoy carrying a message to the rebels whose path he had crossed, urged them to come to London where they would be offered any help they needed. One of Horn's co-conspirators, Walter Sibil, stood on the bridge and, repulsing offers of help to resist the rebels, left the gates open and unguarded, declaring, 'These Kentishmen are friends to us and the king', thus allowing 'the said traitors and their bands free entry and exit into the city although he ought to have prevented them from entering and could have done so easily'. Another alderman, William Tonge, was similarly accused of opening the Aldgate at night so that the Essex rebels could gain entry to the city.[1]

This seems a plausible explanation of how the rebels were able to get into London so easily – not least because Sibil and Tonge were the aldermen responsible for Bridge ward and Aldgate ward respectively – but it is untrue: the inquisitions are a classic case of the malicious laying of false evidence to discredit political rivals. They were held during the mayoralty of John of Northampton, a protégé of Gaunt and a radical outsider who wanted to overthrow the old guard and reform the city constitution. All the aldermen named were members of the powerful group of victuallers against whom his efforts were aimed and each one had held many offices in the city; Sibil, Tonge and Karlille had represented London in parliament and Fresshe had been one of the third poll-tax collectors. Northampton was briefly successful since the charges were repeated in parliament by one of his supporters and all five were imprisoned in the Tower, only to be released through the intercession of William Walworth and John Philipot, who stood bail for them. Three months into the next mayoralty they were all declared innocent when no one could be found to testify against them. Although this could be dismissed as further politicking (Northampton himself was arrested shortly afterwards and would eventually be permanently deprived of his freedom of the city), Tonge, Karlille and Fresshe all resumed their political careers at the heart of the civic administration: Tonge and Karlille both became MPs and Fresshe served as mayor. Sibil was never fully restored to his position as alderman, which suggests that, even if he had not committed the treason attributed to him, he was held culpable for his failure to hold London Bridge against the rebels, but he too continued to enjoy royal favour and served as a councillor and ambassador to Prussia. Only Horn disappears from the record after his release, which might indicate that he was guilty of colluding with the rebels, or that he was too heavily implicated by his dealings with them to be accepted back into the city elite. If he had encouraged the attack on the Marshalsea (not that the Kentishmen needed much encouragement), then most Londoners would have supported him; in the wake of the revolt, however, it would not have been politic for the city government openly to condone such action.[2]

Horn, Karlille and Fresshe were not the only messengers passing between the rebels and those in authority in London. The king too sent his envoys to ask those gathered at Blackheath what they wanted; they responded by sending their prisoner, Sir John Newenton, the constable of Rochester Castle, with a message to Richard that they wished to speak with him, their intention being to tell him face to face 'how all that they have done or will do is for him and his honour' and how his uncles and the clergy, especially archbishop Sudbury his chancellor, had not governed the realm well for a long time and that they should be held to account. Newenton therefore had himself rowed across the Thames to the Tower where, because he was known, he was admitted to the king's presence. According to Froissart, the king's mother, two half-brothers, the earls of Salisbury, Warwick and Oxford, archbishop Sudbury, the treasurer Sir Robert Hales, the mayor of London William Walworth, several burgesses and four Hainaulters, including Froissart's friends Robert, count of Namur and Jean, lord of Gommegnies, were all present when Newenton delivered his message. The constable told Richard that the rebels desired him to come to speak with them at Blackheath, that he need not fear for his safety 'for they hold and will hold you for their king', and asked for a reply that he could take back to appease them 'for they have my children in hostage till I return again to them'. After taking his councillors' advice, Richard told Newenton that he would come the following morning as requested, but would travel by boat and meet the rebels at his Thames-side manor of Rotherhithe, which was less than four miles from Blackheath.[3] It was a sensible compromise: close enough to Blackheath to show willing but on the opposite bank from the city, two miles away from the vulnerable London Bridge and affording Richard the chance to escape quickly by boat if things turned nasty.

Next morning, 13 June, the feast of Corpus Christi, Richard heard mass in the Tower, boarded the royal barge with some of his councillors and, accompanied by his men in four other barges, was rowed downriver to Rotherhithe. If his party had been expecting to meet only a deputation of leaders, they must have been horrified to see a huge and noisy throng of rebels gathering on the river bank to greet their king. Whatever Richard's own views – and he was not lacking in personal courage – his councillors could not allow the fourteen-year-old king to risk being abducted, manhandled or possibly even killed. They therefore refused to land, turned tail and rowed back to the safety of the Tower.[4] According to some chroniclers, Tyler's forces were so enraged by this breach of faith that they decided to take matters into their own hands and storm their way into the city. As they made their way through Southwark their ranks were swelled by substantial numbers of local people, among them such leading lights as John Brenchesley, who had been one of the collectors of the third poll-tax, and at least three others who would serve repeatedly as tax-collectors in future.[5] Like so many in the vicinity of London they joined the revolt not as a protest against taxation but as an opportunity to wreak vengeance on the king's ministers and John of Gaunt in particular.

It was the fact that Londoners themselves were not just willing but eager to take up arms that seems to have paralysed the administration: their loyalty could not be relied upon. Walworth and his aldermen must have given orders for the gates to be shut against the rebels and the drawbridge on London bridge to be raised, but several chroniclers allege that the rebels 'enjoyed free access to and exit from the city' because the inhabitants chose not to prevent them from doing so. The *Anonimalle* specifically accused the men of Southwark of actively forcing the bridge-keepers to let the rebels through and even claims that the Savoy Palace was put to the torch by 'the commons of London ... before the commons of the country arrived'. Walsingham asserts that the rebels 'went in and out', winning over the locals with their talk of liberty, their insistence that they would not plunder at all but buy everything at a fair price 'and that if they discovered anyone guilty of theft, they would execute him because they detested robbers'.[6] The chroniclers' allegations are borne out by the documentary evidence. The private prosecutions brought by Gaunt and Butterwick against the rebels who destroyed their London properties were overwhelmingly brought against people from the city and the list of those excluded from the right to claim a pardon named 150 Londoners (and a further twenty-three from its county, Middlesex), compared with only eleven men from Essex and twenty-eight from Kent and Canterbury combined. Just like their country counterparts, the London rebels came from a variety of social backgrounds from vintners, goldsmiths and innkeepers down through the ranks of the dozens of artisans and craftsmen – weavers, tailors, saddlers and cobblers (including a children's shoemaker) – to the humble servants, water-carriers, porters, boatmen, tinkers and 'travelling-men'. Intriguingly, they include William Brampton, 'formerly gate-keeper of Cripplegate', one of the three gates on the northern side of the city which were near to both Smithfield and the Hospitallers' priory at Clerkenwell. Here, at least, we have direct evidence of a gate-keeper who threw in his lot with the rebels instead of defending the city against them.[7]

Whether the Kentishmen and their local recruits crossed the bridge in dribs and drabs, or swarmed across in an irresistible tide of humanity, by the afternoon of Thursday 13 June they had cleared their first major hurdle by crossing the Thames and were now in the heart of the city. What is more, if Gaunt's and Butterwick's prosecutions are to be believed, they had also been joined by the rebel groups from Essex who, having gathered outside the walls at Mile End, entered the city by the Aldgate.[8] Where or when they made their rendezvous is not known and the chronology of what happened next is so beset with challenges and contradictions that it is almost impossible to draw up a coherent account. The 'official' version prepared for insertion in the city corporation's letter-book notes only that the rebels of both counties 'by the aid within the city of perfidious commoners of their own condition, who rose in countless numbers there, ... suddenly entered the city together', but instead of rampaging and looting through the streets as might have been expected they passed 'straight through' on their way to the Savoy Palace.[9]

Gaunt himself was not at his palace but far away at the other end of the kingdom, negotiating a truce with the Scots, so he escaped the fate of his fellow royal councillors and that of his residence, 'unrivalled in splendour and nobility within England', which was sacked so thoroughly it would never be rebuilt. Much to the amazement of the chroniclers, the rebels did not steal Gaunt's possessions, but simply destroyed them. 'They took all the torches they could find, and lighted them, and burnt all the cloths, coverlets and beds, as well as all the very valuable head-boards (of which one, decorated with heraldic shields, was said to be worth a thousand marks). All the napery and other goods they could discover they carried into the hall and set on fire with their torches. They burnt the hall and chambers as well as all the apartments within the gates of the said palace'. Gold and silver plate, jewels and anything that would not burn was hacked to pieces and thrown into the Thames or the sewers. Since they could not find Gaunt himself, the rebels made do with a representation of him: Walsingham tells us that when they found one of Gaunt's most valuable quilted short tunics they hung it on a lance and then used it as an archery target before finally tearing it apart with their swords and axes.[10] 'And let it be known', wrote the chronicler Henry Knighton, who knew many of Gaunt's officials personally, 'that the keeper of [Gaunt's] wardrobe asserted and swore that he believed no Christian king nor anyone else had a better wardrobe: he said that it was so full of silver vessels and jewels, not counting others gilded or made of pure gold, that five carts could hardly have held them.' Everything there was lost. Inventories of the contents of the Savoy Palace made before 1381 and preserved elsewhere reveal that goods and chattels valued at ten thousand pounds were destroyed; the loss to the chapel alone was later calculated at five hundred pounds. The damage to the fabric of the building could not be quantified but it is a measure of how thoroughly it was gutted that lead from the roof worth one hundred shillings would later be salvaged for the repairs to Hertford Castle.[11]

Despite the rebel leaders' insistence that nothing should be stolen, on pain of execution, some thefts did occur. A man who tried to steal a fine piece of silver was allegedly thrown into the fires, together with his prize, by his fellow rebels, who said that 'they were lovers of truth and justice, not robbers and thieves'. Around thirty-two others became drunk on Gaunt's wine but were then trapped in the cellars when the building above collapsed; in the sort of morality tale beloved of medieval commentators, their cries and lamentations were said to have been heard for the next seven days before they finally expired. The most fascinating incident, however, escaped the chroniclers' attention. Joanna Ferrour of Rochester was later indicted by a Middlesex jury of having been 'a chief actor and leader' in many of the main events in London. Among them was the charge that she had participated in the burning of the Savoy Palace but had also 'taken a certain chest, in which was a thousand pounds sterling belonging to John, duke of Lancaster, and more besides, and she placed the said chest in a certain small boat on the Thames and carried it away and took it all the way to Southwark, and there she divided up the said gold between herself and others'. Her husband John Ferrour, otherwise known as John Marchall, and another Kentishman, Roger atte Wode, were also indicted for the same offences. In 1383 the Ferrours were acquitted and atte Wode pardoned; the indictments may have been malicious or mistaken, but they are unusually detailed and, as we shall see, there were probably good reasons why the charges were eventually dropped.[12]

The chroniclers were so mesmerised by the scale of the devastation at the Savoy Palace that they did not look beyond the physical evidence before them. Yet the financial consequences to Gaunt of the loss of his main residence were not limited to what was lost or destroyed there but affected his income for years to come. For the Savoy Palace was the administrative centre of his estates across the country and the rebels had also burned all the records he kept there and killed the clerks who managed his financial affairs. Ten months later Gaunt was excused having to account to the exchequer and pay back the money he had received for the wages of his Breton campaign in 1378 and his two recent expeditions to the Scottish borders 'because the writings and accounts relating to the same were burnt at his manor of Savoye in the late insurrection, and some of the clerks are dead'. As late as 1388 a general survey of Gaunt's estates revealed that many of his bailiffs in the south had not accounted to him for their judicial revenues since the revolt because all their previous records were destroyed at the Savoy Palace.[13]

The *Anonimalle* chronicler noted that 'the commons of Kent received the blame for this arson, but some said that the Londoners were really guilty of the deed, because of their hatred for the said duke'. Gaunt's prosecutions of those who had been involved in the sacking of his palace reveal his awareness that Londoners were primarily responsible. Perhaps wisely, therefore, he decided not to rebuild his palace and provoke them with a further display of his wealth and power. Whenever he returned to London in future he would instead rent properties from the bishop of Ely or the abbot of Westminster.[14] The Savoy Palace itself would remain a blackened ruin, a stark reminder of the consequences of bad government to all who passed it, particularly those with affairs of state on their mind as they made their way to attend court or parliament at Westminster.

After burning the Savoy Palace the rebels made their way out beyond Smithfield to Clerkenwell. It was here that the Knights Hospitaller had their provincial headquarters, the priory of St John of Jerusalem, which was ultimately responsible for the administration of the order and its properties throughout England, Wales and Scotland. More like a village than a religious house, the priory extended over a ten-acre site at Clerkenwell, while also owning much larger tracts of land farther north in the parish. Even at this period it probably had an outer gated ward enclosing the formal walled quarters. At its heart lay the great church built in 1144–60, with the characteristic round nave favoured by military orders, sixty-five feet in diameter, of which three bays of the vaulted crypt are the only modern survival. Despite its prestige and the grandeur of its buildings, only a handful of Hospitaller knights lived on site, which helps to explain why it was so easily overrun by the London rebels on the evening of 13 June.[15] Since the preceptory at Cressing Temple was the first place targeted by the Essex insurgents it was not to be supposed that the headquarters of the order, where its prior Robert Hales was based, would escape the rebels' wrath. Hales had only been treasurer of England since February 1381 but he was indelibly marked by his association with the military failures of the reign, having been admiral of the fleet west of the Thames in 1376–7 and part of Woodstock's doomed expedition of 1377, and by his assiduous attendance at royal council meetings which had decided government policy in the ensuing years. Although he had not been treasurer when the third poll-tax was granted, he bore much of the personal responsibility for the subsequent heavy-handed enforcement of its collection.[16]

Just like the Savoy Palace, the priory was well and truly sacked: the fire was said to have burned continuously for the next seven days and virtually everything was destroyed apart from the stone church.[17] Hales' successor as prior would bring private prosecutions against men like John Halingbury of Wandsworth, whom he accused of having broken into his close and his houses, 'burnt his charters, writings, court rolls and other muniments, took and carried away his goods and chattels worth £40, and did him other enormities against the king's peace'. Robert Gardiner of Holborn was also indicted, not only for stealing a chalice valued at one hundred shillings but also for killing seven nameless Flemings in Clerkenwell; despite these crimes he was pardoned on 2 February 1382.[18] Several of the priory's own employees were among those indicted, including Hales' servant John Gamelyn, his falconer John Webbe and a former servant, possibly his steward, Richard Mory of Clerkenwell. The last, a relatively prosperous man, was one of three men subject to a special petition from 'certain lords' in the parliament of October 1382 that they should be excluded from the king's grace because they were 'the chief instigators, abettors and procurers of the great and terrible rising and insurrection lately treacherously committed within the kingdom ... and especially the leaders of the firing and destruction of the house and manors of the order of St John of Jerusalem in England'.[19]

While relatively little is known about Mory, and nothing about Richard Dell, the third subject of the petition was one of the few rebels whose actions and motives are well documented. Thomas Farndon was a goldsmith who had represented the county of Middlesex in the parliament of 1377. He was a member of one of the city's leading families which had practised that craft for several generations and become wealthy property owners and aldermen of the city. Farndon himself held properties within the city walls at Wood Street and in the extra-mural suburb of Farringdon Without; he also had a small country estate about twelve miles north of London in Enfield, acquired in January 1378, consisting of eight messuages, 160 acres of land, fifty acres of meadow, sixty-five acres of pasture and sixteen acres of woodland, with a further eight acres of meadow a mile away at Cheshunt. For at least twelve years, however, Farndon had been involved in a bitter legal dispute with his extended family over the ownership of seven shops and a garden in the London suburbs and two dwellings and ten shops in the city. Both claimed the properties were theirs by right of inheritance but his main opponent, Richard Weston, had stalled the proceedings by declaring that Farndon's father was illegitimate. The case had also dragged on because it was caught up in legal arguments over errors in the process and disputes over jurisdictional rights between the crown and the city corporation. Farndon had lost the most recent round but on 6 February 1381 initiated further proceedings.[20]

It was Farndon's deep sense of grievance amounting to monomania on this subject that involved him in the uprising and almost cost him his life. The following day, Friday 14 June, he was among the crowds at Tower Hill and there confronted the king, demanding that he should recognise his title to the property 'which Richard Weston had seized from him' so that he could legally take it back again: 'and he said that, if the lord king did not wish to recognise his legal title to that same tenement, then he would take possession of it on his own authority' using the power of the rebel mob. These rash words were sufficient to get him into serious trouble, but what turned the whole incident into a capital offence was that his enemies, possibly prompted by Weston, later alleged that he had demanded justice from the king against Robert Hales, calling him a 'false traitor' who had 'falsely and fraudulently' deprived him of his tenements and using the same threat that, if the king failed to restore his tenements to him, then 'know that I am strong enough to do justice on my own account and to secure my possession and entry into those tenements'. What is more, to increase the seriousness of Farndon's offence, it was alleged that the incident had taken place at Mile End, which of itself identified him as a rebel, and that, to speak to the king, he had 'criminally, treasonably and irreverently' grabbed the reins of the king's horse, an action which could be construed as lèse-majesty. Weston was thus painted out of the picture and replaced by Hales, creating a plausible reason for Farndon's alleged involvement in the sacking of the Temple, the priory at Clerkenwell and the Hospitallers' manor at Highbury, and justifying the allegation that 'he was the principal cause of the death of [prior] Robert Hales'. Just for good measure, Farndon was accused of being head of a band of rebels which had attacked Cressing Temple and, even more improbably, spending the night of 13 June with a group of Kentish rebels compiling a list of citizens to be executed and their properties destroyed.[21]

In this way a genuine incident was doctored in the retelling to turn a private quarrel into a political one that could have resulted in Farndon's execution. It is possible that Farndon compounded his foolishness by using the general mayhem to seize back his properties, though the charges against him were extremely weak. He was apparently arrested 'in the vicinity of' the house of John Knot in 'Stanynglane' when it was being demolished by the rebels and he was also accused of threatening to demolish the house in St Giles-Without-Cripplegate of Gilbert Prynce, a wealthy portrait painter, but even the jurors who indicted him for this said that he did not actually carry out his threat. Farndon received a pardon on 25 February 1382 at the request of the queen and of the aldermen of London who attested to his innocence, but he was unable to shake off the accusations against him. These resurfaced in the parliament of October 1382 and led to his being excluded from pardon and grace with Richard Mory and Richard Dell.[22] This is the key to Farndon's difficulties for the parliamentary action occurred during the mayoralty of John of Northampton – who had also secured the inquisitions which accused the five aldermen of complicity in the rebels' entry into London – and those same

inquisitions are the source of the fabricated charges against
Farndon. Clearly he had become caught up in the political skul-
duggery between Northampton and his opponents as they
fought for control of the city's administration and his demon-
strable innocence further undermines the case against the five
aldermen. It also removes from the ranks of confirmed rebels
the only member of the city elite whose involvement has hitherto been unquestioned.

The chroniclers imply that it was the same group of rebels
who went from one scene of devastation to the next on that first
day of the uprising in London, and it is indeed possible to plot
a plausible route based on that trail between the city, the Savoy
Palace and Clerkenwell. The Fleet prison, for instance, which
lay just outside Ludgate, was just off Fleet Street, the main route
from the city to the Savoy Palace. Farther along the same street
lay the Temple, then, as now, the hub for London lawyers. The
rebels thoroughly demolished the houses there, stripping the
tiles off their roofs so that they were exposed to the elements,
and forced their way into Temple church, where they 'seized all
the books, rolls and remembrances kept in the cupboards of the
apprentices of the law within the Temple, carried them into the
high road and burnt them there'.[23] It is difficult now to disentangle whether the same bands were responsible for these acts
of violence on their way to or from the Savoy Palace, or
whether once the violence had begun it simply spread from
place to place as others joined in; even contemporary chroniclers seem to have struggled to construct a coherent narrative.
It seems illogical, for instance, that the Essex rebels based at
Mile End should have made a detour through London and out
to the Savoy Palace before returning to attack the priory at
Clerkenwell, which was just three and a half miles from their
starting point; and unless those involved had stayed in London
overnight, time would surely have been against them if they had

participated in all the attacks along the way before nightfall. Given the levels of coordination between them in the past it is not inconceivable that the Kentishmen led the assault on the Savoy Palace and the men from Essex led that on the priory. We do not know: but it is indisputable that Londoners themselves played a major role in these events.

Jack Straw also emerges in person, if briefly, from the shadows at this point. Before daybreak on Friday 14 June, the abbot of St Albans had sent a delegation to the king because he had learned that his tenants from St Albans and Barnet were intending to join the rebels in London. Their road took them through Highbury, where the abbot's men saw the rebel hordes destroying the recently refurbished Hospitallers' manor: 'a multitude of twenty thousand rustics and common people who had set fire to its buildings, already burning inextinguishably, and were striving to pull down with their tools all that the fire could not destroy. They saw men summoned and forced before one of the leaders of the rebels, called "John Strawe", who made them promise that they would adhere to King Richard and the commons'.[24] Other than the 'Rakestrawman' proclamation at Thanet, this is the only credible reference[25] that places Straw in an act of rebellion, though of course the abbey delegates or Walsingham might simply have assumed that this was the leader's identity. The vignette nevertheless confirms the repeated assertion that the rebels compelled all they met to swear allegiance to the king and his 'true commons'. The *Anonimalle*, for instance, describes as their 'wache word' the question 'With whom haldes yow?' to which the reply was 'Wyth kynge Richarde and wyth the trew communes'; 'and those who did not know how to reply or would not do so were beheaded and put to death'.[26]

The London uprising was no different from those in any other town in that once it had been started by the rebel bands from Essex and Kent, local people took it over and made it their own. The Marshalsea, King's Bench and Fleet prisons, all of which housed prisoners from outside London, had already been broken open by the Kentishmen and their supporters; on 14 June it was Londoners who freed the prisoners at Westminster (newly erected by the abbot of Westminster as part of his gate-house to the abbey) and Newgate. Both prisons served the local population but Newgate was said to be packed with people held indefinitely because they were either too poor to find sureties for their good behaviour or were suspicious strangers who had been arrested in the panic caused by the French attacks because they were 'running hither and thither about the place like spies'; those released from Newgate were said to have offered their iron chains in the church of the Friars Minor in token of their gratitude.[27] The release of so many indicted and convicted criminals into the toxic atmosphere must have con-tributed to the violence. John Kirkton, also called Echard, an escapee from Newgate was accused of burning the Savoy Palace, the Hospitallers' manor at Highbury and Stephen Maynard's houses near Highgate. Although acquitted by a jury, perhaps because it was impossible for him to have been at the Savoy Palace since he was not freed until the following day, he remained in prison because he had been excluded from the gen-eral amnesty and, having no possessions, could not afford to buy a pardon. Released on bail because of ill health in October 1382 he failed to appear before parliament a few days later, resulting in orders being issued for his arrest and those of his sureties.[28]

Another escapee, John Benet of Barford St John, Oxford-shire, had been convicted of larceny but was staving off execution by claiming to be a cleric when he was freed by the rebels from the King's Bench prison at Southwark; he partici-pated in the burning of the Savoy Palace and the jail-breaking of the Marshalsea and Newgate but was recaptured and, as a convicted felon, was almost certain of execution. He therefore turned approver, accusing Thomas Wootton of Kent of leading the attack on the Marshalsea and forcing him to hand over six silver spoons which Richard Imworth's wife had allegedly given Benet for safe-keeping. Since the accusation could not be proved before a jury, Wootton was forced to defend himself in trial by combat which he lost, and was therefore executed. In Benet's desperation to escape a similar fate he invented an even more elaborate story, that on 14 June (the day of the Newgate jail-break) he and two other Oxfordshire men had been at Portsmouth where they had received one hundred pounds in gold from an esquire of Jean de Vienne, admiral of France, with a further hundred pounds promised for collection at Rye if they persuaded as many English forces as possible to withdraw from the south coast to facilitate a French invasion. This was an invention too far. The jury declared him guilty of being 'a chief rebel' and he was duly hanged.[29]

There must have been many more Kirktons and Benets on the streets of London after 13 June, even if their stories were less colourful. It was no surprise then that among the first individuals to be attacked was a quest-monger, the medieval equivalent of an ambulance-chaser, who laid information against alleged wrongdoers to encourage petty lawsuits. Roger Leget had been a professional lawyer since at least 1360, witnessing charters for, among others, Sir Robert Knolles, and building up a nice little property portfolio in Holborn, including two dwelling houses and fifteen shops in the parish of St Andrew's. He was wealthy enough to employ his own private chaplain, which was probably a necessity given his trade and his character: a peculiarly nasty manifestation of the latter was his building a new dyke on Fikettsfield next to the Staple Inn to keep out the clerks, apprentices and others who daily came 'to play their common games there'. When that failed to work, he had 'privily put and hidden' caltraps – spiked devices used on military operations to bring down horses – along the top of and all around the dyke. His punishment had been a 'long abode' in the Fleet prison but he bought himself out by paying a fine of twenty marks. He would not be able to buy himself out of the situation he faced in 1381. Knowing he was a target, he had fled to the sanctuary of St Martin-le-Grand while his houses in Holborn were attacked and burned, but he was dragged away from the high altar, taken to Cheapside and there beheaded.[30] Like Richard Imworth, warden of the Marshalsea, who would meet a similar fate the following day,[31] he had made many enemies among the criminal fraternity of London and those whom he had unjustly imprisoned.

Friday 14 June also saw a concerted attack on the properties of another corrupt lawyer with close connections to the King's Bench. The houses at Knightsbridge, Ebury and Tothill of John Butterwick, under-sheriff of Middlesex, were all attacked and burned; among the seven hundred alleged rebels whom he would later privately prosecute in twenty separate actions was William Pecche, the clerk who was also accused of dragging Imworth from sanctuary at Westminster and murdering him. Butterwick's scattergun approach to his prosecutions – he shared information with Gaunt's lawyers in a bid to secure conviction for any crime, rather than specifically identifying those who had committed the offences against him – suggest that he had a casual attitude towards establishing the truth which was hardly compatible with his office.[32] Stephen Maynard, whose properties in West Smithfield and near Highgate were burned down the same day, had been accused in 1378 during an inquisition held by the mayor John Philipot of being a 'common maintainer of plaints', in other words, a quest-monger like Leget.[33]

All these victims of the revolt, and many more besides, were people in whom the Kentish and Essex rebels can have had no interest, even if they knew of their existence, which reinforces the theme that this was now an uprising by Londoners against Londoners. The only person of any broader significance who might have been recognised and attacked by rebels from outside the city was Richard Lyons, whose manor of Overhall at Liston had already been sacked by the combined forces of men from Essex and Suffolk. The fact that he was dragged from his house, however, before being taken to Cheapside to be beheaded again implies local knowledge.[34]

All that distinguished the London revolt from those in other towns was the scale of the violence and the eminence of those victims who, even as the uprising gathered pace across the city, were sheltering in the Tower. From this vantage point they could not fail to see the fires burning on every horizon or hear the shouts of the mob as they raised a cry against their next victim and surged through the streets to burn, demolish and kill. To add to their terror, many knew that their own lives were in danger: the king had already received a petition from the Kentish rebels demanding the heads of Gaunt and fifteen other royal councillors, including the chancellor Sudbury, the treasurer Hales, the keeper of the privy seal John Fordham, the chief justice Robert Bealknapp, the chief baron of the exchequer John Plesyngton, Sir Ralph Ferrers (Gaunt's retainer who had violated the sanctuary at Westminster Abbey to kill John Hawley and a sacristan in August 1378 and had been accused but cleared of treason in the parliament of 1380) and two of the most notorious reassessors and enforcers of the third poll-tax, John Legge and John Bampton. All but Gaunt, who was still in the Scottish marches, were said to have been in the Tower, but this seems unlikely given that most of them escaped unharmed. Fordham may already have had a narrow escape in that the place where he was staying, the bishop of Chester's inn on the Strand close to the Savoy Palace, was raided by rebels who drank the contents of its cellars but left the building itself unscathed.[35]

Also present in the Tower were said to have been William Walworth with several of his aldermen; four earls, Salisbury, Warwick, Oxford and Kent (Richard's thirty-one-year-old half-brother), all of whom had considerable military experience as veterans of the campaigns against the French; the young king's other half-brother John Holland, who had also fought the French; his mother the princess of Wales, who, if Froissart is to be believed, had already been treated disrespectfully by rebels she had encountered on the road to London as she returned from a pilgrimage to Canterbury; and a handful of Hainaulter lords with long-standing connections to the English court. To this list provided by Froissart the *Anonimalle* adds Sir Robert Knolles, one of the most famous and successful professional soldiers of the day, with decades of experience in Brittany; Sir Thomas Percy, another veteran of many a French campaign and a Knight of the Garter; and finally Thomas of Woodstock, Richard's uncle, whose disastrous Breton expedition in 1380–1 had been one of the underlying causes of the revolt. Woodstock's presence seems highly unlikely, given how provocative it would have been to the rebels, but his exact whereabouts at this crucial time are unclear. There was another person there, not mentioned by any of the chroniclers, whose capture or death would have been high on any rebel agenda: Richard's fourteen-year-old cousin Henry Bolingbroke, the only legitimate son and heir of John of Gaunt.[36]

With or without Woodstock, this list demonstrates that Richard had plenty of experienced people around him to advise him on what steps he should now take. Just to focus their minds, a growing crowd of rebels had been gathering to the east of the Tower since the evening of 13 June. This area, known as St Katherine's, was just outside the city wall and home to the hospital of St Katherine by the Tower, a twelfth-century charitable foundation beloved by the king's grandmother Queen Philippa. Run by a master and three priests who said daily masses for the souls of past kings and queens of England, it housed twenty-four poor people including six poor scholars, cared for by a number of sisters. Though the hospital statutes decreed that one thousand poor men were each to receive ½d. on the anniversary of Henry III's death (16 November), this had been abandoned by 1377 owing to the expense of rebuilding the great church which dominated the site. Perhaps the brethren and sisters saw fit to distribute food or offer overnight shelter to the rebels, for all the hospital's buildings were left untouched by those gathering in its shadow.[37]

The king and his councillors appear to have tried various stratagems to persuade the rebels to leave. Richard had it proclaimed to them that they would all receive pardons for any crimes they had committed if they returned home peaceably, only to be met with the response that they would not go until they had captured the traitors in the Tower, received a full account from the chancellor of all the taxes that had been raised over the past five years and been given charters freeing them 'from all manner of serfdom'. Richard prevaricated, repeating his offer in a further proclamation written out in the rebels' presence and sealed with his personal signet, which 'willed and commanded' them to put their grievances in writing to him and promised that he would provide 'such remedy as shall be profitable both to him and to them, and to the kingdom'. This too was rebuffed with contempt. When these attempts at conciliation failed, some of his councillors suggested that they should make a concerted attack at midnight, bringing armed men down four different streets to converge on the sleeping rebels at

St Katherine's and take them by surprise. 'They would all be drunk and could be killed like flies, since not one in twenty of them was armed ... but none of this was done, for fear of the rest of the common people in London'.[38]

Either at some point in the evening of Thursday 13 June or more likely during the following morning, when the rebels launched a renewed assault on the prisons, lawyers and Hospitallers' manor of Highbury, the royal party reached the decision that they would have to negotiate. It would have been safer to have stayed within the Tower precincts and invited rebel delegates in to speak with them, but such was the distrust on either side that this did not happen. Instead, they took the extraordinary decision to send the king himself out to meet the rebels face to face. This was what the rebels had been demanding since their arrival at Blackheath – but it was a highly risky concession which would place the boy-king at the mercy of a volatile and possibly angry crowd. The rebels might not all have been armed but it would only have taken a single rogue archer with a longbow to have brought him down with an arrow through the eye, neck or heart. And if Richard's councillors had been so afraid of his being captured, wounded or killed that they would not allow him to disembark at Rotherhithe the day before, then why were they now prepared to allow him to ride more than two miles through the streets and suburbs of London to a place where the rebels from Essex had been encamped for some thirty-six hours? Even with a heavily armed escort to protect him, an ambush would have been possible at any point, but more especially at Mile End where the rebels were already in possession of the field. The risks were amply illustrated by the fact that William Treweman, a brewer, was able to seize the bridle of Nicholas Brembre's horse as he was riding with the king down Aldgate and, having thus stopped him in his tracks, was able to berate the alderman for the injuries done to him by

Brembre when the latter was mayor. (Later in the day Treweman would bring a band of rebels to Brembre's house to intimidate him into handing over five marks, a sum of such insignificance to two very wealthy men that it can only have been a disputed debt.)[39]

To counterbalance the obvious dangers in leaving the Tower, the king's councillors could take some comfort from the fact that the rebels had always vowed their express loyalty to Richard himself. What finally convinced them that a meeting was now imperative was the escalating violence within the city. The rebels' response to the failure of the king to meet them at Rotherhithe had been to invade the capital, and sack the Savoy Palace and the priory at Clerkenwell. What might they do if he refused to go to them again? Something had to be done if the situation was to be retrieved and order restored. A proclamation was duly made to the people assembled at St Katherine's that if they wanted to speak to the king then they should go to Mile End and he would meet them there without fail. Mile End, 'a fine open space ... situated in the middle of a pleasant meadow, where the people go for recreation in summer', was easily accessible for both parties inside and outside the Tower but it was far enough away to remove the immediate peril posed by the rebels gathered around 'St Katherine's – if they could be induced to leave. It has been persuasively argued that Sudbury and Hales 'were condemned to almost certain death when Richard rode out to Mile End'; his removal from their company effectively granted the waiting rebels permission to seize his hated councillors and carry out their long-expressed determination to execute them; and, with the young king to all intents and purposes a hostage among the rebels at Mile End, those guarding the Tower had no other course but to surrender because 'Richard's life might well be forfeited by any show of opposition on their part'.[40] While all this is undoubtedly true, and some historians have taken the argument even further, contending that Richard deliberately abandoned his ministers to their fate, it all assumes that the king and his councillors knew what was about to happen which, of course, they could not. Any of those in the Tower whose names were on the rebels' list, and particularly Sudbury and Hales, knew what their fate was likely to be if they fell into the rebels' hands, but the Tower was virtually impregnable so while they remained there they must have felt themselves to be as safe as it was possible to be in the circumstances. There is no greater evidence of this than the fact that, among those left behind in the Tower as the royal party rode out to Mile End, was Richard's cousin Henry Bolingbroke.

According to Froissart, Richard's two half-brothers and Jean, lord of Gommegnies, a soldier of fortune who had been in Gaunt's service since 1369, left the king's company before it arrived at their destination because they 'dare not show themselves to the populace at Mile End'. (The fact that no one else made use of this means of escape from the Tower also suggests that those left behind considered it a safer option.)[41] Richard rode into the open fields at Mile End preceded by Aubrey de Vere carrying his sword of state and accompanied by his most experienced military advisers, the earls of Salisbury, Warwick and Oxford, Sir Thomas Percy and Sir Robert Knolles, together with the mayor William Walworth and 'many knights and esquires'; his mother came too, riding in a carriage. Bizarre though it seems that she should have been there, the princess of Wales was widely respected, especially by Londoners, as a conciliator: Gaunt had notably fled to her in the crisis of 1377 and she had sued for peace between him and the rioting citizens of London.[42]

The so-called Mile End conference was a seminal moment in the revolt and an extraordinary one in the course of English history because, having listened to their demands, the king granted the rebels all their requests. In so doing he made concessions which would have radically altered the very fabric of English society. Yet we know next to nothing about what happened: not the time of the meeting, how long it lasted, what form it took or even who acted as spokesman or spokesmen on behalf of the rebels. Froissart, Knighton and the monk of Westminster refer in vague terms only to Richard granting freedom from bondage 'for the sake of peace'; Walsingham does not mention the meeting at all but says the king offered the rebels 'peace' if they stopped burning and killing and went home. The London letter-book's 'official' version has a unique take designed to divert blame away from its own citizens for the murders at the Tower, stating that 'all the men from Kent and Essex ... together with some of the perfidious persons of the city' gathered at Mile End where 'our lord the king granted that they might take those who were traitors against him and slay them, wheresoever they might be found'.[43] Though the crowd was probably predominantly made up of people from Essex, since Mile End was their appointed meeting-place, the presence of Kentishmen is confirmed by the indictment of Thomas Noke from the Sittingbourne area who 'feloniously killed' James French 'at Milende in the county of Middlesex'.[44] The most detailed account of what happened occurs in the *Anonimalle*:

> And when the king arrived and the commons saw him, they knelt down to him, saying 'Welcome our Lord King Richard, if it pleases you, and we will not have any other king but you.' And Wat Teghler, their master and leader, prayed on behalf of the commons that the king would suffer them to take and deal with all the traitors against him and the law. The king granted that they should freely seize all

who were traitors and could be proved to be such by process of law ... And they required that henceforward no man should be a serf nor make homage or any type of service to any lord, but should give four pence for an acre of land. They asked also that no one should serve any man except at his own will and by means of regular covenant.[45]

This is the only evidence we have that Wat Tyler was even present at Mile End. Froissart tells us that the king promised he would have letters drawn up at once, sealed with his Great Seal, setting out all that he had granted them. Two or three representatives from each place should remain behind to receive these letters but the rest of the rebels were to return to their homes immediately. As a symbol of his good faith, he offered them banners of the royal arms, one for each county, and told them that they would be pardoned for everything they had done 'provided that you follow my banners and go back to your own places in the way I told you'. Thirty clerks were then put to the task of writing out the letters.[46]

Richard was patently sincere in what he said and for the most part the rebels believed him. Accepting his word and his banners – of which more later – the crowds began to disperse, leaving only those waiting for their letters. Two of those letters have survived; one is a draft prepared for the men of Somerset, dated from Westminster on 2 July;[47] the second, which varies only very slightly in wording from the first, was copied into his chronicle by Walsingham from the letter 'extracted by force from the lord king' by the men of Walsingham's own county of Hertfordshire:

Richard, by the grace of God, king of England and France, and lord of Ireland, to all his bailiffs and faithful men to whom these present letters come, greetings. Know that by

our special grace we have manumitted all our liegemen, subjects and others of the county of Hertford; and we have
freed and quitted each of them from bondage by these present letters. We also pardon our said liege men and subjects
for all felonies, acts of treason, transgressions and extortions performed by them or any one of them in whatsoever
way. We also withdraw sentences of outlawry declared
against them or any of them because of these offences. And
we hereby grant our complete peace to them and each of
them. In testimony of which we order these letters of ours
to be made patent. Witnessed by myself at London on 15
June in the fourth year of my reign.[48]

The official form and language used here tends to obscure what
a revolutionary document this is: no less than the complete abolition of villeinage, not just on the king's own estates but in
every lordship throughout the land. As the lords and prelates
were quick to point out in the first parliament that met after the
revolt, Richard had no authority to free their serfs 'without the
assent of those who had the chief interest in the matter'. In a
remarkably emotional outburst, they added that 'they had never
agreed to it, either voluntarily or otherwise, nor would they
ever do so, even if it were their dying day'. Though they made
their protest respectfully, they made it as robustly as it was possible to do when contradicting their king, adding, for good
measure, that on this subject they spoke with one voice with the
knights, burgesses and citizens of the House of Commons.[49]
Richard would be left in no doubt that his abolition of serfdom
was not only illegal, it was also actively opposed by all his most
important subjects.

Yet this was not all the young king had conceded. Just eighteen days after he made the original grant, and probably under
the watchful eye of the new hard-line chief justice, Robert

Tresilian, Richard repealed the letters of manumission he had offered at Mile End. In doing so, he recited two extraordinary further concessions he had made which are not mentioned in either of the two extant examples. The first was that he had abolished not just personal villeinage but all villein tenure as well: 'not an acre of land' should be held anywhere in bondage or by customary service but only by paying a rent of four pence per acre, with the corollary that if less had been paid in the past, then that lower rate should stand for the future.[50] As we have already seen,[51] the enforcement of customary dues and services had long been a burning issue, affecting many more people than personal bondage, so the consequences of this act were much more far-reaching than a simple abolition of villeinage by blood. Arbitrary impositions and punitive fines would be a thing of the past and those with the will and capacity to work hard and build up a profitable landholding or business enterprise would be able to do so without hindrance from their landlords. Less than two weeks after the oath at Bocking, the rebels had achieved what their fathers and grandfathers could only have imagined in their wildest dreams.

The second concession revealed in the revocation of the letters Richard had granted to the rebels was, if anything, even more startling. It is not mentioned in any of the chronicles, not even the *Anonimalle*, and it does not feature in any of the lists of rebel demands reported before, or indeed after, the meeting at Mile End. Yet its consequences would have been even more profound than the abolition of villeinage and villein tenure. Richard agreed that all his subjects were to be free to buy and sell within every city, borough, market-town or other place in the realm of England.[52] This would have swept away at a single stroke all the closely guarded monopolies and privileges upon which the economies of every urban community depended. Great religious houses like Bury St Edmunds or St Albans would no longer be able to force their townsmen to use the abbey's mills or impose other restrictive practices. Neither they, nor secular lords of towns, nor even self-governing urban communities would be able to exact tolls and fines on outsiders. This was something for which all those excluded from elite circles of citizenship had fought for generations: not just country people coming into towns to sell their produce and their wares but every urban dweller, every artisan and craftsman, shopkeeper and street seller, would be free to buy and sell whatever and wherever they chose without having to pay someone else for the privilege. It was a radical concept of free trade which did not exist anywhere in Europe – and indeed still does not exist even today. Had the concession been allowed to stand, it would have transformed both the market economy and the structure of society itself, but once again Richard had acted 'without the assent of those who had the chief interest in the matter'. The same lords and prelates, knights of the shire and burgesses who had so vehemently objected in parliament to the abolition of villeinage would have been equally united and adamant in their opposition to a measure which would have removed their highly profitable trading privileges. Nevertheless, the fact that the rebels asked for, and were able to gain, Richard's support for this measure is a further clear indication that the uprising was not just one of the countryside: townsmen were not only involved but had a powerful voice in determining what was at issue.

In this context it is worth noting the two items on the rebel agenda which were not included in Richard's concessions. Despite the *Anonimalle*'s assertion that 'they asked also that no one should serve any man except at his own will and by means of regular covenant', Richard did not revoke the Statute of Labourers. It is possible that he gave an assurance that he would do this in the next parliament, but there is no evidence that he did so, and if he had it is likely that parliament would have rejected it. The second major issue which was not addressed was the poll-tax. The oath that the Kentish rebels were said to have extracted from pilgrims and other travellers in the vicinity of Canterbury included the clause that they would accept no tax in future except the old subsidy of a tenth and a fifteenth 'which their fathers and ancestors had known and accepted'.[53] Whether or not the king promised that there would be no more poll-taxes, this was the only stated rebel aim that was achieved, ironically only through default: fear of a popular uprising to match that of 1381 was enough to prevent any other English government even attempting to levy another poll-tax for almost exactly six hundred years.

Richard's complete capitulation to the rebels' demands has led many historians to believe that it was merely a cynical ploy on the part of the king and his advisers. In their anxiety to get the country rebels away from London they were willing to say and do anything that was required, safe in the knowledge that they could later claim that they had acted under duress and therefore all their concessions were legally invalid. This is exactly what did happen. When the new treasurer Sir Hugh Segrave addressed parliament at the beginning of November 1381, the first to be held after the revolt, he gave a very carefully worded account of what had happened:

It is not unknown to you indeed that our lord the king, during the said troubles, was constrained to make and grant letters of franchise and manumission under his great seal to the villeins of his kingdom and others, knowing full well that he should not do so in good faith and according to the law of the land, but that he did for the best, to stop and put an end to their clamour and malice, for he did not then enjoy his rightful power as king. But as soon as God, by his grace, had restored him to his authority and former state as king, and when the trouble had partly ceased, our same lord the king, by the advice of his council then about him, had the said grants revoked and repealed, for they had been made and granted under compulsion, contrary to reason, law, and good faith, to the disinheritance of the prelates and lords of his aforesaid realm.[54]

Aside from its emphatic reiteration that the concessions were the result of duress, the tenor of this speech is that of a parent making excuses for a wayward child. The young king knew he should not have granted the letters of franchise and manumission but he was motivated by the best of intentions and did not understand the consequences. The implication is clear that Richard had acted entirely alone. It was only afterwards that wiser and older heads had been able to intervene and extricate him from the embarrassing position into which his own naivety had led him. It is the royal councillors, not the king himself, who assert that the concessions were granted 'under compulsion, contrary to reason, law, and good faith'. What follows next is critically important to an understanding of what really happened at Mile End because, through his treasurer, Richard made an appeal to parliament over the heads of those wise councillors:

And now the king wishes to know the will of you, my lords, prelates, lords and commons here present, and whether it seems to you that he acted well in that repeal and pleased you, or not. For he says that if you wish to enfranchise and make free the said villeins by your common agreement, as he has been informed some of you wish to do, he will assent to your request.[55]

This only just falls short of saying that Richard had been forced by his councillors to revoke his letters against his will. It is also an explicit declaration that he was ready and willing to abolish villeinage, even if this time he felt obliged to seek 'the assent of those who had the chief interest in the matter'. All medieval kings were supposed to act on the advice of their councillors as a matter of good governance; as a boy of only fourteen Richard was in a peculiarly difficult position in trying to assert his personal authority and override the views of his council. This very unusual and highly personal appeal to parliament (not the sort of thing normally found in the opening addresses) was clearly an attempt to do just that. And in his mind it was not a question of whether the granting of the letters of manumission was right or wrong that was at issue: it was their revocation.

Richard therefore appears genuinely to have sympathised with the grievances of the rebels he met at Mile End and granted his letters to them in good faith. By using the Great Seal to authenticate them he utilised the most important symbol of royal authority: the more personal privy seal did not carry the same weight, literally or metaphorically. Unusually, Richard had immediate access to the Great Seal, which had been handed over to him two days earlier when Sudbury had resigned; no new chancellor had been appointed, enabling Richard to issue the letters personally without going through the usual formalities of the chancery department – or having to seek the approval of his chancellor. Revoking letters patent issued under the Great Seal was a serious matter and the young king was undoubtedly well aware that, in doing so, he committed a major breach of faith. He had compromised the moral authority of both himself and his government.[56]

Richard's willingness to accept the rebels' demands at Mile End had the unintended consequence of making the situation worse. Admittedly, it achieved the immediate objective in that it persuaded the men of Essex and Hertfordshire, in particular, that they had achieved what they had set out to do and could now go home, thus emptying the capital of many of the rebel bands. On the other hand, it legitimised further action because the rebels now knew that they had the king's sympathy and, more importantly, his authority for what they had done. The Essex band from Manningtree, for instance, speedily returned home declaring that they had royal authority to execute traitors and went to find their persecutor Thomas Hardyng: they were joined by some 275 local people gathered from every social group, from prosperous burgesses and lower gentry down to the humblest craftsmen and villagers, with their wives and families, who, when Hardyng was not to be found, burned down his houses at Manningtree and Mistley instead.[57] Richard Horsman clearly believed he was acting on the king's commission when he put himself at the head of a rebel band in Hertfordshire on 17 June, issued proclamations in the king's name and had a standard of the cross of St George made and paraded before him as he attacked the archbishop of Canterbury's manor of Tring and burned the records there. The rising at Winchester, which also began on 17 June, was triggered by Thomas Faukoner, who had ridden over from Guildford, where news of the king's letters had already arrived. He then went on to raise Farnham by means of 'congregation, debate and proclamation', all of which implies discussion of the king's concessions and a decision to act on them.[58] The major uprisings in St Albans and Cambridge, as well as the taking of Norwich town and castle, similarly all post-date the meeting at Mile End. The fact that so many of the rebels involved in these incidents carried the royal standard, or the standard of St George, suggests that they believed they were acting with the king's approval and under his commission: some of them may even have been bearing the actual banners that he had given them at Mile End.

CHAPTER TEN

Smithfield

It may also have been Richard's concessions at Mile End which effectively signed the death warrants of his ministers in the Tower. The exact sequence of events is not clear and the chronicles give conflicting and confused accounts of what happened. All we know for certain is that the king was not there, but since he did not return to the Tower after the Mile End conference that does not narrow the possibilities down. The likelihood is that the rebels broke into the Tower while Richard was at Mile End: hearing the petitions and granting the specific wishes of the various different communities represented there[1] must have taken a great deal of time, though it is likely that the concession that the rebels 'should freely seize all who were traitors and could be proved to be such by process of law' was early on the agenda since it was a common objective. The *Anonimalle* did not hesitate to make this connection: 'Because of this grant Wat Tyghler and the commons took their way to the Tower, to seize the archbishop and the others while the king remained at Mile End'; the account in the London letter-books also assert this cause and effect. Froissart, however, says that Wat Tyler, Jack Straw, John Balle and four hundred rebels invaded the Tower almost immediately after Richard's departure, while other chronicles blame those rebels who remained around St Katherine's hospital after their fellows had departed for Mile End.[2]

The biggest mystery of all is how the rebels were able to get into the Tower. Bounded by the Thames on its southern side and by a hundred-foot-wide moat which encircled the rest, it had two concentric sets of massive walls each with numerous watch towers and, at its heart, the great Norman keep, the White Tower itself. The only entrances were either from the city on the west side, over the heavily guarded bridge with its gatehouses and towers at each end, or from the river through what is now known as Traitor's Gate; in each case, however, these gates gave access only to the narrow outer ward so a second set of gates, both on the south wall, had to be negotiated. Even then, once inside the inner bailey, access to the White Tower was not at ground level but up a narrow flight of external stairs and through an even narrower doorway into the huge entrance hall which was the guard chamber on the first floor. The only entrance to the living quarters on the two upper floors was via a small internal spiral staircase. This was a castle built to be impregnable, and it had frequently been both a refuge and a stronghold for beleaguered kings with baying mobs of Londoners snapping at their heels.[3] How then was it possible for rebels armed only with hand weapons to break through its defences? The question has baffled both contemporary chroniclers and modern historians. There is no hint that Sir Alan Buxhull, constable of the Tower since 1366,[4] was complicit, either willingly or under duress like John Newenton of Rochester Castle. Even if the garrison consisted of nothing like the twelve hundred men-at-arms and archers whom Walsingham accuses of doing nothing to prevent the invasion, and even if most of them had left to accompany and protect the king on his way to Mile End, the whole point of the castle's defences was that they were designed to be held by a small number of strategically placed soldiers. And however large the rebel group that pierced to the heart of the White Tower itself, they could not have 'stormed' their way in.

The only feasible answer is that the rebels were let in, possibly by sympathisers or collaborators inside the castle, or more likely because the crowds arrived bearing one of the king's royal standards, given to them at Mile End, and possibly also his letters patent with a ribbon hanging from it to which was attached the distinctive wax seal, six inches in diameter, carrying the image of the king on horseback on one side and crowned and enthroned on the reverse.[5] Even the most illiterate guard at the Tower would have recognised the Great Seal of England and none would have dared to refuse entrance to someone bearing what they said was the king's authorisation to seize the traitors hiding there. It should not be forgotten that, despite Walsingham's contemptuous description of the 'filthy' rustics, serfs and swineherds with 'uncouth and sordid hands', 'ribalds and whores of the devil',[6] there were many relatively wealthy, articulate and literate men in the rebel ranks who were accustomed to office and, with the king's commission in their hands, quite capable of arguing their way past the guards. And, just as there had been throughout the revolt, there was evidently both leadership and an element of organisation in the attack. The victims chosen for execution were not selected at random and there were relatively few of them – only five are named by all the available sources. There might well have been other, less prominent casualties, but for all the rampage of destruction described by the chroniclers, none of them suggests that it was accompanied by an orgy of killing.

Having gained access to the White Tower the rebels went from room to room seeking their quarry. Both Walsingham and Froissart claim that they found the king's mother there, which seems unlikely if she had accompanied Richard to Mile End (as Froissart himself says) and neither of them returned to the Tower after the meeting. Walsingham angrily denounces the soldiers who he alleges stood idly by while the rebels 'arrogantly lay and sat on the king's bed while joking; and several asked the king's mother to kiss them' while Froissart has the rebels tear her bed to pieces so that she fainted with shock and terror and had to be carried out to the water-gate by her servants, placed in a boat and taken to her house at La Reole. Though we may doubt the princess of Wales's presence, the attack on the royal bed was true enough: Thomas atte Sole of Gravesend, Kent, confessed that he was in the king's bed-chamber on 14 June and that he 'ran through the bed of the lord king with his sword saying "that was for the traitors found there such as [Nicholas] Heryng and others"'.[7] Atte Sole was not implying any sexual liaison: medieval kings frequently held private audiences with petitioners and courtiers while sitting in state in the royal bed, hence the symbolism of its destruction by the rebels. This was a blow aimed at those who did not do their business openly with the king when he held public courts but secretly, in his private chambers, to which only a favoured few were admitted.

Two of those privy councillors were the most famous victims of the revolt: Simon Sudbury and Robert Hales, chancellor and treasurer of England respectively. That they were both clergymen at the pinnacle of their profession made their deaths even more shocking and the monastic chroniclers, led by Walsingham, did their utmost to portray them as martyrs. Sudbury's death, recounted in the lurid and gruesome detail beloved of martyrologists, is the great set-piece of Walsingham's description of the London uprising and the counterpoint to his equally fictitious accounts of Balle's and Straw's speeches. He describes the archbishop's gentle demeanour towards his murderers, his calm acceptance of his fate (in true martyr's fashion it took eight blows of the sword to behead him: after the first he put his hand to the wound and said 'Ah! Ah! This is the hand of God') and the miracles that occurred through his intercession after death.[8] The *Anonimalle* chronicler, on the other hand, who was probably a Yorkshire chancery clerk, did not fail to inform his readers that Sudbury had made an ignominious attempt to escape by boat through the water-gate but had been forced to turn back when 'a wicked woman' saw him and raised a cry against him. The descendants of Eve were always destined to be the ruin of the sons of Adam in medieval storytelling, but a Kentish indictment reveals that John Rous, and presumably others, were on the archbishop's barge that day, which explains why they were able to prevent him fleeing. The *Anonimalle* gives a pithier but more poignant account of how Sudbury, knowing that he was likely to be executed, presided over masses in the tiny eleventh-century chapel of St John on the second floor of the White Tower, heard the confessions of Hales and others gathered there, then recited the prayers for the dying and the dead, the seven penitential psalms and the litany of the saints. As he reached the words 'All the saints pray for us' the rebels burst into the chapel and dragged him out to Tower Hill, the traditional place of execution, and there beheaded him.[9]

The same fate befell the prior of the Hospitallers Robert Hales, the king's sergeant-at-arms John Legge and two further victims: the Franciscan friar William Appelton, a physician and surgeon who was executed simply because he was much favoured by John of Gaunt; and Richard Somenour of Stepney, one of the petty lawyers targeted by the London rebels who had made the mistake of fleeing for protection to the Tower.[10] That two minor figures such as Appelton and Somenour should have been identified by name as being so brutally murdered alongside such significant political figures suggests that there were no other victims at the Tower – though Richard Greenfield, a servant, was allegedly taken from his house in Bead Street and beheaded in Cheapside for having the temerity to speak well of Friar Appelton 'and the other murdered persons'.[11] The bodies of the men executed on Tower Hill were left where they fell since no one dared remove them for burial: their heads, however, were stuck on poles by the rebels and then displayed on London Bridge, just like the heads and quartered limbs of those whom the state had sentenced to death. The solemn excommunication of Sudbury's murderers, issued by William Courtenay, bishop of London on 1 September, adds the grisly detail that, having beaten, wounded and decapitated the archbishop, the rebels 'carried his head, to which his episcopal hat was affixed by a nail in the brain, through the city shouting, "Here is the predator's head"' before they displayed it with the rest on London Bridge. Once the revolt was over, Sudbury's body was interred in Canterbury Cathedral but, curiously, his head was taken to the collegiate church of St Gregory, which he had founded six years earlier with his brother at Sudbury, Suffolk. The hope that it might become a venerated relic of the murdered archbishop, attracting hordes of pilgrims like the tomb of St Thomas Becket at Canterbury, was disappointed but the skull is still displayed in his church today.[12] The final resting places of those executed with him are not known.

The one that got away was Henry Bolingbroke. If his father's physician had been executed because of his connection to Gaunt, then Gaunt's only son had no chance. Knighton, alone of all the chroniclers, notes his presence in the Tower, perhaps because of his links to Gaunt's household. Yet we know Henry was there, and that he narrowly escaped with his life, because John Ferrour of Southwark was later pardoned by him for his involvement in the rebellion of January 1400, not long after Henry had seized the throne. Ferrour's pardon explicitly states that it was granted because he had saved the life of Henry 'in a wonderful and kind manner' during the attack on the Tower on 14 June 1381.[13] Ferrour was a relatively common name in medieval times but the Gaunt and Southwark connections raise the intriguing possibility that Henry's saviour was none other than John Ferrour, alias Marchall, of Rochester, who like his fellow citizen Thomas atte Raven had business interests in Southwark and, with his wife, had been accused of stealing a chest containing a thousand marks from the Savoy Palace and taking it by boat to Southwark. The Ferrours were also accused of stealing two horses and wool worth six marks from the priory at Clerkenwell, as well as the unpardonable offence of laying violent hands on Sudbury and Hales in the Tower and dragging them out to be executed. Both were acquitted by juries but Ferrour was excluded from the general amnesty because of this last charge against him: he was eventually freed on 11 November 1383 when William Walworth confirmed that he had no case to answer. It is therefore possible that Ferrour's intervention which saved the young Henry's life also procured the dropping of the charges made against him in 1381. If the two are one and the same it is further evidence of a comparatively wealthy man taking part in the invasion of the Tower and the beheading of Sudbury and Hales. Ferrour had already been pardoned on 13 March 1380 for the death of Roger Tibrit of Rochester, whom he had killed a year earlier, so he was perfectly capable of murder, even if he would not kill, or allow to be killed, a fourteen-year-old boy just because he happened to be the son of the most hated man in England.[14]

Richard's concessions at Mile End may have persuaded the more moderate rebels from Essex and Hertfordshire to return home, but the execution of Sudbury and Hales, followed by their heads on poles being paraded through the streets, seems to have sparked off a frenzy of rioting and bloodshed more extreme than anything that had gone before. The main targets, however, were no longer the representatives of law and government but the Flemings. Xenophobia had always been a very English vice and murdering Flemings was a popular medieval pastime. Edward III had encouraged their immigration to bolster the skills of the native cloth trade and they had settled in large numbers in towns up and down the country. Like the Jews, they tended to live in ghettos, which made them easy to find, and, like the Jews, their financial success made them objects of envy. So when the Manningtree rebels were unable to find Thomas Hardyng they murdered a Fleming; when the Norwich rebels broke open the prison at Yarmouth they released an Englishman but murdered three Flemings.[15]

Londoners were especially virulent in their hatred of Flemings – though they did not fail to take advantage of the services of the Flemish prostitutes in the brothels of Cock Lane and Gropecuntlane. One of the first acts of the uprising in Southwark had been the demolition of a Flemish brothel near London Bridge and when Robert Gardiner of Holborn went to burn down the Hospitallers' priory at Clerkenwell he killed seven Flemings there.[16] Despite the king's proclamation that no foreigners were to come to harm, the London mob 'went on to the banks of the river Thames where the majority of the Flemings lived; and they beheaded all the Flemings they found without judgment and without cause. For you could see heaps of dead bodies and corpses lying in the squares and other places'. Thirty-five Flemings who had taken refuge in St Martin Vintry were dragged outside and beheaded in the street; seventeen others claiming sanctuary in another parish church allegedly suffered a similar fate. And it was not just Londoners who committed this slaughter: at least two Kentishmen were later indicted for killing Flemings in London.[17]

The king and his councillors were well aware that the continued presence of the Kentishmen in the capital would only further exacerbate a deteriorating situation. Aside from any political grievances the rebels still hoped to have resolved, any money or supplies of food they might have brought with them must all have been used up; since the Londoners were unlikely to continue to feed them voluntarily, they must have had to resort to theft and extortion simply to eat and drink. Even without this aggravation it was difficult enough to reassert any sort of order when the whole machinery of government had broken down: with the chancellor and the treasurer both dead, and no one willing to step into their shoes, even the basic step of issuing orders by means of writs was in disarray. Richard temporarily entrusted the Great Seal to Richard, earl of Arundel, on Friday 14 June so that the rebels' letters patent could be issued, but the sheriffs and other royal officials in London and its suburbs to whom writs would normally be addressed were now so terrified by the 'uprisings and popular commotions' that they did not dare to carry out the king's commands. Unwilling to return to the Tower after the murder of his ministers there, and in preparation for what was planned for the following day, Richard and his court spent the night on the other side of the city at the Great Wardrobe, in the shadow of Blackfriars.[18] This was a royal residence but, significantly, it was also a store-house for money and arms. Both would be needed for the coming confrontation.

Proclamations were being made throughout the city on both

Friday night and Saturday morning, urging all the rebels to go peaceably to their own counties and homes; one chronicler even claims that, on the advice of Sir Robert Knolles, the king had it proclaimed that John of Gaunt was on his way back from the Scottish borders at the head of an army twenty thousand strong. When these did not have the desired effect, yet another proclamation was made, that if the rebels all made their way to Smithfield on the north-western side of the city the king would come to talk with them there, just as he had done at Mile End.[19] West Smithfield, like Mile End, was a large open field outside the city walls: it was there that the weekly livestock markets and the annual fair were held. At the east end of the field stood St Bartholomew's priory, a wealthy royal foundation with twenty Augustinian canons in residence, and St Bartholomew's hospital, where a master presided over three brothers and three sisters who looked after the poor and sick. Priory and hospital had long been at odds, but in 1373 Simon Sudbury had resolved the main issues by granting the hospital practical independence from the priory and removing the priory's obligation to pay a tithe to the hospital.[20]

At some point, probably around nine in the morning of Saturday 15 June, Richard and his train rode down the Strand, past the smouldering ruins of the Savoy Palace to Westminster Abbey, to pray at the shrine of Edward the Confessor.[21] Having sought the saint's intercession, they then rode up to Smithfield, where Wat Tyler and his Kentishmen were waiting in front of St Bartholomew's hospital. The chroniclers disagree as to details but a member of the royal party, either William Walworth or Sir John Newenton, was sent to bring Tyler before the king, who had taken up a position outside the priory. Tyler trotted across the field on his little horse and Richard asked the rebel leader directly why they did not go home, urging them again to do so. Tyler replied that they would not leave until the king had given them further concessions and amended their letters patent accordingly.[22]

Exactly what these new demands were has proved controversial because they were articulated only by hostile chroniclers, leading some commentators to suggest that the rebels put forward a radical agenda which was so extreme that it was designed to make a negotiated settlement impossible.[23] They were certainly far-reaching reforms, but not actually unreasonable ones, despite the sometimes shocking spin given to them by the chroniclers. More importantly, they were a verbal expression of the issues which had driven the rebels and determined their actions from the start. One of the concessions sought, for instance, was the abolition of all monopolies on the hunting of wild animals, a grievance which had been articulated throughout the revolt by the breaking down of park enclosures and raiding of warrens: 'all preserves of water, parks and woods should be made common to all: so that throughout the kingdom the poor as well as the rich should be free to take game in water, fish ponds, woods and forests as well as to hunt hares in the fields'.[24]

A more fundamental demand was for the reform of the law and the way that it was administered. Walsingham presents this at its most extreme, claiming that Tyler wanted a commission to execute 'all lawyers, escheators and others who had been trained in the law or dealt in the law' and ascribing this to his desire to have 'all things ... henceforward ... regulated by the decrees of the common people; there would be no more law at all, or, if so, it would be determined by his own judgement'. The *Anonimalle* chronicler does not mention killing all lawyers but reiterates 'that there should be no law', adding the important proviso 'except for the law of Winchester'.[25] Quite what was meant by 'the law of Winchester' has long troubled historians: it has been contended that it was a reference to Domesday

Book, which on rare occasions was called 'the book of Winchester', and more plausibly that it referred to the Statute of Winchester (1285), which was regularly recited in the charges to the commissions of the peace.

It has been argued that this was because the statute presented 'an ideal of communal self-policing', setting out the regulations on, and responsibilities of, each community for keeping the peace, and giving 'the people the right as well as the duty ... "to possess the arms of free Englishmen"',[26] but the real explanation is rather more mundane. A rebel petition handed to the commissioners appointed to suppress the revolt in Essex by John Preston of Hadleigh establishes its credentials by opening with the familiar request (and it is a request, not a demand) that 'no one should pay annually for customary land more than 4d. an acre' in lieu of all services and less if less had been paid in the past. It then goes on to state: 'We also beseech that no court should be held in any vill apart from the leet of the Lord King annually and for ever. And also we beseech that if any thief, traitor or malefactor against the peace be captured in any vill, that you will give us a law by which he will be chastised'.[27]

The rebels were not asking for the abolition of all law, but only for the abolition of the private jurisdictions administered by the manorial courts. It is possible that getting rid of justices of the peace and royal commissioners was also on the agenda: they had certainly been one of the main objects of attack during the revolt, not least because their recently increased powers had allowed them to act outside the limitations of the established judicial system by enforcing, for instance, the Statute of Labourers. What the rebels specifically said they wanted to retain was the ancient royal system of criminal justice, founded on the annual view of frankpledge, which empowered local people to bring to account those whom they accused or suspected of crimes. The law by which thieves, traitors and malefactors were to be chastised if captured outside their own administrative area was the Statute of Winchester, the first two clauses of which dealt specifically with this problem. The abolition of outlawry in legal proceedings would also have removed another major source of abuse in the legal system since it was most often used against defendants who, through ignorance or inability, did not turn up at court. It had been regularly used by justices of the peace to punish labourers who flouted the Statute of Labourers and by sheriffs to seize the goods of anyone of the same name.[28]

The remaining demands identified by the chroniclers concerned the Church and are perhaps the only indication of John Balle's possible presence among, or influence on, the rebels at Smithfield. The Church hierarchy was to be swept away except for a single prelate over all England; the clergy should have their goods removed and divided among their parishioners, leaving them only with sufficient to live on; all property belonging to members of religious communities, except enough to provide them with 'a reasonable sustenance', should similarly be taken from them and shared among the commons. The disendowment of the Church was, as we have seen, a hot topic of debate at the time, with advocates ranging from Gaunt to Wyclif, so it should not have been a surprise to find it on the rebel agenda. Irrespective of the moral argument as to whether the Church should own property at all, it was the tenants of ecclesiastical landlords who had felt themselves most aggrieved by the exercise of lordship. That they should seek freedom by disendowing the Church was a logical extension of their rejection of the clergy's right to enforce arbitrary dues and services; it would also, of course, have removed the Church's right to collect annual tithes and the much-disliked obligation to give beasts, produce and cash as fees for christening and burial.[29]

The king's response was evidently more circumspect than it

had been the day before: he said that he would grant all that he reasonably could, saving only the regality of his crown, and reiterated his order that Tyler and his fellows should return home. The confusion of the chroniclers as to what happened next probably reflects the confusion on the day. They are united in their assertion of Tyler's insolent and uncouth behaviour, whether it was riding up to the king and failing to doff his cap to him, seizing the bridle of Richard's horse, addressing him in over-familiar terms or swilling out his mouth with water in the royal presence. This prompted an altercation between Tyler and one of the royal party, who rebuked him and daggers were drawn; either William Walworth or Richard himself responded by ordering that Tyler be arrested. At this point Tyler, perhaps realising the seriousness of his position, is said to have attempted to stab the mayor, but his blade was turned aside by the armour Walworth wore concealed beneath his cloak. Walworth retaliated by striking Tyler off his horse with a dagger blow to the head and one of the king's esquires, correctly identified by Knighton as Ralph Standissh, ran him through with his sword and killed him.[30]

Everything had happened so quickly that the rebels, taken by surprise, did not know how to react. As the situation hung on a knife edge and the cry began to go up that Tyler was dead and some of the rebels began to bend their bows, the young king took the initiative: spurring his horse forward and shouting that he was their king and their leader, he commanded them all, on their loyalty, to leave the field immediately. Both the *Anonimalle* and Walsingham further enhance Richard's bravery by having him order the rebels to follow him and personally leading them away from Smithfield to Clerkenwell fields, though they do not say what he did when he got there or how he managed to get away from the rebels again; it also seems improbable that his bodyguard would have allowed him to go unaccompanied and surrounded by rebels, yet if they had gone with him it could well have turned into a rout. Walworth apparently chose this moment to go back to the city, shouting that the king was in danger and that all able-bodied citizens should go to the fields to rescue him from the rebels. Knolles, with his fellow mercenary captain the Gascon Bertucat d'Albret, took charge of the city levies and soon had the rebels surrounded so that they would all have been slain had not Richard ordered that they should be allowed to depart, leaving behind their banners and any of the letters patent he granted them, but assured of his pardon if they went peaceably.[31]

The involvement of Knolles and d'Albret, both of whom had personal armed retinues at their disposal, suggests that they may have been lying in wait, ready for a signal to surround the rebels and overwhelm them, as had already been suggested they might do to the rebel hordes when they were massed around St Katherine's.[32] Was the Smithfield meeting therefore pre-planned by the king and his councillors as a deliberate plot to trap the rebels and kill their leader? This would have required a complete change of heart in the king which could well have been effected by the murders of his councillors in the Tower, but the fact that he was still willing to abolish villeinage five months later militates against it. And if the plan really had been to murder Tyler, then why do it openly in front of his men, who were bound to react badly? Tyler might have been deliberately provoked into drawing his dagger to provide an excuse for his assassination but a better outcome would have been to humiliate him personally and discredit his cause publicly by taking him alive, putting him on trial and executing him legitimately after due process of law. Why did Walworth have to leave at such a critical moment to raise the citizens – and why did the rebels allow him the time (half an hour, the London letter-books tell us) to do so? And if he could raise them, then why had he not done so before? Why did Richard have to take the enormous gamble of approaching the rebels and commanding them to leave if he knew that they were already surrounded by his own troops? If it was a plot it was highly risky, shambolic in its execution and out of character with the way the uprising had so far been handled. It is much more probable that Richard hoped to repeat the successful conclusion of the Mile End conference by meeting the rebels face to face for a second time: everything that happened was therefore simply a response to events as they unfolded.

Richard lost no time in showing his gratitude to those who had so signally demonstrated their loyalty to him at Smithfield. There on the field, beneath his standard, he personally conferred knighthood on the mayor, three of his aldermen, John Philipot, Nicholas Brembre and Robert Launde, and on Ralph Standissh, who had killed Tyler.[33] Standissh was not a young man, having served the king's father as an esquire for many years; nor was he wealthy, being the younger son who had not inherited the family manor of Standish-and-Langtree, Lancashire. On 14 August, therefore, 'for the better maintenance of his knightly rank', Richard appointed him constable of Scarborough Castle for life and granted him an annual income of ten pounds from the castle revenues, £16 13s. 4d. from the farm of the town and a further twenty marks from a Cheshire manor.[34] Another person was also generously rewarded: Sir John Newenton, who was already a knight and, since 1378, had been constable for life of Rochester Castle. On 16 June, just a day after the dramatic events at Smithfield, Newenton was granted a remission of forty marks in the fifty pounds he paid annually for the farm of Rochester Castle and town. A few weeks later he was also appointed to the highly profitable post of escheator for Middlesex, a county which included much of London.[35]

What had Newenton done to merit such valuable privileges, particularly as his perfunctory defence of Rochester Castle might justifiably have led to his forfeiture of office and imprisonment? It is possible that in his earlier role as emissary between the rebels and the king he had provided important details of the rebels' numbers, armaments and intentions, though not much use seems to have been made of any such information. The dating of his grant, however, is surely significant: it was one of the earliest actions of the chancery department, which was not fully up and running again, after the murder of Sudbury. Newenton must have played a significant role at Smithfield. Walsingham tells us that he was sent to persuade Tyler to come to the meeting – 'to ask rather than order (for Tyler's arrogance was already well known)' – and that it was Newenton who provoked the quarrel with Tyler by refusing to dismount before approaching the rebel leader because the latter was also on horseback. When Tyler angrily drew his 'knife (which we commonly call a "daggere")' and called him a 'traitor' – which would have stung, given Newenton's surrender of Rochester Castle – the latter responded by calling Tyler a liar and drawing his own dagger.[36] It is odd that neither man used a sword, the usual weapon for fighting on horseback: daggers were intended for close combat on foot, and giving the *coup de grâce* in particular, so they would have been inappropriate and difficult to use effectively in the circumstances. It is possible that Tyler was otherwise unarmed and that Newenton chivalrously responded by using the same weapon; on the other hand he may have been trying to draw the rebel leader into close quarters, which would allow him to be surrounded and assassinated. Richard's alleged intervention, urging Newenton to dismount and surrender his dagger to Tyler, certainly suggests that this was not part of a pre-planned strategy. Planned or not, if it was Newenton who succeeded in bringing Tyler to meet the king and manoeuvring him into a position where he could be killed, he deserved the king's gratitude.

With all the country rebels now on their way home Richard and his councillors could turn their attention to securing the city and ending the disorder there. After the slaughter of the Flemings the previous day, this had degenerated into opportune acts of violence committed by those who believed themselves wrongly excluded from their rights. Paul Salesbury, for instance, was a young man who had only just emerged from wardship: on 29 May his guardian had claimed fifty-two pounds from Salesbury's estate for four years' expenditure on his schooling, clothing, bedding, riding 'etc'. On 14 June Salesbury armed himself and his servant and forced entry into two houses which had once belonged to his father but were now owned by two aldermen, William Baret and Hugh Fastolf. Salesbury ejected Baret, his wife and servants into the street, made Baret's wife kneel at his feet for a long time and compelled her and her husband to thank him for their lengthy occupancy of the house and for not killing them; he then seized all the indentures relating to the property and compelled Baret to swear he would release a bond for two hundred pounds which Salesbury's father owed him. Fastolf was not at home (he was alderman for Tower ward and therefore probably caught up in events there) but Salesbury assaulted his wife, who was Salesbury's own kinswoman, compelled her to hand over a chest containing the deeds for the property, a sword, a pair of iron gauntlets and forty shillings, 'wasted' a hundred shillings' worth of wine and ale and finally forced Joan to hand over one penny in acknowledgement of his ownership of the house and its adjacent tenements. Salesbury was fortunate to have other friends among the aldermen and at court because he secured the first pardon of the revolt, on 22 July, through the good offices of Aubrey de Vere: his servant Thomas had to wait another six years to obtain his pardon.[37]

Salesbury was just a high-profile instance of the sort of clashes that were going on throughout the city. Others, too, took advantage of the breakdown of law and order to pursue their own agendas. Walter atte Keye, for instance, a brewer who had no chattels to confiscate, allegedly extorted 3s. 4d. from a fellow brewer Andrew Vernoun by threatening to kill him and burn his house down. More interestingly, he was also a member of a group which set out to find and destroy 'a book of the constitutions of the city of London called le Jubyle'. This was a compilation of reforming ordinances drawn up by a series of committees as a response to the scandal of the impeachment for corruption of Richard Lyons and two other serving city aldermen in the Good Parliament of 1376, the year of Edward III's golden jubilee. Depending on one's political affiliation, therefore, it either 'comprised all the good articles appertaining to the good government of the City' or 'ordinances repugnant to the ancient customs of the City'. Atte Keye and his fellow rebels made determined attempts to find it, breaking into the guildhall and, when they failed to find it there, forcing their way into the king's counting house in Milk Street on Cheapside and ransacking the place in a second futile search. The Jubilee Book was eventually burned in March 1387 on the orders of a specially enlarged common council summoned by the mayor Nicholas Exton, at whose request atte Keye had been pardoned a month earlier.[38]

The attack on the Milk Street counting house is a reminder of how little the London uprising was actually concerned with politically motivated acts of violence. A marginal note in the monk of Westminster's chronicle observes that the rebels attempted to plunder the royal treasury at Westminster on 14 June; the absence of the exchequer receipt rolls and their duplicates for the period Michaelmas 1380 to Easter 1381 from an otherwise almost complete series also suggests that the rebels might have deliberately removed and destroyed this record of the poll-tax returns.[39] However, neither Westminster Palace nor

Westminster Hall were attacked, despite being the centre of government, though it was perhaps fortunate that the law courts were not in session, so the judges of the King's Bench, Common Pleas and Exchequer were mostly away from the city. Westminster Abbey and all the other religious houses and churches in the city were left untouched: the Charterhouse, St Mary's nunnery, St Bartholomew's priory and hospital were all unscathed despite their proximity to the Hospitallers' priory and Smithfield. The Flemings were massacred and the Lombards allegedly robbed but Hanse merchants from northern Germany were protected by their English colleagues who, having just gained valuable reciprocal trading rights, were concerned that these would be withdrawn if anything befell them. In a letter written on 17 June the Hanseatic merchants assured their fellow league members at home that, despite the Londoners having 'killed many foreign people, namely any Flemings they could find ... none of us has suffered as much as a penny-worth of damage' and that their English hosts 'have told us that they will live and die with us'. Significantly, the newly appointed alderman of the Hanseatic guilds in England was one William Walworth.[40]

Fresh from his triumph at Smithfield, Walworth was immediately appointed to a royal commission with his newly knighted aldermen Philipot, Brembre and Launde, and Robert Knolles. They were charged with securing London against further invasion 'by illegal groups', pacifying any riots within the city and its suburbs and ensuring the security of the capital's food supplies, if necessary seizing victuals and bringing them in by land and water. They were given extraordinary and wide-ranging powers to punish anyone 'who makes or presumes to make riots, risings and assemblies against our peace ... either according to the law of our kingdom of England or by other ways and methods, by beheadings and the mutilation of limbs, as seems to you most expeditious and sensible'. The same day, 15 June, they were also appointed to a judicial commission with the chief justice Robert Bealknapp and the recorder of London William Cheyne, charged with pursuing the rebels in London and elsewhere and bringing them to trial; because the king's sheriffs and other officials were too afraid to carry out their duties, the commissioners were given sweeping powers to choose their own executive agents and to arrest and release prisoners at will.[41]

CHAPTER ELEVEN

St Albans and Bury St Edmunds

The London uprising collapsed as quickly as it had started but many of the rebels from outside the city would literally take the standard of rebellion back out to their shires, convinced that they had the king's approval and commission to act against traitors and secure in the knowledge that they had his letters patent granting them their freedoms from local lordship. One of those people was William Grindecobbe, who had travelled to London with the party from St Albans on the morning of 14 June. He had been present at Mile End and there 'had knelt to the king six times' to obtain letters patent for his fellow townsmen.[1] Everything we know about Grindecobbe and the revolt at St Albans comes from the pen of Thomas Walsingham, a monk at the abbey who made no secret of his loathing of the 'fools' who had sought to overturn his house's privileges.

For Grindecobbe to have successfully sued and obtained the very moderate requests he asked of the king was anathema to Walsingham, not least because it undermined his abbot's right to deny those same freedoms: the right to borough status; to pasture their animals freely within the town boundary; to enjoy undisputed fishing, hunting and fowling rights in certain places; and to be able to use their own hand-mills instead of being compelled to use the abbot's mills. These were rights which the townsmen had claimed in vain from the monastery for over a century. The issue of the hand-mills in particular had become a potent emblem of their struggle against the abbot's assertion that they were his villeins. The townsmen had collectively refused to use the abbot's mills in 1274, 1314 and 1326–7 and, on the last occasion, had won a major victory when they appealed to Domesday Book and it was confirmed that St Albans had indeed been a borough in 1086. It was a short-lived triumph. By 1331 the abbot had successfully lobbied the king to get the decision overturned, and restated his authority over the townsmen in a symbolic gesture of humiliation: he seized all their hand-mills, dismantled them and used the stones to pave the floor of the parlour next to the cloisters so that he and his monks could walk over them every day.[2]

It was against this background that Grindecobbe went to Mile End to reassert his town's claim to freedom from the monastery's ownership. In the face of Richard's approval, Walsingham could only lash out by attacking Grindecobbe's character, accusing him of betraying the abbey where he had been brought up and educated, and still had relatives; he did not mention the fact that the abbey had deprived him of an acre of land he had bought by charter in 1377, but attributed his campaign for freedom to a desire for revenge for being excommunicated and made to do penance naked before the brethren as punishment for laying violent hands on two monks who were measuring a tenement in the town. Now, to cap it all, Walsingham made the nonsensical assertion that Grindecobbe had also obtained a promise from Wat Tyler that, if sent for, the rebel leader would come with twenty thousand men to behead the monks, but only on condition that the townsmen would 'absolutely' obey all his commands.[3]

Having achieved what they set out to do without requiring Tyler's aid, Grindecobbe and his lieutenant William Cadyndon (yet another rebel baker) returned from Mile End on the evening of 14 June, leaving Richard Wallingford, 'the greatest of the villeins of St Albans', as their delegate to collect their royal letters. An abbey servant had got there before them, however, and told the monks what had happened to Sudbury and Hales, so the prior, four monks, the steward and some of the other abbey officials had already fled, embarking on a long and arduous journey to the safety of the abbey's daughter-house in Northumberland. On their return from London Grindecobbe and his fellow townsmen immediately set about dismantling the gates and enclosures the abbot had erected around woodland in the vicinity of St Albans and also demolished the 'Thwethonerhous' in the town, which belonged to the sub-cellarer, who was responsible for victualling the abbey and therefore for collecting the dues required as payment for using the abbot's mills. At some point also they attacked the houses of four abbey servants: John Clerk and Richard Scryveyn, who were both probably lawyers or clerks, the forester Robert atte Chambre and Simon Lymbrennere, who, if his name reflects his occupation, was a lime-burner who would have used the abbey woods to collect fuel for his kilns.[4]

The following morning, the day of the Smithfield meeting, the men from St Albans and its rural estates gathered in response to a summons which bore all the hallmarks of the calling out of the county levies. Walsingham says they all joined their right hands in an oath to be faithful to one another before formally reclaiming their ownership of the warrens and common woods and fields, and after catching a live rabbit there they fastened it to the town pillory as a public demonstration of their right to hunt on the abbot's lands. They then returned to the abbey and ordered the porter to throw open the prison, allowing the prisoners to go free 'solely on condition that they owed faith and loyalty to the community and adhered inseparably to them'. John Baron, however, publicly executed one prisoner before the abbey gates for an unspecified crime and stuck his head on the pillory, to the acclamation of the crowd, or as Walsingham put it in a transparent attempt to link the St Albans rebels with the unpardonable offences of the London revolt, 'with a devilish shouting which they had learned in London at the archbishop's execution'. At about nine o'clock that morning, in the wake of a contingent of the abbey's villeins from Barnet, Richard Wallingford arrived bearing a banner of St George, which he fixed in the square before the abbey as a meeting point for the rebels, then went into the church to present the king's letters to the abbot.[5]

Walsingham gives the text of the letters 'extorted rather than obtained' from Richard. They seem innocuous enough, simply ordering the abbot to hand over to the 'burgesses and good men of the town certain charters in your custody made by our ancestor King Henry to the said burgesses and good men concerning common, pasture, fishing rights and several other commodities ... as law and reason requires: so that they may have no reason to complain hereafter to us on this score'.[6] There are two oddities here: the letters are issued under the privy seal, rather than the Great Seal Richard had used for his letters patent, which may be explained by the fact that they were addressed privately to Thomas de la Mare rather than being public documents or charters. They are also dated 15 June, the day after Mile End, which would mean that the king would have had to have issued the letters at dawn for Wallingford to have delivered them at nine. Letters patent and close were usually back-dated by the chancery clerks to the date the king issued the warrant but in the chaos after the chancellor's murder and snowed under by rebel demands, it is possible that this practice was temporarily abandoned. Presumably that is why the king's letters patent conferring freedom on the bondsmen of Hertfordshire, which Wallingford also brought back with him, and Walsingham later copied into his chronicles, were also dated 15 June.

The abbot had little choice but to obey the king's direct orders and hand over the abbey's deeds and charters. What is interesting about the revolt in St Albans, however, is that the rebels were highly selective in what they wanted. They burned in the market-place various bonds, ranging in value from one to three thousand marks, which their predecessors had been forced to give the abbot as security for their good behaviour; they also burned the archdeacon's muniments, rolls and books concerning his civil and canonical jurisdictions. But what they were actively looking for was a specific document, an ancient charter that had two illuminated capital letters, one in gold and one in blue. This very precise description suggests that the townsmen had seen the document before, though the abbot denied all knowledge of its existence and was even prepared to swear on the sacrament that it did not exist.[7]

Yet Walsingham for one thought he knew what they were talking about: a charter of liberties and privileges granted to the townsmen by King Offa, which according to malicious gossip had been withdrawn and suppressed by the abbey. Walsingham denounced the old men who had spread rumours of its existence and proved to his own satisfaction that the charter was a myth because the town of St Albans did not exist until after Offa's death. However, the townsmen may have had a point because Offa, who had founded the abbey in 793, had also established a borough close by called Kingsbury. The growth of an abbey town round the monastery and its frequent clashes with its neighbour eventually led to a later abbot purchasing Kingsbury from King Ethelred and levelling it. The last remaining vestiges of the borough were destroyed by the abbey with King Stephen's permission and the site ploughed, sown and generally absorbed into the suburbs of St Albans, which was unwalled.

The 'lost' charter of King Offa has generally been accepted by historians to be the object of the townsmen's search, and has even been hailed as an important and striking piece of local political folklore,[8] but the specific reference to charters of 'our ancestor King Henry' in the king's letters to the abbot suggests an alternative explanation. In 1253 Henry III had granted legal freedoms to the 'worthy men' of St Albans in a charter which effectively recognised their borough status: this, too, the then abbot had managed to get around by changing the constitution of the town, but as recently as 1353 – well within living memory – the townsmen had succeeded in having it confirmed again by the crown. Five years later the abbot Thomas de la Mare, who was still in post in 1381, won the latest round in the long battle against the town by having the charter and its two confirmations revoked, annulled and cancelled by the Court of Chancery on the grounds that it was expressly contrary to the common law of the land.[9] This, surely, was the charter with the gold and blue initials for which the rebels asked in vain.

The abbot may have been disingenuous in his claim that the charter did not exist but he was determined to prevaricate for as long as possible before making any concessions. In this he was helped by the arrival of the news of Wat Tyler's assassination, the departure of the Kentishmen and the launching of attempts to restore order. No doubt he already had his delegates at court because the same day, 15 June, Richard granted letters of protection to the abbey, prohibiting any 'grievance, damage or molestation' of the monks and their property, though with the corollary that if anyone had a complaint against the abbot or his people 'we ourselves will make him give redress for the same, and make amends, as right shall demand'. As Walsingham gleefully noted, they were issued under the Great Seal, which trumped the men of St Albans's letters under the privy seal. The townsmen, in the meantime, had already demonstrated their new-found freedom in another act of great symbolism: they had dug up and taken away the mill-stones which had been confiscated from their forebears and used to create the monastery's parlour floor. Walsingham adds that they broke them into pieces and passed them round 'as the Holy Bread is accustomed to be broken up and given on Sundays in parish churches', but this was probably a malicious invention intended to taint the rebels with the sin of blasphemy as the stones were later restored to the abbey. He also alleges that the rebels proclaimed that anyone who was owed money by the abbey should come the next morning to claim it and they would receive satisfaction from the burgesses out of the goods of the monastery.[10]

By Monday 16 June the abbot could no longer stave off demands to find the missing charter by claiming fruitless searches and was forced instead to make concessions of his own. The previous day he had confirmed Richard's abolition of villein tenure in a charter relating only to abbey tenants in Barnet and South Mimms, adding that they could buy and sell land by charter unimpeded; his tenants in Rickmansworth had secured a similar concession for a carefully defined piece of land, where in return for specified rents they were given rights of common pasture, except for pigs and geese, and free fishing.[11] Such were the suspicions of the abbot's slippery character that even now the townsmen insisted on dictating their own charter of liberties which granted them rights of common pasture, bridleways through the abbey woods, common fishing and hunting with dogs and hawks, all within strictly defined bounds; they were also permitted to have hand-mills in their own homes and the bailiff of the abbey's liberty was excluded from St Albans unless he had the king's writ. It was hardly the most radical of charters, merely a reiteration of all the privileges that the town had claimed in the past, though the rebels, taking a leaf out of the abbey's own book, also made the abbot sign a bond to them for one thousand marks. Again, the terms were entirely reasonable. The rebels legally bound themselves to return the money if the lost charter was restored to them before 25 March 1382 or if, on that day, the abbot and twelve of the most senior monks swore on the sacrament that it was not in their possession. In a final formal ceremony the townsmen then went in procession to beat the bounds of the borough, marking out the extent of their jurisdiction, just as their forebears had won the right to do in 1327.[12]

Over the course of the next four days the abbot was inundated by tenants from his estates clamouring for their freedoms and was forced to concede twenty more charters in which he recited and confirmed Richard's letters of manumission. Tenants of certain manors also received specific liberties; Watford and Cashio, for instance, not only acquired fishing and hunting rights in their locality but also freedom from all works and tolls connected with the abbot's bridge and park, from having to attend the abbot's manorial court, pay alepenny or use his windmill; they too were now allowed to have hand-mills for their own domestic use.[13] What is striking about the entire 'revolt' at St Albans is not just the absence of violence (not a single person was killed or injured, though several properties belonging to abbey officials were attacked)[14] but the emphasis on legal documentation and due form: this was a quiet revolution by men who knew their rights and were determined to get them legally acknowledged and preserved in written evidence so that they could not be overturned again.

Unfortunately for them, the abbot had friends in high places. On 29 June Sir Walter atte Lee rode into town at the head of fifty men-at-arms and a great number of archers. Atte Lee was a major local landowner who had sat as an MP in the four most recent parliaments and was an experienced soldier, regular commissioner of array and justice of the peace. He was also a knight of the body to King Richard, despite his father having been disgraced and imprisoned in 1368 for abusing his powers as Edward III's steward of the household. Atte Lee used his influence with the king to secure a commission for himself, his fellow justice of the peace and John Sewale's predecessor as sheriff of Essex and Hertfordshire Edward Benstede, and Geoffrey Stukeley 'to make a good peace' between the abbey and its tenants. Though Walsingham says that atte Lee came to save the day because St Albans was in a state of terror and rebellion, technically it was only in 'revolt' because the townsmen were enjoying the concessions they had received from the king and the abbot. By 29 June all was peaceful: the uprisings were over not only in St Albans but throughout most of the country. Atte Lee's interpretation of his commission, if he had one, for there is no evidence of it in the patent or close rolls, was not that he should adjudicate over disputed rights but that he should restore the abbot's supremacy. He therefore ordered the townsmen to surrender their charters and that William Grindecobbe, William Cadyndon and John Barbour (who had also been involved in removing the mill-stones from the abbey parlour floor) be arrested and put in Hertford jail.[15]

What atte Lee had not counted on was the passive resistance he would encounter from the townsmen. A jury he brought together refused to indict anyone; Grindecobbe was released when his neighbours put up three hundred pounds as bail for him; the charters were not handed over. They even spent a small fortune employing the lawyer Sir William Croyser, who was steward of John of Gaunt's household and a member of his council, to plead on their behalf.[16] It was all in vain. Grindecobbe was returned to prison on 6 July to await trial before the king and Chief Justice Tresilian and, as royal justice incarnate approached St Albans, all that Croyser could do was negotiate a settlement between the abbot and his townsmen: the parlour-floor mill-stones would be returned, the house in the town would be rebuilt, the abbey would receive two hundred pounds in compensation for the damage done, and all the charters and bonds the abbot had granted would be handed back to him. Even at this moment, when everything they had achieved was being taken from them, the townsmen took care to make copies of their charters before they surrendered them so that they could be used in the next round of their fight for their freedom.[17]

In the end, all that Grindecobbe and his fellow townsmen had done was what so many other burgesses and would-be burgesses up and down the country had done for centuries. But they had the king's authority for what they did, had avoided violence against individuals and the damage to property had been minimal compared with other regions. There was no suggestion that they had been involved in the sack of the Savoy Palace or the priory at Clerkenwell, nor in the murders of Sudbury and Hales. Yet they were treated with greater severity than many charged with these offences. Even as harsh a critic as Walsingham, who felt personally slighted by their assaults on his abbey's privileges, was evidently shocked and moved by their fate.

Tresilian chose to assert his authority over the townsmen from the start by setting up his court in their moot hall rather than the abbey; the jurors again refused to indict but Tresilian, 'a most experienced judge, a man of great boldness and the cunning of a snake', persuaded them to give him a list of names by offering them the king's pardon for their own misdeeds. When it came to trial, however, the jurors withdrew their indictments, saying that their fellow townsmen were all good and loyal subjects and had always been so. That might have worked before any other judge, but not before Tresilian, who told them that if they did not proceed with their indictments then they would themselves suffer the penalty of those named in them. According to Walsingham, he even empanelled two more juries to confirm the indictments of the first, so that no man was condemned in St Albans except by the witness of thirty-six men, though this might have been one of the chronicler's many attempts to excuse the abbey's liability for what befell those who had opposed it. When some of the jurors charged the abbot with duplicity and having fomented the revolt himself, Tresilian compelled them to tear up their accusation and had it proclaimed that anyone who repeated rumours that the abbot had treated freemen as bondsmen would be hanged.[18] In the circumstances, the moving speech Walsingham had earlier attributed to Grindecobbe when he was bailed from prison seems entirely justified:

Fellow citizens, for whom a little liberty has now relieved the long years of oppression, stand firm while you can, and do not be afraid because of my persecution. For if it should fall to me to die in the cause of acquiring liberty, I will count myself happy to end my life as such a martyr. Act now as you would have acted if I had been beheaded at Hertford yesterday, for nothing could have saved my life ... they had accused me of many things and had a judge partial to themselves and eager to shed my blood.[19]

If even Walsingham could sympathise with Grindecobbe's cruel end, then how much more must his cowed fellow tenants who had dared to challenge one of the most powerful abbeys in the kingdom?

Grindecobbe, Cadyndon and Barbour were just three of the fifteen 'rebels' whom Tresilian hanged at St Albans in July 1381.[20] We do not even know the names of most of them but at least two had substantial properties: John Wylkyn had a dwelling-house, three farms, 164 acres of arable land, seven of wood, three of meadow and rents which brought him 27s. 6½d. and 2lb of cumin every year; Thomas Skot had a farm and garden, fifty acres of land, four of meadow, eight of pasture and two of wood in Little Hadham, twenty-four miles from St Albans, which he had purchased in its entirety eight years earlier.[21] Tresilian and the abbot obviously intended to make an example of the wealthiest men in the town. After rapid convictions the fifteen were drawn through the fields which they had so lately claimed as common pasture to the wood where they had asserted their right to hunt, and there were hanged, with orders that their bodies should remain suspended from the trees for 'as long as they lasted'. Even now some spirit of defiance remained, for Thomas de Wycresley came secretly and cut the cords by which they hung so that the corpses could be spirited away for decent burial. On 3 August the king ordered the bailiffs of St Albans to find the bodies and make iron chains by which they could be re-suspended and the sentence fully implemented. Walsingham delights in telling us that the townsmen were obliged to rehang the putrefying corpses 'with their own hands'. Wycresley's act of charity landed him in Newgate prison, though on 10 October he, or someone acting on his behalf, paid the large sum of eighteen shillings to purchase a royal pardon and obtain his release. Almost a year later, on 3 September 1382, Richard finally relented 'at the supplication of queen Anne' and gave licence that the bailiff and constable of St Albans, 'and any others who may wish to do so', could bury the bones without hindrance.[22]

Eighty other 'rebels' were convicted and sent to prison, among them Richard Wallingford, who had brought the king's letters from Mile End to St Albans, Thomas Peyntor, who had painted a standard of the king's arms for the rebels to carry in St Albans and John Dene who had carried it. The petty nature of some of the alleged crimes reveal the vindictiveness of both Tresilian and Thomas de la Mare (much as Walsingham tried to excuse his abbot by claiming he had interceded for the rebels): Gilbert Taillour was accused of threatening that if any man should die because of the uprising then the abbot's manors would be burned and the abbey itself cast down; John Wayt was similarly indicted for saying that the rebels would not get what they wanted until they had prostrated all the abbot's manors and the abbey too. If men could be punished just for saying such things it was hardly surprising that in August the tenants of the abbey's manors at Watford and Rickmansworth fled in such numbers that the harvest could not be brought in and the abbey faced serious losses: Thomas de la Mare's response was to secure the king's writ ordering the sheriff to round them all up and bring them back. Conciliation was not a word in his vocabulary.[23]

The most important rebel to be tried before Tresilian at St Albans was John Balle. When or where he had been captured remains as much a mystery as his whereabouts during the uprising. He may have been at Mile End or Smithfield, or both, but his presence is not noted by anyone, other than in the chroniclers' general lumping together of the three rebel captains' names wherever there was trouble. Walsingham and Knighton say that Balle was captured in Coventry. This is possible because on 3 August the town received a commission to investigate abuses committed by tax-collectors there, which may have been its reward. He was sent to St Albans so that he could be tried by the most senior judge in the country and before the king himself. They had spent the first seven days of July trying Essex rebels in Chelmsford and reached St Albans on 12 July.[24] Balle was tried the following day. Given that a chronicler of Walsingham's calibre was sitting right there in the abbey when the trial took place, we might have expected a great set piece, a real-life equivalent of his fictional account of Jack Straw's execution. Walsingham does indeed quote a letter allegedly written by Balle 'found in the tunic of a man who was to be hanged for his share in the disturbances', but his description of Balle's appearance before Tresilian could not have been more perfunctory or less informative. 'John Balle confessed that he had written this letter, and sent it to the commons, and he said that he had written many more beside; for this reason, as we have said, he was dragged, hanged and beheaded at St Albans on 15 July, in the presence of the king, and his quartered corpse was sent to four cities in the realm'.[25] And that was all. It is a myth that his execution was delayed at the request of William Courtenay, bishop of London, so that Balle could have time to repent of his sins: it was simply to avoid carrying out such a bloody act on a Sunday.

So John Balle, the fiery radical, excommunicate priest, charismatic torch-bearer for generations of religious and political dissidents, whose ardent words were said to have inspired England's first great popular uprising, went speechless to his brutal end. Did he deserve a traitor's death? What influence he actually had in inspiring the revolt or guiding its course is at best debatable. He cannot be placed with any certainty at any of the key events and his sermon on the mount at Blackheath is a fiction. The letters he confessed to having written were not treasonable in themselves, even if they were found on a rebel.

Tresilian's elastic concept of treason and his determination to impose the ultimate sanction on all those tainted by association with the rebellion meant that Balle would be condemned, whether or not he was guilty of that particular crime. This injustice was compounded afterwards by the way that the chroniclers, and Walsingham in particular, built up a simple wandering critic of privilege and abuse of power into a demonic figure who could be blamed for conjuring up a revolutionary whirlwind which they had feared would sweep them all away. Perhaps, after all, he was not the harbinger of doom but just a convenient scapegoat.

The records suggest that the revolt in Hertfordshire was almost entirely an uprising against the abbey of St Albans by its townsmen and rural tenants, though Walsingham's focus was naturally on events affecting his own monastery, and Thomas de la Mare's determination to crush those who had challenged his authority meant that actions against them are predominant in the legal archives. There are indications, however, that just as in Essex and Kent certain royal officials were also targeted. Hertfordshire shared its sheriff and escheator with Essex: they had already been assaulted on 10 June but now, after the Mile End concessions, three justices of the peace were also attacked. Thomas Longe of Watford, for instance, broke into John Lodewyk's house at Digswell on 15 June and carried off all the 'legal record, processes and indictments' he found there; the next day he did the same to John Kymperle's house but, finding the justice of the peace at home, compelled him to hand over the documents for burning together with 'three books of the lord king he had sought at John Lodewyk's house'. Another group, led by the delightfully named 'Hugo the personesprest of Puttenham', who must have been a stipendiary priest looking after the parish on behalf of the parson, burned the 'charters, letters, rentals and other muniments' of Edmund Stonor 'and other faithful subjects' and threatened to kill anyone who stood in their way or prosecuted them. Stonor, the son of a former chief justice, had little to do with Hertfordshire because his main estates lay in Oxfordshire, but he had served in the latter county as sheriff, MP and justice of the peace, as well as commissioner for the poll-taxes of both 1379 and 1380–1.[26]

The parson's priest of Puttenham was just one of many from the lower ranks of clergy who joined and even led the revolt. Stipendiary priests and chaplains who had no benefice of their own and acted in place of absentee (often pluralist) rectors, or as curates or chantry chaplains, were not above feeling aggrieved at the fact that they had to carry out all the duties of a parish priest without receiving any of the perks: they were paid a small wage but the tithes collected from their parishioners all went to the absentee parson, or to the bishop or religious house which owned the parish church. They were supposed to receive the fees for baptism, churching and burial, but even this was not always the case, and they were often required to teach in grammar schools as well as fulfil their employer's pastoral and spiritual duties. To add insult to injury, the wages of stipendiary chaplains were limited by their archbishop's decrees (most recently by Sudbury in 1378) and, uniquely among clerics, subject to the Statute of Labourers. They had suffered years of heavy taxation, convocation matching parliament's poll-tax grants for the laity and sometimes exceeding them. The notorious third poll-tax had been set at a flat rate of 6s. 8d. for beneficed clergy; the rich were urged to help the poor, as with the lay tax, but 3s. 4d. was still the lowest rate even a poor chantry chaplain or stipendiary priest had to pay.[27] This was not only more than three times the rate for the laity, but also a substantially higher proportion of their income than was paid by wealthier clergy. They shared many of the grievances of their parishioners, including the fact that their money was being taken to pay for an unsuccessful, ill-managed war in which good money was being thrown after bad to no purpose. Literate, numerate, accustomed to leadership but accessible in a way that their superiors were not, these disaffected clergy were naturally the men whom their parishioners would follow into revolt.

It was one such priest, the chaplain John Wrawe, who played a large part in drawing the county of Suffolk into rebellion. According to his own confession, on 12 June he had been present at a gathering of rebel contingents from Essex, Hertfordshire, Suffolk and Norfolk at the village of Liston on the Essex–Suffolk border: he had then sent a message back to his home town of Sudbury, just under four miles away, for reinforcements to join him in sacking Richard Lyons's manor of Overhall at Liston. It is possible that the gathering before the attack was a planning meeting, because the following day Wrawe and his recruits began a concerted attack on the abbey of Bury St Edmunds, one of the wealthiest and most privileged houses in England with vast estates across eastern England from Yorkshire to Kent.[28] The abbey also controlled the liberty of St Edmund, which covered most of west Suffolk. Granted to it by the king in the eleventh century, the liberty was to all intents and purposes run as a separate county by the abbot, who enjoyed not only the exercise of administrative and jurisdictional rights and privileges within the liberty, including the right to appoint officials who elsewhere were responsible to the crown, but also all the profits of government, from court fines down to fees for registering wills. After the rental income from the abbey's rural estates and market tolls, these fees formed the third-largest source of its income. The second-largest revenue stream, market tolls, was growing rapidly. Suffolk was becoming one of the most industrial and urbanised areas of England and, at eighty per cent, had one of the highest proportions of free tenantry – though, significantly, most of the villeins and villein holdings were still to be found on the abbey's manors.[29]

Bury St Edmunds was the administrative centre of the liberty and it too was thriving commercially. It was ideally situated as the hub of East Anglia, with Norwich and King's Lynn less than forty miles away and Ipswich and Cambridge under thirty. It was connected not just by roads but by a hugely important network of navigable rivers, providing power for the fulling mills and cheap bulk transport for goods which could be taken by barges, poled by men or pulled by mules or oxen, through the shallows of the Fens out to the North Sea. The town itself was unusual in having been laid out in a grid pattern before the Conquest with two great squares, one in front of the west door of the abbey and the other, the Great Market, near the Risbygate, where there were permanent shops and stalls as well as a tri-weekly market for the liberty. One of the largest stone buildings on the western side of the Great Market, with a bell tower that was a prominent feature of the townscape, was the abbey's toll house, where the abbot's bailiffs held courts and collected all the tithings, rents and other revenues due from the town. The abbey benefited from all this commercial activity by imposing a second rent above and beyond the lease for water-powered mills, and taking a tithing for all ordinary business transactions and a highly lucrative share of all fish caught in its rivers. Unlike St Albans, it did allow its tenants to use hand-mills for their personal use, but they were forced to pay to use its mills for larger-scale flour production. It had a finger in every money-making pie, from the supervision of a profitable royal mint down to renting out the right to collect all the manure from the streets to interested farmers. A steady stream of pilgrims making their way to the shrine of St Edmund, king of the East Angles, who was martyred fighting the Viking invaders in

869, added to the prosperity of the town and greatly enriched the abbey with its offerings.[30]

The townsmen of Bury St Edmunds had created much of this wealth but, like their peers in St Albans, resented the abbey's milking of their profits and refusal to allow them their independence. Though the townsmen had won the right in 1292 to have an alderman, who was mayor in all but name, they were still obliged to present three candidates to the abbot for him to make the final selection. And just like St Albans there had been disputes between abbey and town for generations. In 1327 these had flared into serious riots in which abbey servants were assaulted, its rural manor houses, barns and town houses were plundered and burned, and the abbey itself was besieged, broken into and looted and the monks seized. The abbot had been forcibly deported to Brabant and the prior and twelve monks held hostage in the guildhall and forced to sign bonds to the townsmen for ten thousand pounds. The abbot later cited around three hundred named individuals for these crimes, including three rectors and nineteen chaplains or assistant parochial clergy: the Franciscan friars, whom the abbey had doggedly refused permission to build a house within the town, paraded through the streets in support of the rebels and were later accused of helping the ringleaders to escape.[31]

The uprising of 1381 bore all the hallmarks of the great riot of 1327 but a more recent dispute had further soured relations between town and abbey. In 1379 the monks, led by their prior John de Cambridge, had elected the sub-prior John Tymworth as their new abbot; before he could be installed, news came from Rome that the pope had already appointed another Bury monk, Edmund Brounfeld, instead. The monks were divided in their support and, after the chapter meeting to discuss the issue degenerated into a brawl, Brounfeld's party enlisted the townsmen to their cause. They responded enthusiastically, not least because they did not wish to see the prior's nominee promoted to an even more powerful position, but partly because Brounfeld was considered likely to be more favourable to them as his brother was a burgess and his cousin Thomas Halesworth was then alderman of Bury. A large party of townsmen, including Halesworth, Robert Westbron, John Clakke and the parsons of Stansfield and Ixworth, forced their way into the abbey church, read the papal bull appointing Brounfeld from the high altar steps and returned a couple of days later formally to install their candidate. At which point, because the installation of a papal appointee was against the Statute of Provisors, Brounfeld and his supporters were arrested and imprisoned, the latter obtaining their release only on being bound over in large sums not to enter the abbey precincts or in any way harass the prior and his monks. This was not an issue that could be forgotten: as recently as 28 May 1381 the king had granted that half the sureties taken from Halesworth and Westbroun, if forfeited, should be given to the prior. And, since the pope did not give way and recognise Tymworth as abbot until 1384, Prior Cambridge was still legally the head of the abbey at the time of the revolt.[32]

The stage was therefore set for further confrontation when John Wrawe and his rebel band arrived in Bury on Thursday 13 June. They had made a detour on their journey to the village of Cavendish, five miles north-west of Sudbury, where Sir John Cavendish owned the manor of Overhall. Cavendish was one of the most hated men in Suffolk: a lawyer who had sat on every kind of royal commission, including those enforcing the Statute of Labourers, he had worked his way up to become chief justice of the King's Bench in 1372. Remembered by the legal profession for his refusal to estimate the age of a lady before him in court on the grounds that 'there is no man in England who can with certainty say whether a woman is of full age or not, for there are women of thirty who try to pass themselves off as eighteen', he was infamous among his contemporaries for being hand in glove with the abbey, which had regularly called on his services since at least 1357.[33] On the day the rebels came calling Cavendish was sitting in Bury St Edmunds, carrying out routine sessions of assize. Whether they looked for him at his manor, or indeed attacked his manor, is not known, though it seems likely as John Peek, keeper of the rolls of the King's Bench, had property in Cavendish stolen that day. All that Wrawe eventually admitted was that they had gone to the parish church and Ralph Somerton of Sudbury, who had stolen the keys, let them in and showed them where Cavendish had hidden his valuables in the tower. Cavendish had obviously taken this precaution because of the unrest already evident just over the border in Essex: only the previous day Richard Lyons's manor at Liston, just four miles away, had been sacked. Cavendish owned the right of presentation to the church, so he would have had no difficulty in persuading the parson to hide his possessions there, though he had not counted on someone betraying their whereabouts. The rebels carried off his silver, including a candlestick worth seven pounds, and a velvet tunic worth 26s. 8d., and went to celebrate at the tavern in Long Melford where they allegedly drank a whole pipe (105 gallons) of red wine and had to leave their haul in pledge until Wrawe returned to pay the bill out of his own money.[34]

News of this incident was carried so swiftly to Bury St Edmunds that by the time Wrawe and his band reached the town later that same day both Cavendish and the prior had fled. Wrawe had it proclaimed that all the able-bodied men of Bury should go immediately to the south gate to join his forces, on pain of execution, and prepared to seek out the fugitives. The chief justice had probably decided to make his way either to Ely or, more likely, given his choice of route, King's Lynn, but when he got to the abbey's manor of Lakenheath on the edge of the Fens, seventeen miles north-west of Bury, he was intercepted. Cavendish was a familiar and deeply unpopular figure in the town because of his suppression of the riots in 1371 and enforcement of the Statute of Labourers which had led to the two constables refusing to cooperate with the King's Bench in 1379. He was recognised and, with the townsmen in hot pursuit, made for a boat drawn up on the bank of the Little Ouse so that he could cross the river into Norfolk. Realising what he planned to do, a quick-thinking woman called Katherine Gamen pushed the boat out into the river, cutting off his only escape route. Cavendish was thus surrounded, overpowered and beheaded.[35] His chamberlain, who may have been with Cavendish at the time, later denounced a fuller, John Potter of Somerton, as one of the murderers; despite protesting his innocence Potter was tried, convicted and himself beheaded. Unless this was a trumped-up charge, Potter's involvement suggests that it was not just locals who committed the murder. Somerton was some twenty-five miles south of Lakenheath but less than ten from Bury, so Potter may have been one of the rebels who joined Wrawe's band in that town; a jury later gave evidence that Wrawe, his lieutenant Geoffrey Parfrey and four hundred men were in the vicinity of Mildenhall on 14 June, searching for Cavendish and John de Cambridge. Since this was the day Cavendish met his end, it would appear that they found him.[36]

According to an account written by John Gosford, the abbey's almoner, the prior may have had a day's start on the chief justice. He had fled by night to the house of a faithful servant at the abbey's manor of Mildenhall, some twelve miles north-west of Bury. There he hid all day before trying again, under cover of darkness, to make his escape by boat across the Fens to Ely, but an angry crowd of locals prevented him from going on board, and he only escaped from them with difficulty.

Instead, he decided to chance his arm by going overland to Cambridge with just a single guide to accompany him. Gosford says that two or three times the locals made attempts to detain him as he left Mildenhall, wounding him in the process, but the pair travelled some six miles before reaching a wood outside Newmarket, where the prior hid while his guide went to get provisions in the town. Instead of going into Newmarket, however, the guide doubled back and returned to Mildenhall, where he betrayed the prior's location to the men from Bury who were searching for him there. They surrounded the wood with cries of 'Where is the traitor hiding?', found the unfortunate man, frog-marched him three miles to Newmarket and allegedly spent the night taunting him as the Jews had taunted Christ on the eve of his crucifixion. (Gosford undoubtedly had his eye on the fact that the abbey had another martyr in the making, so was keen to draw the relevant parallels; in the process he managed to add an extra night to the story which is not borne out by other sources.)

On the morning of 15 June John de Cambridge was escorted back to Mildenhall Heath to be greeted by crowds baying 'Kill the traitor! Kill the traitor!' and forced to descend from his horse while the men from Bury decided his fate. It was a foregone conclusion, since among those present were men who had fought him and lost in 1379, including Thomas Halesworth and Robert Westbron: John Wrawe, who admitted being there himself, claimed in his accusation against the other two that the prior would not have been killed if they had not been present. Cambridge was allowed to make his confession to a priest from Mildenhall, then beheaded. His corpse was left lying unburied on the heath for several days but his head was stuck on a lance and carried back in triumph to Bury, where it was placed on the pillory next to that of Cavendish. In a gruesome piece of theatre, the rebels put the prior's head close to Cavendish's ear 'as though seeking advice', then to his mouth, as if giving the kiss of friendship, 'wishing in this way to taunt them for the friendship and counsel they had shared in life'.[37]

Having gained their two main objects, the rebels in Bury entered the abbey cloisters looking for further victims. They demanded certain monks involved in the administration of the abbey's property by name, and when they could not be found they clamoured for John de Lakenheath, the keeper of the abbey's barony, whom they dragged out to the market-place and beat senseless, then beheaded him too, adding his head to those already on the pillory.[38] Such was the terror instilled in the remaining monks that when the rebels demanded that they should bring all their charters and muniments to the guildhall they did so without demur, handing over also a solid golden chalice and a gilded and bejewelled cross worth three hundred marks as pledges that they would accept Brounfeld as their abbot and that he would confirm the townsmen's ancient liberties and any further concessions they would seek. Brounfeld's brother also pledged all his possessions that, if reinstated, the abbot would grant them all they demanded. His arrival was imminently expected as the Bury rebels believed that their fellow insurgents from Essex had already petitioned the king for his release. Unusually, though the townsmen were looking for ancient charters setting out their privileges, they did not burn or destroy the rest, since they were later able to hand these back intact.[39]

In the meantime, Wrawe's band in Bury had already released the prisoners from the abbey's prison in the Great Market, looted and demolished a tenement and its adjacent buildings belonging to the prior, and ransacked Cavendish's house in the town; Wrawe would later accuse John Talmache, esquire, a scion of what would become the Tollemache family of Helmingham Hall, of stealing the prior's bay horse worth twenty marks and keeping Cavendish's gilded and bejewelled sword, valued at one hundred marks, which Wrawe's own servant had presented to Talmache.[40] Other people connected to the abbey were also targeted. Edmund Herring, a clerk of the King's Bench who acted as the abbot's attorney, had his houses looted, and Thomas atte Ook, whose manor of Barham lay six miles north of Ipswich, was murdered. In 1369 atte Ook had provided sureties for the future good behaviour of the monks after they had secretly buried a monk who had been accidentally killed in a fight in their dormitory. He was not just a friend to the abbey but was also steward of the bishopric of Ely, a regular colleague of John Cavendish on royal commissions throughout East Anglia, a current justice of the peace in Suffolk and, perhaps most tellingly of all, a late addition to the Suffolk commission to assess and collect the third poll-tax.[41]

Just as we have seen before, particularly in Kent and London, the arrival of Wrawe had encouraged the townsmen to take up arms and carry out their own specific aims. Inevitably, after the revolt was crushed, Wrawe would try to save his own life by shifting the blame for the most serious crimes on to the townsmen and vice versa: in fact, the townsmen went so far as to allege that Wrawe's band had entered the town 'in the absence of the people of the said town of Bury'.[42] Not all the crimes could by any means be laid at Wrawe's door. They clearly had some common aims, but Wrawe had a larger picture in mind than just the conflict in Bury. The townsmen had needed little persuasion to join him, but it is worth noting that another agitator had also been at work. In July 1381 the alderman John Osbern accused 'Georgius de Dounesby of the county of Lincolnshire' of coming to Bury and claiming 'that he was the messenger of a great society [who] was sent to the town of St Edmund to make the commons of the town rebel'. Much has been made of this claim. There was indeed a place called

Dunsby in Lincolnshire, where the tenants of the Knights Hospitaller were refusing to perform their services, so it has been assumed that Dounseby travelled the seventy-five miles from his home village to make his pronouncement in Bury and that the uprising must already therefore have been in full swing in Lincolnshire. The more prosaic answer is that he probably lived locally, perhaps in Sudbury, and, like so many 'incomers', had acquired his surname to distinguish him from other Georges in the town: he could well have been the one making the proclamations to the men of Bury on Wrawe's behalf. What has caused palpitations among some commentators is the idea that Dounesby was 'sent by' and acting on behalf of 'a great society', which suggests some large confederacy of political activists with an agreed agenda who had been working underground to bring about the revolution. Other rebels were also accused of speaking on behalf of 'a great society' – Thomas Faukoner at Winchester and Adam Clymme in Cambridgeshire, for example – but the phrase was in common parlance and meant no more than a large crowd or gathering. Reading anything further into it than, at most, a group with a common aim such as the 'great society' raised at Romsey by the men from Winchester to carry out additional specific acts of rebellion, is a historical solecism.[43]

What are we to make of John Wrawe's involvement in the revolt? He has been dismissed as a bandit chief 'ambitious without ideas and greedy without scruples', whose confessions confirm that his 'primary objective was the levying of blackmail and protection money from the surrounding localities'.[44] This is unfair. His confession was probably forced from him by torture, and although he had turned king's evidence in the hope of saving himself he named only four obvious ringleaders among the townsmen of Bury as being involved in the murders of

Cavendish, the prior and John Lakenheath. The two oft-cited examples of his 'extortions' may not be all they seem. All too often in the course of the revolt, what appears on the surface to be a flagrant example of extracting money by threats of violence turns out to be a private quarrel, usually concerning an unpaid debt or a bond held as security, which the donor wanted cancelled. There is probably more than meets the eye, for example, in the fact that a group of Wrawe's associates from Sudbury, including Geoffrey Parfeye the vicar of All Saints church, Thomas his chaplain, Adam Bray, a tanner of Sudbury, and Thomas Munchesy the younger, esquire, whose family manor at Edwardstone lay six miles east of Sudbury, all went to Thetford, Norfolk, on 14 June and 'extorted' twenty marks from the mayor and corporation to save the town from being burned down. It is more probable, given Wrawe's influence and activities elsewhere, that they were trying to raise the town in revolt rather than destroy it. An even more unconvincing alleged act of extortion is Wrawe's accusation that Sir Thomas Cornard had threatened to call in Wrawe's band to kill John Rookwood and burn down his tenements unless he gave him ten marks. Cornard left with only eight marks, but this was almost certainly a family dispute. Cornard was the brother-in-law of Sir Robert Swinburne, a former and future MP for Essex, and the two men regularly helped one another in financial transactions; Swinburne was a close friend of the murdered chief justice, and with his son-in-law John Rookwood was executor of Cavendish's will. Given that Cavendish had been murdered that day, there may be a link to him, but it is inherently improbable that Cornard blackmailed Rookwood in such a way – and for such a small sum.[45]

Wrawe's deeds, rather than his words, mark him out as one of the most important leaders of the revolt in East Anglia, though frustratingly, like Wat Tyler, he seems to have sprung fully formed into action without having left a trace on earlier records. He was evidently a leader whose authority was recognised by rebels both in Suffolk and elsewhere, particularly in Norfolk. On 19 June Martin Mannyng, who was then staying in Sudbury, sent letters 'ex parte Johannis Wraw' to three men in East Dereham, Norfolk, which was more than fifty miles away, ordering them to return a freehold to Mannyng; the following day John Ikesworth and others broke into the rectory at Wickmere, Norfolk, 'by the command and warrant of John Wrawe' and by the same authority took goods valued at ten pounds from Brother Thomas de Hengam, a canon of the Premonstratensian abbey of West Dereham, who was probably an absentee.[46] Most significantly of all, on 25 June the Norfolk rebels who had compelled the burgesses of Great Yarmouth to hand over their charter of liberties cut it in two and sent one half to John Wrawe and other named leaders by whose 'abetting, consent, procuration and maintenance' they had achieved their aim.[47]

CHAPTER TWELVE

Ely, Huntingdon and Cambridge

The murder of Thomas atte Ook was an indication of the way the Suffolk rebellion, which had been centred on Bury St Edmunds, was now spreading across the county towards Ipswich. Adam Rogge, the son of a villein who, despite an early career of violence which included raising the hue and cry against his own mother, had risen to become bailiff of the earl of Oxford's manor of Aldham, led a band of men on 14 June to attack and rob the house of the local escheator William Gerard at Wattisfield; next day he stole goods worth one hundred marks from Roger Usshefield's house.[1] The quasi-official status of these acts committed by a bailiff was matched on 15 June by James, a younger son of Sir Peter de Bedyngfeld, who took a large body of men to the house of William Rous, the chief constable of Hoxne hundred, and allegedly compelled him under threat of instant beheading to give him ten archers from the district. He then rather undermined his supposed menaces by undertaking to pay them six pence a day while they were in his service.

Bedyngfeld employed them against Edmund de Lakenheath, a deeply unpopular justice of the peace who acted in an official capacity for the abbeys of both Bury St Edmunds and Ely, serving as constable of the liberty of St Edmund and steward of Ely's estates in west Suffolk. Lakenheath had already lost property in a suspicious fire at Lakenheath in 1378 which had destroyed many houses, cottages, market stalls and the prior of Ely's dovecot and grange and caused extensive damage to the priory manor. Now Bedyngfeld would lead his men to Stoke Ash, where he looted Lakenheath's house and held his bailiff to ransom for ten pounds, then to Gislingham where he again pillaged the house and stole ten cows, a bull, cloth and wool. Bedyngfeld would later return everything he had taken, but Lakenheath was not a man to forgive and forget: Bedyngfeld was pursued through the courts, excluded from the general amnesty and did not obtain his pardon until the Earl Marshal interceded for him in 1389. Even though the properties of the two men were a few miles apart, this was not a dispute between neighbours but part of a concerted attack on all Lakenheath's many properties within an eighteen-mile radius of Bury St Edmunds, in which his goods were stolen and his court rolls burned. Lakenheath himself was personally pursued with as much vigour as Cavendish. He did make it to the coast and was even able to board a boat to make his escape – only to be captured by the French whose admiral was cruising off the Suffolk coast. So, to add insult to injury, Lakenheath was obliged to pay a five-hundred-mark ransom for his release, bringing his total losses to one thousand pounds.[2]

The fact that so many of Edmund de Lakenheath's properties were attacked, even though they were some forty miles apart, suggests an agreed plan of action had been drawn up by John Wrawe, either in Bury St Edmunds or in Sudbury. His hand can certainly be seen in Ipswich, where Richard Talmache of Bentley, one of his lieutenants involved in events in Bury St Edmunds, spread the revolt. Perhaps because he was a locally respected figure, an esquire of good family, Talmache was able to recruit John Battisford, parson of Bucklesham church, just outside Ipswich, and Thomas Sampson, a collector of the second and third poll-taxes for Suffolk who served on the same commission in 1381 as the murdered Thomas atte Ook. Sampson was one of the wealthiest rebels to have his property confiscated for his crimes. In Suffolk alone he had land in at least three parishes, including 137 acres under cultivation, seventy-two horses and cattle, three hundred sheep, one hundred either hoggets or boars,[3] an eighth-share in a ship called the *Waynpayn* of Harwich and goods valued by the escheator at £65 12s. 8d., including silver dishes and plates and three beds with their linen. The parson, by contrast, had goods worth only five pounds.[4] Given Sampson's wealth and close involvement with the third poll-tax his decision to rebel is odd, but he was evidently opposed to the Statute of Labourers as he stood as a pledge on behalf of two of his servants who were fined for taking excess wages in 1380. He and Battisford were both excluded by name from the general amnesty offered in parliament in November 1381 and both were condemned to death. Sampson, however, turned king's evidence and, probably because he could afford to buy his way out of trouble, received a pardon on 14 January 1383; Battisford's fate is unknown.[5]

Battisford and Sampson went together to Ipswich on 15 June and there issued proclamations that everyone from Ipswich and the surrounding villages should on pain of death prepare to go with them whenever called upon to do so. The following day Talmache, Battisford and Sampson led their recruits out of Ipswich into the surrounding villages, where they took goods worth ten pounds from Christiana atte Ook, presumably a relative of Thomas, and one hundred marks from

Roger de Wolfreston, the former escheator. At Melton they broke into the property of William Fraunceys and carried off everything they could find, from gold and silver to his rings, kitchen utensils and beasts, amounting in value to one hundred marks. The reason why Fraunceys had attracted their particular attention is not mentioned, but next day Talmache 'on his own authority' arrested him in Ipswich, which led to his execution: it is unclear whether Talmache ordered this, whether Battisford was complicit or even, as some juries alleged, whether Fraunceys was then murdered by a pedlar John (or William) Dene.[6]

The rebels attacked and plundered several houses in Ipswich, including those of John Cobat, an assessor and collector for the second and third poll-taxes, a lawyer John Gerard and the archdeacon of Suffolk, the non-resident Roman cardinal bishop of Sabina, who still collected his ecclesiastical dues despite never setting foot in his archdeaconry. Inspired by these examples, rebels from slightly farther afield rose up in their own localities and broke into the manor houses of John Staverton, Lady Margaret de Sutton and the countess of Norfolk, stole their court rolls, charters and other muniments and ceremonially burned them. Agitators like John Genour and Simon Bullok rode northwards from Ipswich up to Framlingham, calling on each village through which they passed to rebel, so that by 16 June the whole of eastern Suffolk was in turmoil. There were serious riots in Lowestoft on 18 June which, unusually, were supposed to have been provoked and led by a foreigner, Richard Ressh of Holland, and, in a final act of defiance, as late as 28 June, when the earl of Suffolk was already in session trying rebels at Bury St Edmunds, the men of Bawdsey carried off and burned all his court rolls from his nearby manor of Hollesley.[7]

While some of Wrawe's ambassadors were spreading the

revolt across eastern Suffolk, others were crossing the border from west Suffolk into northern Cambridgeshire. Two of the principal leaders in this region were Robert Tavell of Lavenham and William Cobbe of Gazeley, who had been with Wrawe's band on 14 June when they looted the property of the prior and John Cavendish in Bury St Edmunds. They may well have been members of the group that went out to seek the fugitive pair the following day and been present at the prior of Bury's execution on Mildenhall Heath because on 15 June their band was at neighbouring Chippenham where they seized household goods, cloth, wool and cattle from the Hospitallers' preceptory and infirmary for sick brethren. They then made their way to Ely where rebels led by William Combe had already seized the only bridge and causeway into the town over the Great Ouse. Combe would later be tried and condemned to death for holding the bridge against the men of the king and bishop, but he freely admitted these Suffolk rebels.[8]

On 18 June, reinforced by recruits from Ely, Tavell and Cobbe's party struck out farther west intending to raise the town of Huntingdon, some twenty miles away. It is possible that they had been summoned by a sympathiser because John Smyth of Huntingdon was later beheaded there for treason. As the rebel band approached the town they discovered that the only bridge across the Great Ouse was held against them. This time there was no friendly bridge-keeper to greet them but William Wightman, a royal yeoman since 1357 and sealer of chancery writs since 1363, who had sat in all but four parliaments since 1361 as member for the town. Although his chancery role meant that he was rarely resident he had acquired property there, including most recently a tenement in 1379, and was one of Huntingdon's most important people. Unfortunately for the rebels, he happened to be at home, rather than in London, because it was the legal vacation. Learning of the rebels' approach, he had blocked off the bridge and, with the aid of the town bailiffs Walter Rudham and John Burtenham, called out the burgesses to defend it. There was a skirmish in which Walsingham tells us two or three of the rebels were killed and the rest put to flight.[9]

The escheator's records confirm that Robert Ffyppe was beheaded there and that his grey horse and goods worth 63s. 4d. were confiscated; he would later share the dubious honour of being listed with Wat Tyler, Jack Straw and John Hauchach as a 'captain, leader and chief' of the revolt, in his case in Huntingdonshire, who had been executed without due process but for legal purposes would still be treated as though he had been a tried and convicted felon. If he genuinely was a leader of the revolt his activities have not been recorded but it is possible that Wightman, as an influential chancery official, made sure that Ffyppe's name was included simply to prevent his family reclaiming his property. Wightman spent several years fighting the escheator and exchequer over the ownership of goods which the people of Huntingdon had seized from the rebels until in 1385 Richard intervened and gave them all to Wightman personally, except for 13s. 8d. belonging to John Smyth, which had been granted to the prior of Huntingdon. The king expressed his gratitude for this first act of concerted resistance in the history of the revolt by confirming to the burgesses all their borough's royal charters 'in consideration of the[ir] good and laudable action' and by granting Wightman himself a pension of six pence a day for life 'for his service in repelling certain commons of the realm lately in insurrection'.[10]

Tavell and Cobbe cannot have been too cast down by this setback as they did not return to Suffolk but decided instead to try their luck at Ramsey, ten miles north of Huntingdon, where they found shelter in the town and sent to the great tenth-century abbey for food and drink. The abbot, Edmund of

Ellington, was not a man blessed with any firmness of character (he would later be censured for allowing his monks to keep 'too many' hunting dogs) and, not daring to do anything else, he sent them large quantities of food, wine and ale, which they were said to have consumed with gusto and then slept until late the next morning. In the meantime, an armed force had gathered to resist them, led either by the men from Huntingdon, or by the energetic bishop Despenser of Norwich, who was hurrying back from Burley, Rutland, to suppress the rising in his own diocese. On the way, Despenser had already crushed a revolt against the abbey of Peterborough by its neighbours and tenants, pursuing even those who had fled to the church for sanctuary and, as Knighton tells us with great glee, smiting them down with swords and lances inside and outside the church walls and near the altar. Ramsey was also en route and only twelve miles from Peterborough, so it is likely that this 'agent of divine mercy' would have sprung to the defence of another beleaguered abbey. Tavell's band was taken by surprise as they slept and twenty-four of them were killed; the rest were either captured or fled, some of them being cut down as they tried to escape and their heads 'placed on high trees to serve as an example to others'.[11]

The accounts of the escheator tell us that Tavell himself was beheaded at Ramsey where his bay horse, worth thirty shillings, was acquired by John Grateford of Ramsey; the abbot was in possession of seventeen horses, nineteen saddles and bridles, six swords, two shields, one corselet, one short sword or dagger and further unspecified goods valued at £8 12s. which had belonged to Tavell, Cobbe and the other rebels. The goods of John Brux, who was also beheaded at Ramsey, were partly in the hands of his widow but mostly in those of Sir Hugh la Zouche, head of the commission to suppress the rebellion in Cambridgeshire and Huntingdonshire.[12] It is unclear whether

Tavell and Brux were captured and then formally tried and convicted, or summarily executed, though the wording of the escheator's account suggests the latter. Despenser had no compunction in these matters and Zouche himself was just the sort of royal official whose behaviour had sparked the revolt in the first place. Not only did he dispense summary justice to the rebels, ordering the beheading without trial of John Hauchach at Cambridge, he had no scruples about appropriating their possessions: he would later have to answer before the exchequer for acquiring goods worth at least a hundred pounds from Brux's estate which did not appear in the escheator's accounts.[13]

Three rebels from Cambridge were also executed in Huntingdonshire, though whether at Huntingdon or Ramsey is not known; four men from Ely escaped[14] and crept back home, where the revolt had already fizzled out because the rebels had made a clean sweep of all the 'traitors' in their vicinity. The uprising there had begun on 15 June when news of Richard's concessions at Mile End reached the town. John Michel, a chaplain who had left the Isle of Ely to join Wrawe's band, returned that day to become what his indicting jurors described as 'a sub-leader' in his home town. The day of his return, and possibly at his instigation, Richard de Leycester and John Buk went through the streets of Ely bidding the people to rebel and making proclamations to the same effect. Next day, it being Sunday, Leycester urged a crowd of townsmen to go with him into the monastery 'and there standing in the pulpit of the said monastery he would publicly show to them, the things to be performed on the part of the King and the commonalty against traitors and other unfaithful'. As a result of that proclamation Leycester and Buk led a company the following day, 17 June, to open up the bishop's prison in Ely, releasing all the prisoners, burned the bishop's books and then inverted the usual order of things to sit in judgment on Edmund de Walsyngham, a regular colleague of John Cavendish on royal commissions, most recently as a current justice of the peace for both Cambridgeshire and the university of Cambridge. Walsyngham, whose manor of Great Everdon, on the far side of Cambridge, had been plundered and the buildings demolished the previous day by rebels from that town, was sentenced to death. John Buk was accused of dragging him to the place of execution, violently assaulting him and stealing his purse containing 42½m., from which Buk gave twelve pence to John Deye of Willingham 'for his trouble' in beheading the justice. Walsyngham's head was placed on public display on the Ely pillory.[15]

Leycester and Buk were both condemned to death for their part in the Ely rebellion. Almost to the end Leycester retained his belief that he had his king's approval for his actions: at his trial he asked to be acquitted on the basis that he had chancery letters of protection for his person and property (perhaps issued at Mile End), but was told that they were not sufficient to save him. He refused to offer another plea when ordered to do so, saying that he believed himself to be pre-judged and condemned already. He was therefore found guilty, drawn to his place of execution and hanged as a traitor. Buk claimed first that he had only gone with many others to witness and hear the reasons for Walsyngham's execution, then that he had acted under compulsion, but when pressed further for the names of those who had forced him to attend he replied irritably that 'the devil had made him go' and, like Leycester, refused to say anything more and suffered the same fate. The escheator's records reveal that Leycester owned a tenement, a dovecot and two shops in Butchers' Row, Ely, and Buk four shops in Walpole and two dwelling-houses near the castle mound, so both were men of standing before the revolt. All their property and goods were confiscated to the crown, though twenty-seven shillings' worth of 'fish called Pykes' taken from Buk were given to John White, the sacristan of Ely, who had narrowly avoided the fate of the prior of Bury St Edmunds: the rebels had tried to hunt down and kill him, aided by the constable of Sutton who claimed to have been acting under duress, but White had managed to evade capture and lived to enjoy his persecutor's pike.[16]

Just as it had done in Ely, the revolt in and around Cambridge began on 15 June[17] and once again we are reminded that the king's concessions made at Mile End a day earlier led many otherwise law-abiding subjects to commit acts which would be classified as rebellion once those concessions had been cancelled. Geoffrey Cobbe, for instance, was married to the widow of Sir John Norwich and held substantial estates in seven places in Cambridgeshire and possibly others in neighbouring Huntingdonshire.[18] Yet on Saturday 15 June he personally led a band of his servants and retainers in breaking into Thomas Haseldene's adjacent manors at Guilden Morden and Steeple Morden, where he demolished all the buildings, seized all their contents, including his stores of malt, peas and dredge (a mixture of oats and barley), and sold them off to the crowd. What is more, he publicly proclaimed that this was being done with the king's authority. He did the job so thoroughly that it took two days, even though they were joined on both days by large contingents who had ridden down from Cambridge. Together they managed to inflict on Haseldene damage valued at one thousand pounds. The particular object of their hatred was intimately connected to John of Gaunt, being controller of his household, steward of his manor of Bassingbourn three miles from the Mordens and lessee of another, Babraham, some fifteen miles away. His properties in Essex and Hertfordshire were also ransacked by rebels in those counties and his horses, oxen, cows, pigs, sheep and other draught animals 'of no small value' were stolen, as he later complained to the king.[19] Two of Cobbe's servants were involved in another incident on 15 June, breaking into John Walter's house at Croydon, the village where Cobbe was lord of the manor, assaulting Walter's wife, stealing the keys to his chamber and making off with goods and chattels worth forty shillings. Cobbe himself must have believed he had fulfilled his remit because he did not take any further part in the revolt after attacking Haseldene's properties and was one of the first to sue for and receive a pardon: it cost him forty pounds but his forfeited lands were restored to him on 24 October 1381.[20]

Cobbe's happy ending contrasts sharply with that of another Cambridgeshire gentleman who joined the revolt. John Hauchach came from an old-established family with extensive landholdings in the south-east corner of the county; though much of his property was only a fifth-share in various manors and parcels of land, and even his title to one of the manors in Shudy Camps, where the family seat lay, was disputed by the parson of Fulbourn, he still enjoyed a comfortable income comparable to most gentry in the shire.[21] How or why he was recruited as the 'chief leader' and the 'person giving out instructions', as he was described in various inquisitions throughout the county is not explained – though his widow improbably asserted that he had been 'compelled' to do so by other rebels.[22] But again we come back to the point that he believed he was acting with the king's authority. He was certainly in contact with John Staunford, since both men were involved in an attack on 15 June on property belonging to Thomas North at Abington, where Hauchach himself held lands. Staunford's relevance was that he was a saddler from London who also had a small estate in Barrington, some eighteen miles west of Shudy Camps; whether or not he was genuinely present at the Mile End meeting, he carried around with him in Cambridgeshire 'a certain deed-box' which he told everyone contained the king's commission to destroy traitors.[23] And less than fifteen miles north of Shudy Camps was the home of another agitator, John Greystone of Bottisham, who had definitely been in London and Kent during the uprisings there, and had allegedly been in the company of those rebels who killed Sudbury and Hales. Just like Richard de Leycester of Ely, however, Greystone had genuine letters of protection for himself and his property, issued and sealed by the chancery, which, on his return, he not only showed to people in his home town but also travelled about to display in other places as far afield as Wilbraham, Swaffham and Burwell, explaining to everyone that they gave him complete royal power to raise and gather together the people of these places so that they could destroy traitors. Adam Clymme too had travelled about in this locality carrying 'a sign to gather rebels', which may have been a standard rather than a document, but he knew that the king had abolished villeinage and villein tenure because everywhere he went he gave out orders to all free and bond tenants, on pain of execution, immediately 'to cease performance of all dues and services'.[24]

It is usually assumed that men like Staunford and Greystone were fraudulently using documents already in their possession to raise rebellion, fooling people into believing that they were royal commissions. That might have worked with illiterate commoners who might only recognise the royal seal, but men like Leycester and Hauchach would not have been so easily deceived. Staunford, Greystone and Clymme were only spreading the news of the king's genuine concessions and it is not beyond the bounds of possibility that the letters of protection that Leycester and Greystone carried were issued at Mile End: though the pardons Richard had granted there were only for deeds already committed, rather than licences for future action, there was a widespread belief that he had authorised that traitors to the crown should be punished, with or without the king's caveat that this only be by due process of law. Even if

these protections had been issued before Mile End, it is understandable that their recipients would feel able to rely on them
as authority for their actions. Both Greystone and Clymme
would be tried and executed for their part in spreading the
revolt; Staunford, perhaps because of his London business, was
able to escape justice in Cambridgeshire, bought his pardon on
4 November 1381 and had his country estate restored to him
on 26 November 1381.[25]

If Hauchach was responsible for organising the action
against traitors in his part of the world, he did a very thorough
job of it. In addition to the attacks on Thomas Haseldene's
properties, Saturday 15 June also saw the sacking of the
Hospitallers' wealthy manor and preceptory at Shingay, which
had two dovecots, a watermill, a windmill and a preceptor who
shared a name with the late chief justice John Cavendish. The
Hospitallers' little house at Duxford, which, since being taken
over from the Templars in 1313, had always been let out at
farm, was also demolished. The current lessee, Richard
Maisterman, had been one of the collectors of the third poll-tax
for Cambridgeshire so was a target in his own right: he lost not
only his house but also goods worth twenty pounds, which
were stolen.[26] At least three of Maisterman's fellow poll-tax
collectors were also victims of the violence. Edmund Forester,
who had also been a collector in 1377 but was now a supervisor, was threatened and had to pay twenty shillings to prevent
his house being burned down;[27] John Sibil, who was both a
supervisor and a commissioner for reassessing and enforcing
the tax, had his manors of Horseheath, just over two miles
from Shudy Camps, and Upwer on the edges of the Isle of Ely
invaded, the houses and buildings despoiled or burned, his livestock stolen, including a valuable breeding herd of twenty-four
cattle and a bull, and even the fish from his fishponds which the
rebels dismantled.[28]

Like Sibil, Roger Harleston had also been both a supervisor of the third poll-tax and then appointed a commissioner to reassess and enforce it. A professional lawyer, justice of the peace, former sheriff and MP for Cambridgeshire in 1377, he was one of the most hated figures in the county and a perfect example of the sort of corruption that made lawyers a particular target of the revolt. As long ago as 1368 he had been summoned before the king's council to answer detailed charges that he had taken bribes, acted against his own clients' interests to obtain money and land for himself and committed 'frauds, deceptions and other ambidextries'. As a sample of his dealings (several of which involved rare matrimonial cases), he had been hired to procure a divorce for a woman but secretly cooperated with her husband until he received a further payment from the woman's father; in another case, acting as legal counsel for the sale of a manor, he had delayed completion until the purchaser paid him forty pounds, then arranged for the purchaser to buy the manor for much less than it was worth. Harleston did not deny any of the charges against him and was fined two hundred and fifty marks, but his career was unaffected and indeed prospered thereafter.[29] His house and guesthouse in Cambridge were demolished and looted of goods and chattels, including woollen bedclothes, an expensive blue and black striped coverlet, malt and corn, and his dovecot was burned down with its inhabitants still inside. His manor of Cottenham, on the edge of the Fens, was plundered of its livestock and wool which, together with the timber and lead stripped from the buildings, were all sold off on site to the highest bidder. (John Deye, who had executed Edmund de Lakenheath at Ely, bought six oxen, a horse and a bull.) Similar treatment was meted out to Harleston's tenements at Milton and Denny, north and east of Cambridge, and his barns containing corn and barley at Haslingfield, south of the town. Fortunately for him, Harleston himself could not be found, though rebels from Ely scoured the countryside hoping to kill him.[30]

All the usual suspects were attacked: the sheriff Henry English, whose Essex manor of Birdbrook had been one of the earliest targets of rebels in that county, had his Cambridgeshire manor of Woodditton sacked on 15 June; the king's bailiff William Margrete was obliged to hand over several large sums of money to prevent his house and buildings at Bottisham being pulled down; the escheator's rolls in the custody of Thomas Somenour were taken and burned.[31] Local justices of the peace and royal commissioners, such as William Bateman, who would be appointed to the commission to suppress the revolt, Sir Thomas Torell and of course Edmund de Walsyngham, who was beheaded at Ely, all had their estates ransacked and demolished.[32] The prior of Ely had his court rolls burned at West Wratting, as did the bishop of Ely at Balsham and the prioress of Ikelington at Ikelington itself.[33] John Hauchach was blamed for leading many of these attacks personally and accused of riding with a standard borne before him by John Peper, his henchman from Hauchach's manor of Linton. The only crime Hauchach was accused of committing in Cambridge was an attack on the properties of John Blankpayn, a wealthy burgess who had represented the town in parliament four times between 1373 and 1377, as mayor in 1374–5 and 1379–80 and as its assessor and collector of the third poll-tax in 1380–1. This last office might have been the reason why he was targeted, but his close association with Roger Harleston was probably a weightier factor, particularly since his fellow collector Richard Martyn was one of the town's leading rebels and personally led a force out to attack Harleston's manor at Cottenham.[34]

Although many of the townsmen and even some of the burgesses had joined in the sacking of country estates belonging to people like Haseldene and Harleston, the uprising in

Cambridge itself was largely an internal affair. And just like St Albans and Bury St Edmunds, it was dictated by tensions between the burgesses and the great institution which dominated the town: in this case it was not a religious house as such but the university. Founded in 1209, the university had been expanding rapidly since the first college, Peterhouse, was established in 1284 because a university education in 'learned law' had by then become a prerequisite for practising in English ecclesiastical courts. It was also the starting point for ambitious clerics eager to climb the career ladder in government service: both King's Hall and Trinity Hall were founded specifically to train up future lawyers as chancery clerks and diplomats. As the university prospered its powerful patrons also granted it many privileges, which made it independent of the borough, leading to constant friction between town and gown and causing serious outbreaks of violence in 1304, 1322 and 1371.[35] Tensions were already building again before the uprising in 1381. In November 1378 the university petitioned the king in parliament and obtained permission to hold the assizes of bread, wine, ale and other victuals in the town 'if the mayor and bailiffs be negligent or remiss'; the grant was extended for five years in 1379 and then for a further seven years on 4 December 1380, at which point the king had to order the mayor and bailiffs to enforce the peace because 'roberdesmen' and 'wastours' were plotting together and causing disorder. In February 1381 the king had to intervene once more, binding over five Cambridge men one hundred pounds each to keep the peace and sixteen prominent burgesses to obey and not obstruct the king's justices and commissioners by holding their conventicles. Among this last group were the mayor, Edmund Redmeadow, also known as Lister, John Mareschall and John Trippelowe, all of whom would play a leading role in the revolt (though John Blankpayn, one of their victims, was also bound over).[36]

It was alleged in parliament that the attack on the university was planned at a meeting held by the mayor, bailiffs and burgesses at the town's 'tollbooth' or town hall after their return from the raids on Shingay and Haseldene's properties on 15 June. They had elected an unwilling 'Jakes de Grancestre' as their leader and captain, with threats of death if he refused to act, but making him and his brother Thomas free burgesses of Cambridge as his reward. A John de Grauncestre was commissioner of array for Cambridgeshire in March 1380 and a James de Grauncestre would sit on the commission in August 1381 to identify the rebels who attacked the university: they were probably one and the same man, the oddity of the rebel leader being appointed to investigate his own attack on the university being explained by the fact that his involvement (if true) was not revealed during the assizes in July but only in parliament in December.[37] The plan of action was discussed and decided upon at a further meeting, held at ten o'clock that night, after which it was proclaimed that everyone should go to the house of the university bedel William Wigmore to destroy it and kill him. As bedel, Wigmore was the administrator responsible for keeping the rolls and other records, and collecting fines and fees due to the university; his house was duly sacked and his records removed but Wigmore himself was not apprehended and so escaped with his life. It is possible that he was hidden by sympathisers among the townsmen as, earlier the same day, Roger Blaunkgrene had only been saved from beheading by the active intervention of parishioners in the church of St Giles, where he had fled for sanctuary.[38]

The next focus was the newest college, founded in 1352 as an act of piety after the Black Death by the Guild of Corpus Christi, which met in the tiny Anglo-Saxon church of St Ben'et's. Because of its connection with the guild it was known as St Ben'et's College or Corpus Christi, and it had profited from bequests by the members to build up rapidly such a large property portfolio that an estimated sixth of the townsmen owed it rent in some form or another. This had become a source of tension, as had the college's links with its powerful patron John of Gaunt, who, in January 1381, had just secured Corpus Christi a royal licence to acquire even more lands and rents.[39] The rebels stormed the court of the college and the dwellings of its scholars, smashing down doors and windows and carrying off all the 'charters, writings, books and other muniments' as well as any valuables and other goods they could find.[40] The next day, led by the burgess John Giboun junior, the rebels broke into St Mary's parish church during mass and seized and broke open the university chest which was stored there and contained money and jewels. Giboun's father, perhaps hoping to save his son from the consequences of his actions, persuaded him to leave it alone by giving him a ten-shilling ransom for it, but Giboun simply went to the Carmelite friary, where the second university chest was kept, and made off with it and its contents. In a sad little corollary to this story, when Giboun was indicted for his part in the revolt he freely admitted being involved in the destruction of Haseldene's estates at Morden but denied breaking into the church to seize the chest. In the bald words of the assize roll, 'But John Giboun senior was called as a witness against him, and he was found guilty and hanged'.[41]

Just as their fellow burgesses in St Albans and Bury St Edmunds had done, the rebels in Cambridge forced the masters and scholars of the university to hand over all their charters, privileges and letters patent, including those granted by Richard himself. They took them to the market-place, smashed the seals with sticks and knives, heaped them up into a bonfire with all of the university's archive that they had taken from the bedel and burned the lot. In one of the more picaresque moments of the revolt, an elderly woman called Margery Starre gathered up the ashes and scattered them into the wind, shouting 'Away with the learning of clerks! Away with it!' Then, again like their fellow rebels in St Albans and Bury St Edmunds, the Cambridge rebels drew up a comprehensive new charter which forced the chancellor, all the masters and wardens of the colleges and the university scholars to renounce 'for us and our successors in perpetuity, any privileges whatsoever granted to us by any kings of England from the beginning of the world until the making of these presents', promised to pay three thousand pounds on Christmas Day to clear the bonds for good behaviour that the townsmen had been obliged to make and undertook to pay the expenses of having the new charter sealed in the king's chancery. (A clear indication, yet again, that the 'rebels' believed that the king would support their actions.) A second charter renounced in perpetuity the right to take legal action, real or personal, against any person in Cambridge on the basis of those bonds or any other obligations. Both were sealed with the university seal and the seals of each college. Curiously, given the care that had been taken to ensure that they were as legally binding as possible, the first charter was dated 1 May and the second 29 April; this is unlikely to have been a mistake, so we can only assume that it was a deliberate back-dating, though the reason remains obscure.[42]

Having thus gained a complete victory over one ancient adversary, the rebels turned their attention to another. The neighbouring priory of Barnwell, which offered accommodation to university students from the Augustinian order, had enclosed a piece of land called 'the Grenecroft' over which the men of Cambridge claimed ancient rights of common pasture; in doing so, the priory also blocked the road along which the townsmen had always driven their cattle. On Monday 17 June, therefore, the mayor Edmund Redmeadowe issued a proclamation to his townsmen and led them out to reclaim the

Grenecroft by force: they tore down the walls, fences and gates, cut down trees worth four hundred pounds, demolished the water-gate and carried off the fish, as well as sedge and turf cut from the land. The prior later claimed that they had also compelled him to enter a legal bond for two thousand pounds so that he would not prosecute them.[43]

There were a few more isolated acts of violence that day, including, ironically, the burning at Duxford of manorial court rolls and other muniments belonging to Sir William Croyser, who defended the rebels at St Albans; at about the same time his manor at Wrestlingworth, just over the border in Bedfordshire, was also raided and livestock and goods seized. Like the good lawyer he was, Croyser would later bring two private actions and secure a royal commission to obtain restitution of his lost property.[44] By the time the wrath of God descended on Cambridge in the shape of bishop Despenser, however, the uprising was already over. The rebels had achieved their dreams, punishing corrupt royal officials, regaining ancient liberties and setting out a brave new world order which would enable the king and his faithful commons to face a harmonious future together.

CHAPTER THIRTEEN

Norfolk

O f all the counties involved in the great revolt, it was Norfolk which produced the largest number of known rebels: 1214 have been identified from the existing records, compared with only 954 for Essex, 456 for Kent, 299 for Suffolk, 242 for Cambridgeshire and 389 for London and the rest.[1] Yet of those counties, Norfolk was the last to rise in rebellion, even though its economic conditions were much the same as in Suffolk, with a large proportion of its workforce employed as craftsmen and tradesmen or working for wages as servants and labourers. These were exactly the sort of people, as we have seen, who felt most trapped and exploited by the manorial system and government legislation, particularly the Statute of Labourers and the introduction of poll-taxes. Norfolk's slowness to respond cannot therefore have been for lack of motive, as the enthusiasm with which its inhabitants eventually responded to the call to arms indicates. What it does point to, however, is that potential rebels were not willing to rise until they learned the king had granted his concessions at Mile End. The early attempt on 14 June by John Wrawe's lieutenant Geoffrey Parfeye, vicar of All Saints, Sudbury, to raise the town of Thetford, close to the border with Suffolk, met with rebuff.[2] The Suffolk rebels were given money, perhaps just to persuade them to leave, but, unlike the townsmen of Huntingdon, the people of Thetford were not prepared to take a stand against the incursion of rebels from another county.

Despite this early failure, it was from the adjoining counties of Suffolk and Cambridgeshire that the uprising eventually spread into Norfolk. The first band to take action was drawn mainly from the Suffolk towns of Mildenhall and Lakenheath and their surrounds, and its principal objective was John of Gaunt. The group was led by three men: William Metefield, whose father was a free tenant leasing almost twenty acres of land in the bishop of Ely's manor of Brandon, where he was the main seller of bread and ale and served regularly as a manorial official; John Phillip, who was also a substantial leasehold tenant in Brandon and had held the two key manorial posts of bishop's warrener since 1368 (Brandon rabbits were a highly sought after delicacy) and his bailiff since 1374; and John Gelder of Feltwell, six miles from Brandon and just over the border in Norfolk, who had been living in Bury and had probably been with John Wrawe at Mildenhall.[3] Their first act, on 15 June, was to raid across the Little Ouse river from Brandon to attack the house at Weeting of John Strakour, an official of Gaunt who, in a village where everyone else had paid four or six pence in the 1379 poll-tax, had alone been assessed at two shillings. The rebels carried off his goods worth twenty pounds, which they left overnight with Metefield's father. Like John Giboun's father, William Metefield senior attempted to forestall any evil consequences for his son by returning the items to Strakour next day, but it was already too late.[4]

That same day, Sunday 16 June, his son's band burned the court rolls at Gaunt's manor of Methwold, eleven miles away, and destroyed goods and chattels belonging to both Strakour and Gaunt before moving on to Langford and West Dereham where they did the same to John de Methwold, Gaunt's steward for the manor of Castle Acre. He had paid the large sum of 6s. 8d. in the 1379 poll-tax and was described as a gentleman in the 1381 returns: he would later bring private actions against eighty-five of the rebels involved.[5] Having also attacked Binham Priory, this band made a concerted attack on the properties of Richard Holdych, who had served as sheriff of Norfolk and Suffolk in 1367–8, MP for Norfolk in 1369 and regular royal commissioner since then, including investigating tax evasions in 1379.[6] The rebels demolished Holdych's houses at Tottington, where they killed Thomas atte Brigge and Roger Davy, the manor's lessee, looted and demolished his residence at Didlington, making off with three hundred sheep, then took further property from his estate at Foulden. Perhaps as a result of this experience, though claiming it was 'on account of age', Holdych would petition for, and receive on 7 February 1382, an exemption for life from serving as any kind of royal officer ever again.[7]

His fellow royal commissioner Edmund Gurney, an 'apprentice-at-law', active justice of the peace and, more importantly, steward of Gaunt's estates in Norfolk, had his houses at West Lexham destroyed by the same band.[8] Fortunately, he was not there because, in one of the first acts of the Norfolk rebellion on 15 June, a proclamation had been made by John Rychmond of Walton, near King's Lynn, that if anyone captured either Gurney or his fellow justice of the peace John Holkham he should have twenty shillings as his reward. With a nice touch of irony, Rychmond had taken the money from Gurney's servant William Dauntre, telling him

that his master and Holkham were 'traitors and common pil-
lagers of the lord king's people', a phrase which echoed the
terminology of the law courts. Gurney and Holkham took
fright and fled to the coast, where they were lucky enough to
find a boat prepared to take them on board. News got out that
they were making their escape, however, and Thomas Kenman
of Holme-next-the-Sea commandeered another vessel and with
a crew of volunteers set out in pursuit for what the terrified
men alleged, with pardonable exaggeration, was over fifty
miles, though they managed to disembark safely at Burnham,
just ten miles along the coast. Another proclamation, this time
by a Walter Tyler living in Kettlestone, that Holkham was
hiding at the house of William de Ellerton, parson of St
Andrew's church, Thursford, was sufficient to send a gang of
men scurrying over to seize and kill him, but it turned out to
be a false alarm.[9]

On Monday 17 June Metefield's band arrived at Rougham,
twenty-three miles north of their original setting-out point,
where they would meet up with other rebel groups which had
worked their way up the county. Among them were recruits
drawn from Mildenhall, Suffolk, and Littleport, Cambridgeshire, who had entered Norfolk to burn the manorial court
rolls of the abbey of Bury St Edmunds at Southery and of
Gaunt at Hilgay. Another unpopular justice of the peace,
Nicholas de Massyngham, who was also one of the Norfolk
reassessors and enforcers of the third poll-tax, had his house at
Hilgay ransacked at about the same time. Massyngham could
not say that he had not been warned: John Coventry, a bowyer
from King's Lynn, had already sent him a letter threatening
that if he did not send ten pounds to King's Lynn, Coventry
would bring a troop of two hundred men to kill him and burn
down his houses. Massyngham had staved off that threat by
sending the money, but could not avert the attack by the other

band of rebels.[10] Another group which converged on Rougham was locally raised and led by John Bettes, alias John Creyk, of Wymondham, one of the most active rebels in western Norfolk; though he would eventually obtain a pardon in 1383 by pleading that he had been falsely accused by his enemies, he was indicted by so many juries across the county that his exclusion (twice, under both names) from the general amnesty in 1381 seems justified.[11] Yet another group came from the Diss area and was led by Thomas Gyssing, son of Sir Thomas Gyssing, the MP for Norfolk in 1379 and 1380.[12]

The rebels who gathered at Rougham on 17 June were therefore drawn from a wide range of places throughout west Norfolk, as well as from just over the border in Suffolk and Cambridgeshire. They included people from all ranks in society: gentry such as Gyssing; members of the village elite like John Clerk of Whissonsett, who was bailiff to the earls of both Arundel and Richmond and Andrew, bailiff of the bishop of Ely at Bridgham; and members of Rougham manor's tenantry, who had virtually all paid the lowest rate of tax in 1379. Forty of these rebels, including five women, were later brought before the manorial court on charges of violent breaking, entering and assault.[13] The object of their united hatred was John Rede, a professional tax-gatherer who had served on almost all of the tax commissions for Norfolk since 1377, most recently as a collector of the third poll-tax; not only that, but he was a professional money-lender, with debts owed to him throughout west Norfolk. Rede's personal residence was at Rougham and it was thoroughly looted and demolished: goods worth one hundred shillings were taken, including grain, horses (four of which were acquired by Thomas Gyssing), his pigs and even his mill-stone. It is a measure of the man that, despite what had happened to him during the revolt, less than six weeks later, on 25 July 1381, he had no qualms about accepting the post of escheator of Norfolk and Suffolk. Perhaps he saw it as an opportunity to exact his revenge.[14]

Monday 17 June may have been the climax of the revolt in west Norfolk, but in the east of the county it was just beginning. Agitators had been riding throughout the county for several days preparing the way for a major gathering at Mousehold Heath on the north-eastern outskirts of Norwich. John Bokelerman, for instance, who had stolen a horse at Holkham belonging to the abbot of West Dereham, travelled a distance of around fifty miles on his road from Rougham to Winterton-on-Sea. Henry Sherman and Simon Cook carried messages to Wighton and Walsingham in the north. John Gentilome and Richard Felmond, both from Buxton, were the 'principal instigators' in north-east Norfolk: they began their work on 14 June, the day of the Mile End meeting, were still riding from village to village calling on everyone to rise up three days later and may even have been doing so as late as 21 June.[15] In their indictments it was claimed that they were working for a dyer from Felmingham, a village fourteen miles north of Norwich, named Geoffrey Lister or Litster, though in the poll-tax return for 1379 he appears as 'Galfridus Lestere': all three were variant spellings of his occupation. It is recorded that he paid six pence in that poll-tax, one of thirty-eight to do so, compared with thirty-two who paid four pence and three who paid twelve; when his goods were confiscated after the revolt the escheator assessed them at 33s. 9d.[16] Though by no means poor, Lister was therefore not even in the top rank of his own village society, let alone a man of standing like Thomas Sampson in Suffolk or John Hauchach in Cambridgeshire. Yet, like Wat Tyler and John Wrawe, he apparently emerged from obscurity to become a major leader of the revolt.

Like Lister, most of those designated in the indictments as 'captains of the malefactors' who gathered at Mousehold Heath came from the area around North Walsham, including his messengers Gentilome and Felmond. John Trunch came from an old established family at Trunch on Gaunt's manor of Gimingham and had property there worth twenty pounds forfeited because of his role in the revolt.[17] Thomas Skeet and William Kybyte were both from Worstead: Skeet paid four pence in the 1379 poll-tax; Kybyte was a 'clericus' or clerk (in minor orders or a layman, one assumes, since in 1381 he paid 2s. 6d. poll-tax for himself and his wife) who possessed goods in Worstead worth sixty shillings.[18] But there were other leaders at the gathering who had come from much farther away, including Gyssing, who must have ridden hard (perhaps on one of his newly acquired horses) to get there after his attack the same day on Rede's property at Rougham thirty miles away. The most surprising new recruit was one of the highest ranking rebels of the entire revolt. Sir Roger Bacon of Baconsthorpe, just over twenty miles north of Norwich, was newly returned from south-west England, where he had spent many long weeks hanging around waiting to be deployed to Brittany as one of the ten knights out of twenty-four captains recruited by Sir Thomas Felton to lead his companies to the aid of Thomas of Woodstock. Bacon had recruited a retinue of four men-at-arms and five archers to accompany him and was personally responsible for paying their wages throughout the period of their 'service', whether or not he received due reimbursement from the crown.[19] Whether the mishandling of the war was his main motive for joining the revolt, or, as his later actions suggest, he had personal grievances to redress, Bacon was the only member of the Norfolk gentry who admitted voluntarily doing so.

The rebel gathering at Mousehold Heath, like that on Blackheath, was preparatory to entering the town. Norwich was the fifth largest town in the country with a tax-paying population of 3952 in 1377, which was probably at least double that in real terms. Surrounded by walls with more than fifteen towers, and with the huge square bulk of the Norman keep of the castle looming over the centre, it must have been a formidable sight. Fortunately for the rebels, the warlike bishop Despenser, whose episcopal palace stood next to the cathedral, was still making his way back from Rutland. Nevertheless, the bailiffs had made extra provision for defence, ordering all but three gates to be closed, reinforcing the guards at those that remained open and adding two extra constables to every ward. They had also sent messengers to William Ufford, earl of Suffolk, begging him to come to their rescue, but he had already fled: according to Walsingham, the rebels had had the same idea of putting him in charge of their forces but, on learning of their approach, he had leapt up from table, leaving his meal half-eaten, disguised himself as a groom of Sir Roger de Boys (one of his feoffees of Mettingham Castle) and made his way 'circuitously and through lonely areas to St Albans'. Though this smacks of romantic fiction it is possibly true, since Walsingham, as a monk at St Albans, would have been among the first to know if the earl had arrived there in such a fashion.[20]

At some point there was a confrontation between the rebels and Sir Robert Salle. Froissart, who turned this into one of his great chivalric set pieces, said that Salle was in charge of Norwich's defences and had gone out alone to parley with Geoffrey Lister to stop him burning the town: when Lister asked him to remember his humble birth as the son of a mason and join them, Salle responded angrily and tried to remount his horse to ride away but his foot slipped from the stirrup, the horse took fright and he was left on foot to face a crowd baying for his blood. Despite 'a marvellous display of swordsmanship', in which he killed or wounded anyone who came too close, he was eventually overwhelmed by numbers (sixty thousand, according to Froissart) and brutally murdered. As with so many of Froissart's heroic tales of noble knights, it is virtually impossible to disentangle what is the truth from the fiction. Salle may have had a hand in organising the city defences, though the burgess records suggest that it was done on their initiative and by the bailiffs. Norwich Castle was a prison and Salle had no role there. It is unlikely that he would have gone out of the city gates alone as no knight travelled without his retinue, least of all in such a situation, but the indictments confirm that he was indeed killed outside the leper hospital of St Mary Magdalene, about a mile north-east of the city on the edge of Mousehold Heath; Adam Pulter, otherwise known as Adam Martyn, was himself beheaded for having been one of those who 'feloniously killed and beheaded' Salle there.[21]

Salle was not the son of a mason; his family were well-to-do burgesses of Norwich. Nor was he a model chivalric hero, even though he had been knighted by Edward III. In 1360 he was pardoned all felonies, trespasses and any consequent outlawry for which he was indicted or appealed because of his good service fighting in France; two years later he was accused of assaulting and maiming the parson of Stanhope at Horsfield and on 28 January 1381 he had finally received a pardon for killing Robert Luce of Oxnead in 1369.[22] Despite all this, he had been created a king's esquire in November 1363 on a pension of ten marks a year for life. In 1373 he was entrusted with the custody of the English castle of Merck in the Calais marches, only to blot his copybook once again by going home to England without licence, allowing the garrison to mutiny and change sides so that the constable of Calais was forced to bring an army to recover it. Salle was pardoned this offence too, in May 1378, but everything he had left in the castle remained confiscate, except for a complete suit of armour and weapons for war, which were probably among his most valuable assets. It is tempting to think that this uncommon exception was made because the armour itself was unusual: Froissart says that Salle was physically one of the biggest and strongest men in England, but that was probably just poetic licence.[23]

Whether Salle was murdered as he tried to negotiate with the rebels, or more probably as he tried to evade capture by them, it was a salutary lesson to the burgesses that they could not look to the natural defenders of the realm for military help in their plight. An emergency council meeting in Norwich therefore decided that two of the bailiffs, together with eleven leading citizens, should offer the rebels large sums of money to persuade them to spare the town from pillage and fire. (News of what had happened to the Savoy Palace and the Hospitallers' preceptory at Clerkenwell, as well as the murders at the Tower, must have been common knowledge by this time.) The burgesses' offer was duly accepted and on Monday 17 June the rebels were able to make their way into Norwich unimpeded, either because the burgesses opened the gates themselves, or because so many of the townsmen had joined the revolt that effective resistance was impossible. Sir Roger Bacon may still have had some of his troops recruited for Brittany with him as his indictment states that he marched into the city at the head of the rebels 'with pennons flying and in warlike array'. They did indeed spare Norwich the general pillage and arson which the burgesses had feared but, as in every other town rebels had entered, they immediately set about administering their own kind of justice against the 'traitors' to the crown. Their first victim was Reginald de Eccles, a servant of the earl of Suffolk and an assiduous justice of the peace who was regularly appointed to the same commissions as John Cavendish, including those investigating Salle's assault on the parson in 1362 and enforcing payment of dues to the crown which the men of Lakenheath had forcibly resisted in 1371. Eccles had been captured in his lodgings at Heigham, on the outskirts of Norwich, by a group which included one of Salle's murderers: Adam Pulter, who came from Heigham. All his rolls, records and documents pertaining to his office were burned, his furred gown and other goods were stolen and Eccles himself was dragged to the pillory in Norwich, stabbed in the abdomen and then beheaded. At least one indictment accused Bacon of delivering the fatal blow and cutting off his head, though other less well-known figures were also blamed.[24]

The 'day of bloodshed and plunder'[25] in Norwich was nothing of the sort. Salle and Eccles appear to have been the only ones who lost their lives. Salle's house in the city was plundered of goods worth two hundred pounds, which suggests there was something more to his death than simply refusing to cooperate with the rebels; this is supported by the fact that his murderers would later claim that they had acted on the king's orders, suggesting that they identified him as one of the traitors to the crown who was to be punished.[26] The house of William de Swynflet, archdeacon of Norwich, the diocesan administrator and second-in-command to bishop Despenser, was also ransacked. Henry Lomynour's residence was looted of goods he alleged were worth a thousand marks. Lomynour was a wealthy merchant and one of the most important burgesses of Norwich, having served two terms as bailiff and being currently both a justice of the peace and a member of the Norfolk reassessment and enforcement commission for the third poll-tax. Despite being an obvious target, he had been one of the eleven burgesses chosen to talk with the rebels and bribe them not to burn the town. He was neither physically threatened nor personally harmed in any way – though that did not stop him bringing actions against six hundred people from a hundred places in and around Norwich whom he accused of attacking his house.[27] Walter Bixton, who had served four times as both MP and bailiff for Norwich, was a surveyor and controller of the collection of the third poll-tax in the city: his house was sacked and he was forced by one of his debtors to hand over 6s. 8d. in cash and remit seven pounds from the debt he was owed. Another tax-collector, John Fychet, was pursued to Mousehold and threatened with death until he promised that he would never levy another tax again.[28]

Terrifying and traumatic though the events of 17 June must have been to those unwillingly caught up in them, they paled into insignificance compared with the violence in other towns. What was genuinely unusual about the revolt in Norwich was that at least four prominent members of the local gentry were said by Walsingham to have been taken hostage and forced to act as servants to Geoffrey Lister, 'who called himself "King of the Commons"'. Salle's fate had taught them the need to dissimulate, so 'they praised all that the rebels praised and cursed everything the rebels disliked', and waited upon him with bended knee. The captives were all knights, though as Walsingham confused the names at least two cannot be identified with any certainty. They appear to have been the sire de Scales, who could have been any one of several members of that extensive family,[29] and probably Sir Thomas de Morlee, whose manor of Great Bromley, Essex, had been invaded by its own bond tenants, who had insulted the lessee Lady Anne de Leyre 'in her hall and threatened her' then carried away all the court rolls and burned them. The third knight was Sir John de Brewes, a former sheriff of Norfolk and Suffolk, who had fought in the French wars since the siege of Calais in 1346–7 and whose court rolls at his Norfolk manor of Heydon would be burned by rebels on 21 June; he was a member of the third poll-tax reassessment and enforcement commission.[30] The fourth and most important of these captives, according to Walsingham, was Sir Stephen de Hales, whom Lister was said to have forced to cut up and taste his meat before he ate it – a menial job

normally reserved for an esquire in a noble household. Hales
was in his fifties, a man with a long professional career as a soldier in France, who had been retained by the Black Prince in
1372 for the huge sum of a hundred marks a year for life. This
grant had been confirmed by Richard, who had also relied on
him, as he relied on his father's other retainers, for administration in the shires. Hales had thus become MP for Norfolk in
1377 and 1380, sheriff in 1378–9, a justice of the peace in 1380
and both a controller and surveyor of the third poll-tax and
then a reassessor and enforcer.[31]

Why, then, were Brewes and Hales in particular spared the
fate of Reginald de Eccles? If Walsingham's story is true – it is
not corroborated by any other source – then the only reason
can have been publicly to humiliate them. Sir John Newenton
was not, so far as we know, treated in such a way by his
Kentish captors. To have one of the greatest men in the county
compelled to serve a humble dyer was an inversion of the hierarchy of medieval society. It has rightly been compared to
folklore customs which similarly reversed the social order, such
as the election of Lords of Misrule during the Christmas fes-
tivities and, more particularly, the 'somergamen', the revels held
around midsummer, in which mock kings were crowned amid
much feasting and drinking. John atte Forth, for example, was
heavily fined in 1363 because he entered the precincts of his
local lord of the manor at Polstead, Suffolk, 'and together with
others played in the lord's hall a game called a somergamen'.
Since Hales's humiliation and Lister's elevation occurred
between Whitsuntide and Midsummer's Day, they would naturally fall into the pattern of the customary year, just as the
rebels' carefully staged public burnings of court rolls and insti-
tutional records echoed the midsummer ritual of lighting great
parish bonfires.[32] Yet there was also another element to Hales
and his fellow prisoners being forced to wait on Lister. It was

a custom more honoured in the breach than the observance that enemies captured in battle should wait upon the victors: the Black Prince, for instance, garnered much praise for refusing to do this after the battle of Poitiers, allowing the king of France and his other prisoners to sit while he chivalrously waited upon them.[33]

The possibility that the four knights willingly collaborated with the rebels and then claimed coercion, as so many others would do when faced with the consequences of their actions, should not be dismissed out of hand. One piece of evidence which might support their claim comes from the Norfolk commission appointed to suppress the revolt and deal with the rebels. When William Tayllour appeared before them he was identified by John Brewes as one of those who had threatened to behead him on 18 June in Norwich, in the presence of Stephen Hales and Sir Thomas Gyssing. Since both Brewes and Hales were members of the commission, and Hales, Gyssing and others confirmed the truth of Brewes's accusation, Tayllour was immediately convicted and executed on their word alone.[34] Beyond the lack of due process involved, the oddity of this is that Sir Thomas Gyssing should have been in Norwich that day and observed Brewes being threatened. Unless it is a confusion with his son, who admitted being there with the rebels at this time, either Gyssing senior was also a hostage or he too had joined the insurgents.

The younger Gyssing appears to have remained in Norwich when Bacon, Lister, Thomas Skeet, William Kybyte, John Trunch and a large group of rebels set out for the coast on 18 June. Lister's messengers, Felmond and Gentilome, went on ahead to raise the village of Billockby, while the main group made its way to Great Yarmouth. The town had been granted borough status by King John and was a hugely important centre for the herring trade: catches were landed there for distribution throughout the east of England and also for export abroad. Yarmouth had always had a prickly relationship with its neighbours on the east coast and with the Cinque Ports, but these had worsened considerably in recent years. This was due to the fact that in 1372, as other approaches to the town silted up, Edward III had granted the burgesses a further charter annexing the seaboard harbour of Kirkley Road, six miles away in Suffolk, with the right to levy tolls and customs on all trade passing through and, more importantly, prohibiting any vessels, English or foreign, from loading or unloading herrings or any other merchandise for sale within twenty-one miles of Yarmouth. In effect, the charter gave the town a complete monopoly on all sea-borne trade and forced the fishermen and traders of Lowestoft and other ports along the coast out of business, unless they chose to pay the tolls and use the quays at Kirkley Road. If the wind was against them, however, and they could not land there, they were not allowed to enter Yarmouth, so had to dump their catches at sea. In 1376 the Good Parliament repealed the charter as being 'contrary to the common profit of the realm' and impeached and imprisoned William Elys, the farmer of customs at Yarmouth, for extortion and corruption. Two years later, parliament reversed the decision and Richard granted a new charter, confirming the monopoly: when the under-sheriff tried to proclaim it at Lowestoft he was stoned and run out of town by the furious inhabitants.[35]

As recently as April 1381 the king had appointed yet another commission to inquire into the complaint of the commons of Norfolk and Suffolk that the burgesses of Great Yarmouth were using their charter to prevent them buying or selling victuals at Kirkley Road at any time of year. When Bacon and his cohorts rode into Great Yarmouth on 18 June they came expressly to right this wrong. They confronted the burgesses, compelled them to hand over their precious charter and proceeded to cut it in two, sending one half to John Wrawe, Edmund Hemmyng and many others in Lowestoft and the wider county of Suffolk to show them that this had been done with their help, consent and advice. The following day Hemmyng was to be found at Kirkley Road, collecting in the tolls and customs on behalf of the rebels according to the proclamation of Roger Bacon.[36] While in Yarmouth the rebels broke open the town prison and freed John Cook of Coventry but beheaded three Flemings they found there; Bacon also freed two thieves in the custody of the local constables for stealing a cow because, the indictment alleged, Bacon 'was obedient to all the laws and orders of Geoffrey Lister'. He then broke into the houses of Hugh Fastolf and William Elys and carried off their goods, chattels, two hundred pounds in cash from Fastolf and four hundred from Elys, as well as the king's customs rolls.[37] Fastolf was targeted because, like Elys, he had been impeached for corruption in the Good Parliament. He was a local merchant who had forged a spectacularly successful career as a burgess and merchant in Great Yarmouth, as a sea captain in the king's wars against France (it was his ship, the *Waynpayn* of Harwich, in which the Suffolk rebel Thomas Sampson had an eighth-share) and finally, as a fish-monger, breaking into the merchant oligarchy in London. He had cultivated royal favour with his loans and his seafaring abilities and had already served Yarmouth as bailiff five times, MP four times, lieutenant to successive admirals of the Fleet since 1362, collector of customs, justice of the peace and, most recently, as a Norfolk reassessor and enforcer of the third poll-tax. He had still found time to amass a huge fortune and build up great estates in both Norfolk and London, making many enemies along the way. The 'poor men' of Yarmouth had added their voices to the complaints in the Good Parliament about the oppressions and extortions committed by Fastolf and Elys, so Bacon's band found many willing helpers in their destruction of the two burgesses' properties, both in Yarmouth itself and in Caistor, four miles up the coast, where Fastolf and his brother John were building up family estates. It was one of John Fastolf's own servants, Robert Strongehobbe, who led the demolition and looting at Caistor, removing even the lead from the chapel roof and the drain-pipes.[38]

Roger Bacon's actions to this point had appeared to be altruistic in so far as they fulfilled the general aims of the revolt and were in line with the concessions granted by Richard at Mile End: even the destruction of Yarmouth's charter was in accordance with the king's abolition of tolls and customs throughout the land. While in the town, however, Bacon determined to settle a personal score by abducting William Clere, the son-in-law and co-heir through his wife of William Wychingham, a professional lawyer and justice in the Court of Common Pleas. By fair means or foul, Wychingham had used his legal abilities to acquire a large portfolio of properties in eastern Norfolk, including the manor of Antingham which Bacon had allegedly sold him 'by charter and king's licence'. Wychingham had died just before the revolt (his will was proved on 25 March 1381) and Bacon, who obviously felt that he had not parted with the manor willingly, much less permanently, decided to seize the opportunity to recover it. He imprisoned Clere until he signed a legal document giving up his claims to Antingham on behalf of himself and his wife, duly witnessed by three guarantors, upon which Bacon triumphantly took immediate possession again. Three days later, however, he sold it back to Clere, again by written charter, though presumably on different terms.[39]

Over the course of the next few days rebels who had been at Mousehold Heath and their local recruits conducted a mass invasion of the religious houses of north-east Norfolk, seizing and burning their manorial court rolls: Carrow Priory, West Dereham Abbey, St Benet-at-Holme Abbey and Binham Priory all lost their records, as did manors belonging to Bury St Edmunds Abbey and Norwich Cathedral Priory. Bishop Henry Despenser, John de Brewes, John of Gaunt and many other secular lords also suffered. In almost every case it was not a single attack on the main religious house or secular lordship but separate attacks on individual manors. St Benet-at-Holme lost the records in nine of its manors, including three where one of those accused of taking part in the burning was Clemence Paston, ancestor of the famous letter-writing family. Gaunt's archives on nine different manors were similarly destroyed. It has been calculated that documents were destroyed at fifty-six places in Norfolk and that there were other incidents connected to the revolt at ninety-five further places. And, of course, these figures do not include the events that went unreported or for which the records have been lost.[40]

On 21 June Geoffrey Lister was at Thorpe Market, some six miles north of his home in Felmingham. There he was alleged to have held a court in which both oral and written complaints were brought before him for judgment so that action (or vengeance as the indictment claimed) could be taken against alleged wrongdoers. Other indictments tell us that Lister received a request for men to assist in burning the court rolls of Binham Priory, which was carried out later that same day, and that John Barkere, Robert atte Moor and others also asked for help in hunting down certain 'traitors' whose names they had written down in a schedule and presented to Lister. The traitors included the parson of Thursford, who had been suspected of sheltering Edmund Gurney. This was by no means the first time that Lister had received requests of this kind: on 17 June Simon Cook and Henry Sherman had come to Mousehold Heath to ask him to bring his forces to Walsingham, where they lived.

Lister was also said to have held a court while in residence at Norwich Castle. Simon Silk had allegedly arrested Thomas Soppe of Burnham and sent him more than thirty miles to Norwich for trial before Lister on charges of stealing a horse worth twenty shillings from the abbot of Dereham's house at Holkham; Lister apparently decided he had no case to answer, presumably because the abbot's goods were considered fair game. These may genuinely have been instances of Lister acting in a judicial capacity, as his enthronement as 'king of the commons' would have entitled him to do, but it is equally possible that the accusations were simply made to suggest he had usurped royal power, a treasonable offence. Apart from the isolated case of the horse thief, where some sort of trial or at least judgment was involved, the 'courts' Lister held seem to have been little more than planning meetings to decide the next target to attack.[41]

Less than a week after the gathering at Mousehold Heath the revolt in eastern Norfolk had run its course. The same was true of the uprising in the west of the county, in and around King's Lynn. John Spayne, a cobbler and shoemaker in 'le gres market' of that town, had led a crowd of his fellow townsmen to raise revolt in Snettisham, some twelve miles away, urging a pogrom against the Flemings and ejecting Nicholas Mawpas from his free tenement at Barwick and installing in his stead John Coventry (the bowyer who had threatened Nicholas Massyngham). On 22 June Spayne's band had surprised Sir Edmund de Reynham, one of the controllers and surveyors of the third poll-tax, in the woods near Castle Rising; having no cash to hand he was obliged to ransom himself with fourteen quarters of oats, which, surprisingly, the rebels meekly accepted. Spayne would later be excluded from the general amnesty but, claiming that he had been falsely accused of murder and pillage through the enmity of people in his part of the county, he would be pardoned in 1383 after bishop Despenser testified to his innocence.[42]

News that Despenser was on his way back to Norfolk at the head of an armed force had already begun to circulate. It was probably for this reason that the rebels decided that they would send a group of delegates to the king in London, or wherever he was to be found, to secure confirmation that they had the royal sanction for their actions and to procure a pardon which would protect them from Despenser's wrath. The money they had obtained from the citizens of Norwich to prevent them burning down the town was to be used for this purpose, and handed over to their chosen representatives. These were three of Lister's trusted lieutenants, John Trunch, Thomas Skeet and the clerk William Kybyte, and two of their noble prisoners, John de Brewes and Thomas de Morlee, who, like Sir John Newenton, were expected to act as intermediaries and procure an audience with the king. Either because they were willing collaborators, or because Hales and Scales remained as hostages in rebel hands, Brewes and Morlee set off with the little group on the road to London. When they reached the village of Icklingham, Suffolk, on the London side of Thetford, they unexpectedly encountered Despenser and his troop, who were travelling the same road back from Cambridge after executing John Hauchach and other leaders of the revolt there and imprisoning the rest. No doubt surprised to see Brewes and Morlee in such company, Despenser interrogated the pair and eventually extracted from them an admission of their plight. Walsingham tells us that they had initially resisted, fearing that the bishop would be unable to help them if they betrayed their companions. Despenser had no such qualms, promptly beheading the two rebels who were with the knights and hunting down the third, who had left them to get food for their meal, to administer the same summary justice. Pausing only to order that the three heads should be put on public display in Newmarket as a warning to others, the belligerent bishop continued his journey to Norwich 'dressed as a knight, wearing an iron helm and a solid hauberk impregnable to arrows as he wielded a real two-edged sword'.[43]

Despenser enjoyed – in every sense of the word – a reputation as a military man. He came from a family with a long and distinguished record of military service to the crown, though his father had also acquired notoriety as one of the favourites of Edward II. As a teenager his family connections had procured him a canonry, a rectory, a degree from Oxford and a place at the papal curia where he fought in Urban V's military campaign against Milan. His reward was to be promoted to the bishopric of Norwich in 1370, which required a papal dispensation because, being still in his twenty-seventh year, he was under the canonical age. In June 1377 he had provoked a riot in King's Lynn, which was then known as Bishop's Lynn, by trying to assert his episcopal lordship over the town: this was a long-standing dispute, but Despenser had not hesitated to wade in personally and was wounded in the fighting. It was no surprise, then, that news that 'the war-like priest' was on his way put heart into the local gentry who, having laid low during the uprising, now allegedly flocked to join him. Nor that it alarmed the rebels who, in the early hours of 23 June, attempted to storm the abbey of St Benet-at-Holme in the belief that Despenser was staying there. The abbey, an Anglo-Saxon foundation, was virtually a fortress because of its inaccessible position on the Norfolk Broads: it could only be reached along a narrow causeway across the surrounding marshland, so it is significant that the assault was led by someone who knew the route well, the abbot's own carter William Kymberley. He was joined, however, by several veterans, including John Bettes alias Creyk, who had led one of the first rebel bands in the Wymondham area, John atte Chaumbre of Potter Heigham, who was accused of murdering Reginald de Eccles, and Adam Pulter (alias Martyn), who had been involved in the murder of Robert Salle. The abbot and his monks were at matins, the first service of the day held between midnight and three in the morning, but they abandoned their prayers, armed themselves, manned the walls and were able to hold off the rebels so that they did not gain entrance.[44]

Despenser probably arrived in Norwich on 24 June to be greeted with enthusiasm, feigned or otherwise, by the inhabitants: the burgesses held an immediate meeting and diplomatically voted to make the bishop a present of their money which he had recovered from the executed rebels Trunch, Kybyte and Skeet. When or how the two remaining knightly prisoners in rebel hands were released is not mentioned in any source. While Despenser made enquiries to find out where the rebels were gathered, the rebels themselves were sending out messengers in an attempt to rally support. In the north of the county Robert Fletcher, for example, brought a band of archers from Hunstanton to Heacham on 24 June and urged the locals there to join his company against the bishop, an action for which he was later beheaded. John Gylding of Heydon rode through several villages to the north-west of Norwich raising rebel levies and proclaiming that it would be a good thing and of great profit to the commons to seize or arrest the bishop and put an end to his malice. There were also gatherings against Despenser in villages in the north-east of the county and it was here that the rebels finally came face to face with their nemesis.[45]

Walsingham, again, is our only contemporary source for what happened next, and his account owes more to his model Tacitus than to what must have been the reality. According to Walsingham, the rebels had built a primitive military stockade at North Walsham, digging out a ditch, topping it with a

14. The month of November in the duke of Berry's Book of Hours (see plate 5) is illustrated by an example of pannage, the customary right of villagers to let loose their domestic pigs in woodland so that they could be fattened up on acorns, nuts and beechmasts ready for killing. A pig, or its equivalent value, was usually demanded by the landlord in return. The enclosure of many woods to create private parks in which their owners could hunt wild game but from which the villagers were excluded was a major grievance which fuelled the great revolt.

15. Clerics hunting rabbits with dogs and bows and arrows. The right of free warren (to hunt game within a specified area) was a valuable privilege enjoyed only by the aristocracy which the rebels of 1381 sought to abolish. Although clerics were officially prohibited from hunting by canon law, many of them did so, and monastic houses and episcopal landlords often kept warrens for the rabbit meat and fur. An illuminated initial from the *Omne Bonum* (see plate 6).

16. Miraculous healing powers were attributed to the relics of St Alban, the first English martyr, which were preserved in a shrine at the Hertfordshire abbey of St Albans. In this drawing by the historian and chronicler Matthew Paris (c.1200–59), himself a monk of St Albans, the shrine is carried in procession by the monks and crippled beggars pray to it for a cure.

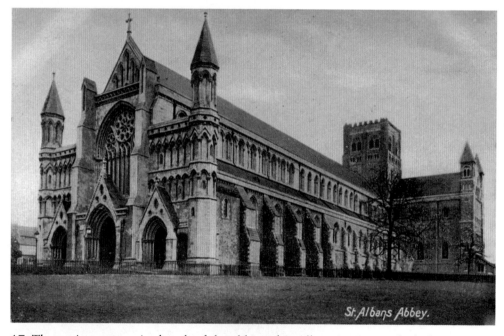

17. The ancient monastic church of the abbey of St Albans, now a cathedral, is virtually all that remains of one of the most powerful Benedictine houses in England. It has the longest nave of any English cathedral and a square central tower dating from the eleventh century. A gatehouse built in 1365 is the only other part of the abbey to have survived the Dissolution of the Monasteries in 1539; it is now part of St Albans School. There is no trace of the infamous parlour floor constructed out of the hand-mills seized from the rebellious townsmen.

18. The Abbey Gate, Bury St Edmunds, which opened into the great courtyard of the abbey, was used by the abbey servants and was the main access from the town. Built in the mid-fourteenth century, it replaced the original building which was attacked and destroyed by the townsmen during the riots of 1327 as part of their long-running feud with the abbey.

19. An illuminated initial from the *Omne Bonum* (see plate 6) for the entry on Cessio Actionis. The man on the left is handing over the deeds to a property while the man on the right offers him payment. Only freemen were legally permitted to acquire or sell land by charter and the confiscation of properties bought by villeins without their landlord's permission was a source of anger and frustration among tenants.

20. Two sergeants-at-law, the medieval equivalent of barristers, wearing their distinctive dress of a white coif or close-fitting cap and a furred gown, argue their case before two judges. Lawyers were a prime target of the rebels in 1381 because they were frequently involved in oppressive and sometimes venal administration of the shires and aristocratic and monastic estates. An illuminated initial from the *Omne Bonum* (see plate 6).

21. An illuminated initial from the *Omne Bonum* (see plate 6) for the entry on Confession, depicting a prisoner confessing his crimes before a judge.

22. A watercolour painting by Thomas Girtin (1775–1802), copied by J. M. W. Turner (1775–1851), of the ruins of the chapel in John of Gaunt's Savoy Palace on the Strand, London, which was destroyed by the rebels on 13 June 1381.

23. The Tower of London and its distinctive White Tower, where Richard II and his councillors took refuge as the rebels from Kent and Essex approached the city. Richard is said to have climbed one of the turrets on 13 June to see the devastation they were wreaking on his capital. London Bridge, with the chapel dedicated to St Thomas Becket in the centre, can be seen in the background. An illumination from a 1483 manuscript volume of poems by Charles d'Orléans (1394–1465) who spent thirty-five years as a prisoner in the Tower after his capture at the battle of Agincourt.

unt ce vint le ven
dredy au matin ce
euple qui estoit

24. Archbishop Sudbury kneels bare-headed as his murderer makes to strike off his head: his mitre lies on the floor beside him. John Hales, prior of the Knights Hospitaller, similarly kneels to meet his fate while behind him another rebel stabs the Franciscan friar William Appelton, who was John of Gaunt's physician. In this miniature from a copy of Froissart's *Chronicles*, commissioned by a Flemish nobleman in the 1470s, the murders are depicted taking place inside the Tower whereas, in reality, the victims were dragged out of the chapel and beheaded on Tower Hill.

25. The skull of Archbishop Simon Sudbury is preserved in the collegiate church of St Gregory which he had founded with his brother in Sudbury, Suffolk. After his murder on 14 June his head, with his mitre nailed to it, had been put on a pole and paraded through the streets before being displayed above London Bridge. The head was taken to Sudbury after the revolt was over but his body was buried in Canterbury Cathedral.

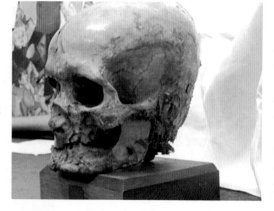

26. This highly stylised and anachronistic miniature from a manuscript of Froissart's *Chronicles* (see plate 24) depicts John Balle riding at the head of his troops to meet Wat Tyler, who is standing in the foreground in front of his army. Both sets of rebels display the royal standard and the banner of St George to illustrate their loyalty to King Richard and the fact that they believed they were acting with his authority.

27. This miniature from the same manuscript (see plate 24) illustrates the meeting at Smithfield on 15 June, where Wat Tyler was struck down and killed by members of the king's party. Richard takes centre stage as Tyler is murdered but is also shown riding to confront the rebels and demand that they show their loyalty to him by following him from the field.

**WHEN ADAM DELVED AND EVE SPAN
WHO WAS THEN THE GENTLEMAN?**

28. Edward Burne-Jones's iconic frontispiece for the
1892 edition of William Morris's *A Dream of John Ball*
immortalised the famous couplet which Balle used as the text
for his alleged sermon at Blackheath. The book became a
socialist classic and was published throughout the English-
speaking world.

makeshift wall of tables, shutters and gates held together by stakes and placing their carts and carriages behind them. This was indeed standard military practice for armies caught in the field during the Hundred Years War, and though Sir Roger Bacon was not with them the rebels may well have had other soldiers with this type of military experience among their ranks. On the other hand, if a last stand was to be made, then there were many more suitable places in the locality, including castles, fortified manor houses and churches, all built of stone and eminently more defensible. Walsingham tells us that the warrior-bishop, 'like a wild boar gnashing its teeth', threw himself upon the rebel force and in the close hand-to-hand fighting that followed was always to be found in the place of greatest danger. In the end, the rebels, weighed down by their guilty consciences, lost any remaining resolution to fight and took to their heels, scrambling over the rampart of upturned carts to escape, only to be cut down by their implacable foe 'until he achieved total victory'. A number of the rebels were killed but some, including Geoffrey Lister, were captured, tried and then executed. Despenser displayed his 'mercy and piety' by hearing Lister's confession himself, absolved him and then accompanied him to the gallows, during which journey he 'held up the rebel's head to prevent it knocking on the ground while he was being dragged to the place of his hanging'.[46]

As a fellow clergyman whose own abbey had suffered at the hands of the rebels, Walsingham naturally had good reasons to admire Despenser's role in suppressing the revolt (though he did not like the man) and to portray him as an avenging angel leading his men into battle to destroy the forces of evil. But it stretches credulity to believe that there was anything like a 'battle' at North Walsham. The two sides were too unequal. Despenser and his men-at-arms were all clad head to foot in steel-plate armour and wielding lances, swords, poleaxes and other knightly arms; the rebels at best would have had long-bows, short swords and makeshift halberds, and their only protection would have been an iron kettle hat and boiled leather arm and chest armour; the wealthier ones might also have had an iron breastplate. If Walsingham is right, and there was no time for either side to deploy their longbows before the close fighting began, then the rebels would not have stood a chance, even if they outnumbered Despenser's forces several times over. An alternative version of the 'battle' is given by John Capgrave, the prior of the Augustinian friary at King's Lynn, who had the advantage of being a Norfolk man, but the disadvantage of writing many decades after these events, since he was not born until 1393. Capgrave followed Walsingham in most of his account of the rising but says that Despenser went to North Walsham on learning that Lister had called out all the able-bodied men of the area to take a stand there. The bishop found the roads blocked with barricades, but 'by good management' he and those with him were able to persuade everyone to surrender and withdraw peacefully. Lister, however, jumped over a wall and hid in a cornfield, only to be betrayed by his former colleagues and taken prisoner. Walsingham's version certainly seems more in keeping with Despenser's character, though he was wrong in his description of Lister's death: the escheator's accounts confirm Capgrave's assertion that he was beheaded, not hanged, so Despenser's alleged 'mercy and piety' at the scene of execution are probably as fictitious as Walsingham's account of Jack Straw's confession at the gallows.[47]

It has been argued that legal records corroborate Walsingham's account of a skirmish at North Walsham. In January 1382 the escheator John Rede, whose property at Rougham had been looted and destroyed in the uprising, held an inquisition at Worstead and recorded that six local men had all been killed the previous June by 'gentiles', or noblemen. 'The wording in the record – "*interfectus est*" – makes it quite clear that these people were killed in battle', we are told. While it is true that this wording was a deliberate attempt to distinguish between those executed after trial and those executed without due legal process, it does not necessarily mean that the six were 'killed in battle', only that they were killed. And since two of those on the escheator's list were William Kybyte and Thomas Skeet, both of whom were summarily executed by Despenser after he intercepted them at Icklingham, it is not necessarily the case that Richard Hobbesson and Geoffrey Coleman of North Walsham, Thomas Radbote of Sco Ruston and Robert Smyth of Ridlington were killed in battle either. The same argument holds true for the cases cited from the local manorial court rolls. One of them is John Trunch, whom we know was killed with Kybyte and Skeet at Icklingham; another, John Buk, 'made insurrections against the peace of the king ... insulted Henry Spenser, Bishop of Norwich' and was killed ('*occissus fuit*') at North Walsham 'by the same Henry'. One could well imagine that a proffered insult would have been enough to provoke Despenser into killing his abuser and maybe even launching an assault on others with him, but Buk and Nicholas de Orforde of Hoveton St John are the only ones cited whose deaths are explicitly stated to have taken place at North Walsham.[48] And two deaths in the same place do not necessarily add up to corroboration of a battle taking place. On the balance of probabilities it is likely that at least some rebels were cornered and put up a fight, just as they would do a couple of days later near Billericay, Essex, but the available evidence does not prove that the Norfolk rebels fought a battle or skirmish against Despenser in a last stand at North Walsham.

Lister's capture was swiftly followed by a rounding-up of the other rebel leaders. Bacon and Gyssing were both arrested, tried and imprisoned in the Tower of London. Gyssing was released on 20 November 1381 'by advice of the council and with the king's assent'. Bacon was only released after he was pardoned at the intercession of the queen, Anne of Bohemia, whom Richard had married in January 1382. He was among those privately prosecuted by Hugh Fastolf for the destruction of the latter's property in Great Yarmouth and, when he appeared to face the charges (the only one to do so), he was found guilty and ordered to pay one hundred marks in compensation: it was a pyrrhic victory as Bacon never paid Fastolf a penny.[49] Eighteen Norfolk men were eventually excluded from the general amnesty, among them Lister's messengers Richard Felmond and John Gentilome; the murderers of Robert Salle and Reginald de Eccles, Henry Royse, Thomas Aslak, John atte Chaumbre, John of Norwich (a cook) and Adam Pulter (who had already been executed under his alias Adam Martyn); and the local leaders John Spayne and John Bettes alias Creyk, who would both obtain pardons.[50]

Bishop Despenser's prompt and decisive actions undoubtedly stopped the momentum of the revolt in Peterborough, Cambridge and Norfolk. They won him many admirers, not least in the House of Commons, which would enthusiastically support his plan to launch a crusade against Count Louis de Mâle of Flanders in 1383. This sordid exercise qualified as a crusade because the count, like his overlord the king of France, supported the schismatic pope Clement VII (though his subjects did not), thus allowing Despenser to sell the idea as a way of continuing the war against France without raising the spectre of having to raise more taxes from the laity. In the wake of the great revolt, that was a very attractive proposition, and Despenser's particular brand of muscular Christianity, which he had so singularly demonstrated during the uprising, promised greater success than the military alternatives proposed by Gaunt and his brothers, which simply re-trod the well-worn paths that had led to a decade of failure and humiliation. Plus, of course, there was the added attraction of having a legitimate, papally endorsed reason to slaughter the Flemings, with the bonus that personal salvation could be won while doing so. Despenser led the crusade in person, since no professional soldier of any standing would take that responsibility, and enjoyed spectacular initial success, defeating a combined Flemish and French army at Dunkirk and accepting the surrender of a number of Flemish towns, but the enterprise petered out in an abortive siege of Ypres, where the 'crusaders' were besieging supporters of their own pope, Urban V. It was a disaster to match all those that had preceded it. Having squandered all the kudos he had won during the revolt, Despenser was impeached and deprived of his temporalities, though not his liberty or his see, until he regained favour two years later by fighting against the Scots.[51]

Despenser's crusade would probably never have got off the ground had he not acquired his reputation as a decisive and effective leader in suppressing the great revolt. Yet it is worth asking why he alone, out of all the nobility and gentry whom medieval society had designated as its defenders of the peace, should have risen to the challenge. Contemporaries were quick to blame the inaction of these lords, knights and esquires on cowardice. Historians have been kinder, demonstrating how the rebels' removal of the chancellor and treasurer at the highest levels of government and the shrievalty and justices of the peace in the shires caused paralysis which prevented all the normal administrative responses taking place. What has not been taken into account properly is that, without that administrative structure, no one had any *authority* to act. This might not have mattered so much if the uprising had been just a simple case of attacks on royal officials, unpopular individuals or oppressive institutions: these could have been dealt with at a local level if those who had the means to do so had not either themselves been under attack or were uncertain as to the legitimacy of the rebels' actions. What happened at Mile End on 14 June complicated everything. When the young king agreed that traitors to the realm should be punished, issued written letters under his seal abolishing all personal and tenurial villeinage and granted all his subjects freedom from paying tolls, he effectively gave royal authority to the rebels to act as they did. It would have been a brave or foolhardy man who tried to intervene or prevent such action – just such a man as Despenser, who was confident enough in his own social status as both aristocrat and bishop, and arrogant enough in his personal character, to assume that he could dispense summary justice as he thought fit, with or without royal authority. For anyone else to have acted as he did would have been to run the risk of usurping royal authority, just as the rebels would later be accused of doing. And the problem was that when it really mattered, when the revolt was in full swing, no one really knew if the king had granted his concessions willingly and would stand by them – in which case opposing the acts of his agents would in itself have meant countermanding the king's will. Ironically, that would have been an act of rebellion. So it is not surprising that so many of the shire gentry chose either to join the rebels, believing that they had the king's support, or, more prudently, to lie low and wait to see how events would turn out.

CHAPTER FOURTEEN

North and south

It was not until 18 June, four days after the Mile End meeting and the murders in the Tower of London, that the king finally issued writs to the country's sheriffs, mayors and bailiffs ordering the resistance to begin. Yet even this was not the rallying call to crush the revolt that might have been expected.

> Because we understand that various of our subjects have risen in various counties of England, against our peace and to the disturbance of the people, and have formed various gatherings and assemblies in order to commit many injuries against our faithful subjects, and because they affirm and inform our people that they have made the said assemblies and risings by our will and with our authority; we hereby notify you that these risings, assemblies and injuries did not and ought not to derive from our will or authority, but that they displease us immensely as a source of shame to us, of prejudice to the crown and of damage and commotion to

our entire kingdom. Wherefore we command and order you to have this publicly proclaimed, in the places where it seems to you this can be best and most quickly done to pre-serve the peace and resist the said insurgents against our peace; you are to do this to the limit of your ability and with force, if necessary, so that for lack of such proclamations and resistance, damages and ills shall not continue to be perpetrated by the said assemblies and risings ... and you must command all and each of our liegemen and subjects to desist completely from such assemblies, risings and injuries and return to their homes to live there in peace, under penalty of losing life and limb and all their goods.[1]

Apart from the denunciation of the rebels' claims that their gatherings were made by the king's will or with his authority, this was no stronger than any other writ against riotous assembly. Reading it in isolation, one could be forgiven for not realising that the country was in the grip of the most serious and widespread popular rebellion in its history. There is no mention of the murders, the abductions, the invasion of religious houses, the demolition of buildings and the burning of records, just a rather pallid reference to 'many injuries' having been committed. This might well be because the government did not want to give any ideas to places as yet untouched by revolt – but the purpose of the writ was to put a stop to such activities by removing any justification for them.

The suggestion that force should be used to resist the rebels 'if necessary' sits oddly with the general perception created by the chroniclers that the revolt was a maelstrom of uncontrollable mob violence. If indeed this were the case, then it is surprising that the king did not call on his retainers to provide him with military assistance: the prime purpose of paying pensions to knights and esquires was, after all, that they were always in readiness to come to the king's aid when required. Richard, his father and his grandfather all had substantial numbers of such retainers and this was just the sort of crisis in which the king should have been able to rely on them. It would appear, therefore, that he did not summon them, leaving them in as much a state of uncertainty as to his intentions as the rest of the gentry. Richard could also have called on the assistance of at least two armies already in the field, fully arrayed and ready for deployment. His uncle Edmund of Langley had some three thousand men at Plymouth and Dartmouth waiting to take ship for Portugal, among them trusted captains like Sir William Beauchamp and Sir Matthew Gournay, both veterans of the Hundred Years War.[2] The winds from the south-west which prevented these forces sailing to Portugal could have borne the army, or a substantial detachment from it, down the Channel to Kent, Essex or indeed London itself. Again, they were not called upon, and eventually sailed to Portugal at the end of June, so a full-scale military operation against the rebels was clearly not crown policy.

The second army was in an even better position to intervene since it was awaiting orders as to where it was to be deployed. This was the remnant of Felton's two thousand men recruited to reinforce Woodstock's abortive Breton expedition and mustered at Dartmouth since April. As we have already seen, many of them had deserted or officially returned home after Felton's death, including the rebel leader Sir Roger Bacon, but there was still a substantial force in arms available. It was to these soldiers that the government turned, sending a writ under the privy seal ordering Sir Peter de Veel and Sir Robert Passelowe, former MPs for Gloucestershire and Kent respectively, to make their way to London with their retinue of sixty knights and the same number of archers. When the writ was issued, or when they arrived in London, is not known, but they remained with the king until 26 June, at which point he sent them to restore order and peace in Hampshire and Wiltshire. It is just possible, though unlikely, that this troop might have arrived in time to confront the rebels at Smithfield: riding hard on good horses they should have been able to cover the two hundred miles in twenty-five hours, though they would have needed to take breaks along the way; a messenger carrying the writ would have been able to travel faster, especially if he was able to use relays of horses, but since we do not know when he was despatched we cannot begin to work out when they might have arrived. They later claimed their wages for this service, saying that they had remained in Hampshire and Wiltshire 'for a long time', though their contract ended on 20 August.[3]

Of the other armed companies used to quell the disturbances we know remarkably little. John Gosford, the chronicler of Bury St Edmunds, tells us that the earl of Suffolk arrived in the town on 23 June with five hundred lances to put down the revolt. This must be an error of fact or transcription.[4] A 'lance' varied in meaning from a single man-at-arms to a unit composed of a man-at-arms, an esquire or other lightly armed horseman and an archer, but the essential component was the heavily armed man-at-arms, who was also the soldier in shortest supply. For his major French campaign of 1355–6 the Black Prince himself had only 433 men-at-arms, and that was more than double the size of the largest retinues provided by the wealthiest earls.[5] Even with all the resources at his command the king himself could not have found five hundred men-at-arms to send with Suffolk – and indeed could raise only sixty from the residue of Felton's army. It is much more likely that Suffolk's retinue was fifty strong, like the one that Sir Walter atte Lee took to St Albans on 29 June. Walsingham tells us that Despenser's retinue which slaughtered the rebels at Peterborough, Ramsey and North Walsham consisted of just eight lances 'and a tiny number of archers'. This might seem a ridiculously small number to suppress a revolt, though not inappropriate for providing protection for a bishop travelling through dangerous country, yet when Sir Thomas Trevet (a seasoned campaigner) left London on 17 June to put down the rebellion in Kent he took only twelve men-at-arms and twenty-five archers with him. The Essex rebels who had gathered in great numbers near Billericay on 28 June were 'easily dispersed by only ten lances (to use the common term)'.[6]

Such small numbers tell us two things: that the rebels were completely outclassed in terms of armour and weaponry so that fielding armies against them was not necessary; also that, by the time the soldiers were deployed, they were doubly unnecessary because the revolt was for the most part at an end. The pattern across the board had been a few days of violence in which the rebels had got rid of, or punished, corrupt officials and burned the records used to oppress them. After that, apart from a few agitators determined to spread the revolt elsewhere, the rebels had usually gone home to enjoy their newly won personal liberty and freedom from customary dues, services and tolls. Even a major leader like John Wrawe, whose activities had taken him far from his locality and spread the revolt throughout East Anglia, was arrested back at home in Sudbury. He was taken to London, where he was tried and condemned to death despite turning king's evidence. It is possible that the sentence was never carried out: in 1395 the son and heir of Robert Bracy, who had been appointed marshal of the Marshalsea in place of Richard Imworth, was excused the old debt his father owed the crown as a fine for the escape of five men, one of whom was 'John Raude alias Wrawe of Sudbury'.[7]

There were some isolated acts of resistance sparked by the appointment of the commissioners to suppress the rebellion, the most significant being what is usually described as the battle or skirmish near Billericay on 28 June. The indictments do indeed record that John Geffrey, the bailiff of East Hanningfield and a major leader of the revolt in the locality, had summoned all the men of the neighbouring villages to meet in arms at Great Baddow church to resist the forces of Thomas of Woodstock. The only source for the 'battle' is Walsingham and even he describes nothing of the sort. He says that the rebels took cover in Rettingdon Wood, near Billericay, and barricaded themselves in with ditches, carts and stakes, but scattered and fled when attacked by just ten lances of the advance party; when the main troops arrived they surrounded the wood, hunted down and killed five hundred rebels and captured eight hundred of their horses, numbers which are clearly hugely exaggerated. Those that fled tried to raise Colchester, but were rejected and, while trying their luck at Sudbury, were ambushed and slaughtered. A series of writs issued on 3 July confirms that the government feared that rebels from Essex and Kent were trying to revive the rebellion but, if so, they signally failed. Geffrey himself was captured, tried and hanged at Chelmsford: when his goods were confiscated it was noted that he owned nothing 'of his own' because he was a serf by blood.[8]

Most of the commissioners appointed to suppress the uprising met with no resistance because the revolt was already over: they were simply there to round up and punish those who had committed what were now defined as acts of rebellion. On 20 June Woodstock (whose own lands in East Anglia had been attacked) and Robert Tresilian, who would be appointed as chief justice to replace the murdered Cavendish on 22 June, were given over-arching authority with powers extending throughout England. The first county commissions were set up for Kent and Hampshire the same day. On 23 June a writ was issued to newly appointed commissioners for the northern counties, Norfolk and Suffolk, Cambridgeshire and Huntingdonshire, and in

Bridgwater, Somerset, ordering them to issue a further proc-lamation concerning the murders of Sudbury, Hales and Cavendish and forbidding unlawful assemblies; the commissioners were empowered to resist and punish the rebels and those for Cambridgeshire, led by Hugh la Zouche, were also given authority to seize 'notorious offenders' without delay. Lincoln, the south-western counties, Bath, Bristol and Oxford followed the next day and writs for the rest of the country were gradually rolled out between 3 and 10 July.[9]

The problem for the government at this stage was not so much suppressing acts of violence in places where the rebellion had already taken hold but preventing the revolt spreading further. How far and wide it had already spread is indicated by the appointment of the special commissioners. Bridgwater, for example, sits oddly with Norfolk, Suffolk, Cambridgeshire and Huntingdonshire, but it was included because, despite its distance from the heart of the revolt, the townspeople had risen up on 19 June under the leadership of Thomas Engilby and attacked the Augustinian Hospital of St John, which lay in their borough. The hospital was dedicated to caring for the sick and providing hospitality for pilgrims but it had acquired property in the town and both lands and churches throughout the area; it was, therefore, like the abbeys of Bury St Edmunds and St Albans, the most powerful institution in the locality. Trouble had been brewing for several years over disputed jurisdictional rights and over the hospital's claim to the church of Bridgwater. On 14 April 1380 the master William Cammell had obtained a special protection for the brethren and hospital because of an unsettled 'controversy' between the previous master, who had resigned, and the people of Bridgwater. In February and July of the same year he had also brought charges against the townsmen, alleging that they had broken down the door of the hospital church and held him and his brethren prisoner; the townsmen had responded in February 1381 by obtaining a royal confirmation of their free borough status and their rights to a free market and yearly fair.[10]

When the revolt broke out in London, several men from Bridgwater, including its vicar Nicholas Frompton, were in the city pursuing their legal case against the hospital. Richard's concessions at Mile End sent them hurrying back home where, according to an extraordinary appeal in parliament in November 1381, they persuaded a local justice of the peace, Sir William Cogan, to negotiate a settlement with the hospital. When that failed, Frompton and Engilby, bearing banners of the royal arms, broke into the hospital buildings and compelled Cammell to hand over the bonds he held from the townsmen, release all his rights and profits in the church, apart from the corn and hay tithes, to Frompton and pay a two-hundred-mark fine. Richard de Clyvedon, the esquire who appealed Cogan, also accused him of leading this band and offered to prove his charge with his body in accordance with the law of arms: 'For he said that the said Sir William was a rich man, and he poor; and therefore he would not be able to prevail by inquest against the said Sir William, even though his cause was as true as there is God in heaven above'. Parliament had no appetite for a duel to the death so the case was referred to the courts, where it sank without trace. Whether Cogan was involved is impossible to assess but it seems unlikely, if only because he was both a surveyor and controller of the third poll-tax for Somerset and a commissioner to reassess and enforce its collection.[11]

Engilby, however, admitted his role at the hospital and then, over the next two days, demolishing one house and raiding another belonging to John Sydenham, the steward of two unpopular local landlords, whose manorial court rolls, together with other documents relating to Engilby's own inheritance he tore into pieces, removed the seals and burned. He also burned down the houses of a clerk, Thomas Duffeld, and Walter Baron. The latter he 'treasonably caused ... to be beheaded', together with Hugh de Lavenham, a government informer whom he abducted from prison at Ilchester, placing both their heads on lances over the bridge at Bridgwater. Engilby and twelve other Somerset men (among them a soothsayer) were excluded from the general amnesty but Engilby eventually obtained a pardon in March 1383, thirteen months after Frompton, for whom William Courtenay, now archbishop of Canterbury, had interceded.[12] What makes the Bridgwater uprising particularly interesting is that letters of manumission and pardon, almost word for word the same as those issued at Mile End, were drawn up for the men of Somerset. Dated from Westminster on 2 July, the very day that Richard revoked his other letters (when he was actually in Chelmsford), the letters are a draft prepared for his approval. It is possible that either Frompton or his representatives obtained them at Mile End, but no royal clerk would have post-dated a written pardon to cover crimes not yet committed. A more probable scenario is that they were drafted by Frompton's attorney in London, who copied their wording from others he had seen; he could not have known that Richard would withdraw those already granted on the same day and that they would therefore become redundant before they had even been approved.[13]

Bridgwater was the furthest outpost of south-west England where incidents connected with the general uprising are recorded.[14] Winchester had a three-day rebellion of its own after the arrival of Thomas Faukoner of Winchester, alias Thomas Palmer of Surrey, from Guildford on 17 June with news of the rebellion in Surrey and the Mile End concessions. This was the excuse William Wygge and his supporters needed to rise again; they rang the town bell and blew the communal horn to summon the townsmen to their aid then the following day broke into the king's Staple, stole all the rolls and records stored there and publicly burned them in the high street. Walter Hogyn, who may have been the Staple clerk, was killed. This appears, once again, to have been caused by a long-running jurisdictional clash. The town's merchant guild, of which Wygge was a senior member, resented the Staple's independent administration of commercial contracts and debts involving their members, and in 1377 the mayor and community had been prosecuted for pulling down tenements in Winchester which the king had designated for an expansion of Staple business. With banners flying the Winchester rebels also went out to Romsey, some eleven miles away, presumably to raise the tenantry and burn the charters and rolls of the Benedictine nunnery there; eight men from Romsey were later indicted for revolt and one of them hanged. Faukoner and Wygge were among the six Winchester rebels excluded from the general amnesty; both were eventually pardoned, though Faukoner, who had fled, did not receive his until 1398.[15]

The Midlands remained relatively quiet, though there was a farcical situation in Leicester, where rumours that the rebels from London were marching on the town to attack Gaunt's castle there led the mayor to order all able-bodied townsmen to take up arms and assemble on the hill outside the town. For two days around twelve hundred men, 'some good and others less so', waited for the onslaught that never came. In the end, all that happened was that the keeper of the duke's wardrobe arrived from London, loaded as many of Gaunt's belongings as he could into carts and waggons and took them to the abbey for safe-keeping. The abbot, however, afraid that the rebels would sack his abbey instead of Gaunt's castle, refused to accept them, so they were dumped in the churchyard of St Mary de Castro 'to await divine providence'. In Northampton William Napton, who was probably a butcher, led an uprising against the mayor and was still considered an agitator in July 1382.[16] The university at Oxford, unlike Cambridge, appears to have escaped unscathed, though the arrests were ordered on 28 June of seven rebels from Abingdon, just seven miles away, and the earl of Warwick hurried back to Warwickshire at the beginning of July on unconfirmed rumours of an uprising there.[17]

Farther north, Derbyshire was affected by the antics of the five sons of Goditha de Stathum who had a long-standing dispute with Gaunt over their mother's ownership of property in the manor of Morley. Unable to win their case by legitimate means against such a powerful opponent, the Stathums had been drawn into an escalating quarrel which had resulted in murder, theft of livestock, wanton destruction of property, poaching, outlawry and the appointment of royal commissions that Gaunt packed with his own supporters. On 18 June, therefore, as news of the revolt arrived in Derbyshire, the Stathums attacked Breadsall Priory, an impoverished house of Augustinian canons which held one of the four manors of Morley: Gaunt, the Stathum family and the abbot of Chester held the others. The prior and his two canons took refuge in a strong chamber, and when the rebels grew bored with laying siege to it they broke into the church, where they were accused of burning a pyx containing the sacred Host, images, books, vestments and other precious items before burning down the prior's kitchen and another chamber. They then took themselves off to Horston Castle, a few miles away, which was held by Gaunt's chamberlain and leading retainer Sir Robert Swillington. Rather than destroy it, they seized the castle and flaunted their victory by flying a standard of St George from the ramparts. There is no suggestion that records were burned, and though two men were killed they were linked to the property dispute rather than an assault on corrupt royal officials. The Stathums' actions were typical of those that marked their feud with Gaunt and could just as easily have taken place at any time during the previous few years: it is only the timing and the adoption of the standard of St George which links them specifically with the great revolt, though the knowledge that Gaunt was a major target of the rebels may have encouraged them to strike again.[18]

The furthest north that the revolt spread was Yorkshire. As we have seen,[19] York was already in turmoil as Simon Quixley's supporters fought, sometimes literally, for a say in the city government. Newly installed as mayor in February 1381, Quixley had tried to exploit grievances among the townsmen to bolster his authority. News of the revolt, and possibly even the Mile End concessions, reached York swiftly, probably through its mercantile connections with the crown and London, and on 17 June more than a hundred people attacked three major religious institutions in the city: St Leonard's Hospital, St George's Chapel and the Dominican friary. The hospital, said to be the largest in the north of England, stood in the shadow of the Minster; eight brothers and eight sisters provided daily alms for thirty poor people at the hospital gate, prisoners and lepers in the city and up to 206 sick staying in their infirmary. A visitation in 1376–7 had noted that the master had spent over £1116 on repairs to the roof but a further thousand pounds needed to be spent on repairs to the dormitory, hospital church and tower.[20] The hospital, like the Dominican friary and royal chantry near York Castle, enjoyed extensive privileges within the city, such as exemption from secular taxation, which were a source of tension with the city government.

The attacks seem to have had Quixley's approval, and possibly his authorisation, because he held a meeting of 'all the commonalty' the same day in the guildhall to issue an ordinance designed to protect York should the king intervene. Gisburn and his supporters were accused of a further incident at the city's Bootham Bar on 1 July, in which they rode armed through the streets, assaulted and threatened their opponents with iron bars and other weapons, swore oaths of loyalty to one another and handed out liveries. John Gisburn's followers retaliated by accusing Quixley of seizing and imprisoning their people at the time of the 'diabolical insurrection in the counties of Kent and Essex', threatening to execute them 'just like the chancellor and treasurer of our said lord the king' until they handed over large sums of money and bonds to the guildhall treasury. Both sides were quite deliberately trying to tarnish the other with the much more serious charge of rebellion, rather than simply the petty crimes resulting from their bitter feud.

Richard ordered Gaunt and the archbishop of York to sort out the affair, but in the meantime, in November 1381, he issued royal confirmation of the friary's charters that granted it various plots of land within the city, with power to enclose them, which suggests that the wall within its precincts demolished by the townsmen was a disputed enclosure: the confirmation of the charters was duly recorded in the York civic records, together with the fact that earthen walls against the city walls and two of the great gates which had been demolished and carried off were to be restored. On 3 March 1382 Quixley, as mayor, was forced to offer security of five thousand pounds pledged on his own goods and lands, that before midsummer he would compel 120 named townsmen to repair the closes, walls and doors of the hospital and chapel, and the wall within the friary which they had broken down, and take bonds of one hundred pounds from each of them that they would keep the peace in future. It was not until November 1382 that Richard cancelled these bonds and issued a pardon to the city, though its people still had to pay a collective fine of one thousand marks.[21]

Much of the antipathy between the two factions had arisen

because the old guard, represented by Gisburn, was so closely identified with the crown and abuse of royal power. The same would be true of two other Yorkshire towns, Beverley and Scarborough, where uprisings are recorded in the summer of 1381. Beverley was an important centre for both the woollen industry and for pilgrimage: its Minster housed the shrine of St John of Beverley, the seventh-century bishop of Hexham who had ordained the Venerable Bede. With a tax-paying population of 2663 in 1377, Beverley was the second largest town in the north of England but it was riven by urban conflict and had within its walls three separate and frequently rival jurisdictions exercised by the crown, the archbishop of York and the provost and chapter of the Minster. The archbishop was already at loggerheads with the canons of the Minster and launched a bitter and prolonged attack on their privileges in June 1381. This further escalated tensions within the civic government where, at the end of May, a 'formidable if temporary coalition' of the 'ordinary' people, or lesser craftsmen, had succeeded in ousting the self-perpetuating twelve keepers, who were all members of rich merchant families: the two wealthiest and most powerful, Thomas Beverley and Adam Coppendale, had both served as poll-tax collectors in 1377, antagonising local people by obstructing streets with their new buildings and, in the case of the former, by acting as steward of the Minster chapter. The rebels not only expelled the keepers from office but then reformed the constitution to ensure their own place in future civic government by instituting a single alderman, two chamberlains, a recorder and a council of twenty-four. The new regime promptly arraigned the most hated members of the old for their abuses of power and forcibly extracted such huge bonds from them that many fled in terror of their lives. The violent aftermath of reprisals and counter-reprisals continued for over a year; it was not until

June 1382 that the archbishop and sheriff were able to restore some sort of order by taking pledges for good behaviour from four hundred of the townsmen of both parties. Beverley finally obtained its letters of royal pardon in October 1382, though it had to pay 1100m. for the privilege, a fine even higher than that imposed on York.[22]

Scarborough, with a tax-paying population of 1393 in 1377, was a borough on the east coast overlooked by a royal castle. There had been conflicts between the two jurisdictions for over a century, resulting in 1312 in the town being confiscated into the king's hands for fifteen years, though its liberties were restored by Edward III and confirmed by Richard on his accession. Resentment against the crown had grown in recent years because of its increasingly heavy naval demands which were at odds with the town's vulnerability to Scottish and French raiders. In 1378 the son of a Scot held prisoner in the castle managed, with French and Spanish help, to capture all the ships in the harbour; the situation was only saved by the London merchant John Philipot, who raised and equipped a fleet at his own expense, recovered the English ships and booty and captured fifteen of the Spanish ships. The following year Scarborough appealed to parliament for royal protection from the French ships which constantly threatened the town, causing it to lose a thousand pounds in captures and ransoms over two years.[23]

The revolt in Scarborough began on 23 June with a gathering of some five hundred townsmen who, having heard of the uprising elsewhere, bound themselves by oath to redress each other's wrongs and adopted a livery of white hoods tipped with red. That night they deposed one of the bailiffs, Robert Acclom, who fled to sanctuary in the house of the Friars Minor, only to have the rebels attempt to break down the doors to get him. Acclom belonged to the most powerful family in the borough and was notoriously corrupt: he had already been accused of a number of violent crimes and manipulating the local food markets, and his son John was no better, sharing his father's misdeeds and being outlawed for murder in 1384. Various leading burgesses were besieged in their homes and imprisoned until they swore to be faithful to the commons and paid fines for their release: among them were John Acclom and William Scott, who were both assessors of the third poll-tax, and Robert Pad and John Stokwyth, the controllers and assessors of the tax. Stokwyth was dragged from his house by 'a great crowd of men called *rowtes*' and led from street to street 'with a great shout called *hountays*' to prison; kept there for several days and threatened with beheading he offered money but was only saved by his son-in-law Henry de Ruston (another poll-tax collector) who had it proclaimed throughout Scarborough that he would personally make amends for any complaint against Stokwyth, 'even if he had to sell his lands, tenements, goods and chattels' to do so. The rebels were led by William Marche, himself a wealthy Scarborough merchant, against whom the Accloms duly took their revenge three years later by robbing his ships and home and stealing his flock of two hundred sheep, a crime which went unpunished. Scarborough itself was compelled to pay a fine of four hundred marks but it was not pardoned until 1391.[24]

There can be little doubt that other towns throughout the kingdom were also caught up in the revolt, though documentary evidence as to the course of events is currently lacking: royal writs ordering rebels to be resisted, arrested and punished were issued on 23 and 24 June not just to York, Beverley, Scarborough and Bridgwater, but also to Kingston-upon-Hull, Newcastle-upon-Tyne, Bath, Bristol and Oxford.[25] The revolt had spread so far and so fast that the government was in danger of being overtaken by events even as it tried to suppress them.

By 10 July, however, even Scarborough had its commission empowered to put down the uprising, with force if necessary, and to restore to their posts any royal officials removed by the rebels.[26]

CHAPTER FIFTEEN

Suppression

Throughout the kingdom commissioners were now actively at work, so much so that the monk of Westminster observed that 'the royal judges were now everywhere to be seen in session, inquiring into the activities of the conspirators and giving the guilty short shrift. Gibbets rose where none had been before, since existing ones were too few for the bodies of the condemned. Many who had been privy to the insurrection took to flight to avoid sharing the arrest and bitter fate suffered by others'. Melodramatic though the monk's comments may seem, they are borne out by other evidence. The earl of Arundel, for example, was given permission on 9 July to keep prisoners in his own castles of Arundel and Lewes because Guildford Castle, 'the chief gaol of the counties of Surrey and Sussex, is not sufficient for the safe custody of all the late insurgents indicted before him and his fellow justices'. Other counties had faced similar problems and responded by granting bail to those indicted; this was swiftly stamped upon, and from 10 July onwards commissioners were ordered on pain of forfeiture not to release anyone arrested on charges connected with the revolt; the sheriff of Oxfordshire and Berkshire was even ordered to re-arrest and re-imprison all rebels who had been released on bail. The problem identified by the monk of so many rebels fleeing to avoid punishment was addressed in Essex and Cambridgeshire by granting the commissioners additional powers to pursue and arrest indicted rebels found outside their counties. As late as 26 October the king granted the petition of the collectors of the third poll-tax on the clergy in the archdeaconry of Essex that they should not have to answer for the sums which ought to have been levied on a great number of chaplains and clerks who, 'fearing impeachment for the insurrection and being perhaps guilty, have withdrawn thence and fled to places unknown'.[1]

To add weight to the commissions and give physical expression to the king's opposition to the rebels' actions, it was decided that Richard himself should accompany Chief Justice Tresilian into Essex, where the rebellion had first begun. Between 1 and 7 July they were at Chelmsford, hearing indictments and deciding cases. Significantly, given Tresilian's hard-line reputation, it was here on 2 July that Richard was finally persuaded that he must formally revoke all his letters abolishing personal and tenurial villeinage, granting liberty from tolls and customs and pardoning all offences. The concessions he had granted at Mile End were thus to be repealed and everything was to return exactly to the way it had been before the uprising. The fact that it had taken so long for Richard to do this – eighteen days after he had made the original grants – is surely a clear indication that he was reluctant to do so. If he had no intention of standing by them it would have made far more sense to have revoked them immediately after the Kentishmen had left London. This would have sent a powerful message that the letters had been granted under duress and could not be used to legitimate or justify future actions by the rebels. Instead, by remaining silent on the subject, even as he was appointing commissioners to resist the rebels and restore the peace, Richard effectively continued to condone the rebel agenda. This not only encouraged the spread of the rebellion but also drew into the rebel fold many people who would not have acted as they did except in the belief that they were doing so with the king's authority. With the young king now in his company and observing the consequences of his generosity in the stream of rebels brought before the court, Tresilian no doubt applied such pressure that Richard conceded defeat. The fourteen-year-old king now stated that, on mature reflection and advised by his council, he realised that his grants prejudiced and disinherited the crown, the state, the nobles and the Church; he therefore 'revoked, quashed, invalidated and annulled' them, ordered all letters of manumission and pardon to be returned to the chancery for cancellation and commanded that each and every freeman and bondman should again perform all his usual works, dues and services 'without contradiction, complaint, resistance or difficulty'.[2]

This proclamation must have crushed any remaining hope harboured by the rebels that the king might intercede for them or support them. According to a famous passage in Walsingham's chronicle, a group of Essex rebels had already visited the king while he was at Waltham (22 June) to ask if he intended to stand by his grants to them and for a further liberty that, like the lords, they should not be compelled to attend any courts except the biannual view of frankpledge. While the king's councillors hesitated over how to reply, Richard himself had rounded on the rebels for their temerity which, he said, deserved death. 'Give this message to your colleagues from the king', he allegedly told them: 'Rustics you were and rustics you are still;

you will remain in bondage, not as before but incomparably harsher. For as long as we live and, by God's grace, rule over the realm, we will strive with mind, strength and goods to suppress you so that the rigour of your servitude will be an example to posterity'. No account of the so-called Peasants' Revolt is complete without this vivid 'quotation' from the king – yet it is as much a fabrication as Jack Straw's speech at the gallows or John Balle's sermon at Blackheath. All of which, it should be noted, come from Walsingham's pen. Richard's own deeds belie the words Walsingham put into his mouth, in particular the fact that, as late as November 1381, he was still prepared to plead with parliament to allow the abolition of villeinage.[3]

The mixed messages emanating from the king before his public revocation of his letters on 2 July were poignantly displayed time and again in the judicial proceedings that followed the revolt. We have already seen how Richard Leycester thought he could rely on his royal letters of protection when he was brought to trial at Ely. Equally naïve was John Preston of Hadleigh, Suffolk, who appeared before Woodstock and the Essex commissioners at Chelmsford on 25 June with a petition reiterating the rebel demands at Mile End: it asked on behalf of 'the commons' that no one should pay more than four pence an acre for customary land in lieu of services, that all courts should be abolished apart from that of the king and that provision should be made for punishing malefactors from outside the area where they were captured. The commissioners immediately ordered his arrest and interrogated him as to who had drawn up the petition. When Preston admitted that he had done so, and personally delivered it to the court, they ordered that he should at once be beheaded. It is difficult to see what crime he had committed to deserve instant execution without trial, especially as this all took place a week before the revocation of Richard's concessions, so the king's own letters patent were still in force. The terrible injustice of it led two days later to a group of Essex rebels threatening to kill the abbot of St Osyth in retaliation for Preston's execution.[4]

The problem was that the commissioners' powers were defined so loosely as to allow them carte blanche to act as they saw fit: they not only had the power to round up, arrest and imprison those suspected of rebellion, but also sometimes acted as prosecution, judge and jury. Those appointed to the county commissions were the old guard, many of whom had seen their friends, neighbours and patrons attacked or had themselves been victims of the revolt. The commission for Kent, for example, included Thomas Trevet and the sheriff William Septvans, both of whom had been abducted, coerced and put in fear of their lives by those whom they were now supposed to arrest and imprison; the sire de Scales, John Brewes and Stephen de Hales, who had all been forced to wait on Geoffrey Lister, were on the one for Norfolk and Suffolk.[5] Impartiality was hardly to be expected of such men. The earl of Suffolk's commission, on which Scales, Brewes and Hales served, was particularly high-handed in its approach, sometimes denying suspects the right to a jury and accepting private accusations as the equivalent of a legal indictment by a jury. These resulted in many executions, among them that of William Taylor of Norwich who, when he appeared before the commission on other charges, was accused by Brewes and Hales of having threatened to behead Brewes when he was held captive. Their word, corroborated by Sir Thomas Gyssing, was sufficient to secure Taylor's immediate execution without due process or recourse to a jury.[6]

Hugh la Zouche's commission in Cambridgeshire cut through the bureaucratic process of outlawry which allowed the escheator to seize the property of convicted rebels. Instead of non-appearance in response to the customary summons to attend up to four county courts, which could take many months, Zouche decreed that if indicted rebels – not convicted ones, it should be noted – had fled the county and did not answer a single summons to appear before the commissioners then their lands and goods could be taken into the king's hands. (We have already seen that he had no qualms about acquiring some of these goods for himself.) He was also reluctant to release defendants who were acquitted by trial juries, ordering proclamations to be made asking if there were any further charges against them and then requiring four sureties for future good behaviour before allowing prisoners to go free.[7]

The arbitrary nature of many of the commissioners' judgments was to some extent due to a determination on their part to push the definition of treason as far as it would go, and beyond. Although it was the presenting juries at the inquisitions who indicted their peers, the actual charges were drawn up by clerks employed by the commissioners, and it was upon this wording that the defendants were tried. At its most basic, the definition of treason was a violation of the loyalty owed by one individual to another: a servant who killed his master, a husband his wife or a cleric his superior thus committed petty treason and his goods were forfeited to his lord. High treason, in which the forfeiture was to the crown and the additional penalties of drawing to the place of execution and quartering the body were imposed, was defined in the Statute of Treasons (1352). This had been introduced to stop royal judges extending the common law of treason to cover all sorts of simple felonies such as murder, arson, rape, wounding and robbery. The statute limited high treason to planning or attempting the death of the king, his consort or his heir; raping his consort, his eldest unmarried daughter or the consort of his heir; raising war against the king or allying with his enemies; counterfeiting the Great Seal or the coinage; and killing senior royal officials such as the chancellor, treasurer and justices empowered to hear and determine cases, but with the significant proviso that this was only treason if they were actually killed while they were performing their official duties. It was therefore a moot point whether the deaths of justices of the peace such as Edmund de Walsyngham and Thomas atte Ook were high treason, since they were not sitting in court when killed, though they were in office at the time. It was also an almost insuperable legal difficulty that treason was personal to the royal family, yet the rebels had consistently expressed their loyalty to the king and had never envisaged harm to him or waged war against him personally. The statute made no mention of 'treason against the realm', rather than against the person of the king and his immediate family and senior officials, but some of the indictments resurrected this older crime; they also introduced the words 'treacherously' to describe acts which would otherwise have fallen into the less serious categories of felony or trespass, particularly when this covered riding armed with the intention of slaying, robbing, capturing or kidnapping, even though this type of offence had been specifically excluded from the definition of treason by the statute.[8]

This elastic interpretation of treason by the commissioners introduced anomalies whereby rebels might find themselves charged with either treason or felony despite being indicted for the same crime. The murderers of Chancellor Sudbury, Treasurer Hales and Chief Justice Cavendish were all considered traitors by the crown and specifically excluded from any grant of pardon, yet a jury sympathetic to the rebels in Westgate hundred, Kent, found that the archbishop's execution was only a felony. Much depended on the attitude of the commissioners themselves and nowhere was this more obvious than those cases heard by Tresilian: 'whoever was accused before him on the grounds of rebellion,' observed Henry Knighton, 'whether justly or out of hate, immediately suffered the sentence of death'.[9]

Tresilian's hearings at Chelmsford, where he sat in judgment on those Essex men who had been involved at the beginning of the revolt, resulted in thirty-one executions of which twelve included the drawing to the scaffold, which was the penalty for treason; at St Albans he sentenced fifteen townsmen to death and eighty others to imprisonment, despite there having been no killings and no significant acts of violence. The contrast with Bury St Edmunds, where there had been numerous murders, including the abbey's prior and the former Chief Justice Cavendish, as well as demolition of buildings in the town and assaults within the abbey precincts, could not be more striking. The inhabitants of Bury St Edmunds were the only ones to be collectively excluded from the general amnesty in November 1381, together with five named individuals, John Clakke, Robert Westbron, Thomas Halesworth, Robert Sad and Thomas Yoxford. On 22 December, however, the king accepted the town into his grace on condition that it paid a two-thousand-mark fine, a sum which took its inhabitants four and a half years to raise; 722 of them, including forty-five clerics and twenty-two women, were also obliged to bind themselves in the sum of ten thousand pounds for future good behaviour. Financially onerous though all this was, the townsmen escaped with their lives and liberty. Clakke, Westbron and Halesworth were all pardoned in 1385, despite the latter two having been present at, if not actually giving orders for, the prior's murder.[10]

Tresilian was in a league of his own when it came to handing down death sentences. Thomas of Woodstock's commission for Essex heard some four hundred indictments but only tried thirty-five people, of whom ten were executed; three-quarters of the indictments brought before Hugh la Zouche's commission in Cambridge did not proceed to trial. Even so, it comes as a blessed relief in the midst of so much arbitrary and bloody justice to find a justice behaving with calm and reasoned impartiality. 'You are not charged with rebellion', Chief Justice Bealknapp informed a defendant before him. 'For although this event occurred in London, where the rebellion was located, and at the same time, it does not follow that you did it by rebellion, for it could well be that there is a rebellion in some place in a town, but not in another'.[11] Not everyone was willing or able to make such nice distinctions. Just as the revolt itself had been the ideal cover for those seeking to pursue private quarrels, so the judicial process afterwards proved to be an effective way of exploiting old grudges or obtaining vengeance. In Beverley, Yorkshire, where there had been a power struggle between the old oligarchy and the 'middle men' artisans and craftsmen, several of the latter were indicted for the murder of William Haldene on 6 July on the evidence of Haldene's widow, who had been bribed to accuse them by a leading member of the oligarchy. The widow of William Brag similarly gave evidence to the Hertfordshire commissioners that her husband, a servant of Edmund Stonor, had been killed at Gubblecote on 18 June by the rebels who had burned Stonor's archives. This accusation led to Hugo the persone-sprest of Puttenham and seven others being sent to the Tower. Yet in other evidence Anna Brag stated that her husband was murdered on 10 December 1381, several months after the revolt. By falsifying the dates she had procured a much less rigorous legal process and swifter punishment for those whom she accused. All were eventually acquitted when the discrepancies came to light, but one of them did not receive his pardon until 1391.[12]

Injustices like these must have been multiplied many times over, especially when professional extortionists like Thomas Hardyng of Manningtree, Essex, brought his expertise to bear, ruthlessly and unscrupulously abusing the system repeatedly to blackmail his neighbours into giving him money to avoid prosecution.[13] The situation was not helped by government attempts to help those who had suffered losses at the hands of the rebels. Royal licences were granted to the likes of John Gildesburgh, Thomas Haseldene, the sheriff of Norfolk and Suffolk William de Kerdeston, the prior of Barnwell, Hugh Fastolf, John Bampton and the executors of both Reginald de Eccles and Richard Lyons, allowing them to take back any goods they could prove to be theirs 'howsoever they please from those who detain them, without hindrance from the king or his ministers'. This was an extraordinary tool to put into the hands of powerful and sometimes corrupt men, giving them free rein to act outside the law without fear of retribution. Haseldene, Fastolf, Bampton and the prior of Barnwell also obtained royal commissions which were empowered to inquire into the destruction and theft they had suffered, but also to arrest offenders and compel restitution and the payment of compensation, thus putting the full force of the law behind their attempts to recover their property and receive damages. One of the first off the mark in obtaining this kind of commission was John Herlyng, an esquire of the royal household, steward of the liberty of Bury St Edmunds and castellan of Castle Rising, Norfolk, but he was swiftly followed by William Crosyer, John Sibil, the abbot of Stratford Langthorne, the warden of Cressing Temple and the university of Cambridge.[14] These again were dangerous tools to put into the hands of those seeking revenge since impartiality could hardly be expected when so many of those appointed to these local commissions had themselves been targeted by the same rebels. What is more, the summary nature of the proceedings and the power to recover goods from anyone in possession of them, not just those who had taken them, naturally lent themselves to abuse: Ralph Barbour, for example, was prosecuted because he had bought several valuable items, including a psalter, which were later found to have been pillaged from

Henry Lomynour's house in Norwich. The fact that the commissioners were 'unlawfully oppressing the people beyond measure by extortions and other intolerable grievances' was eventually recognised by the crown; on 12 September sheriffs were ordered to proclaim that all proceedings under these commissions were to cease and to set free all those imprisoned by them: in future, anyone who wished to reclaim stolen property or recover damages should do so through the normal processes of the king's courts.[15]

Private prosecutions continued unabated, however, until the House of Commons successfully petitioned that no new actions should be brought after 8 July 1383 and allowed anyone accused to be acquitted if three or four men of good repute gave testimony in their favour before the court. This intervention, again, was an attempt to remedy the abuse of process by people like Hardyng, who brought thirty-nine separate actions against people who could afford to pay him off, or John Sibil, who inflated the value of the crops stolen from his Cambridgeshire manor at Horseheath to obtain higher damages. Almost three hundred private prosecutions were brought against alleged rebels by around one hundred and twenty-five plaintiffs, the majority of them being actions for trespass in Essex, Norfolk and London/Middlesex. There is clear evidence to show that plaintiffs such as Gaunt and Butterwick, for instance, supported each other by sharing information and listing as many names as possible in the hope that at least some would be convicted.[16] Despite being singularly unsuccessful as far as obtaining judgment against the defendants was concerned, they were an effective means of harassing enemies and extorting money from those accused, falsely or otherwise, of participation in the revolt. They created an atmosphere of fear and suspicion which the introduction of a time limit on future actions was intended to address, enabling 'peace and tranquillity to be nourished and augmented throughout the realm and to cease strife and contentions'.[17]

The final weapon in the government's armoury for crushing the revolt or, more correctly, overturning what it had achieved, was the issuing of writs to compel tenants to render all their customary dues and obligations. This was happening even before Richard formally revoked his letters patent: on 30 June the commissioners in Lincolnshire were ordered to make proclamations without delay that all tenants, bond and free, should 'without gainsaying, murmuring or resistance perform the works, customs and services due to their lords, as they used to do before the disturbance now arisen in divers counties', nor were they 'to delay them on any pretence, or to claim other privileges or liberties than they formerly had', on pain of arrest and imprisonment. The same writ was issued on behalf of the abbot of Stratford the same day, and the litigious Margaret, countess of Norfolk, followed suit on 1 July. Over the course of the next few weeks, as the harvest approached and the need for labour grew more intense, many more were issued, mostly to religious houses, such as the abbeys of St Albans and Ramsey, but also to individuals. Richard, earl of Arundel, for example, whose rebellious tenants had allegedly caused him a thousand pounds' worth of damage when they invaded Lewes Castle on 16 June and burned his records, was now facing a labour strike and obtained one for his lands in Sussex on 2 July. The king himself had to acquire one on 22 July for his Hertfordshire manor of King's Langley, to which he added a clause commanding his tenants to return 'a charter made to them concerning manumissions and pardons' so that it could be cancelled.[18]

Many tenants proved remarkably stubborn: the harvest came and went but Stratford Langthorne Abbey, the Knights Hospitaller (whom Richard had taken into his special protection after their prior's murder) in Lincolnshire and the vacant archbishopric of Canterbury all had to apply for further royal assistance to force their tenants back to work – and not always successfully.[19] On most manors, however, landlords and tenants had to come to some sort of pragmatic accommodation. All the villeins on the manor of Moze, Essex, for example, were deprived of their holdings because they had burned the court rolls but they were allowed to have them back again on paying fines of ten or twenty shillings; the record of the re-grant states that it was also made to 'their heirs and assigns', indicating that these villeins effectively held by hereditary tenure just like freemen. The tenants of the bishop of Norwich's manors where court rolls were burned were ordered to return any damaged ones and to make new custumals, rentals, extents, terriers and lists of those tenants owing suit of court on pain of a five-pound fine.[20]

When parliament met in November 1381 the revolt was over but the atmosphere was still tense. The opening was delayed by several days to settle 'a great dispute' between Gaunt and the earl of Northumberland, both of whom had brought large retinues of armed men with them. Gaunt had been at Berwick, Northumberland, negotiating with the Scots when the revolt broke out; on 18 June he concluded an eighteen-month truce then, two days later, moved south to the royal castle of Bamburgh, where he received messengers from the earl bearing letters advising him to remain at Berwick 'until you may be better apprised of the state of the king and the affairs of the realm'. Gaunt took this, or verbal messages given at the same time, to mean that the earl refused him admission to his castles: it is even possible that Gaunt was already virtually outside the walls of the earl's castle of Alnwick when he received these messages, which made the latter's action even more offensive and the dispute more explicable. Given the rumours that Gaunt had been declared a traitor and the rebels wanted his head, it seems clear that Northumberland did not want to be tainted by association. Gaunt may also have felt that the king had abandoned him as he then fled over the border to seek sanctuary with the Scots, only re-emerging after 3 July when Richard issued writs declaring his uncle 'to be most zealous in his cause' and commanding royal ministers and his subjects alike to give Gaunt their assistance in conducting him safely back again. Even so, Gaunt had remained skulking around his northern English power bases until the revolt was over. Determined to seek revenge for at least some of these humiliations, Gaunt had fixed on Northumberland and the earl was forced to make a formal apology in full parliament for his 'disloyalty'.[21]

There could have been no stronger reminder of the events of the summer than the fact that neither Sudbury nor Hales were at parliament to give the opening addresses: instead they were given by William Courtenay, archbishop-elect of Canterbury, and the new treasurer Sir Hugh Segrave. The latter invited the Commons, on Richard's behalf, 'to investigate and search for the causes, motives, and principal reasons for the aforesaid uprising and insurrections, so that having discovered and learnt them, and having entirely rooted them out, people will place the greater trust in the remedy to be ordained, should the commons ever again wish or wickedly propose to perpetrate evil in such a manner'.[22] Richard's acceptance that the rebels had genuine grievances is evident in this determination to seek out and remedy the root causes of the revolt, and perhaps even more so in his offer to abolish villeinage again, which he obviously recognised as one of those root causes. His remarkable appeal to the Commons,[23] over the heads of his councillors, as to whether his revocation of his 'letters of franchise and manumission' had been right, clearly caused consternation. It is a measure of just how unusual it was that the Commons did not know how to respond to their charge to go away and discuss these matters. Unable to come to a conclusion they asked, through their speaker Sir Richard Waldegrave, for the charge to be repeated 'so that we may well understand it'. It was reiterated, with due emphasis on the abolition of villeinage, but the Commons was not prepared to take such responsibility on itself: it was only after consultation with the prelates and lay peers that they were able to reject the king's proposal and say 'with one voice' that the king's revocation of his letters had indeed been 'well made'.[24]

Waldegrave's speech analysing the causes of the revolt has often been hailed as a penetrating and daring critique of the state of the realm. In fact, it is little more than a rehearsal of all the old complaints which resurfaced whenever there was political trouble of any sort. Waldegrave blamed excessive numbers of servants in the royal household and in the king's courts, too many 'embracers of quarrels and maintainers, who act so much like kings in their shires that right and justice are scarcely administered to anyone' and the excesses of the king's household purveyors. None of these things had featured on the rebel agenda, though quest-mongers and lawyers had been among the main targets of the revolt. It is true that other things of which he complained had more relevance to the revolt: the forcible levying of subsidies and tallages, the continual levying of great sums for defence which failed to secure the realm from attack and the 'evil officers and counsellors' who ought to be dismissed. The fact remains that none of the rebel demands, from abolition of all forms of villeinage and freedom from tolls and customs to the revocation of the Statute of Labourers, was even mentioned. This was hardly surprising given that so many of the knights of the shire (and indeed burgesses) had suffered personally in the revolt and that it was their vested interests which had been under attack. Nevertheless, the Commons presented petitions to the king requesting that the chancery, treasury and judicial benches should all be purged of corrupt officials since 'there was and is a great murmuring throughout the realm that they are for the most part too fat in body and in purse, and too well provided, and their benefices ill managed, through the grievous oppressions done and practised by them against the people, by colour of their office'. The chancellor himself was replaced by the Commons' preferred candidate Sir Richard Scrope, but otherwise it was business as usual in all these departments.[25]

The Commons also petitioned for the general amnesty that was granted in this parliament. They asked for three pardons: first for those 'lords, gentles, and others' who had killed rebels without due process of law; secondly for those who had committed treason and felonies during the revolt, with the exception of the principal instigators whose names would be submitted to parliament; and finally for those who had not rebelled. The king, of his grace, granted all three general pardons, excepting only those who had murdered Sudbury, Hales or Cavendish, the towns of Canterbury, Bury St Edmunds, Beverley, Scarborough, Bridgwater and Cambridge (though later in the same parliament he was persuaded to include all except Bury St Edmunds) and without prejudice to private prosecutions. The list of 'principal instigators' excluded from grace comprised 287 named individuals, the vast majority of them from London. There were two catches, so far as anyone seeking a pardon was concerned: the first was that it had to be sued for, which made the applicant vulnerable by admitting his guilt; the second was that it had to be paid for, which many of those in more menial positions could not afford to do, even if they were innocent. A year later, another parliament would remedy this by petitioning the king to issue a second general pardon, excluding only those on the list and Bury St Edmunds:

this was the first comprehensive general pardon which did not require individuals to sue for and buy their own letters – a generous concession given that at least two thousand pounds had been raised so far by their sale.[26]

Other measures were taken to deal with the revolt. Inundated with complaints from the university of Cambridge, the king summoned the mayor, bailiffs and burgesses to appear before him. In September Richard had ordered the borough to quash its election of John Mareschall, a prominent leader of the revolt, as its new mayor and to replace him with 'a fit person'. The replacement, Richard Maisterman, despite being a victim of the rebels, proved no more conciliatory and refused to surrender the charters the university had granted during the revolt. It took the full force of the king sitting in parliament to compel the borough to hand them over for cancellation and, as punishment, the town was deprived of many of its lucrative market franchises, which were granted to the university.[27] All bonds, releases and other deeds, together with any acquisitions of land or rents, made under duress during the revolt were quashed, voided and cancelled by statute. Those who could provide proof that they had lost 'charters, releases, bonds, statutes-merchant, court rolls, or other evidences' during the rising were offered remedies, including free copies of any charters which had been enrolled in chancery. There was one small victory for the rebels: the king repealed Great Yarmouth's charter which Bacon, Lister and their band had cut in two. It proved a pyrrhic victory, however, as Richard reinstated it in 1384, only to repeal it in 1385, then reinstate it again permanently in 1386.[28]

Perhaps the most important measure of the parliament, however, was the drawing up and enrolment of a form of commission which could be used to deal with any future popular uprising. Based on the commissions to keep the peace, it gave extraordinarily wide powers for the commissioners to arrest anyone who arranged or participated in

> conventicles or gatherings contrary to our said peace, and all others whom you or any one of you know for certain to be persuading, encouraging, and inciting our people, whether by word, deed, act, cunning, or any other art, to rise up and rebel in such conventicles and gatherings ... and punish and destroy them at your discretion if they rebel against you or resist you, and ... crush, extinguish, and oppose all such illicit conventicles and gatherings by any methods or means within your power, even by force and armed might if necessary.

The commissioners were given authority to enter liberties normally exempt from such intrusions, to raise as many knights and men-at-arms as seemed necessary to them to oppose, punish and destroy such rebels and to execute justice on all perpetrators of 'treasons, murders, felonies, or arsons, or who be found in the act of committing thefts and robberies'. No future king of England, facing a popular revolt, would be without the legal administrative tools to suppress it.[29]

What parliament did not do was grant another poll-tax or even an old-fashioned subsidy, despite the king's plea that he was greatly in debt and Gaunt's extraordinarily insensitive demand for a loan of sixty thousand pounds for six months' wages for two thousand men-at-arms and two thousand archers to bolster his brother Langley's failing expedition in Portugal. This caused 'great argument and altercation in the said parliament' but the Commons stood firm: 'bearing in mind the ill will which the common people still express in rancour throughout the kingdom, they did not dare nor wish to grant tallage in any way, or anything else for which the said commons would be liable or responsible'. What they did grant was a four-year extension of the wool subsidies, with the heartfelt but hopeless prayer that the burdens of war might soon be abolished so 'that the poor commons may live in peace and tranquillity'.[30]

CHAPTER SIXTEEN

The aftermath

Any account of the great revolt raises more questions than it answers. We still do not know exactly how long the rebels had been planning their action: the confrontation at Brentwood was undoubtedly a catalyst but we do not know whether rebellion was already being discussed or how long the rebels of Essex and Kent had been in communication with each other. Wat Tyler, Jack Straw and John Balle, despite their iconic status, remain shadowy figures. Nor is it clear why Straw, in particular, earned such an enduring reputation whereas other rebel leaders about whom we know much more, such as John Wrawe, William Grindecobbe and Geoffrey Lister, have been virtually forgotten.

It is obvious now that the rebels were far more sophisticated than contemporary chroniclers gave them credit for: they were not just servants and labourers but craftsmen, artisans, wealthy tenant farmers, even members of the gentry, with more to lose than gain from revolt. Apart from the slaughter of the Flemings, especially in London, there was none of the indiscriminate mob violence which characterised other medieval uprisings. A number of royal officials were killed, but the eminent rank of Sudbury, Hales, Cavendish and the prior of Bury St Edmunds should not obscure the fact that the great revolt was not like the French Revolution of 1789 to which it is often compared. These rebels were highly organised and disciplined enough to target particular officials and not others: many of their victims were involved in the collection of the third poll-tax but that was not in itself sufficient to attract retribution – indeed some collectors, like Thomas Sampson in Suffolk and Richard Martyn in Cambridge, were to be found among the leaders of the revolt. The rebels were not a ragged bunch of agricultural workers forced to march on foot but were capable of covering long distances on horseback, spreading the revolt quickly and maintaining the element of surprise. They understood the workings of local government and were often part of it, acting as bailiffs, constables and other 'worthy men', so they were therefore able to utilise its systems for their own cause, calling out the local levies for instance, which in other circumstances would have been used against them. They were sufficiently sophisticated and organised to employ a watch-word to identify themselves as sworn members of a movement with coherent aims; the answer to the question 'With whom haldes yow?' was simple to remember – 'Wyth kynge Richarde and wyth the trew communes' – but it powerfully articulated their loyalties and political ideas. They were not rebels against their king but against those who abused his royal authority; they, and not those supposed to represent them in parliament, were his true and faithful commons. Above all else, they or their leaders were sufficiently literate to be able to read letters, write petitions and dictate charters of liberties.

The great revolt is often characterised as a reaction against the written record, but this is simplistic. While it is true that burning the returns of the third poll-tax, manorial court rolls, judicial records and legal archives was a major part of the revolt and was often an act of great symbolism, manifested by bonfires in public places, the rebels did not seek simply to destroy the written record but to replace it with a new one. At every point, whether it was the king's concessions at Mile End, those of the abbots of religious houses like St Albans or Bury St Edmunds, or those of private individuals compelled to sign bonds, the rebels wanted the documentation in place so that they had their new-found freedoms enshrined in letters patent or charters. They were not destroying the past but securing their future, and they knew that had to be done in writing.

At the heart of the revolt, in every sense, were the concessions made by Richard II at Mile End. It is difficult to imagine what would have happened if he had refused to grant them. Would the rebels have sacked Westminster itself? Or taken the boy-king hostage? But the fact that he did grant them and was then so slow to revoke them gave the rebellion legitimacy, which persuaded many otherwise unlikely rebels, such as John Hauchach and Geoffrey Cobbe at Cambridge, Richard de Leycester at Ely and Thomas Sampson in Suffolk, to join the revolt. What is more, these men's standing in their own local communities gave added authority to the rebels' actions and encouraged others to swell their ranks. One only has to look at the charter of liberties granted by the abbot of St Albans on 15 June to see that Richard's concessions persuaded people who might otherwise have resisted the revolt that the king was in favour of the rebels' proceedings. Walsingham's transcript, which he provocatively titles 'extorted by the villeins of Barnet', records among its list of witnesses both John Lodewyk, JP, whose 'records, processes and indictments' were being removed from his house that very day by rebels, and Sir Thomas Hoo.[1]

Walsingham gives no hint that they were compelled to act as witnesses (and he would have been the first to do so) so we can only assume that they signed voluntarily having seen the king's own letters granting freedom to the people of Hertfordshire.

The many examples of rebels riding with banners of the king's arms displayed – banners which, in at least some instances, were given to them at Mile End – demonstrate that they believed they were acting as the king's agents, as does the repeated insistence that they were acting 'on the king's commission'. The gruesome beheadings of so many victims and the displaying of their heads on London Bridge or local pillories mimicked the usual practice of the state when dealing with traitors. On the odd occasion when a victim was killed by another method, like Reginald de Eccles at Norwich, who was stabbed in the abdomen, his head was still cut off for public display as that of a traitor. When we learn that the rebels in Cambridge compelled the university's representatives to undertake to pay for the enrolment of their new charter in the king's chancery, we cannot be in any doubt that they believed that they had the law and the king on their side.[2] Richard's futile attempt in November 1381 to persuade parliament to reinstate his abolition of villeinage suggests that they were right, at least in so far as the king's personal wishes went.

The great revolt was over and the inquest had been held, but little would be done to redress the grievances that had inspired it. John of Gaunt would continue his Spanish adventures, oblivious to, or careless of, the financial cost to the kingdom. Corrupt and oppressive royal officials remained in place and even, in cases like the Accloms of Scarborough, managed to pass the baton on to the next generation. The townsmen of places in the lordship of powerful abbeys did not gain their independence until after the monasteries themselves had been abolished by Henry VIII: St Albans eventually got its charter of incorporation in 1553, Bury St Edmunds in 1606.[3] In the countryside those holding by villein tenure reverted to their former methods by which they tried to throw off the yoke of lordship. In 1385, for example, the villeins on the abbey of Bury St Edmunds' manor of Littlehawe, Suffolk, were found guilty of withholding their customary services for three years and fined three pounds. Led by their parson and chaplain, they had formed an association and raised money to buy exemplifications from Domesday Book to prove their free status; significantly, despite withholding their services, they had paid the abbey four pence an acre throughout their labour strike, exactly the sum which the rebels had persuaded the king to accept as the value of customary land.[4]

Villeinage was never formally abolished, but lingered on into the sixteenth century: manumission for the villeins of the duke of Norfolk was one of the demands of Kett's rebellion in 1549 and as late as 1575 Queen Elizabeth I sold off three hundred of her villeins in an attempt to shore up her depleted finances.[5] In the years immediately after the revolt it was actually the House of Commons which would lead a rearguard action to enforce villeinage more rigorously. The king granted its petitions in 1385 for the right to reclaim and extradite villeins who left their manors for towns, and in 1388 that villeins' children should not be allowed to leave the manor after the age of twelve. A further petition in 1391 demanding that they should not be permitted to send their children to school because education was a means to ordination, and ordination automatically bestowed manumission, was rejected. On most estates, however, a combination of economic pressures as grain prices dropped, outright refusal by tenants to perform collective services and an inability to find anyone willing to take on tenancies burdened with labour dues led to a gradual withering away of villein tenure and its replacement by leasehold and cash rents.[6]

In the immediate aftermath of the revolt, parliament and the Church would act in concert to ensure that no popular revolt could again be stirred up by renegade preachers: orthodox churchmen had been quick to point the finger of blame at John Wyclif. William Rimington, for instance, a Cistercian writing in 1382–3, claimed that Wyclif's 'pestiferous teaching was probably a cause that lately moved the community to rise against the king and nobles of this realm'. Walsingham went further, seeing archbishop Sudbury's death as punishment for his 'lukewarmness' and 'negligence' in suppressing Wyclif and his followers, among whom he placed John Balle, who 'taught, moreover, the perverse doctrines of the perfidious John Wycliffe, and the insane opinions that he held'. The Carmelite author of *Fasciculi Zizaniorum*, a fifteenth-century compendium of anti-Lollard material, blatantly fabricated a 'confession' by Balle 'that for two years he had been a disciple of Wycliffe and had learned from the latter the heresies which he had taught' and that he had been part of a 'secret fraternity' which had travelled the country preaching Wyclif's 'perverse doctrine [and] ... if they had not encountered resistance to their plans, they would have destroyed the entire kingdom within two years'. The chronicler Henry Knighton, who was in the embarrassing position of having one of Wyclif's most eminent former disciples as his abbot, found his way out of the difficulty by describing Balle as Wyclif's John the Baptist: 'Balle prepared the way for Wycliffe's opinions and, as is said, disturbed many with his own doctrines ... [Balle] was the real breaker of the unity of the church, the author of discord between the laity and clergy, the indefatigable sower of illicit doctrines and the disturber of the Christian church'.[7]

Wyclif's personal response to the great revolt was ambivalent. He condemned the murder of Sudbury because it was carried out without trial and was an excessive punishment for his crime in assuming the chancellorship, which Wyclif described as the most secular office in the land; however, Wyclif pleaded for mercy for the rebels because their grievances cried out for redress and had been ignored.[8] The Church, however, had no intention of allowing his voice to be heard in public again. In May 1382 the Blackfriars Conference (which was appropriately struck by an earthquake while in session) condemned a list of twenty-four propositions attributed to Wyclif and his followers, including his heretical beliefs about Church property and the impotence of priests in mortal sin, which were shared by Balle. A few days later parliament issued a statute requiring sheriffs and other royal officials to imprison unauthorised preachers and those who defended the propositions. Wyclif and his supporters were prohibited from any further preaching or teaching until they renounced their heresy and did penance for it. As a result of the combined action of Church and state the apparatus was put in place for punishing heretics which would eventually lead to legislation in 1401 allowing them to be burned at the stake. Balle could not have envisaged that his preaching would have had such terrible consequences but his role in stirring up the revolt, however much exaggerated by the chronicles and the authorities, could not be ignored and gave the Church the excuse it needed to seek and gain the state's assistance in repressing future dissent in matters of faith.

Despite having lost everything they set out to achieve, and despite the thoroughness of the suppression of the uprising, the rebels did not give up easily. On 29 July sixteen bondsmen by blood of the abbot of Chester held secret meetings in woods and the fields around Backford, just north of Chester, and made a collection of money to pay for legal advice on how to obtain their freedom. Was this a very late outbreak of the great revolt, a very early example of a new one or, as the 'rebels' themselves would have claimed, not a revolt at all but simply a non-violent way of trying to gain their liberty? Nevertheless, because the systems were now in place to suppress rebellion, it was identified and treated as such by the authorities.[9]

A more serious attempt to revive the rebellion apparently occurred in September in a group of villages south of Maidstone, Kent. Allegedly inspired by the unlikely report by pilgrims travelling from northern areas of England to Canterbury that Gaunt was about to free his villeins, Thomas Harding gathered a group of sympathisers in the local brewery and plotted to seize and kill three members of the Kentish gentry, enlist armed assistance from Romney Marsh and elsewhere and compel the king to reinstate the concessions he had made at Mile End or kill him too. They even agreed to send one of their number as a spy to the royal court to report on any planned moves against them and an agitator into Essex to raise rebels there. We cannot tell now whether this was a genuine attempt to restart the rebellion, or talk prompted by the drink, or the inventions of the approver who betrayed the alleged plot to John Frenyngham, one of the Kent commissioners to put down the rebellion. What we do know is that the response was swift and savage. Frenyngham had already suffered at the rebels' hands earlier in the year, when he had been seized and compelled to swear the oath of loyalty to king and commons. Now he arrested the ringleaders and brought them before Tresilian, who held a special session of the King's Bench just to try them: nine were executed and Harding's head was fixed to the outer gate of Westminster Palace. A jittery government appointed a string of commissions to investigate, arrest and punish agitators from Kent who were rumoured to be stoking up further revolts in counties throughout the south-east.[10]

A year later, in September 1382, another conspiracy was uncovered in Norfolk, this time with the objective of capturing and killing bishop Despenser and other magnates, probably as a preliminary to raising another rebellion. The plan was to raise recruits at the three-day fair of Horsham St Faith near Norwich then lead them to occupy the abbey of St Benet-at-Holme, which was to become a rebel fortress. This plot too was nipped in the bud by the commissioners for Norfolk, led by Thomas de Morlee, who had so ignominiously been held captive by Geoffrey Lister. As senior judge in Despenser's absence, Morlee was able to exact his revenge by condemning ten of the men to death. Morlee, it appears, had learnt nothing from his experiences, since at about the same time he was able to clear himself of the charge of having taken prisoner Thomas, son of Philip Gervays, and kept him hidden away by claiming that the man was his serf.[11]

In May 1383 six men were charged with making a 'new insurrection' in Suffolk because they had raised a large band of people to attack the houses of George Glanvyll at Hollesley and the rector of Parham: they had allegedly compelled Glanvyll and his wife to pay them a fine of ten pounds and looted their house, which had previously been broken into during the great revolt. Three of the accused were condemned to death but two claimed benefit of clergy and therefore escaped execution. A couple of months earlier, an attempt to kill the sheriff of Devon at Tavistock was judged to be insurrection and treason – though the murder of a royal tax-collector at Goldsworthy, Devon, was tried only as a felony.[12]

Much of the north was in a state of semi-permanent disorder throughout the late 1380s and 1390s, with numerous uprisings recorded in Yorkshire and Cheshire, but these were by and large local affairs, far enough away from London for the government to regard them as lacking the potential to inspire a second nationwide revolt.[13] John Berwald, junior, of Cottingham, Yorkshire, for instance, was indicted in 1392 because he had composed 'a certain rhyme in English words' which he had proclaimed at Beverley on 28 July and in Hull a week later. Like the letters attributed to John Balle, his rhyme was considered revolutionary and incendiary: it urged people to stand together as brothers, maintain their neighbours and, if wrong were done to one of them, it should be held a wrong to all 'and on that purpose we stand'. The rhyme was linked with disturbances on the manor of Cottingham, which belonged to Thomas Holland, the king's half-brother, in which there had been

> sworn conspiracies, assemblies, taking of fines and ransoms from the people without reasonable cause, liveries of hoods ... contrary to the ordinance, confederacies, ambushes to beat, maim or kill people of the country-side, assaults on William Holme, late escheator in that county, in the exercise of his office, and false alliances by confederation that each would maintain the other.

Despite these crimes, all those involved were pardoned a year later.[14]

The great revolt of 1381 achieved none of its stated aims – though no government would dare to impose another poll-tax for six hundred years. Nevertheless, the idea that ordinary people could spontaneously rise up and join forces against an oppressive regime to better their condition has gripped the popular imagination ever since. From Jack Cade in 1450 to the Revolutionary Socialist Workers' Party and the poll-tax rioters of the 1980s, generations of rebels and political idealists have looked back to the great revolt for inspiration and affirmation of their own struggle. Wat Tyler, Jack Straw and John Balle have been mythologised and elevated to the status of ideological martyrs for their cause – a cause which, bizarrely, has largely been misunderstood. Radical though the rebel demands were, they did not include equality for all, redistribution of wealth or the destruction of the political system; even the poll-tax, as we have seen, was not a flat-rate imposition levied on one and all regardless of rank or personal means.

It is one of the great ironies of history that the man who did more than anyone else to ensure that the rebel leaders would be remembered was one of their bitterest and most implacable foes. Thomas Walsingham had wanted to create martyrs of archbishop Sudbury and the prior of Bury St Edmunds. Instead, he made popular heroes out of Tyler, Straw and Balle. It is not the pious phrases he put into Sudbury's mouth as he faced his brutal execution that ring down through the centuries but the words of the fictitious sermon he gave John Balle:

When Adam delved and Eve span
Who was then the gentleman?[15]

We can question whether Tyler, Straw and Balle were as key to the revolt as their fame would suggest, but what is beyond doubt is that they, and many others like them, emerged as leaders of a popular uprising the likes of which had never before been seen in England. Previous rebellions had always been led by members of the aristocracy: it was the barons who united against King John to obtain Magna Carta in 1215, fought the civil wars against Henry III in the 1260s and deposed Edward II in 1327. The same was to hold true for much of the future, as Richard II would learn to his cost when he too was removed from the throne by a coalition of magnates led by his cousin Henry Bolingbroke. In 1381, however, there was not a single member of the nobility, secular or ecclesiastical, who identified with the grievances of the general population and was prepared to act to remedy them. For the lay aristocracy war with France was a matter of honour and a way of life: its financial cost was an irrelevance. The senior clergy might protest in congregation at being forced to contribute money to the king's wars but, like their lay peers, they did not voice opposition to the war in principle. And also, like their secular counterparts, they were beneficiaries of the systems which those at the lower end of the social scale so resented.

Parliament, as an institution, was quite capable of taking a stand against bad governance, insisting on changes in government personnel and imposing tighter controls on spending and auditing royal accounts, but the merchants and shire gentry who sat in the House of Commons were the same men who served in civic office and as stewards of great estates, sheriffs and, above all, as justices of the peace. They were therefore part of the problem. They might express concern about the effect of continual and heavy taxation on the 'poor commons' and even attempt to mitigate its worst effects on the poorest, but only once in six assemblies since 1377 had parliament refused a request for taxation. Their conviction that wage-earners, such as labourers and servants, were cash-rich and ought to be brought within the tax net, encouraged them to enforce regressive and unrealistic legislation controlling wages and to impose the poll-taxes, despite their disproportionate effect on the less wealthy in society. Neither parliament as a whole, nor even the Commons, which purported to represent the people of the shires and towns, was prepared to voice or redress the grievances of the general population.

Since the natural leaders of the kingdom could not be called upon to provide remedies, others had stepped into the breach. These were what we might now call the middle class, or more specifically the aspirant middle class: those who had no real voice or role in the administration of urban government, or who were caught in the middle of agrarian society between the traditional defined ranks of landlords on one side and villeins on the other. Whether free or unfree, though generally the former, they were the ambitious, hard-working and lucky who had bettered themselves by seizing the economic opportunities offered in the years after the Black Death. It was these people who had become the village elite, rich enough to pay wages to employ others outside their own families, and serving in manorial and county administration as jurors, constables and bailiffs. And it was overwhelmingly these people – hitherto respectable men like William Gildeborne, John Geffrey and Thomas Sampson – who led the revolt of 1381.

They were joined by the artisans and craftsmen whose skills enabled them to earn their living in a growing market economy outside the narrow confines of the traditional, manorial, agricultural relationship of landlord and tenant. Men like Henry Bongay and William Grindecobbe were wealthy enough to expect that they had earned a right to play a part in civic government or to avoid the humiliation of being obliged to perform archaic customs and services at the whim of their social superiors. Yet they had no legitimate means of expressing their dissatisfaction and frustration, and their relatively modest earnings and savings were increasingly being targeted by a government determined to squeeze as much as possible from the populace into its ever-empty coffers. Repeated demands for taxation took their toll, particularly when the burden of supporting their poorer (and possibly more feckless) neighbours was added to their own personal liability. Many of them were doubtless sufficiently educated to be both numerate and literate in English, if not in the French or Latin which remained largely the preserve of professional clerks. They were just the sort of people who, in the decades after the revolt, would reject orthodox religion to become Lollards, subscribing to the popular heresy, based on Wyclif's ideas, which encouraged lay literacy and reading the Bible in English, questioned the Church's monopoly on salvation and championed the rights of the individual. The government ignored such people at its peril and, in 1381, it paid the price.

CHAPTER SEVENTEEN

The legacy

The great revolt played out over a remarkably short period of time; its suppression was swift and thereafter, to all appearances, life returned to normal. We even read of former rebels, charged with rebellion in their manorial courts, levying amercements and entry fines against themselves in order to be able to pick up the threads of their old lives as if nothing untoward had happened.[1] Yet for others the effect of being caught up in the revolt was profound and even life changing. We have already seen, for instance, how some royal officers in the shires resigned their posts and retired from public life; and there must have been others who, like the sheriff of Kent William Septvans, responded to what had happened to them by taking the decision to free all their own villeins.[2]

One person above all others must have been marked for life by his experiences, and that was Richard II. He had stood in a turret of the White Tower and watched as the rebels overran London and the flames consumed his uncle's Savoy Palace and the preceptory of the Knights Hospitaller. He had parted from his two most senior advisers, his chancellor and treasurer, after the council meeting in the Tower and the next time he would come face to face with them was at the entrance to London Bridge, where their severed heads were displayed for all to see. He had met the rebels and their representatives twice in person, at Mile End and Smithfield, had talked to them, listened to their grievances and offered remedies. And he had witnessed not only the murder of Wat Tyler but also the judicial execution of John Balle. These were events which would have tried the mettle of the most experienced medieval monarch but Richard was still a boy, at the impressionable age of fourteen, and facing an unprecedented political crisis before he had even fully assumed the reins of government.

Unfortunately we have no means of knowing for certain what impact these events had on the boy-king as he left no personal account or comment, either public or private. What we can perhaps deduce from Richard's subsequent behaviour is that the great revolt instilled in him, or reinforced, his own ideas of kingship. The rebels had attacked his government's policies, his ministers and his officials but they had remained unswerving in their loyalty and devotion to Richard himself. His name had been on their lips as their watch-word and even when he was at his most vulnerable, riding through the streets of London or meeting them at Mile End and Smithfield, they had treated his person as sacrosanct. In granting them their freedoms he had acted solely on his own royal authority – a moment of empowerment for him as much as it was for them – only to be forced by his councillors, and later by parliament, to retract and revoke his charters of manumission in what he clearly felt was an act of bad faith. The significance of this moment, when Richard's appeal to parliament to reinstate his abolition of villeinage was so crushingly rejected, was perhaps that the young king learned then that he had a better understanding of, and greater rapport with, his 'true commons' who, even in rebellion, had demonstrated their love and reverence for him personally, than he had with the representatives of his kingdom in parliament who, like his councillors, were not prepared to allow him to do what he, their divinely appointed monarch, deemed to be right.

In the immediate aftermath of the revolt Richard was still subjected to the conciliar government which had been the hallmark of his minority. It was not until he was seventeen that he began to assert his right to exercise his kingship in person. He was now an imposing six feet tall, though he retained the pale complexion, blond hair and effeminate caste of countenance of his childhood; he was also said to have suffered from a stammer. He shared the medieval nobility's passion for hunting, riding and hawking although, unlike most other medieval kings, he declined to participate in jousts or tournaments for fear of damaging his regal dignity by taking a fall or being defeated. Richard deliberately cultivated a sense of separateness and uniqueness that set his divinely ordained royal status apart from and above the rest of his subjects, even the most mighty of them. He was highly conscious of his own self-image and so preoccupied with it that more portrayals of him survive than of any other monarch before the similarly narcissistic and despotic Henry VIII. Although realistic in the new renaissance style, they also contribute to his plan of semi-deification by what has been aptly described as their 'icon-like' representation.[3] Autocratic, vindictive and capricious though he was by nature, Richard was also capable of selfless acts of kindness, particularly towards those who could not reciprocate, paying the debts of all the prisoners held in Newgate in 1388, for example, and pardoning a thief who had been sentenced to death after being caught red-handed in Westminster Hall in 1397. He also had an affinity with children, showering his child-bride with gifts and treating the future Henry V, a hostage for his father Bolingbroke's good behaviour, with a generosity that he would later repay by ensuring Richard's honourable reburial.[4] Perhaps Richard recognised in these young political pawns some of the difficulties he had himself faced during the years of his minority.

From the outset of his personal rule, however, Richard was determined to shake off the limitations imposed on his authority by having to consult his magnates in council or his Commons in parliament. This was not just because he believed it was his right to do so but because he believed that the aristocracy had mismanaged his kingdom throughout the years of his minority. In what we can see to be echoes of the grievances articulated during the great revolt, he held them responsible for prolonging the war with France out of self-interest and failing to achieve either military or political success, for conceding royal powers to the Commons to win their support for this fruitless war and for the repeated demands for heavy taxation to pay for it which had driven the populace to rebel. 'For the twelve years since I became king,' Richard declared to his great council in 1389, 'I and the entire kingdom have been under the control of others and my people burdened year by year with taxes'. Now that he intended to assume control himself, he promised that he would 'work tirelessly so that my subjects shall live in peace and the realm prosper'.[5]

A crucial part of that work was a radical political realignment which again echoed one of the themes of the great revolt by placing the king in a more direct relationship with his subjects. He wanted to free the crown from the control of the magnates, replacing them with men about him who 'owed their position solely to the king's will and favour'.[6] In the shires he recruited a royal affinity to match those of his leading noblemen, directly retaining knights and esquires not just for military service but to exercise influence over local administration by securing their appointment as sheriffs and justices of the peace. At court he built up a small group of trusted intimates, some of them from his father's household, others from among his own contemporaries, but almost all of them courtiers of lesser birth, rather than the aristocrats who would naturally expect to have such privileged access to the king's person and patronage. By promoting the likes of Robert de Vere to a dukedom (a rank previously enjoyed only by members of the royal family) and Michael de la Pole, the son of a Hull merchant, to an earldom, Richard demonstrated his belief that the crown alone had the power to confer titles and land at will, but showed a flagrant disregard for the custom, convention and sensitivities of the aristocracy which would ultimately be his undoing.[7]

By asserting his royal prerogative to rule alone Richard excluded those who felt that they had an equally God-given right to share in the responsibility of ruling the kingdom and set himself on a collision course with the traditional supporters of the crown, including his own family: two of the five Lords Appellant who temporarily deprived him of his powers in 1386–9 were his own uncle Thomas of Woodstock and cousin Henry Bolingbroke. The nobility's traditional chivalric role was also emasculated by Richard's decided reluctance to engage in the war with France. Unlike either his predecessor or his two successors Richard preferred to pursue a policy of appeasement which would end the crown's continual need to come cap in hand to parliament for taxes and subsidies. His ultimate success in this – in the teeth of opposition from his magnates – led in 1396 to his marriage[8] to the six-year-old daughter of Charles VI of France and the conclusion of a twenty-eight-year truce which could have brought a premature end to the Hundred Years War.

In the end, however, Richard's insistence on his royal prerogative would lead to his downfall. He expected the loyalty of his subjects, great and small, but did not appreciate that he had to earn it by inspiring either affection or respect, and preferably both. Although he succeeded in building up a substantial retinue in the shires, his failure to accord his magnates their accustomed place at the heart of government drove them into overt opposition. When Bolingbroke returned from exile in 1399 to claim his father's inheritance, which Richard had seized on John of Gaunt's death, he was able to rally enough support among his fellow peers and in parliament to seize the crown as well. Compelled under duress to abdicate, despite continuing to protest the sanctity of his kingship, Richard was despatched to imprisonment in the Lancastrian castle at Pontefract, Yorkshire, where he was almost certainly murdered in February 1400 in the wake of a failed rebellion by his supporters.

Richard's deposition undermined not only the legitimacy of the monarchy but also its sacral nature, which he had promoted so vigorously. It brought a premature end to the direct line of Plantagenet rulers of England that led back to the accession of Henry II in 1152. That line would have ended with Richard's death in any case, since he left no child, legitimate or even illegitimate, to claim his throne, but Henry IV's usurpation effectively disinherited Richard's preferred heirs in the more senior line, the Mortimers, and their struggle to reassert their rights would be a cause of future dissent, rebellion and ultimately the Wars of the Roses. The weakness of Henry's claim to legitimate kingship also made him dependent on those very institutions and policies which Richard had decided were an impediment to his rule: the magnates, parliament and the war with France.

The challenge to Henry's rule he perhaps could not have expected, however, was actually a lingering legacy of the great revolt: the loyalty among the 'true commons' towards King Richard. Henry was unable to shake off persistent and widespread rumours that his predecessor was not dead, but had escaped to

Scotland and would return to raise his people against the usurper. Although there was political advantage in spreading such rumours (Charles VI of France sent his valet to Scotland to investigate this 'common report' in 1402), what is noticeable is that so many of those involved were what we might term 'ordinary' people who had nothing to gain personally by a change of regime: John Lancaster, a piper, who claimed to have seen Richard at Berwick-on-Tweed; Franciscan and Dominican friars; John Sparrowhawk, 'a wandering man of Wales'. Letters allegedly from Richard circulated at the parliament of 1404, and as late as 1416 Henry V was embarrassed by the presentation of a petition to his guest Sigismund, the Holy Roman Emperor, asking him to depose Henry by force of arms and restore Richard to his rightful throne. While it is not surprising that committed loyalists clung to the belief that the former king was alive, or that the Scots found it convenient to maintain Thomas Warde of Trumpington as a pseudo-Richard II, it is surely significant that the idea that Richard had sympathised with the plight of his 'poor commons' was still powerful enough to make his name once more a rallying cry for potential rebels years after his deposition and death.[9]

It was this ability to utilise, interpret and reinterpret the great revolt to suit contemporary political ideas that has given it such resonance down the centuries. As soon as the rebellion was over it was appropriated by those in authority seeking to extrapolate its lessons for their own purposes. The parliamentary Commons in 1381 blamed the revolt on their perennial complaint about the oppressions caused by aristocratic livery and maintenance. The Church establishment blamed heresy and Wyclif's teachings in particular. Michael de la Pole, in his role as Richard's chancellor in 1383, lectured the Commons on the necessity of obedience: the revolt, he said, had begun as a rebellion first against the king's shire officers, then his ministers of state and then finally the king himself. From this he argued that 'true obedience to the king and his ministers is the foundation of all peace and tranquillity'.[10]

What united them all, however, was the belief that the revolt was an object lesson in the anarchy that ensued when the normal rules of society were suspended and broken. To question one's rank or place in the social order was, in their eyes, an affront to God himself, who had appointed each man to his station in life, and it would be duly punished by Him. A horrifying and hellish maelstrom of chaos, violence and disorder was the inevitable consequence of defying the divinely ordained social structure of the world. This was the theme of virtually all accounts of the revolt for the next four centuries: the spectre of present or future popular insurrection ensured that historians and commentators of all kinds would have little or no sympathy with the rebels of 1381. For the late-sixteenth-century Holinshed's *Chronicles*, drawing on the works of Walsingham and Knighton, they were 'barelegged ribalds' and 'vile rascals' who were 'set on by some divelish instinct and persuasion of their own beastlie intentions, as men not content with the state whereunto they were called'.[11] The anonymously authored play *The Life and Death of Jack Strawe*, published in 1593, has Walworth call Straw a 'dunghill bastard born' and an 'accursed villain'; the rebels demand 'wealth and liberty' as the price for peace and when Richard grants them liberty but does not offer wealth, Straw tells the men from Essex that they may go tamely home if they wish, but he 'came for spoil' and spoil he would have.[12]

In the seventeenth century Tyler's was still a name with which to conjure up the horrors of anarchy. In 1642, when parliament presented Charles I with their Nineteen Propositions demanding greater parliamentary oversight of, and involvement in, government, the king responded that to grant them would upset the historic balance of power between the three estates: 'this excellently distinguished form of government will end in a

dark, equal chaos of confusion,' he warned, 'and the long line
of our many noble ancestors in a Jack Cade or a Wat Tyler'.[13]
Some of the most extreme radical Puritan sects active during the
ensuing Civil War and republican Commonwealth found parallels between their ideas and those circulating during the great
revolt, introducing another enduring popular misconception,
that the rebels wanted to abolish distinctions of rank and property and create a proto-communist state in which goods were
held in common. Thomas Fuller, a royalist parson writing in
1655, identified the rebels of 1381 with the Leveller sect of his
own day. 'These [rebels] were all pure levellers,' he claimed,

> ... who, maintaining that no gentry was *jure Divino*, and all
> equal by nature,

> 'When Adam delved, and Eve span,
> Who was then the gentleman?'

> endeavoured the abolishing of all civil and spiritual degrees
> and distinctions. Yea, they desired to level men's parts, as
> well as their purses; and, that none should be wealthier or
> wiser than his fellows, projected the general destruction of
> all that ... could write or read.[14]

Disillusion with Cromwell and the other army leaders who had
beheaded the king and abolished the monarchy only to seize
power themselves united those of disparate political views. John
Lilburne, who had fought for the parliamentary cause and was
a prolific pamphleteer and passionate advocate of freeborn
rights, wrote in 1649 that the crimes of the general and his
council far outweighed those of Jack Straw, Wat Tyler and 'all
those famous men mentioned with a black pen in our histories
and called rebels and traitors'. John Cleveland, the royalist

poet, historian and author of *The Idol of the Clownes, or, Insurrection of Wat the Tyler, With his Priests Baal and Straw* (1654), later given the even more inflammatory title *The Rustick Rampant, or Rurall Anarchy Affronting Monarchy* (1658), saw Tyler as a prototype of Cromwell, 'the future monarch, who had designed an Empire for himselfe'. 'The world cannot exist without Order and Subjection', Cleveland's Richard declared, 'men cannot be freed from Lawes'. For Cleveland, like Lilburne, the revolt of 1381 was abhorrent but paled into insignificance compared with the events of their own times, in particular what they saw as Cromwell's great betrayal.[15]

It was not until the final two decades of the eighteenth century that Wat Tyler began to shed his bogeyman image and emerge as the champion of the people. Even as late as 1780, the *Gentleman's Magazine* could draw attention to the 'so strikingly a resemblance' of the great revolt to the recent anti-Catholic riots in London which had led, once again, to the breaking open of Newgate prison and the Clink. Indeed, Lord George Gordon, president of the Protestant Association which had inadvertently instigated the riots by presenting its petition to parliament, declined to step down from his post on the grounds that 'there might spring up some Wat Tyler who would not have patience to commune with Government, and might very possibly chuse to embroil the nation in civil war'.[16]

What changed popular perceptions of the great revolt was the advocacy of Thomas Paine, author of *The Rights of Man* (1791–2), promoter of colonial America's independence from Britain and enthusiastic supporter of the French Revolution. His most famous intellectual adversary Edmund Burke was himself no admirer of absolute monarchy, but had argued that the only security for English law and liberty was its ancient constitution, not abstract principles and notions about 'the rights of man'. He had no time for revolutionaries, English or French. He dismissed

John Balle as 'that reverend patriarch of sedition, and prototype of our modern preachers' and mocked his propagation of the same message as the French National Assembly 'that all the evils which have fallen upon men had been caused by an ignorance of their "having been born and continued equal as to their rights"'. Burke scoffed that Balle's 'sapient maxim' (the Adam and Eve couplet) was 'in learning, sense, energy, and comprehensiveness ... fully equal to all the modern dissertations on the equality of mankind; and it has one advantage over them – that it is in rhyme'.[17]

Paine's response was a spirited defence of the rebels of 1381. Tyler, he argued, was 'an intrepid disinterested man' whose 'proposals' to Richard II were made 'on a more just and public ground' than those made by the Magna Carta barons to King John. Walworth, so long celebrated as the hero who had saved the king from the importunate rebel, was merely 'a cowardly assassin' and it was Tyler who deserved a national memorial to be erected in his honour at Smithfield, not the barons at Runnymede.[18] Paine's intervention ensured that Tyler would be taken up by other enthusiasts for the French Revolution, including the future Poet Laureate Robert Southey who, in 1794, aged nineteen, dashed off his three-act play *Wat Tyler: A Dramatic Poem* in just three days and celebrated by drinking the toast, 'May there never be wanting a Wat Tyler whilst there is a Tax-gatherer'. (After the revolution turned into a bloodbath Southey changed his mind and became an equally ardent critic; he therefore spent the rest of his long life regretting having written his play and trying unsuccessfully to suppress it. Nevertheless, such was its popularity that unlicensed copies of it outsold by three times to one the rest of Southey's considerable output combined.)[19]

There were two reasons why the great revolt, or 'Wat Tylerism', as its later interpretations have been christened, acquired such a hold over the popular imagination after 1789. The first was that it gave radicals and reformers across party and political divides a plebeian lineage or tradition which they could claim to validate their own efforts to obtain change or 'liberty', especially by direct action. This counterpointed nicely with the 'aristocratic' version of history espoused by the likes of Edmund Burke and many nineteenth-century historians, which venerated Magna Carta, Simon de Montfort and the Glorious Revolution of 1688 as the sacred foundations of the English constitution. The second was that radicals from 1789 onwards appropriated the story of the great revolt for their own particular causes and, more importantly, enabled their politically charged versions of it to reach a wider audience by mass producing cheap and accessible printed chapbooks, pamphlets and leaflets to circulate among an increasingly literate working class. Southey's *Wat Tyler* was first printed, without his knowledge, in 1817, to coincide with government repression of popular dissent, and was quoted frequently thirty years later by Chartist agitators who printed selections from it on ballad sheets distributed at their public assemblies and radical camp meetings.[20] Chartist poets such as Thomas Cooper celebrated Tyler's name in enthusiastic if execrable verse ('They'll tell his fair fame, and cheer his blythe name, When a thousand years are gone!') and Pierce Egan's 1841 novel *Wat Tyler*, which gave its hero an entirely spurious backstory as a 'Freeborn Englishman' and veteran of the Hundred Years War, enjoyed widespread success among readers with Chartist sympathies. In 1848, as in 1817, Wat Tyler clubs were founded in London, together with a Wat Tyler Chartist Brigade, and Tyler's name and image were regularly reproduced on Chartist banners, including, most appropriately, that flown at the Hyde Park meeting of 1867 which asserted the people's right to enter royal parks.[21] The most famous and enduring image, that of Tyler the blacksmith striking down the tax-gatherer with his hammer, was instantly recognisable and, like the later Communist hammer and sickle, immediately apposite as a wronged working man using the tool of his trade to destroy his oppressor. The story behind the image was a sixteenth-century invention[22] but its powerful symbolism ensured that it would never lose its emotional appeal and it still enjoys popular currency today.

Another re-invention, that of John Balle, has proved equally enduring. William Morris, the Victorian medievalist, designer, writer and political activist who co-founded the Arts and Crafts movement, recruited Balle for his crusade against the capitalist exploitation of his own age by claiming him as an early socialist. In *A Dream of John Ball*, Morris's time-travelling narrator explains to the rebel chaplain that the injustices of the feudal system have been replaced by those of the Industrial Revolution and that Balle's dream of an egalitarian society remains unfulfilled. The novel was serialised in 1886–7 in *The Commonweal*, then republished in a single volume with an iconic frontispiece based on the Adam and Eve couplet by Morris's friend the Pre-Raphaelite Edward Burne-Jones. It became a socialist classic, reprinted countless times in cheap editions in Britain, and published throughout the English-speaking world. Less influential, but equally anachronistic, was Balle's appropriation by anarchists as a teacher of 'distinctly ... anarchist character' and by Bede Jarrett, head of the Dominican order in England, as 'the preacher of communism' in his *Medieval Socialism* (1913).[23]

Despite such misinterpretation of both Tyler's demands and Balle's preaching, their appeal to revolutionaries has never faded. For those on the political left, in particular, reclaiming the rebel leaders' reputations from 'the thousand defamatory pens' that have 'lied away' their characters, places them at the forefront of the historical march towards an inevitable socialist utopia.[24]

They are the epitome of popular history and the great revolt itself the first direct action by an oppressed and voiceless people who felt they had no constitutional means for redressing their wrongs. Tyler's name is still shorthand for resolute resistance to the iniquities imposed by government and society: hippies in 1970s London set up a counter-cultural squatting agency with the slogan 'established by Wat Tyler, 1381' over its doorway, and anti-poll-tax rioters in 1990 blazoned 'Avenge Wat Tyler' across their campaigning leaflets.[25] Establishment reactions were as horrified in the twentieth century as they were in the fourteenth.

Even today the great revolt remains a point of reference for almost every radical political movement, from socialism through to the extremes of communism, republicanism, anarchism and environmentalism. The passage of more than six hundred years may have blurred popular notions of what it was all about but it continues to exercise a fascination far beyond narrow political factional interests. What makes this so extraordinary is that the great revolt achieved none of its stated aims: villeinage and villein tenure were not abolished; neither were market tolls and restrictive practices; nor were manorial courts. There were no fundamental reforms in society, law or government. Even though the great revolt failed in its specific historic objectives, however, it articulated much wider ideas which continue to resonate today. For the first time in English history ordinary people had defied authority and tradition, taken matters into their own hands and asserted what they conceived to be their basic human rights. Their concepts of personal liberty, articulated so powerfully in the Adam and Eve couplet attributed to John Balle, transcend the limitations of their age and play into what we now consider to be the rights of the individual: to be heard and to be respected. That surely is the reason why the great revolt continues to speak to us all.

APPENDIX 1

Wat Tyler

One of the major frustrations of writing about the great revolt is that the rebels destroyed so many of the records which would have given us valuable information about them as individuals. Nowhere is this more disappointing than in the case of Wat Tyler, or Tegheler, as his name was generally set down at the time. Neither his identity nor his place of origin can be pinned down with any certainty and the few snippets of evidence that do survive seem contradictory. In a petition of 1383–4 from the House of Commons to the king in parliament, for instance, Tyler was described as being 'a captain, leader and chief ... of the county of Kent'. This does not necessarily mean he was a Kentishman, though the *Anonimalle* chronicler, writing after 1385, goes further, identifying him as 'Watt Teghler of Maidstone'.[1] He is the only chronicler to attribute a place of origin to Tyler, and he may have assumed he was from Maidstone since that was the place where the rebel first emerged as a named leader in his account.

Opposing evidence comes from Kent itself. In the inquisitions made immediately after the revolt several juries from the county, giving testimony at the beginning of July 1381, declared him to be 'of Essex'. More tellingly, on 4 July, less than a month after the events they were describing in Maidstone, the jurors of that town specifically identified him as being 'of Colchester'. While it was clearly in the Kentishmen's interest to blame outsiders for causing the revolt, the same juries had no hesitation in correctly identifying the places of origin of other rebel leaders in their own county, such as Abel Ker of Dartford.[2] It is tempting to give more weight to the Kent sources, since they were better placed to know the truth about their own people and they are as close to contemporaneous as it is possible to get on this subject. The poll-tax records might have given us more material but all the 1381 returns for Kent, except those for Canterbury, 'were burnt by the commons' and none of the detailed earlier rolls for Maidstone have survived. In Colchester the sole extant return is for 1377, and no Wat Tyler appears there.[3]

It is possible that 'tegheler' was Tyler's occupation rather than his family name; the two were not always synonymous, even at this period. If he were a tiler by trade, as some chroniclers claim,[4] he could have been either a simple layer of floor or roofing tiles or a skilled craftsman involved in their production. Making tiles, particularly decorative ones for flooring, required wooden stamps with a proud design to create a depression in red clay which was then filled with white clay to create the pattern. The tiles were then glazed and fired in a kiln. Tilers were either itinerant, like the masons who worked on major ecclesiastical and aristocratic buildings, or associated with a particular large-scale production site like Battle Abbey's ten kilns at Wye, Kent, twenty miles from Maidstone, which in 1374 alone produced some 190,000 flat, ridge and corner tiles for flooring and roofing the Sussex abbey, but also for sale elsewhere at prices between two shillings and 2s. 6d. per thousand. It is tempting to think that Tyler might have been drawn to Kent to work in such a place, but there is no hard evidence at all, other than his name, to suggest that he did follow that occupation.[5]

We reach a similar dead-end with the only other potential source of information. Froissart tells us that Richard Lyons was murdered as an act of revenge by Tyler, who had once been his servant 'during the wars in France'. Sadly, this is a typical Froissartian fabrication, colourful but untrue, if only because the chronicler is unaware that Lyons was a merchant-financier and had never performed military service in France. Given Tyler's methods and leadership skills it does seem possible that he might have been a soldier, perhaps newly returned from Brittany, or one of Felton's disbanded recruits who had mustered in Dartmouth earlier in the year. Again, however, we draw a complete blank in the muster rolls of the period.[6] In the end, all that we can say about Tyler is that his activities in the revolt, so far as the record stands, relate to Kent and London, but there is no reason to suppose that he was not originally from Essex, or even Colchester. He may have been one of the band of Essex men recruited by Abel Ker and brought over to Kent at the beginning of the revolt, but there was considerable movement of individuals between the two counties long before this, and he may simply have been living in Maidstone by 1381, just as John and William 'Kentissh' and their wives were resident in Colchester.[7] Tyler's origins are not immaterial. If he did come from Essex, his prominent role in events in Kent might help to explain how and why the rebels of both counties were able to coordinate their movements so closely.

Jack Straw

Some commentators have argued that Jack Straw was a pseudonym adopted by Wat Tyler, and not a separate individual. Henry Knighton, a monastic chronicler writing in Leicester in the 1380s, was the first to suggest this, telling us that the king was approached at Smithfield on 15 June 'by the rebels' leader, properly called Watte Tyler but now known by the different name of Jakke Strawe'. Fifteenth-century London chroniclers and a couple of contemporary political poems also assume that it was Straw who was killed at Smithfield, but they do not make any reference to Tyler who has no role at all in the revolt in their accounts.[1]

Folklore historians have added weight to this elision of the two captains by drawing attention to the fact that 'Jack Straw' is a name traditionally associated with seasonal revelries and therefore an appropriate pseudonym for a rebel captain to adopt. In 1517, for instance, after the damage caused during the Christmas revels at Lincoln's Inn, the authorities declared that

'Jack Straw and all his adherents be from henceforth utterly banyshed and no more to be used in Lincolles Inne'. Mummers and revellers with straw-stuffed or straw-clad figures are not uncommon features in folk custom, from the mischievous Strawboys of All Hallows Eve in Ireland to the Plough Boys' plays of Lincolnshire.[2] Yet the point that seems to be missed here is that all these verified examples post-date the great revolt and it cannot be proved that they belonged to an earlier tradition, pre-dating 1381. Is it not more likely that later revellers adopted the troublesome leader of the rebellion as an iconic figure of mischief, just as the real Guy Fawkes who tried to blow up parliament in 1605 became the guy for whom pennies are begged on Mischief Night? Straw's name was certainly remembered in connection with the great revolt and to such powerful effect that rebel leaders of even very minor uprisings in Warwickshire in 1407 and North Yorkshire in 1485 chose to call themselves 'Jack Straw'.[3]

It is true that 'Jack Straw' chimes well with other generic names from popular culture, such as Hobbe the Robber, Jack Carter and, most famously of all, Piers Plowman, all of which were circulating at the time of the revolt. It may even have been a pseudonym adopted by one of the rebel captains who wished to conceal his true identity. But it was not an alias of Wat Tyler who, as we shall see, was an entirely different man. So who was Straw, or 'Rakestraw', as he sometimes appears in the records? The simple answer is that we do not know. He first comes to public notice on 13 June when a group of rebels including the chaplain, clerk and sacristan of St John's Church at Margate on the Isle of Thanet, Kent, made a proclamation in the church 'by commission of John Rakestraw and Watte Tegheler, of Essex' that an attack should be made on the house of William Medmenham, the coroner of Kent; a similar proclamation was made on the same day, four miles away, in St Laurence's church on the outskirts of Ramsgate.[4] The suggestion here that Straw, like Tyler, was 'of Essex' is noteworthy and is confirmed by Walsingham, who notes that men from his abbey saw Jack Straw commanding the Essex rebels who burned down the Hospitallers' manor at Highbury on 14 June.[5]

Another reference, this time to Rakestraw's 'meynee', or company, occurs in the records of Battle Abbey's manor of Wye, site of the tile factory and at the heart of the rebellion in Kent: at least five of the manor's demesne servants had been 'ensnared by Rakestrawesmayne' and abandoned their haymaking to join the rebels, so that others had to be paid to take their place.[6] A further source again links Straw and Tyler personally but as separate individuals. In 1384 Nicholas Est of Heston, Middlesex, accused a group of men of having broken into his house during the revolt, carried away his chests, goods and chattels, beaten him with swords and staves and finally imprisoned him until he paid a ransom of forty shillings. The accused admitted the offences but justified themselves by saying that they had no evil intent and that they had only acted under duress from 'Jack Straw, Wat Tyler, and other rebels', an excuse which entitled them to a pardon under the general amnesty.[7] Though their claim is dubious at best, it shows that the names of the two leaders were common currency and endorses their different identities.

The final piece of evidence is perhaps the most convincing. The parliamentary petition of 1383–4 concerning four rebel captains who were put to death without due process of law to prevent their being rescued and for the swifter suppression of the revolt lists 'Jakke Strawe' as captain, leader and chief 'in Essex' after Wat Tyler 'of the county of Kent'. The inclusion of Straw's name among those of other verifiable individuals (the other two were John Hauchach in Cambridgeshire and Robert Ffyppe in Huntingdonshire) not only confirms his separate existence but also discredits Walsingham's fanciful account of Straw's public confession at the gallows after his alleged capture and trial by the mayor of London. It reiterates the Essex connection which seems to bind all three of the main rebel leaders and makes it clear that Straw was not John Wrawe, the rebel chaplain from Sudbury, despite the similarity of their names. Wrawe's activities are well documented and were all confined to Suffolk; the legal record concerning his trial and execution, which includes his lengthy confession, is one of the most detailed to have survived.[8]

APPENDIX 3

John Balle

In one of the letters circulating in Balle's name during the revolt, he refers to himself as 'som tyme seynte marie prest of ork. and now of colchestre'. Quite why Balle should have been in York before he came to Colchester is unclear, though there were long-standing links between the two places. Both had Benedictine abbeys and in 1096–7 the abbot of St Mary's Abbey in York had sent thirteen of his monks to found St John's Abbey at Colchester, one of whom went on to become its first abbot; a continuing relationship between the two houses would not have been unusual. As a 'St Mary priest', Balle may have been either a vicar in one of the many churches owned by the abbey (seven within the city of York and a further thirty-three in the county) or, more likely, a chaplain or chantry priest associated with the abbey – all professions which tended to foster religious radicalism and were well represented among the rebels in 1381.[1]

Balle was not an uncommon name and there were at least

two clerical John Balles active in Colchester at the time. One was the rector of the twelfth-century parish church of St James in the 1370s, who lived in the rectory near the church; the other was one of two chaplains who shared a lodging house in East Street in the same parish in 1377.[2] Neither of these seems likely to be the rebel since by this stage in his career Balle had no permanent residence and is likely to have eluded this type of official record. If we go further back, however, there is another possibility. On 3 October 1362 'Johannes Balle', parochial chaplain of Layer de la Haye, was alleged to have verbally and physically abused Henry, son of Thomas Waryn, lifting him up and throwing him down so that he broke his right leg, for which Waryn claimed damages of one hundred pounds. Balle, who appeared in person before the court of King's Bench in Colchester to answer the charges, explained that Waryn was 'his clerk and pupil', and that he had only chastised him in the way teachers do so that he learned his lesson. Upon which perfectly satisfactory explanation he was fully acquitted of all charges and allowed to go free. If this chaplain is indeed our John Balle it raises interesting questions. The church at Layer de la Haye, a village five miles south of Colchester, belonged to the town's priory of St Botolph, the oldest Augustinian house in England, and its chaplains would therefore have been members of that order. A year after the incident, the prior led an armed band of his canons and laymen which invaded St John's Abbey and assaulted one of the monks, allegedly because of a dispute concerning Layer de la Haye, which was settled in 1364 after papal intervention.[3]

Was the John Balle of the great revolt involved in any of these things? The first incontrovertible reference to our man occurs in the royal writ of 25 February 1364 by which the king withdrew the special protection he had granted to 'John Balle, chaplain, on his petition setting forth that he feared bodily injury from some of his enemies in the prosecution of his business'. This all fits neatly with the possibility of the Waryns seeking revenge for the injuries inflicted on young Henry and even with the fracas between the priory and the abbey. However, the reason Edward III gave for withdrawing his protection was that he had learned that Balle was 'not prosecuting any business but wanders from country to country [*sic*] preaching articles contrary to the faith of the church to the peril of his soul and the souls of others, especially of laymen'.[4] While it is possible that Balle had fled his parish for fear of reprisals, the fact that he was already a vagabond preacher at odds with church teaching and taking his controversial message directly to the laity suggests that personal conviction, rather than a fear of reprisals for his schoolmastering methods, lay behind his choice of career.

APPENDIX 4

John Balle's letters

John Balle was neither unique, nor even particularly unusual, in his beliefs and his methods of disseminating them. Where he is without parallel for this period is that as many as six of his letters have survived, copied by Walsingham and Knighton into their chronicles as examples of Balle's revolutionary rhetoric which caused the revolt. Unlike the spurious confessions attributed to Balle and Straw, these seem to be authentic. Walsingham has only preserved one, which he says was found in the tunic of a man who was to be hanged for his part in the revolt, adding that Balle, who was tried, convicted and executed in Walsingham's home town of St Albans, 'confessed that he had written this letter and sent it to the commons; and he admitted that he had written many others'. One might take this with a pinch of salt were it not for the fact that Knighton, writing independently at Leicester, transcribes five further examples. He does not explain how or why they came into his hands but they share not only the same images and vocabulary as Walsingham's, but the same turn of phrase. Knighton only identifies two of his as Balle's letters; the rest he puts into the mouths of Jakke Mylner [Miller], Jakke Carter and Jakke Trewman as speeches addressed to the assembled rebels at Smithfield.[1] His reason for doing so, even though textually they all appear to be letters and each one begins in similar fashion with the sender's name, can be attributed to his treatment of them as real people, not pseudonyms, and his assumption that, as labourers, they were illiterate – unlike the priest John Balle.[2]

Whether or not Balle was personally responsible for composing each of the letters, they were circulating at the time of the revolt and were in the vernacular which ought to give them extraordinary significance as an insight into their author and the rebel mentality. Their survival is not a matter for uncontained joy, however, as the 'letters', though written in English, are so obscurely phrased as to be impenetrable. Even Walsingham, while commenting that the letter to the men of Essex urged them 'to finish what they had begun', admitted that it was '*aenigmatibus plenam*', which might best be translated as 'full of enigmas' or 'full of riddles'. For once he was telling the unvarnished truth. Walsingham's letter, which he titled in Latin, 'A letter of John Balle. Sent to the commons of Essex', is worth quoting in full to get a flavour of the sort of riddles we are dealing with.

> Johon schep some time seynte marie prest of ork. and now of colchestre. Greteth well johan nameless and johan the miller and johon carter and biddeth them that they be wary of guile in borough and standeth [together] in God's name. and biddeth Piers Plowman. go to his work. and chastise well hobbe the robber. and taketh with you johan trewman and all his fellows and no more. and look shape you to one hewed ['on heued'] and no more.

Johan the miller hath ground small small small
the king's son of heaven shall pay for all.
be ware or ye be woe
knoweth your friend from your foe.
haveth enough. And saith 'Ho!'
and do well and better and fleeth sin.
and seeketh peace and you therein.
and so biddeth johan trewaman and all his fellows.[3]

Many scholars have tried to unpick the allusions, identifying Hobbe the Robber as Robert Hales, the treasurer, for instance, and Piers Plowman as the eponymous hero of William Langland's great English poem. While the latter, in particular, is tempting, it is surely a step too far to argue that the poem – which only circulated in manuscript copies – 'was talked about enough for the name of ... Piers Plowman to be taken up by the insurgents as a rallying cry'.[4] He is actually only mentioned in two of the six letters, and even then as one among several names representing particular trades, so his was hardly a name to inspire rebellion. It might rather be argued that the significance of the ploughman is that, like the carter and the miller, he is involved in the production of bread from grain, sowing the seed from which the harvest will grow, be reaped and carted to the mill where it will be ground into the flour from which bread, the staff of life, will be made. Such images were familiar not just from agricultural practice but because they abound in the New Testament as symbols of the true Christian. The idea that Christ himself was spiritual food, grain milled for the salvation of mankind, had been represented visually in the windows and carvings of churches since the twelfth century, but it had acquired new significance with the inauguration in 1264 of the feast of Corpus Christi, a day for venerating the Eucharistic host, which the Church taught was the body of

Christ miraculously present in the bread after it had been consecrated.[5] The first two lines of the rhyme quoted in Balle's letter would appear to reference this idea:

> Johan the miller hath ground small small small
> the king's son of heaven shall pay for all.

Though the link is tenuous, it may be significant that the rebels from Essex and Kent chose to converge on London on the eve of the feast of Corpus Christi, which in 1381 fell on 13 June, and entered the city on the day of the feast itself.[6] Contemporary commentators certainly made the connection, though given that barely a week went by in medieval times without some feast day or saint's day being celebrated, the rebels might have been hard put to find a day which had no sacred relevance.

We are, however, in the realms of speculation. Though it remains a minority view, it does seem more likely that both Langland and Balle drew on a common heritage, oral and written, of what is known as complaint literature. *Piers Plowman* shares with Balle and the rebels of 1381 a conviction that power was wielded only by 'wikked men' and that all men, regardless of social rank, are of one blood; he even advocates, with them, the removal of traitors and looks to the king to amend all that is wrong. But as one critic has shrewdly observed, the poem 'represents nothing more nor less than the quintessence of English medieval preaching gathered up into a single metrical piece of unusual charm and vivacity'.[7] The same (except for the charm and vivacity) is true of Balle's letters. Take the 'Jakke Trewman' letter, for example:

> Jakke Trewman doth you to understand that falseness and
> guile have reigned too long and truth hath been set under a

lock and falseness reigneth in every flock. No man may come to truth but he sing '*si dedero*'. Speak, spend and speed quoth Jon of Bathon and therefore sin fareth as wild flood. True love is away that was so good and clerks for wealth work them woe. God give remedy for now is time.[8]

The impetus of the letter and the wording of the last sentence might be interpreted as a call to arms but the whole composition, like the letter copied by Walsingham, is in fact a cobbling together of the sort of popular adages beloved by medieval preachers and the friars in particular. The phrase 'To sing *si dedero*' (the Latin translates as 'if I will have given') was in widespread usage from morality plays to the works of Gower and Lydgate and, together with 'speak, spend and speed', alludes to judicial corruption and the common belief that bribery was the only way to secure a favourable judgment.[9]

The phrase 'now is time' occurs in three letters, two of which Knighton attributes to Balle himself. These two are the ones which most lend themselves to being read as an incitement to rebellion. The first, described as an 'exemplar' or transcript, is the least obscure in its phraseology of all the letters.

> Jon Balle greeteth you all well and doth you to understand he hath rung your bell. Now right and might, will and skill. God speed every idle person ['dele'/'ydele']. Now is time lady help to Jesu thy son, and thy son to his father, to make a good end, in the name of the Trinity of that is begun. Amen amen for charity's sake amen.[10]

Taken out of the context of the revolt, this could just as easily be the sort of vernacular prayer or devotional rhyme popular among the laity, with its threefold repetition of amen to replicate the Trinity and its appeal for a good death.[11] On the other hand, it is equally open to interpretation as Balle's general summons to arms in order to finish what the rebels had begun. The 'first letter of John Balle', transcribed by Knighton, begins in similarly promising fashion but then falls back into the familiar pattern of moralistic aphorisms:

> John Balle Saint Mary priest greeteth well all manner of men and bids them in the name of the Trinity, Father and Son and Holy Ghost. Stand bravely [literally 'like men'] together in truth and help truth and truth shall help you. Now reigneth pride in highest regard ['in pris'], and covetousness is held wise and lechery without shame and gluttony without blame. Envy reigneth with treason and sloth is everywhere ['in grete sesone']. God give remedy. For now is time amen.[12]

Even if we assume that recipients of any of these letters were sufficiently literate or knowledgeable to decipher their message, it seems unlikely that they would leap instantly into action. If the letters are genuinely by Balle – and even that is not beyond question – then it is surprising that they are not less allusive and more overtly political or more obviously focused on issues which were at the heart of the rebels' demands. Had Walsingham and Knighton not specifically stated that the letters surfaced at the time of the revolt, we could have been forgiven for thinking that they could have been written at any time in the fourteenth century, or even earlier, and that it is only because of their associations with the revolt, and with one of the rebel leaders in particular, that the letters lend themselves to a more sinister interpretation.

It is ironic that in the absence of so many records that might have fleshed out and breathed life into the bare biographical bones of the rebel captains, this extraordinarily rare survival of vernacular medieval letters, purportedly written by John Balle, adds so little to our knowledge of the man. If we accept that he was their author, we can see that he shared the medieval scholarly predilection for cryptograms, mnemonics and riddles, and that he was well versed in proverbs, type-figures and allegory. Perhaps more important than any of this, even more important than any overt or covert radical message he intended to convey, is that he chose to write, as he preached, in English: the language of the people. That in itself was sufficient to condemn him in the eyes of the authorities of Church and state as an agent provocateur.

NOTES

PREFACE

1 Dan Jones, *Summer of Blood: The Peasants' Revolt of 1381* (HarperPress, London, 2009); Melvyn Bragg, *In our Time*, BBC Radio 4, 16 November 2006.
2 *See* 324–5.
3 Palmer (2), 164, 189.
4 *CPR 1377–81*, 599.
5 *OCL*, 365; *see* 316–17.
6 Hilton, xviii.
7 Réville, cxiii n. 1, 189, 205, 273.
8 *See* 365–6.
9 Oman, 146; Dobson, 284. *See* 366–7.
10 *See bibliography for the other links.*
11 Dobson, 243.

CHAPTER ONE: THE END OF AN ERA

1 *ODNB*, 'Edward III'; Ormrod (4), 578; Walsingham, 32; Sumption, 271.
2 *ODNB*, 'Edward III' and 'Perrers, Alice'; Sumption, 270–1; Ormrod (4), 575–6; Barker, 109.
3 *ODNB*, 'Perrers, Alice'; Walsingham, 32; Ormrod (4), 583–4.
4 Walsingham, 32; Froissart, 195–6.
5 Sumption, 268–9.
6 Ibid., 279; Saul, 22, 31–3.
7 Searle, 380–1; Walsingham, 32, 36–7, 46; Froissart, 196–7; Dobson, 92–3.
8 Walsingham, 36–7, 46 and n. 5; Sumption, 286; Searle, 381.

Lewes Priory later appealed to the pope for licence to appropriate churches in an attempt to recoup some of their losses.

9 Keen, 201–5.
10 Ibid., 204.
11 Barber, 228; Keen, 201.
12 Barber, 16, 18, 20, 41, 177; *ODNB*, 'Edward, prince of Wales and Aquitaine'.
13 Ibid. An older son, Edward, born at Angoulême, had died the previous year.
14 Walsingham, 27.
15 Barber, 239.
16 *PROME*, v, 315; Saul, 17; *ODNB*, 'John of Gaunt'.
17 Ibid.
18 *ODNB*, 'Edmund of Langley'.
19 *ODNB*, 'Thomas of Woodstock'.
20 Bennett, esp. 582–5, 593–4.
21 Crouch, 124–7.
22 Saul, 17, 22.
23 Ibid., 28; *ODNB*, 'John of Gaunt'.
24 Saul, 32–4.

CHAPTER TWO: THE STATE OF THE NATION

1 Saul, 24–6, 310.
2 Sargent, 257–61.
3 Rich, 137–8.
4 Shakespeare, *Richard II*, Act 2, Scene 1, ll. 43–9.
5 Hewitt, 70; Ohler, 40–1; Harriss, 225.
6 Dyer, 77–99, esp. 96–8.
7 Keen, 137–9; Butcher, 94; Ravensdale, 198; Campbell, 96; Bailey, 179.
8 Saul, 6; Harriss, 218.
9 Jewell, 61; Butcher, 98; Gottfried, 248; Schofield, 7; Young, 24–6, 28.
10 Dyer, 133–65, esp. 140–3, 148–9; Schofield, 83.
11 Ibid., 224–5, 256–7; Britnell (2), 74–7.
12 Chaucer (2), 20; Russell, 178 n. 3, 179, 212; *OCL*, 124.
13 Dyer (6), 32, 36; Harriss, 311–12.
14 Owst, 159–61, 178–9, 223, 282.
15 Ibid., 68, 72–5, 196; Réville, lxvii; *PROME*, v, 230–1.
16 At the end of 1380, a panel of Oxford doctors chaired by the

chancellor had condemned his most recent treatise, *On the Eucharist*, which argued that Christ's body and blood were only 'figuratively' present in the bread and wine at mass, not physically and corporeally as the Church taught. Anyone holding such beliefs, the panel decreed, was to be excommunicated and banned from teaching. Yet the fact that the panel reached its decision by the slimmest possible majority of just seven to five was a clear indication that there was still room for debate on the subject. Had Wyclif confined his highly academic arguments to university circles he might have flourished undisturbed. But by his unholy alliance with John of Gaunt in the autumn of 1376 he had entered the public arena of secular anti-clericalism and his preaching – in English – that the crown could legitimately seize the Church's property to fund the defence of the realm meant that the ecclesiastical authorities could not ignore him, because his sermons played into ideas that were already circulating not just among the educated and literate but also among the 'commons'. Harriss, 377–83; *ODNB*, 'Wyclif, John'.

17 *See* 280.
18 Orme, 136.
19 Ibid., 168, 249; Orme (2), 243–4, 264.
20 Ibid., 30.
21 For a discussion of the content of the letters *see* Appendix 4.
22 Chaucer (2), 5; Barker (2), 262–3; Heath, 29.
23 Chaucer (2), 3–21; Fenwick, ii, 558, 562.
24 Chaucer (2), 14; Staley; Dobson, 133, 324.
25 Brown, 28.

CHAPTER THREE: LANDLORDS AND TENANTS

1 Fenwick, i, 173; *Domesday Book*, 988; Rippon and Wainwright, 2, 12, 14, 16, 21.
2 *ODNB*, 'Canville, Sir Thomas' and 'Felton, Sir Thomas'; Thornbury, 'Westminster Abbey: Chapels and Royal Tombs', states that Eleanor de Bohun wears the conventual dress of a nun of Barking Abbey in her monument at Westminster Abbey but she may simply be wearing a widow's veil: *ODNB*, 'Thomas of Woodstock'.
3 *VCH Essex*, 'The Abbey of Barking'; Hanawalt, 135.
4 *VCH Essex*, 'The Abbey of Barking' and 'The Hundred of Becontree'; Dyer (3), 39. *See* 159–60.

5 Dyer (5), 22; *VCH Essex*, 'The Abbey of Waltham Holy Cross'.
6 *VCH Essex*, 'The Abbey of Coggeshall'; Sparvel-Bayly, 218.
7 Dyer (5), 22; *see* 15.
8 Dyer (3), 16 n. 23; 18; Fenwick, i, 185; Réville, 226.
9 *ODNB*, 'Joan, countess of Kent' and 'Brotherton [Marshal], Margaret'; Réville, 220, 288.
10 *VCH Essex*, 'The liberty of Havering-atte-Bower'; P&T, 17–18; Dobson, 148–9.
11 *ODNB*, 'Vere, Aubrey de'; Sparvel-Bayly, 216–17; *CCR 1369–74*, 8.
12 Dyer (5), 22.
13 Wood, 68.
14 Harriss, 94.
15 *OCL*, 578; Saul (2), 96–7, 169; Harriss, 94–6.
16 Ibid., 130, 172, 264; Fryde (3), 24.
17 Dunn, 19; Poos, 243; Fryde (3), 17; Dyer (5), 31.
18 SC8/45/2242, SC8/109/5419, TNA; *CPR 1377–81*, 130; Arnold, 56, 167–70. *See* 424.
19 Harriss, 223; *PRH*, 60–1.
20 Dyer (3), 25–6.
21 Fryde (3), 15, 18, 26.
22 Ibid., 18; Dyer (3), 24; Dyer (4), 36; *PRH*, 63, 65. A messuage was a dwelling-house with its own buildings and surrounding land: *OCL*, 837.
23 Chaucer, pt. 3 (Avarice); *PRH*, 65; Dyer (5), 32.
24 Dyer (3), 27–8; Poos, 245–6.
25 Bailey, 196–7; Fryde (3), 16; *PRH*, 56–8.
26 Dyer (3), 32–3; Dyer (5), 31, 32.
27 Ibid., 32; Dyer (3), 16, 36; *PRH*, 55, 56, 74.
28 Chaucer, pt. 3 (Avarice).
29 *PROME*, vi, 47; Faith, 48–9.
30 Ibid., 47–9; *PROME*, vi, 47.
31 Dyer (2), 277; Faith, 52, 56.
32 Ibid., 44–5, 47–8; Fryde (3), 40.
33 Müller, 3–5, 7–10.
34 Faith, 45; *PROME*, vi, 47; Dodd, 173.
35 Faith, 45, 54–8.
36 *PROME*, vi, 47–8.
37 Faith, 43, 45, 71–3. *See* 167–8, 172, 182, 183, 254, 367, 369.
38 Fenwick, i, xiv.
39 Dodd, 172–4.

40 *VCH Middlesex*, 'Middlesex: Social and Economic History'; Dodd, 99.
41 Müller (2), 5–7.
42 Dyer (2), 280; Bailey, 186–8.
43 Poos, 246; Dyer (3), 24–5, 8.
44 *PRH*, 68–9.
45 Dyer (3), 24 and *see* 64.
46 Dobson, 126–7.
47 Saul, 15–16; *CPR 1377–81*, 192–3. The *Anonimalle* does not identify the villein by name.
48 Réville, 186–8.
49 www.ghs.org.uk.

CHAPTER FOUR: URBAN SOCIETY

1 Dyer, 265; Schofield, 149; Bailey, 169–70; *CPR 1374–7*, 157; Aston, 12. For Sibil *see* 226–7; for Philipot *see* 117, 273, 277, 369.
2 Fenwick, ii, 61.
3 Harriss, 49; Saul (2), 110.
4 Harriss, 302; Dyer, 260–1.
5 Barron, 45–6; Brown, xiii; Chaucer (2), 229.
6 Barron, 49.
7 Ibid., 47–8; Bellot, 23–5.
8 Barron, 49, 52.
9 Ibid., 44, 53; Knoop, 32–3.
10 *See* 226–7.
11 Barron, 53, 55; Barker, 99–100, 109; *see* 267 ff.
12 Barron, 46–7; Thrupp, 133, 138, 140.
13 Barron, 51; Thrupp, 130–3.
14 Sabine, 28–33, 40; Thrupp, 137 n. 113; Wood (2), 384.
15 Sabine, 22–5, 29, 40; Thrupp, 137 n. 112.
16 Barron, 45; Thrupp, 136; Barker (2), 349–51.
17 Saul, 332–3; Wright, 43.
18 Thrupp, 127, 141–2.
19 Ibid, 39; Bird, 13, 27–9, 46–50; *ODNB*, 'Walworth, Sir William'.
20 Ibid.; HOPOL, 'Askham, William',
21 Thrupp, 208, 209–16, 218.
22 Ibid., 1–4, 6; Barron, 56.
23 Fenwick, i, 174; Grieve, 38–9; Harriss, 239; Bailey, 244–5; Grenville, 320; Dyer, 124–5.

24 Fenwick, i, 223–4; Grieve, 38–9; Quiney, 80.

25 Schofield, 57–8, 147; Bailey, 118, 122.

26 Ibid., 245–6.

27 Dyer, 173–4; Dyer (3), 24–5; Dyer (4), 39.

28 Goldberg (2), 109; Smith, 36, 37, 53 n. 78.

29 Goldberg (3), 5–6; Poos, 159, 200–3.

30 Britnell (2), 54–7, 60, 63–4, 74–5, 81–2, 87–8.

31 Fenwick, i, 173; *VCH Essex*, 'Medieval Colchester: Growth of the Town'.

32 *OCL*, 144; Harriss, 281–2, 284.

33 Britnell (2), 115–20, 159–60; *VCH Essex*, 'Medieval Colchester'.

34 Poos, 236 n. 14; Britnell (2), 124–5; *VCH Essex*, 'Medieval Colchester' and 'The abbey of Colchester'; Réville, 217–18; Fenwick, i, 201.

35 *See* Appendix 1.

36 *CPR 1361–4*, 470.

37 Hinck, 122 nn. 67–9, 123.

38 Bellamy, 94; Réville, 280 n. 3.

39 *CPR 1377–81*, 579, 631–2; *CPR 1381–5*, 1–2; *CCR 1377–81*, 486; Holt, 241.

40 *PROME*, vi, 205–6; Liddy, 1–2, 27.

41 Ibid., 6–7, 11–12, 16–17, 20, 20 n. 102, 22.

42 Ibid., 23–5; SC8/103/5139, TNA.

43 Liddy, 29–30; Fenwick, iii, 132.

44 *See* 433.

CHAPTER FIVE: WARS AND TAXES

1 Figures for 2013: www.ukpublicspending.co.uk/year_spending_2013UKbn_13bc1n_30#ukgs302.

2 Keen, 208–11; *PROME*, v, 292, 294, 315.

3 *PROME*, v, 390; Fenwick, i, xiii; Ormrod (2), 130.

4 Ormrod (3), 61–3, 69–70, 77, 73, 35; *CCR 1369–1374*, 489; Dyer (2), 280. The warden of the Cinque Ports was also issued with an ultimatum ordering him to collect and pay the assessment there two years after parliament had granted the tax: Ormrod (3), 77.

5 *PROME*, v, 390, 400; Dyer, 168; Dyer (5), 24.

6 Four pence was half the fifteenth which the poorest country households had to pay when a subsidy was collected.

7 *PROME*, v, 390.

8 McHardy, 81, xviii; Fenwick, i, 197, 199.
9 *ODNB*, 'Courtenay, William', 'Wyclif, John' and 'Percy, Henry, first earl of Northumberland'; Walsingham, 31.
10 McHardy, xvii. The final amount raised by the clerical poll-tax of 1377 is not known.
11 *See 7.*
12 Saul, 34; *ODNB*, 'Thomas of Woodstock'.
13 *PROME*, vi, 15; *ODNB*, 'Philipot, Sir John' and 'Walworth, Sir William'.
14 Liddy, 11–13; *CCR 1377–1381*, 32–3. The Calais Staple was also ordered to provide a balinger: ibid., 33. *See 106.*
15 Saul, 34–6; Walsingham, 68–9; *PROME*, vi, 89.
16 Ibid., 78–9.
17 Ibid., 89–90, 101, 98, 99–100, 90.
18 Ibid., 75–7. The king's household steward informed the Commons that the king spent £24,000 and £8000 annually in defence of Calais and Brest respectively: ibid., 73.
19 Saul, 36–8; *PROME*, vi, 79–80; *ODNB*, 'Wyclif, John'.
20 Saul, 43; *PROME*, vi, 108, 111.
21 Ibid., 114–16; McHardy, xviii–xix.
22 Ibid., xx; *PROME*, vi, 116.
23 Ibid., 142, 147–9; McHardy, xx. Fryde, 77, says the second poll-tax raised just £18,600.
24 *PROME*, vi, 165; Walsingham, 325–39; Saul, 44. Walsingham's allegation that the soldiers raped local nuns is not supported by the parliamentary petition, which complains of theft and destruction but makes no mention of rape or nunneries being attacked.
25 Saul, 48; *PROME*, vi, 165–6, 168–9, 179–80.
26 Ibid., 142–3, 149–53; *ODNB* and *HOPOL*, 'Gildesburgh, Sir John'.
27 Saul, 52–3; *ODNB*, 'Knolles, Sir Robert'.
28 *ODNB*, 'John of Gaunt'; *PROME*, vi, 184–5, 187–8.
29 Ibid., 189–92, though the first collection date is wrongly given as 28 January; Fenwick, i, xxv.
30 *PROME*, vi, 191–2; Fenwick, i, 173; Fryde, 78–9.
31 *PROME*, vi, 192.
32 Ibid, 192, 199; Saul, 54–5; Fryde, 78.
33 Fenwick, i, xvi, xix–xx; Tout, iii, 359–60, 359 n. 2.
34 Ibid., 360–1; Fryde, 81–2.
35 Fenwick, i, 173, 388; ii, 75, 499.

36 Ibid. and iii, 234; i, 115, 90, 80; Grieve, 41.
37 Goodman, 76; Sumption, 409–11; *ODNB*, 'Thomas of Woodstock' and 'Felton, Sir Thomas'.
38 *CFR*, 248–50; Tout, iii, 362–3; Oman, 183–5; Dobson, 120–2.
39 *CFR*, 250; Dobson, 135; Dunn, 101, 115, 126. The story is usually taken to refer to Legge, but Knighton actually says only that 'one of the commissioners' did these things.
40 Fryde, 82; Fenwick, ii, 75, 499; i, 250, 308–13, 311, 290.
41 Ibid., ii, 532–3 for Chevington and Brockley returns.
42 *PROME*, v, 231; Allmand, 391–2.

CHAPTER SIX: RESISTANCE

1 *CFR*, 247; Tout, 364–5; *CLBCL*, cxxib, cxxxii; Réville, xlii.
2 McHardy, xxiii–xxiv.
3 Dobson, 123–5 (*Anonimalle*), 135–6 (Knighton); Taylor, 136, 141–3; *ODNB*, 'Knighton, Henry'.
4 *See* 159.
5 Harriss, 164–6; *OCL*, 1139–41; Harding, 174; Ormrod, 12.
6 *CFR*, 249; *CCR 1377–81*, 135; *see* 8.
7 Harriss, 166; Saul, 92; *PROME*, vi, 201.
8 *CPR 1377–81*, 38, 40, 358, 474.
9 Ibid., 472; *ODNB*, 'Waldegrave, Sir Richard'; *see* 386.
10 *CPR 1377–81*, 38, 40, 474; *VCH Essex*, 'Ongar Hundred'; Prescott, 300; Dyer (3), 39; Eiden, 14 n. 38.
11 *ODNB*, 'Gildesburgh, Sir John'; *CPR 1377–81*, 40, 514, 571, 575.
12 Stubbs, 469–74; Harding, 165–6; *OCL*, 1276–7.
13 Harding, 175; *PROME*, v, 44.
14 Harding, 170; *PROME*, v, 133; Chrimes, 82–3.
15 Keen, 146; Harriss, 223.
16 *Statutes of the Realm*, i, 307.
17 Palmer, 17–18; Dyer (4), 33.
18 *PROME*, v, 28–30; Palmer, 19–21; Fryde (3), 35, 38.
19 *See* 23–5.
20 *PROME*, vi, 97, 97–8, 100.
21 Ibid., 98; Harriss, 226.
22 Britnell, 29–30; Musson, 248–9; Harriss, 227.
23 Musson, 249; Fryde (3), 34, 36; Hatcher, 21–4, 31; *PROME*, v, 29.
24 Hatcher, 20.

25 Fryde (3), 42; Jewell, 71; *PROME*, v, 28; Fenwick, i, 209; Britnell (2), 136–7.

26 Dobson, 161.

27 Musson, 148–9, 243.

28 Fryde, 85 n. 29; Dobson, 124–5, 136; Sparvel-Bayly, 218–19. The *Anonimalle* chronicler claims that three of Bampton's clerks were captured, beheaded and their heads carried around on poles for several days afterwards 'as an example to others' but this is a confusion and conflation of events after 10 June when the revolt began in earnest: two clerks of the escheator and an 'auditor' of Aubrey de Vere were then murdered at Brentwood by a band of rebels from Manningtree: *see* 198. The absence of any reference in the indictments even to wounding suggests that this was a show of force, rather than a violent assault. The idea that Bampton, who died the following August, was mortally wounded in the attack (Ormrod, 12) would therefore appear to be wide of the mark.

29 *See* 72–3; Hinck, 123 n. 74. For Winchester *see* 103.

30 The *Anonimalle*'s claim that Sir Robert Bealknapp, chief justice of the Common Bench, was sent on a commission of trailbaston to deal with the Brentwood rioters and was forced by them to abandon his sessions, to swear on the Bible not to repeat them and to return home is untrue: Bealknapp was then holding routine assize sessions. On 29 May he was in Maidstone, Kent; he spent the next few days on a circuit round the outskirts of London, taking in Stratford Longthorne, Essex, where he was on the day Gildesburgh and Bampton were attacked, Barnet, Hertfordshire, and Southwark. By 3 June he was back in Kent holding assizes at Dartford as normal; these were followed by rioting (*see* 174) which may have caused the chronicler's confusion: Dobson, 125; Prescott, 128–9; Eiden, 11 n. 30; Musson, 261 n. 150 where, sadly, since it might have offered confirmation of the *Anonimalle*, Southwark is misread as Brentwood.

CHAPTER SEVEN: ESSEX AND KENT ARISE

1 KB 9/166/2 fo.4, TNA. Not every man is given a place of origin but the groupings suggest particular locations.

2 Prescott, 134–5; Brooks, 274; Poos, 236.

3 Sparvel-Bayly, 214.

4 KB 9/166/2 fo.4, TNA; Réville, 189.
5 KB 9/166/2 fo.5, TNA; Fenwick, i, 208.
6 Brooks, 271.
7 *CPR 1361–4*, 470.
8 Aston, 21–2; *ODNB*, 'Ball, John'.
9 Aston, 22; *CPR 1374–7*, 415. Sudbury's writ of 21 September 1377 ordering the arrest of Balle 'a priest of Norwich diocese' appears to be a confusion with another chaplain of the same name in Norfolk: *CPR 1354–8*, 304; *CPR 1396–9*, 67.
10 Aston, 22–3; McHardy (2), xviii n. 37, 86; Logan, 63 n. 119; *see* 211–13.
11 Brooks, 272 n. 18. My translation.
12 Ibid., 272, who omits 'of divers lords'.
13 *See* 440 n. 37.
14 The Whitsuntide link has been noted by Musson, 243 and Dyer (2), 281 but not in terms of its religious significance.
15 Hutton, 19–26, 34–6.
16 Justice, 15.
17 *ODNB*, 'Hereford, Nicholas'; Barr, 204.
18 *See* 166.
19 Schofield, 188.
20 Réville, 183–4; Fenwick, i, 409; *Westminster*, 3.
21 *VCH Kent*, 'The Abbey of Lesnes or Westwood' and 'Wennington'.
22 Prescott, 116, 143; *CPR 1377–81*, 199, 358, 514, 571; Brooks, 272; *CCR 1381–5*, 394–5.
23 *See* 74–6.
24 The *Anonimalle* says that a commission of trailbaston had been issued to quell the disturbances in Gravesend and the surrounding area which was 'turned back by the commons'. The chronicler was mistaken, as he had been when recounting events in Essex: there is no evidence of any such commission operating in Kent around this time, only Bealknapp's routine assize session in Dartford: Dobson, 126; Prescott, 129.
25 Dobson, 126; *CFR*, 250.
26 *See* 139.
27 Dobson, 130, 134; *CCR 1369–74*, 172; *CCR 1377–81*, 80, 221, 309.
28 P&T, 4, 7–9; Réville, 185, 187; Prescott, 143–4.
29 Réville, 185–6; Prescott, 16; *see* 221–2.
30 Réville, 184, 186–8, 211; *CCR 1396–99*, 171–2; Prescott, 359.

31 *TSLME*; Allen Brown, 18–20; Brooks (2), 221–2, 256.

32 Dobson, 141–4; *CPR 1377–81*, 395; Barker (3), 89–90, 142–3.

33 Froissart, 38, 402; Dobson, 142; *see* 227–8, 273–4.

34 Mate, 3; Campbell (2), 28; HOPOL, 'Maidstone'.

35 Prescott, 143; P&T, 6–7, 9; Réville, 187–8.

36 *CPR 1381–5*, 132; SC 8/300/14959, TNA; Coulson, 86.

37 Réville, 187; Flaherty, 77; Fenwick, i, 402; P&T, 7, 11.

38 *CCR 1377–81*, 510; *CCR 1396–9*, 26.

39 *CPR 1377–81*, 424; *see* 176.

40 P&T, 6; Réville, 187; *CPR, 1377–81*, 409. Shardelowe was a witness to the document signed at Dartford on 6 April 1381: *see* 180.

41 P&T, 7, 12.

42 Réville, 185, 187; HOPOL, 'Cobham, Sir Thomas', 'Freningham, John', 'Peckham, James'; P&T, 5.

43 Réville, 211; *see* 176–7, 180.

44 P&T, 9; Flaherty, 76, 78, 89, 92; *ODNB*, 'Trevet, Sir Thomas'.

45 *See* Appendix 1.

46 Dobson, 127; P&T, 9; Brooks, 276–7.

47 *CFR*, 250; *see* 197.

48 The precise timing of the attack on Canterbury is not known, so the rebels may have taken longer to get there than the four hours minimum suggested by riding good horses.

49 Flaherty, 77–8, 88–9, 90–1; P&T, 9, 11.

50 Butcher, 100–4; Fenwick, i, 388.

51 Butcher, 88–9, 98–9, 104.

52 Ibid., 105–6; *CCR 1374–7*, 412; *CPR, 1377–81*, 304, 471.

53 CHAS, 'Canterbury Castle'; Flaherty, 89, 92–3.

54 Hasted, 'Parishes: Milton'; Battely, ii, 32.

55 *See* Appendix 2.

56 Brooks, 285; Butcher, 107, 109; Flaherty, 72–3, 76.

57 De Saxe, esp. 151–6; Flaherty, 81–3; De Saxe, 153 says Kempe was awarded one hundred shillings in damages, Prescott, 263, says one hundred marks.

58 Flaherty, 76, 83–4; *CFR*, 236.

59 Brooks, 285 who mistakenly confers a knighthood on Holt; P&T, 9; Flaherty, 74, 76, 86; HOPOL, 'Holt, William'.

60 Butcher, 105, 107, 109; *CFR*, 250; Flaherty, 74.

61 Ibid., 74–5; Butcher, 108; Fenwick, i, 411, 420; *PROME*, vi, 246–7; *CPR 1381–5*, 573.

62 *CPR 1377–81*, 304; *CCR 1377–8*, 357; Fenwick, i, 431; Flaherty, 74, 76; P&T, 11; Réville, 189.

63 *CPR 1377–81*, 93, 166, 467; Flaherty, 86, 88, 92–4.

64 HOPOL, 'Fogg, Sir Thomas'; P&T, 4, 11; Flaherty, 75–6; Federico, 170 n. 40.

65 Butcher, 109; *CPR 1377–81*, 166, 467; Flaherty, 75.

CHAPTER EIGHT: TO LONDON

1 KB 9/166/2 fo.5, TNA; Sparvel-Bayly, 218–19; Poos, 236 n. 12; Dyer (3), 17, 35; Eiden, 14.

2 *VCH Essex*, 'The Preceptory of Cressing'; *CPR 1381–5*, 76; Napier, 14.

3 *ODNB*, 'Hales, Sir Robert'; KB 9/166/2 fo.5, TNA; Sparvel-Bayly, 217–18; Prescott, 109; Dobson, 125; Dunn, 105; Poos, 237; Eiden, 13.

4 *See* 145–7.

5 Brooks, 274; Prescott, 294.

6 Sparvel-Bayly, 217–8; Brooks, 280, 284 n. 51.

7 Ormrod, 12; *CFR*, 261; Eiden, 13 n. 34.

8 Prescott, 135; KB 9/166/2 fo.5, TNA; *CPR 1381–5*, 79.

9 HOPOL, 'Bataill, Thomas' and 'Fitzsymond, Sir John'; *CPR 1377–81*, 571; Brooks, 287.

10 Prescott, 109; *CCR 1381–5*, 365; *CPR 1391–6*, 721.

11 Poos, 237; Brooks, 281–2.

12 Eiden, 14; Prescott, 136; *see* 51.

13 Sparvel-Bayly, 217–18; Justice, 46. De la Mare must have been a deputy, rather than an admiral, since there is no record of his appointment; there may have been a connection to Robert Hales, prior of the Hospitallers, who had been admiral in 1376 and 1377, given that Ralph atte Wode had been involved in sacking Cressing Temple before going to Peldon.

14 HOPOL, 'English, Henry'; Fenwick, i, 222; Eiden, 14, who wrongly says English paid three shillings poll-tax; Powell, 41, 44.

15 Bird, 18–21, 24; *ODNB*, 'Lyons, Richard'; Eiden, 14.

16 Réville, 177.

17 *PROME*, vi, 241; Réville, 175–82; Dobson, 248–54.

18 Réville, 75 nn. 1, 2; Powell, 24 which wrongly dates Wrawe's attack on Mettingham to 19 June, thereby creating two separate events; *ODNB*, 'Ufford, William, second earl of Suffolk (c.1339–1382)'; Suckling, 'Ringsfield'; *CPR 1361–4*, 294.

19 *See* 331.

20 Suckling, 'Ringsfield' and 'Beccles'.
21 Eiden, 15; Réville, 221–2.
22 Eiden, 14–15; Wood, 74–6; L&W, 87–8.
23 Eiden, 10 n. 26; 13. Some of the same names appear on both lists.
24 KB 9/166/2 fo. 4, TNA; Réville, 189.
25 Ibid., 216–17.
26 Prescott, 299–301; *CPR 1374–7*, 28.
27 *See* 211–13.
28 Prescott, 281–3, 301–10.
29 Ibid., 293–8; *PROME*, vii, 202.
30 Prescott, 312–18.
31 Dobson, 129, 134, 160, 188; Eiden, 10 n. 26.
32 Réville, 183–8. *See* 221–2.
33 Dobson, 136–7; Logan, 63 n. 119; Flaherty, 74, 81.
34 Prescott, 303–4; *ODNB*, 'Ball, John'. Prescott discovered the indictment and wrote the *ODNB* article: the text is given in Brooks, 285 n. 58.
35 *VCH Hertford*, 'Bishop's Stortford'; *CPR 1391–6*, 45, 345; *CPR 1399–1401*, 501.
36 Federico, 167.
37 *See* 291–2.
38 Dobson, 374–5.
39 Froissart, 212–13.
40 Genesis, ix: Ham had seen his father naked: Noah therefore cursed his descendants to slavery.
41 Froissart, 312–3.
42 Dobson, 364–6; *Rot. Parl.*, iii, 175. *See* Appendix 2.
43 For the following description of Southwark see Carlin; Walford.
44 Dobson, 98.
45 Kelly, 345, 347; Karras, 408–11; Fenwick, ii, 564.
46 Sparvel-Bayly, 214; Dobson, 155; *OCL*, 812–13; Dunn, 103.
47 Réville, 185–6; *CLBCL* fo. cxc; Fenwick, ii, 563.
48 Réville, 212–13; Dobson, 202.
49 Bird (2), 125; Dobson, 129 (*Anonimalle*) has Windsor: Westminster is more logical.
50 Dobson, 155, 199–200; *Westminster*, 4–5.
51 Palmer, 381; Fenwick, ii, 562; Réville, 213–14.

CHAPTER NINE: MILE END

1 Dobson, 213–17; Oman, 206–10.
2 Bird, 50–3, 56–61, 143–7; *CLBCL*, fo. cxxxii.
3 Dobson, 141–3.
4 Ibid., 130–1, 144.
5 Prescott, 316–17; Fenwick, ii, 559.
6 Dobson, 156, 169, 182, 188.
7 Prescott, 318; *PROME*, vi, 241–7.
8 Prescott, 292 ff.; Dobson, 209.
9 Ibid., 156, 209.
10 Ibid., 157, 169–70.
11 Ibid., 184; Dunn, 110.
12 Dobson, 184; Réville, 199–200; *CCR 1385–9*, 248–9. *See* 264–5.
13 *CPR 1381–5*, 124; Fryde (3), 78.
14 Dobson, 156; Dunn, 110.
15 *SOLO*, 'South and East Clerkenwell'.
16 *ODNB*, 'Hales, Sir Robert'.
17 Dobson, 170, 185.
18 Prescott, 268; Réville, 203.
19 Prescott, 207–8, 245; *PROME*, vi, 284.
20 *CCR 1377–81*, 106, 116, 177, 238; *CPR 1377–81*, 88, 127; *CLAN*, 612; *CPMROCL*, A20 m. 6b, A23 mm. 8 and A24 m. 5b; *CLBCL Henry VI*, K fo. 122.
21 Réville, 195, 203–4; Dobson, 219.
22 Réville, 195, 203; *PROME*, vi, 284.
23 Dobson, 156–7, 170.
24 *GA*, 298. A mistranslation of '*visi*' in Dobson, 171 wrongly makes Walsingham himself an eye-witness.
25 The continuator of the *Eulogium Historiarum* has Straw at Blackheath sending for the bishop of Rochester to address the rebels but Straw was from Essex, not Kent, so is unlikely to have been at Blackheath and Thomas Brinton was not a sympathiser: Dobson, 206.
26 Ibid., 130.
27 Dobson, 158, 206; Sumption, 290–1.
28 Réville, 210.
29 Prescott, 238–9; Dobson, 321–2; Réville, 201.
30 Dobson, 158; *CCR 1360–4*, 136; *CCR 1374–7*, 210–11; *CCR 1385–9*, 315; McHardy (2), xvii–xx; Réville, 202–3.
31 *See* 222–3.
32 Prescott, 208, 292–3, 323; Réville, 210–12.

33 Ibid., 210; *CLBCL*, cii–cii b.
34 Dobson, 185, 210.
35 Ibid., 130, 157.
36 Dobson, 139, 142; *ODNB*, 'Henry IV'.
37 *VCH London*, 'Hospitals: St Katherine by the Tower'.
38 Dobson, 159–60, 189–90; Froissart, 218–19.
39 Réville, 207.
40 Froissart, 219; Wilkinson, 22–4, 24 n. 1.
41 Dobson, 191–2; Sumption, 292; E30/256, TNA.
42 Dobson, 161, 209; *ODNB*, 'Joan, suo jure countess of Kent'; *see* 115.
43 Dobson, 176, 183, 192, 201, 210.
44 Réville, 216; Flaherty, 95.
45 Dobson, 161.
46 Froissart, 221.
47 Harvey, 89–91.
48 Dobson, 180–1.
49 *PROME*, vi, 215–16.
50 Walsingham, ii, 20–22.
51 *See* 55 ff.
52 Walsingham, ii, 21.
53 Dobson, 133.
54 *PROME*, vi, 215.
55 Ibid.
56 Harvey, 89; Bird (2), 125.
57 Prescott, 294–6, 298, 378.
58 *PRH*, 105–6, 107 n.7; Hinck, 114–15.

CHAPTER TEN: SMITHFIELD

1 *See* 250, 279.
2 Dobson, 161, 171, 183, 191, 201.
3 Hibbert, 164–7.
4 *ODNB*, 'Buxhull, Sir Alan'.
5 Dobson, 172; *OCL*, 536.
6 Dobson, 172.
7 Ibid., 172, 191; P&T, 10 says 'Thom' Heryng, but Nicholas is clearly meant: *see* 175–6.
8 Dobson, 172–5.
9 Taylor, 133; Dobson, 161–2; P&T, 10.
10 Dobson, 162, 210; *CPR 1381–5*, 16.

11 Dobson, 163.
12 Ibid., 162, 174, 191, 201, 210; McHardy (2), no. 650; *ODNB*, 'Sudbury, Simon'.
13 Dobson, 182; *ODNB*, 'Henry IV'.
14 Réville, 199–200; *CPR 1377–81*, 456: *see* 232.
15 Prescott, 294, 310; Réville, 112 n. 2, 216.
16 Hanawalt, 73–4; Dobson, 156, 203.
17 Ibid., 162, 175, 201, 210; Powell, 4, 11.
18 Dobson, 162; Bird (2), 125; Réville, 236 n. 2.
19 Dobson, 163, 207.
20 *VCH London*, 'The Priory of St Bartholomew, Smithfield'; Webb, 'The Hospital'.
21 Dobson, 163, 176, 193, 202; *see* 222.
22 Dobson, 164, 177, 195, 203.
23 Ibid., 164–5, 177; Fryde (3), 48–50.
24 Dobson, 186.
25 Ibid., 164–5, 177.
26 Harding, 166–7.
27 Prescott (2), 13–14.
28 *Statutes of the Realm*, i, 96; Fryde (3), 49–50.
29 Dobson, 164–5; *see* 32–4, 115. The rebels were probably not against paying tithes to support their parish priest *per se*: what they objected to was the compulsory element which forced them to pay tithes in full to absentees or to distant monasteries leaving the day-to-day care of the parish in the hands of poorly paid and often inadequate clergy.
30 Dobson, 165–7, 186, 195–6, 203, 207. The *Anonimalle* claims that Tyler was only badly wounded and that the Kentishmen carried him into the hospital, where he was later found alive by Walworth, dragged outside, beheaded in front of the rebels and his head paraded on a pole 'to subdue the commons'. Why the king's company should have failed to finish him off when they had him in their power is not explained: ibid., 167.
31 Ibid., 166, 179, 186, 196, 203–4, 207–8, 211.
32 *See* 245–6.
33 Dobson, 186, 211. Knighton wrongly adds Nicholas Twyford to the list of new-made knights.
34 *VCH Lancashire*, 'Standish-with-Langtree', n. 23; *CPR 1377–81*, 124; *CPR 1381–5*, 32, 47. Standissh had died by October 1382: ibid., 180.
35 *CPR 1381–5*, 18; E153/2314 and E153/999, TNA.

36 Dobson, 177–8.
37 Riley, 'Memorials: 1381'; Réville, 207–9; *CPR 1381–5*, 30–1; *CPR 1385–9*, 280–1.
38 Réville, 206; *CPR 1385–9*, 280; *CLBCL* (H), fo. cciv b and n. 12; Barron (3).
39 Dobson, 201–2; *Westminster*, 9; Musson, 244–5.
40 Pedersen, 93.
41 Réville, 234–6; Dobson, 317–18; *ODNB*, 'Cheyne, Sir William'.

CHAPTER ELEVEN: ST ALBANS AND BURY ST EDMUNDS

1 Dobson, 271.
2 *PRH*, 86–7; Dunn, 40–2, 139–40.
3 *GA*, 300, 369.
4 Ibid., 300–2, 304; *PRH*, 89–90, 94–5, 101 n. 45.
5 *GA*, 303–4; *PRH*, 90–1, 101 n. 26.
6 *GA*, 305–6.
7 Ibid., 291–2, 308, 311.
8 Faith, 63–4.
9 *GA*, 365–6; *VCH Herts.*, 'The City of St Albans: "Introduction" and "Borough"'.
10 *GA*, 309, 311, 315–16.
11 Ibid., 324–7.
12 Ibid., 318–22; *VCH Herts.*, 'The City of St Albans: "Borough"'.
13 *GA*, 325, 330–1.
14 *PRH*, 94–5, 101 n. 44.
15 *GA*, 334–41; HOPOL, 'Lee, Sir Walter' and 'Benstede, Sir Edward'.
16 *GA*, 335–6, 338, 341, 345; HOPOL, 'Croyser, Sir William'.
17 *GA*, 342–7; SC8/20/955, TNA.
18 *GA*, 347–9.
19 Ibid., 340–1; Dobson, 277.
20 I have been unable to find any evidence that the trials were broken off and recommenced in October as most historians claim: the bodies had been removed by 3 August 1381 (*see* n. 22) so it is impossible for the executions to have been carried out in October.
21 *CPR 1381–5*, 125; *CCR 1381–5*, 168–9.
22 *GA*, 303, 350, 354–5; *CCR 1381–5*, 5; *CPR 1381–5*, 43, 168.
23 *PRH*, 100 nn. 20, 22, 118–19, 120.
24 Dobson, 314; Bird (2), 125.
25 Dobson, 381. For the text of the letter *see* Appendix 4.

26 *PRH*, 107 nn. 4, 9; *ODNB*, 'Stonor Family'; *CFR*, 226.

27 Putnam, esp. 13–14, 32.

28 Dobson, 249–50.

29 Gottfried, 75, 78–9; Bailey, 41, 50.

30 Gottfried, 15, 18, 23–5, 30, 79–83.

31 *VCH Suffolk*, 'Abbey of Bury St Edmunds' and 'Franciscan Friars: Bury St Edmunds'.

32 Powell, 14–16, 142; Gottfried, 233, 270.

33 Dobson, 251–2; *ODNB*, 'Cavendish, Sir John'. The often-repeated statement (most recently Dunn, 153, 157–8) that Cavendish was chancellor of the university of Cambridge is an error: the John Cavendish who appears in the list for 1380 in *VCH Cambs. and the Isle of Ely*, 'The University of Cambridge: Chancellors' cannot be the chief justice as the post was held by resident academics at this period. I am grateful to Dr Benjamin Thompson for pointing this out.

34 Dobson, 251–2; Prescott, 152–3; *see* 201–3.

35 Dyer (2), 280; Powell, 13.

36 Prescott, 49, 154–5; Powell, 126–7; Dobson, 250.

37 Powell, 139–41.

38 Ibid., 141; Dobson, 245–6.

39 Powell, 141–3; Dobson, 245–7. I have preferred Gosford's account to Walsingham's which exaggerates for dramatic effect, eight blows being required to behead Lakenheath, for instance, and the abbey chalice and cross rising in value to over one thousand pounds.

40 Prescott, 153–4; Dobson, 251.

41 Prescott, 154; *CFR*, 237; Powell, 133.

42 Hinck, 125 n. 84.

43 Powell, 49, 57, 127; Réville, 251; Hinck, 119, 127, 129; Prescott, 105–7.

44 Réville, 74–7; Dobson, 248–9.

45 Ibid., 252–3; *HOPOL*, 'Swinburne, Sir Robert'; Prescott, 238.

46 Powell, 36–7, 133; Blomefield, 'Wickmere'.

47 Réville, 110 n. 1.

CHAPTER TWELVE: ELY, HUNTINGDON AND CAMBRIDGE

1 Dyer (2), 284–5; Powell, 21; Prescott, 106.

2 Powell, 21–2, 130–1; Bailey, 188–9; Réville, 83, 155; *PROME*, vi, 241; *CPR 1389–92*, 6.

3 The word 'hoggastres' translates either as hoggets (two-year-old sheep) or boars (pigs); Sampson kept both sheep and pigs so which these are is unclear.

4 Prescott, 343–4; Dyer (2), 285; *CFR*, 237; Réville, 79.

5 Dyer (2), 285; Réville, 156, 158.

6 Powell, 22–3, 127–8; Réville, 80 and n. 4; Prescott, 101, 160.

7 Powell, 22–5, 128; Réville, 80–3.

8 Dobson, 250–1; *VCH Cambs. and the Isle of Ely*, 'Preceptory of Chippenham'; Powell, 44; Palmer, 98, 212.

9 Dobson, 235; Palmer, 246–7; HOPOL, 'Wightman, William'.

10 Ibid.; Palmer, 247; *Rot. Parl.*, iii, 175; *CPR 1381–5*, 120; *CChR*, 276; *CCR 1385–9*, 113; Réville, 250.

11 *VCH Hunts.*, 'The Abbey of Ramsey'; Dobson, 236, 238.

12 Powell, 46–7; Palmer, 245–6; Prescott, 179.

13 Palmer, 99; Prescott, 345.

14 Palmer, 169, 234.

15 Ibid., 168, 211–12, 234–5.

16 Prescott, 51–2; Palmer, 234, 246; *CPR 1377–81*, 513; *CCR 1377–81*, 483.

17 Internal evidence demonstrates that the actions attributed to 9 June in the assize rolls (Palmer, 209) were a clerical error for 16 June.

18 *VCH Cambs. and the Isle of Ely*, 'Croydon cum Clopton'; *CCR 1381–5*, 14; *CCR 1399–1402*, 409.

19 Palmer, 101–2, 167–8; *CCR 1381–5*, 76.

20 *CCR 1381–5*, 14, 92.

21 Palmer, 245–6; Prescott, 345–6.

22 Palmer, 98–9; SC/8/116/5754, TNA.

23 Powell, 43 n. 2; Palmer, 100; Prescott, 172–3.

24 Palmer, 81, 212.

25 Ibid., 246; Powell, 49; Réville, 242.

26 Palmer, 99, 102, 137, 170; *VCH Cambs.*, 'Preceptory of Shingay' and 'Preceptory of Duxford'; HOPOL, 'Maisterman, Richard'.

27 Fenwick, ii, 75; Palmer, 83; *CFR*, 231.

28 Palmer, 98, 137; *CFR*, 231, 249; Réville, 222; *CPR 1381–5*, 76.

29 Powell, 52; Palmer (2), 273 n. 24.

30 Palmer, 137–8, 168–71, 209–10, 235.

31 Ibid., 81, 82–3, 97–8, 168, 171, 212.

32 Ibid., 83–4, 99, 102, 210.

33 Ibid., 99, 168–9.

34 Ibid., 98, 99, 101–2, 138, 170; HOPOL, 'Blankpayn, John'.
35 Musson, 38; VCH *Cambs.*, 'The City of Cambridge'.
36 Ibid.; *CPR 1377–81*, 289, 349, 582; *CCR 1377–81*, 513.
37 *PROME*, vi, 234; *CPR 1377–81*, 472; *CPR 1381–5*, 72.
38 Palmer, 135, 138, 170.
39 www.stbenetschurch.org/history2.html; Dunn, 158.
40 *PROME*, vi, 234; Palmer, 135–6, 138, 170.
41 Ibid., 135–6, 167, 171.
42 *PROME*, vi, 232–5; Crane, 221 n. 51. It is possible that the revolt began much earlier in Cambridge than elsewhere, particularly given the problems in February 1381, but the burning of the university records and the attack on Corpus Christi occurred on 16 June, after the dating of the charters.
43 Palmer, 138, 235–6; *CPR 1381–5*, 75.
44 Palmer, 168; *CPR 1381–5*, 76; Prescott, 255–6.

CHAPTER THIRTEEN: NORFOLK

1 Eiden, 10 n. 26.
2 *See* 305.
3 Dyer (2), 284; Müller (2), 12; Prescott, 163. Gelder is not in the 1379 poll-tax return for Feltwell so I assume he was living in Bury by then.
4 Müller (2), 12; Fenwick, ii, 106 where the name appears as 'Johannes Stratour'. Prescott, 163 dates this attack to 16 June.
5 Eiden, 18; Fenwick, ii, 150, 196; iii, 543; Müller (2), 13–14.
6 Ibid., 14; *CCR 1369–74*, 100; *CPR 1374–77*, 157, 160, 322.
7 Müller (2), 13–14; Prescott, 164; Fenwick, ii, 178–9; Réville, 87; *CPR 1381–5*, 93.
8 Eiden, 18; *CPR 1377–81*, 87–8, 96.
9 Powell, 35, 135–6. Ellerton's grave lies in the chancel of his church with the French inscription, 'From earth I was made and formed and to earth I have returned ... Ellertune was my name parson of Thursford, Jesu have pity on me': Blomefield, 'Thursford'.
10 Prescott, 163–4; Müller (2), 14; *CFR*, 248; Eiden, 18; Réville, 93 n. 5.
11 Eiden, 18; Prescott, 165, 167; SC/8/262/13099, TNA; *PROME*, vi, 241.
12 Eiden, 18; Powell, 26.
13 Eiden, 19; Powell, 134; Müller (2), 14; Fenwick, ii, 151. Clerk also

paid only four pence; despite allegedly being the second wealthiest man in Whissonsett after Adam de Billingford (who paid forty pence), whom he was accused of threatening with death.

14 Müller (2), 14; Réville, 89; Eiden, 19; *CFR*, 262.

15 Réville, 85–6, 89, 117; Powell, 27.

16 Fenwick, ii, 161; Powell, 28 n. 1.

17 Ibid.; Blomefield, 'Trunch'; Eiden, 21 n. 77.

18 Powell, 28 n. 1; Fenwick, ii, 166, 198. Ormrod, 16 asserts that Skeet was coroner of Norfolk because on 7 July 1381 the sheriff was ordered to elect another in place of 'Thomas Skete who is dead' (*CCR 1381–5*, 4) but it is unlikely that a man paying the lowest rate of poll-tax had sufficient property to qualify for the office.

19 *TSLME*; E101/68/9/209 and E101/54/20, TNA.

20 Fenwick, ii, 75; Blomefield, 'The City of Norwich'; Dobson, 257–8.

21 Froissart, 222–4; Powell, 132. Walsingham has a more prosaic take, that Salle was captured but could not refrain from criticising the rebels' actions and so was 'knocked on the head by a rustic who was one of his own serfs and soon died': Dobson, 258.

22 *CPR 1358–61*, 371; *CPR 1361–4*, 211; *CPR 1377–81*, 590. Bartholomew Salle bought an exemption for life in 1347 from holding office as mayor, sheriff, escheator etc, so must have had sufficient rank and money to qualify for such posts: *CPR 1345–8*, 250.

23 *CPR 1361–4*, 436; *CPR 1370–4*, 350; *CPR 1377–81*, 201.

24 Blomefield, 'The City of Norwich'; *CPR 1361–4*, 211; Bailey, 186–7; Powell, 30, 131–2; Réville, 105 n. 4; *ODNB*, 'Ufford, William, second earl of Suffolk (c.1339–1382)'; SC/8/21/1028, TNA.

25 Prescott, 167.

26 Powell, 30; Réville, 103 n. 4.

27 Powell, 30; Blomefield, 'The City of Norwich'; HOPOL, 'Limner, Henry'; *CPR 1377–81*, 630; Eiden, 23.

28 HOPOL, 'Bixton, Walter'; Réville, 106; *CFR*, 233.

29 Possibly Sir Roger de Scales, a commissioner to suppress the revolt: *see* 376.

30 Dobson, 258; Walsingham calls him Sir William de Morlee, but he was dead by 1379 and his heir was Thomas: Eiden (2), 375 n. 1; Wood, 73–4; Powell, 31; *CPR 1377–81*, 630.

31 HOPOL, 'Hales, Sir Stephen'; *CFR*, 229, 248.
32 Dyer (2), 281; Hutton, 9–10, 30–1, 56, 71.
33 Froissart, 143–4; Barker (2), 337–8.
34 Prescott, 50; Réville, 103 n. 4.
35 Powell, 131; Blomefield, 'Great Yarmouth: Kirkley Road'; *PROME*, v, 307–10, 314–15; vi, 105, 254.
36 *CCR 1377–81*, 633; Réville, 110 nn. 1, 2; Powell, 32–3.
37 Réville, 110 n. 2, 111 n. 1.
38 HOPOL, 'Fastolf, Hugh'; *CFR*, 248; Powell, 33, 132; *see* 309.
39 Powell, 33; HOPOL, 'Clere, Robert'; Blomefield, 'Witchingham Manor'.
40 Powell, 31, 33–7; Eiden, 22.
41 Powell, 35; Eiden, 20.
42 Powell, 35–6, 135; *PROME*, vi, 241; Prescott, 25, 358–9.
43 Dobson, 259–60; Powell, 38; Eiden, 21 n. 75.
44 *ODNB*, 'Despenser, Henry'; Powell, 34: Prescott, 169, 260–1, 278.
45 Blomefield, 'The City of Norwich'; Powell, 135, where Fletcher's actions are wrongly dated 8 July; Réville, 138 n. 1.
46 Dobson, 260–1.
47 Powell, 39; Réville, 139 n. 1; *see* 217, 424–5.
48 Eiden, 21.
49 *CCR 1381–5*, 26; Prescott, 264.
50 *PROME*, vi, 241; Réville, 105 n. 4, 162; SC/8/262/13099, TNA.
51 Saul, 102–7; *ODNB*, 'Despenser, Henry'.

CHAPTER FOURTEEN: NORTH AND SOUTH

1 Dobson, 309–10. It does not appear in *CPR 1381–5* but the same text, under the same date, appears in the Chester Indictment Rolls with the notice that it was proclaimed in Chester on 23, 27 and 28 July [sic]: P&T, 13–14.
2 Sumption, 431.
3 Sayles, 821–2, 826–7.
4 I suggest '*quinquaginta*' instead of '*quingentis*'.
5 Powell, 25, 141; Hewitt, 35.
6 *GA*, 336; Dobson, 259, 310; Prescott, 44, 45.
7 *CPR 1381–5*, 20; *CPR 1391–5*, 643.
8 Dobson, 311–12; Poos, 236; Eiden, 14 n. 37; *CCR 1381–5*, 80–1; Wood, 76–7.

9 *CPR 1381–5*, 23, 69–71.

10 *VCH Somerset*, 'Hospitals: St John the Baptist, Bridgwater'; *CPR 1377–81*, 597.

11 *PROME*, vi, 229–30; *CPR 1381–5*, 270; *CFR*, 229, 249.

12 *CPR 1381–5*, 95, 270; HOPOL, 'Sydenham, John' and 'Cole, John'; Reading, 178, 346 n.

13 Harvey, 89–91.

14 A revolt in Cornwall was an invention in false indictments quashed in 1390: Prescott (2), 23 n. 74.

15 Hinck, 113–21; *PROME*, vi, 245–6; Réville, 280.

16 Dobson, 278–9; Réville, 276–7; A81, Andrew of Harlestone Collection, Northampton Record Office.

17 *CPR 1381–5*, 72; Réville, cvii.

18 Crook, 9–23.

19 *See* 104–8.

20 *VCH York*, 'The Hospital of St Leonard, York'.

21 Liddy, 29–31; *CPR 1381–5*, 58, 137; Réville, 272–4.

22 Fenwick, iii, 160; Dobson (2), 124–30.

23 Fenwick, iii, 241; Liddy, 30–1; *VCH Yorks.*, 'The Borough of Scarborough'.

24 *CPR 1381–5*, 77; HOPOL, 'Acclom, John'; Dobson (2), 130–8; Fenwick, iii, 251; *CFR*, 232–3.

25 Réville, 286–7.

26 *CPR 1381–5*, 74.

CHAPTER FIFTEEN: SUPPRESSION

1 *Westminster*, 15; *CPR 1381–5*, 72, 73; *CCR 1381–5*, 1, 17, 82.

2 *HA*, 20–2.

3 Dobson, 310–11; *see* 213 ff, 217, 424–5.

4 Prescott (2), 13–14; *see* 269.

5 *CCR 1381–5*, 8; Prescott, 44; *see* 183, 187–8, 338–9.

6 Prescott, 49–50.

7 Ibid., 46–7; *see* 313–14.

8 *OCL*, 464, 1232; Musson, 238; Bellamy, 87, 90–1, 100, 207–8.

9 Ibid., 103; Dobson, 314.

10 Prescott, 56–7; *PROME*, vi, 241; Oman, 136–7; Réville, 164–71; *CPR 1381–5*, 547; Dobson, 250.

11 Prescott, 54; Prescott (2), 24 n. 93.

12 Réville, 261–2; Prescott, 242; *CPR 1381–5*, 87, 276; *CPR 1389–92*, 384.

13 *See* 209–10, 257.
14 *CPR 1381–5*, 24, 26, 71–2, 75–6; Ormrod, 12.
15 Prescott, 70–1; Réville, 155; *CCR 1381–5*, 85.
16 Prescott, 260–1, 292–3.
17 *PROME*, vi, 315; Prescott, 260–2, 287 n. 40.
18 *CCR 1381–5*, 2, 74–5; *CPR 1381–5*, 73; Prescott, 266.
19 *CPR 1381–5*, 32, 71–2, 75, 77–8.
20 Fryde (3), 50.
21 Walker, 68–74; *ODNB*, 'John of Gaunt'; *CPR 1381–5*, 25–6, 30.
22 *PROME*, vi, 215.
23 *See* 254–6.
24 *PROME*, vi, 215–16.
25 Ibid., 217–20.
26 Ibid., 222–4, 240–7, 257, 260–1; Lacey, 60–1.
27 *CCR 1381–5*, 13; *PROME*, vi, 230–6.
28 Ibid., 249, 253; Blomefield, 'Of Kirkeley Road'.
29 *PROME*, vi, 227–8; Bellamy, 105.
30 *PROME*, vi, 225–6, 247–9.

CHAPTER SIXTEEN: THE AFTERMATH

1   *GA*, iii, 324; *see* 293.
2   *See* 325, 336–7.
3   *VCH Herts.*, 'The City of St Albans: The Borough'; *MSS of Lincoln*, 'The Corporation of Bury St Edmunds: Royal Charters', 122–3.
4   Réville, cxxxii; Oman, 153–4.
5   Fryde (3), 248–9; Dunn, 188. The purchaser, Sir Henry Lee, bought the queen's villeins so that he could profit from selling them their manumissions.
6   Réville, cxxvii; Bailey, 197–202.
7   Aston, 37; Dobson, 367, 374, 376, 378.
8   *ODNB*, 'Wyclif, John'; Wyclif, xxxiii, 190, 194–7.
9   P&T, 15–16.
10 Prescott, (2), 16; Prescott, 61–2, 203–4; Réville, 239–40.
11 Eiden (2), 371–5; *CCR 1381–5*, 15–16, 85–6.
12 Powell, 24–5, 25 n. 1; Eiden (2), 370–1.
13 Bellamy (2), 259.
14 P&T, 19–20; *CPR 1391–6*, 249.
15 Dobson, 374.

CHAPTER SEVENTEEN: THE LEGACY

1 Justice, 194.
2 *See* 188, 198.
3 Saul, 447, 450, 452–3.
4 Ibid., 457–8.
5 Harriss, 468, 490.
6 Ibid., 483–4.
7 Harriss, 450–3.
8 Richard's beloved first wife, Anne of Bohemia, had died on 7 June 1394; the marriage was childless: Saul, 258.
9 Walker (2), 37–8, 41, 43.
10 *PROME*, vi, 324–5; Justice, 194–5.
11 Djordjevic, 85, 87. The enduring myth, based ultimately on Knighton's story about John Legge, that it was the latter's assault on the daughter of 'John Tyler of Dertford, Kent' which provoked the infuriated Tyler to kill the poll-tax commissioner and begin the great revolt was first published by John Stow in his *A Summarie of our Englysh Chronicles* (1566) but then repeated, elaborated and popularised by Holinshed: Matheson, 121–4, 127–8; for Legge *see* 139, 174–5, 262.
12 Adkins, 64, 66. Adkins argues that the rebels are nevertheless portrayed in a more favourable light than previous accounts and that they share a mutual respect with the king, though they have no rapport at all with the nobility; Richard's highly sympathetic portrayal is informed by the idea that he, like Elizabeth I, is a wise, just and merciful sovereign who feels his obligations to rich and poor alike.
13 Dunn, 191.
14 Fuller, i, 451–2. The Protestant Fuller also argued that it was nonsense to blame Wyclif for causing the revolt, arguing instead that the Franciscan friars were responsible 'because some of these, belike, were the rebels' white-boys … to be spared in a general destruction': ibid., 456.
15 Woodhouse, 353; Dobson, 354–5; Dunn, 190–1.
16 Matheson, 135 n. 27; Linebaugh, 347.
17 Dobson, 393–4.
18 Ibid., 395–6.
19 Storey, 67; Taylor, 28. A brief extract is printed in Dobson, 397–8.
20 Taylor, 21, 29, 44–5.
21 Ibid., 20, 34, 37–8.

22 Ibid., 31; *see* n. 11.
23 Taylor, 23, 25–6; *see* plate 28. Morris was a disciple of H. M. Hyndman, who in *The Historical Basis of Socialism in England* (London, 1883), had argued that the great revolt provided a powerful revolutionary precedent for the nascent socialist movement in England and urged the propaganda value of identifying an indigenous socialist tradition, epitomised by leaders of popular rebellions such as Balle and Tyler, 'to show that the idea of socialism is no foreign importation into England'. The historian J. R. Green's *History of the English People* (London, 1878) similarly anticipated Bede Jarrett by stating that Balle 'openly preached the doctrines of communism': Salmon, 30, 34.
24 Taylor, 22.
25 Ibid., 23.

APPENDIX 1: WAT TYLER

1 Réville, cxviii n. 2; *Rot. Parl.*, iii, 175; Dobson, 127.
2 Flaherty, 92–3; Sparvel-Bayly, 211–12; Powell, 9.
3 Fenwick, i, 198, 387.
4 Froissart, Walsingham and the Continuator of the *Eulogium Historiarum*, the last describing him as 'a tiler from Essex': Dobson, 138, 176, 206.
5 Dobson, 176; Froissart, 213; Stopford, 93–108; www.hereshistorykent.org.uk (Wye).
6 Froissart, 218; *TSLME*.
7 Fenwick, i, 197, 202; for Ker *see* 171 ff.

APPENDIX 2: JACK STRAW

1 Dobson, 186; Brie, 106–11 esp. 107–8.
2 Pettitt, 3–20 esp. 8–9, 18 n. 50. Pettitt, 9 is certainly wrong in identifying 'Tronche', named in a political poem as a leader of the revolt, with the club-bearing figure of folk-plays: John Trunch was a genuine rebel captain from Norfolk: *see* 333, 340, 346, 351.
3 Dunn, 190.
4 Sparvel-Bayly, 211–12; Flaherty, 71–3.
5 Dobson, 171; *see* 239.
6 Dyer (3), 18–19.

7 Arnold, 56, 167–8; *VCH Middlesex*, 'Social and Economic History'; *see* 57–8.
8 *Rot. Parl.*, iii, 175; Dobson, 364–6; Réville, 175–8.

APPENDIX 3: JOHN BALLE

1 Justice, 14; *VCH Essex*, 'The Abbey of Colchester'; *VCH York*, 'St Mary's Abbey, York'.
2 Bird, 288.
3 Palmer, 156 n. 11; *VCH Essex*, 'The Priory of St Botolph, Colchester'.
4 *CPR 1361–4*, 470.

APPENDIX 4: JOHN BALLE'S LETTERS

1 Dobson, 380–3; Green, 181–2; Justice, 13–15.
2 Ibid., 15–17.
3 Ibid., 14–15; Dobson, 381. My translation.
4 *ODNB*, 'Langland, William'.
5 Aston, 29–33.
6 Justice, 15; Aston argues for the significance of the Corpus Christi links.
7 Barron (2), 95; Aers, 438–9; Owst, 295.
8 Justice, 13; Dobson 382. My translation.
9 Green, 183–5.
10 Justice, 14; Dobson, 382. My translation.
11 For example, Duffy, 80.
12 Justice, 15; Dobson, 383. My translation.

BIBLIOGRAPHY

Only those works cited in the text are included in this bibliography; reasons of space prohibit a more general bibliography of all works consulted or relevant which may lead to some apparent anomalies by the omission of certain standard texts on the subjects discussed.

Abbreviations

BHO: British History Online: www.british-history.ac.uk.

CCR: *Calendar of Close Rolls: Edward III–Richard II* (HMSO, 1896–1927): BHO and www.medieval genealogy.org.uk.

CChR: *Calendar of the Charter Rolls, Preserved in the Public Record Office: 15 Edward III–5 Henry V* (HMSO, 1916), vol. 5.

CFR: *Calendar of the Fine Rolls, Preserved in the Public Record Office., ix, Richard II, AD 1377–1383* (HMSO, 1926): www.medievalgenealogy.org.uk.

CHAS: Canterbury Historical and Archaeological Society: www.canterbury-archaeology.org.uk.

CLAN: Helena M. Chew and William Kellaway (eds), *London Assize of Nuisance 1301–1431: a Calendar* (London Record Society, 1973): BHO.

CLBCL: *Calendar of Letter-Books of the City of London: H: 1375–1399* (Corporation of the City of London, 1907): BHO.

CPMROCL: A. H. Thomas (ed.), *Calendar of the Plea and Memoranda Rolls of the City of London: vol. ii: 1364–81* (Cambridge University Press, 1929): BHO.

CPR: *Calendar of the Patent Rolls, Edward III–Richard*

II (HMSO, 1891–1916): www.medievalgenealogy. org.uk.

Domesday Book: Ann Williams and G. H. Martin (eds), *Domesday Book: A Complete Translation* (Penguin Books, 1992).

Froissart: Geoffrey Brereton (ed. and trans.), *Jean Froissart: Chronicles* (Penguin Books, 1978).

GA: Thomas Walsingham, *Gesta Abbatum Monasterii Sancti Albani: 1349–1411*, ed. H. T. Riley (London, 1869), vol. 3.

HA: Thomas Walsingham, *Historia Anglicana*, ed. H. T. Riley (Longmans, Green and Co., 1863–4), 2 vols.

H&A: R. H. Hilton and T. H. Aston (eds), *The English Rising of 1381* (Cambridge University Press, 1984, repr. 2007).

HOPOL: J. S. Roskell, L. Clark, C. Rawcliffe (eds) *The History of Parliament: the House of Commons 1386–1421* (Boydell and Brewer, 1993): www.historyofparliamentonline.org.

L&W: W. H. Liddell and R. G. E. Wood (eds), *Essex and the Great Revolt of 1381* (Essex Record Office, 1982).

MSS of Lincoln: *The Manuscripts of Lincoln, Bury St Edmunds etc.: Fourteenth Report, Appendix; Part viii* (Historical Manuscripts Commission, 1895): BHO.

OCL: David M. Walker (ed.), *The Oxford Companion to Law* (Clarendon Press, 1980).

ODNB: *Oxford Dictionary of National Biography* (Oxford University Press, 2004); online edn, Jan 2008: www.oxforddnb.com.

P&T: Edgar Powell and G. M. Trevelyan (eds), *The Peasants' Rising and the Lollards: A Collection of Documents Forming an Appendix to 'England in the Age of Wycliffe'* (Longmans, Green and Co., 1899).

PRH: *The Peasants' Revolt in Hertfordshire: The Rising and its Background: A Symposium* (Hertfordshire Publications, 1981).

PROME: Chris Given-Wilson (gen. ed.), *The Parliament Rolls of Medieval England 1275–1504* (The Boydell Press, 2005).

Reading: James Tait (ed.), *Chronica Johannis de Reading et*

	Anonymi Cantuarensis, 1346–67 (Manchester University Press, 1914).
Rippon and Wainwright:	Stephen Rippon and Adam Wainwright, 'Our Wetland Heritage: An Integrated Approach Towards Managing Coastal Landscapes': https://eric.exeter.ac.uk.
Rot. Parl.:	*Rotuli Parliamentorum, ut et Petitiones, et Placita in Parliamento* (London, 1767–77), 6 vols.
SOLO:	*Survey of London Online:* BHO but links to particular volumes also available at: www.english-heritage.org.uk/professional/research/buildings/survey-of-london/survey-of-london-online.
Statutes of the Realm:	*The Statutes of the Realm* (London, 1810), vol. i.
TNA:	The National Archives, Kew, London.
TSLME:	*The Soldier in Later Medieval England* database: www.medievalsoldier.org.
VCH:	*Victoria County History*: BHO.
Walsingham:	David Preest (ed.) and James Gordon Clark (trans.), *The Chronica Maiora of Thomas Walsingham* (The Boydell Press, 2005).
Westminster:	L.C. Hector and Barbara F. Harvey (eds), *The Westminster Chronicle 1381–1394* (Clarendon Press, 1982).

Cited by author's surname

Adkins, Mary G. M., 'A Theory about "The Life and Death of Jack Straw"', *The University of Texas Studies in English*, 28 (1949), 57–82.

Aers, David, '*Vox Populi* and the Literature of 1381' in David Wallace (ed.), *The Cambridge History of Medieval English Literature* (Cambridge University Press, 1999), 432–53.

Allen Brown, Reginald, *Rochester Castle* (HMSO, 1969).

Allmand, Christopher, *Henry V* (Yale University Press, 1997).

Arnold, Morris S., *Select Cases of Trespass from the King's Courts 1307–99*, Seldon Society, 100 (1985) and 103 (1987).

Aston, Margaret, 'Corpus Christi and Corpus Regni: Heresy and the Peasants' Revolt', *Past and Present*, 143 (1994), 3–47.
Aston (2): 'Lollardy and Sedition 1381–1431', *Past and Present*, 17 (1960), 1–44.

Bailey, Mark, *Medieval Suffolk: An Economic and Social History 1200–1500* (The Boydell Press, 2007).

Barber, Richard, *Edward, Prince of Wales and Aquitaine* (The Boydell Press, 1978).

Barker, Juliet, *The Tournament in England, 1100–1400* (The Boydell Press, 1986).

   Barker (2): *Agincourt: The King, The Campaign, The Battle* (Little, Brown, 2005).

   Barker (3): *Conquest: The English Kingdom of France in the Hundred Years War* (Little, Brown, 2009).

Barr, Helen, 'Wycliffite Representations of the Third Estate' in Somerset, 197–216.

Barron, Caroline, 'The Later Middle Ages: 1270–1520' in Mary D. Lobel and W. H. Johns (eds), *The City of London from Prehistoric Times to c.1520* (Oxford University Press, 1989), iii, 42–56.

   Barron (2): 'William Langland: A London Poet' in Hanawalt, 91–109.

   Barron (3): 'The Burning of the Jubilee Book' (Lecture to the Guildhall Historical Association, 2002): www.guildhallhistoricalassociation.org.uk/docs.

Battely, Nicholas, *The Antiquities of Canterbury* (London, 1703), 2 vols.

Bellamy, J. G., *The Law of Treason in England in the Later Middle Ages* (Cambridge University Press, 1970).

   Bellamy (2): 'The Northern Rebellions in the Later Years of Richard II', *Bulletin of the John Rylands Library* (1965), 254–74.

Bellot, Hugh H. L., *The Inner and Middle Temple* (Methuen, 1902).

Bennett, Michael, 'Edward III's Entail and the Succession to the Crown, 1376–1471', *English Historical Review*, 113 (1998), 580–609.

Bird, Brian and David Stephenson, 'Who was John Ball?', *Essex Archaeology and History*, 3rd ser., 8 (1976), 287–8.

   Bird (2): W. H. B. Bird, 'The Peasant Rising of 1381: The King's Itinerary', *English Historical Review*, 31 (1916), 124–6.

   Bird (3): Ruth Bird, *The Turbulent London of Richard II* (Longmans, Green & Co., 1949).

Blomefield, Francis, *Essay Towards a Topographical History of the County of Norfolk* (1806–7): BHO.

Brie, Friedrich W. D., 'Wat Tyler and Jack Straw', *English Historical Review*, 21 (1906), 106–11.

Britnell, R. H., 'Feudal Reaction after the Black Death in the Palatinate of Durham', *Past and Present*, 128 (1990), 28–47.
Growth and Decline in Colchester, 1300–1525 (Cambridge University Press, 1986).

Brooks, Nicholas, 'The Organization and Achievements of the Peasants of Kent and Essex in 1381' in Brooks (3), 266–89.
Brooks (2): 'Rochester Bridge, AD 43–1381' in Brooks (3), 219–65.
Brooks (3): *Communities and Warfare 700–1400* (The Hambledon Press, 2000).

Brown, Peter (ed.), *Geoffrey Chaucer* (Oxford University Press, 2011).

Butcher, A. F., 'English Urban Society and the Revolt of 1381' in H&A, 84–111.

Campbell, Bruce M. S., 'Population Pressure, Inheritance and the Land Market in a Fourteenth-Century Peasant Community' in Smith (2), 87–134.
Campbell (2): 'Agriculture in Kent in the High Middle Ages' in Sweetinburgh, 25–53.

Carlin, Martha, *Medieval Southwark* (The Hambledon Press, 1996).

Chaucer, Geoffrey, The Parson's Tale: http://classiclit.about.com/library/bl-etexts/gchaucer/bl-gchau-can-parson-m.htm: (my translation).
Chaucer (2): *Canterbury Tales: Nine Tales and the General Prologue*, ed. V. A. Kolve and Glending Olson (Norton Critical Editions, 1989): (my translation).

Chrimes, S. B. and A. L. Brown, *Select Documents of English Constitutional History* (Adam and Charles Black, 1961).

Cole, Andrew, 'William Langland and the Invention of Lollardy' in Somerset, 37–58.

Coulson, Charles, 'Hierarchism in Conventual Crenellation: An Essay on the Sociology and Metaphysics of Medieval Fortification': www.archaeologydataservice.ac.uk.

Crane, Susan, 'The Writing Lesson of 1381' in Hanawalt, 201–21.

Crook, D., 'Derbyshire and the English Rising of 1381', *Historical Research*, 60 no. 141 (1987), 9–23.

Crouch, David, *William Marshal: Knighthood, War and Chivalry, 1147–1219* (Pearson Education, 2002).

De Saxe, David, 'The Hundred of Wye and the Great Revolt of 1381', *Archaeologia Cantiana*, 127 (2007), 143–61.

Djordjevic, Igor, *Holinshead's Nation: Ideals, Memory, and Practical Policy in the Chronicles* (Ashgate, 2010).

Dobson, R. B., *The Peasants' Revolt of 1381* (Macmillan, 1970).

Dobson (2): 'The Risings in York, Beverley and Scarborough, 1380–1381' in H&A, 112–42.

Dodd, Gwilym and Alison McHardy (eds), *Petitions to the Crown from English Religious Houses c.1272–c.1485*, Canterbury and York Society, 100 (2010).

Duffy, Eamon, *Marking the Hours: English People and their Prayers 1240–1570* (Yale University Press, 2006).

Dunn, Alastair, *The Peasants' Revolt: England's Failed Revolution of 1381* (Tempus Publishing, 2002, 2004 edn).

Dyer, Christopher, *Everyday Life in Medieval England* (The Hambledon Press, 1994).

Dyer (2): 'The Rising of 1381 in Suffolk: Its Origins and Participants', *Proceedings of the Suffolk Institute of Archaeology and History*, 36 (1988), 274–87.

Dyer (3): 'The Social and Economic Background to the Rural Revolt of 1381' in H&A, 9–42.

Dyer (4): 'Work Ethics in the Fourteenth Century' in James Bothwell, P. J. P. Goldberg and W. M. Ormrod (eds), *The Problem of Labour in Fourteenth-Century England* (York Medieval Press, 2000), 21–41.

Dyer (5): 'The Causes of the Revolt in Rural Essex' in L&W, 21–36.

Dyer (6): *Standards of Living in the Later Middle Ages* (Cambridge University Press, 1989, revised edn, 1998).

Eiden, Herbert, 'Joint Action Against "Bad" Lordship: The Peasants' Revolt in Essex and Norfolk', *History*, 83 (1998), 5–30.

Eiden (2): 'Norfolk, 1382: A Sequel to the Peasants' Revolt', *English Historical Review*, 114 (1999), 370–7.

Faith, Rosamund, 'The "Great Rumour" of 1377 and Peasant Ideology' in H&A, 43–73.

Federico, Sylvia, 'The Imaginary Society: Women in 1381', *Journal of British Studies*, 40 no. 2 (2001), 159–83.

Fenwick, Carolyn C. (ed.), *The Poll Taxes of 1377, 1379 and 1381* (Oxford University Press, 1998, 2001, 2005), 3 vols.

Flaherty, W. E., 'The Great Rebellion in Kent of 1381 Illustrated from the Public Records', *Archaeologia Cantiana*, 3 (1860), 65–96.

Fryde, E. B., 'Parliament and the Peasants' Revolt of 1381' in E. B. Fryde, *Studies in Medieval Trade and Finance* (The Hambledon Press, 1983), 75–88.

Fryde (2): 'The Financial Policies of the Royal Governments and

Popular Resistance to Them in France and England' in E. B. Fryde, *Studies in Medieval Trade and Finance* (The Hambledon Press, 1983), 824–60.

Fryde (3): *Peasants and Landlords in Later Medieval England* (Alan Sutton and St Martin's Press, 1996).

Fuller, Thomas, *The Church History of Britain, from the Birth of Jesus Christ until the year MDCXVIII* (3rd edn, Thomas Tegg, 1842), vol. 1.

Goldberg, P. J. P. (ed.), *Woman is a Worthy Wight: Women in English Society c.1200–1500* (Sutton, 1992).

Goldberg (2): '"For Better, For Worse": Marriage and Economic Opportunity for Women in Town and Country' in Goldberg, 108–25.

Goldberg (3): 'Marriage, Migration, and Servanthood: The York Cause Paper Evidence' in Goldberg, 1–15.

Goodman, Anthony, *John of Gaunt: The Exercise of Princely Power in Fourteenth-Century Europe* (Longman, 1992).

Gottfried, Robert S., *Bury St Edmunds and the Urban Crisis: 1290–1539* (Princeton University Press, 1982).

Green, Richard Firth, 'John Ball's Letters: Literary History and Historical Literature' in Hanawalt, 176–200.

Grenville, Jane, 'Houses and Households in Late Medieval England: An Archaeological Perspective' in Jocelyn Wogan-Browne *et al* (eds), *Medieval Women: Texts and Contexts in Late Medieval Britain. Essays for Felicity Riddy* (Brepols, 2000), 309–28.

Grieve, H. E. P., 'The Rebellion and the County Town' in L&W, 37–54.

Hanawalt, Barbara (ed.), *Chaucer's England: Literature in Historical Context* (University of Minnesota Press, 1992).

Harding, Alan, 'The Revolt against the Justices' in H&A, 165–93.

Harriss, Gerald, *Shaping the Nation: England 1360–1461* (Clarendon Press, 2005).

Harvey, Barbara, 'Draft Letters Patent of Manumission and Pardon for the Men of Somerset in 1381', *English Historical Review*, 80 (1965), 89–91.

Hasted, Edward, *The History and Topographical Survey of the County of Kent* (Canterbury, 1797–1801), 12 vols: BHO.

Hatcher, John, 'England in the Aftermath of the Black Death', *Past and Present*, 144 (1994), 3–35.

Heath, Sidney, *Pilgrim Life in the Middle Ages* (T. Fisher Unwin, 1911).

Hewitt, H. J., *The Organization of War under Edward III*

(Manchester University Press, 1966; repr. Pen and Sword, 2004).

Hibbert, Christopher, *Tower of London* (Newsweek Book Division, 1971).

Hilton, Rodney, *Bond Men Made Free: Medieval Peasant Movements and the English Rising of 1381*, with a new introduction by Christopher Dyer (Routledge, 2003).

Hinck, Helmut, 'The Rising of 1381 in Winchester', *English Historical Review*, 125 (2010), 112–31.

Holt, Richard, 'Thomas of Woodstock and Events at Gloucester in 1381', *Bulletin of the Institute of Historical Research*, 58 (1985), 237–41.

Hutton, Ronald, *The Rise and Fall of Merry England: The Ritual Year 1400–1700* (Oxford University Press, 1994).

Jewell, Helen, '*Piers Plowman* – A Poem of Crisis: An Analysis of Political Instability in Langland's England' in John Taylor and Wendy Childs (eds), *Politics and Crisis in Fourteenth-Century England* (Sutton Publishing, 1990), 59–80.

Justice, Steven, *Writing and Rebellion: England in 1381* (University of California Press, 1994).

Karras, Ruth Mazo, 'The Regulation of Brothels in Later Medieval England', *Signs*, 14 (1989), 399–433.

Keen, Maurice H., *England in the Later Middle Ages* (2nd edn, Routledge, 2003).

Kelly, Henry Ansgar, 'Bishop, Prioress, and Bawd in the Stews of Southwark', *Speculum*, 75 (2000), 342–88.

Knoop, D. and G. P. Jones, *The Medieval Mason* (Manchester University Press, 3rd edn, 1967).

Lacey, Helen, '"Grace for the Rebels": The Role of the Royal Pardon in the Peasants' Revolt of 1381', *Journal of Medieval History*, 34 (2008), 36–63.

Larsen, Andrew E., 'Are All Lollards Lollards?' in Somerset, 59–72.

Liddy, Christian D., 'Urban Conflict in Late Fourteenth-Century England: The Case of York in 1380–1', *English Historical Review*, 118 (2003), 1–32.

Linebaugh, Peter, *The London Hanged: Crime and Civil Society in the Eighteenth Century* (Verso, 2003).

Logan, F. Donald, *Excommunication and the Secular Arm in Medieval England* (Pontifical Institute of Medieval Studies, 1968).

Mate, Mavis, 'The Economy of Kent, 1200–1500: An Age of Expansion, 1200–1348' in Sweetinburgh, 1–10.

Matheson, Lister M., 'The Peasants' Revolt through Five Centuries of Rumor and Reporting: Richard Fox, John Stow, and their Successors', *Studies in Philology*, xcv (1998), 121–51.

McHardy, A. K., (ed.), *Clerical Poll-Taxes of the Diocese of Lincoln 1377–81*, Lincoln Record Soc., 81 (1992).

McHardy (2): *The Church in London 1375–1392*, London Record Soc., 13 (1977).

Müller, Miriam, 'The Aims and Organisation of a Peasant Revolt in Early Fourteenth-Century Wiltshire', *Rural History*, 14 (2003), 1–20.

Müller (2): 'Conflict and Revolt: The bishop of Ely and his peasants at the manor of Brandon in Suffolk c.1300–81', *Rural History*, 23 (2012), 1–19.

Musson, Anthony, *Medieval Law in Context: The Growth of Legal Consciousness from Magna Carta to the Peasants' Revolt* (Manchester University Press, 2001).

Napier, Jill and Chris, 'Essex Historic Buildings Group Study Day at Cressing Temple', *Norfolk Historic Buildings Group Newsletter*, 10 (2005), 14.

Ohler, Norbert, *The Medieval Traveller* (Boydell Press, 1989).

Oman, Charles W. C., *The Great Revolt of 1381* (Oxford, 1906, repr. Forgotten Books, 2012).

Orme, Nicholas, *Medieval Schools: From Roman Britain to Renaissance England* (Yale University Press, 2006).

Orme (2): *Medieval Children* (Yale University Press, 2001).

Ormrod, W. Mark, 'The Peasants' Revolt and the Government of England', *Journal of British Studies*, 29 (1991), 1–30.

Ormrod (2): 'The West European Monarchies in the Later Middle Ages' in Richard Bonney (ed.), *Economic Systems and State Finance* (Clarendon Press, 1995), 123–60.

Ormrod (3): 'An Experiment in Taxation: The English Parish Subsidy of 1371', *Speculum*, 63 (1988), 58–82.

Ormrod (4): *Edward III* (Yale University Press, 2011, pbk 2013).

Owst, G. R., *Literature and Pulpit in Medieval England* (Oxford, 1961).

Palmer, W. M., 'Records of the Villein Insurrection in Cambridgeshire', *East Anglian* (Dec 1896), 81–4, 97–102, 135–9, 167–72, 209–12, 234–7, 243–7.

Robert C. Palmer, *English Law in the Age of the Black Death, 1348–1381: A Transformation of Governance and Law* (University of North Carolina Press, 1993).

Pedersen, Frederik, 'The German Hanse and the Peasants' Revolt of 1381', *Bulletin of the Institute of Historical Research*, 57 (1984), 92–8.

Pettitt, T., '"Here Comes I Jack Straw": English Folk Drama and Social Revolt', *Folklore*, 95 (1984), 3–20.

Poos, L. R., *A Rural Society after the Black Death: Essex 1350–1525* (Cambridge University Press, 1991).

Powell, Edgar, *The Rising in East Anglia in 1381* (Cambridge University Press, 1896).

Prescott, Andrew, *Judicial Records of the Rising of 1381* (PhD. thesis, Bedford College, University of London, 1984): *Ethos* 319371.

    Prescott (2): 'Writing about Rebellion: Using the Records of the Peasants' Revolt of 1381', *History Workshop Journal*, 45 (1998), 1–27.

Putnam, Bertha H., 'Maximum Wage-Laws for Priests after the Black Death, 1348–1381', *American Historical Review*, 21 (1915), 12–32.

Quiney, Anthony, *Town Houses of Medieval Britain* (Yale University Press, 2003).

Ravensdale, Jack, 'Population Changes and the Transfer of Customary Land on a Cambridgeshire Manor in the Fourteenth Century' in Smith (2), 197–225.

Réville, André, *Le Soulèvement des Travailleurs d'Angleterre en 1381* (Paris, 1898).

Rich, E. E., 'The Mayors of the Staples', *Cambridge Historical Journal*, iv (1933), 120–42.

Riley, H. T. (ed.), *Memorials of London and London Life: In the 13th, 14th and 15th Centuries* (Longmans, Green and Co., 1868): BHO.

Russell, Josiah Cox, 'The Clerical Population of Medieval England', *Traditio*, 2 (1944), 177–212.

Sabine, Ernest L., 'City Cleaning in Mediaeval London', *Speculum*, 12 (1937), 19–43.

Sargent, Frank, 'The Wine Trade with Gascony' in George Unwin (ed.), *Finance and Trade Under Edward III* (Manchester University Press, 1918), 256–311.

Salmon, Nicholas, 'A Reassessment of *A Dream of John Ball*': www.morrissociety.org/publications/JWMS/SP01.14.2SalmonBall.

Saul, Nigel, *Richard II* (Yale University Press, 1997, pbk 1999).

    Saul (2): *The Batsford Companion to Medieval England* (Barnes and Noble, 1983).

Sayles, G. O., 'Richard II in 1381 and 1399', *English Historical Review*, 94 (1979), 820–9.

Schofield, Phillipp R., *Peasant and Community in Medieval England, 1200–1500* (Palgrave Macmillan, 2003).

Searle, Eleanor and Robert Burghart, 'The Defense of England and the Peasants' Revolt', *Viator*, 3 (1970), 365–88.

Smith, Richard M., 'Geographical Diversity in the Resort to Marriage in Late Medieval Europe: Work, Reputation, and Unmarried Females in the Household Formation Systems of Northern and Southern Europe' in Goldberg, 16–59.

Smith (2): (ed.), *Land, Kinship and Life-Cycle* (Cambridge University Press, 1984).

Somerset, Fiona, Jill C. Havens and Derrick G. Pitard (eds), *Lollards and their Influence in Late Medieval England* (The Boydell Press, 2003).

Sparvel-Bayly, J. A., 'Essex in Insurrection, 1381', *Transactions of the Essex Archaeological Society*, n.s. 1 (1878), 205–19.

Staley, Lynn (ed. and trans.), *The Book of Margery Kempe* (W. W. Norton & Co, 2001).

Stopford, J., 'Modes of Production among Medieval Tilers', *Medieval Archaeology* (1993): www.archaeologydataservice.ac.uk.

Storey, Mark, *Robert Southey: A Life* (Oxford University Press, 1997).

Stubbs, W., *Select Charters and Other Illustrations of English Constitutional History* (Clarendon Press, 1895).

Suckling, Alfred, *The History and Antiquities of the County of Suffolk* (John Weale, 1846–8), 2 vols: BHO.

Sumption, Jonathan, *Divided Houses: The Hundred Years War III* (Faber and Faber, 2012).

Sweetinburgh, Sheila (ed.), *Later Medieval Kent, 1220–1540* (The Boydell Press, 2010).

Taylor, Antony, *London's Burning: Pulp Fiction, the Politics of Terrorism and the Destruction of the Capital in British Popular Culture, 1840–2005* (Bloomsbury Academic, pbk 2013).

Taylor, John, *English Historical Literature in the Fourteenth Century* (Clarendon Press, 1987).

Thornbury, Walter and Edward Walford, *Old and New London* (Cassell, Petter and Galpin, 1878), 6 vols: BHO.

Thrupp, Sylvia L., *The Merchant Class of Medieval London (1300–1500)* (University of Chicago Press, 1948).

Tout, T. F., *Chapters in the Administrative History of Mediaeval*

England: The Wardrobe, the Chamber and the Small Seals (Manchester University Press, 1928), vol. iii.

Walford, Edward, *Old and New London* (Centre for Metropolitan History, 1878), vol. vi.

Walker, S. K., 'Letters to the Dukes of Lancaster in 1381 and 1399', *English Historical Review*, 106 (1991), 68–79.

    Walker (2): 'Rumour, Sedition and Popular Protest in the Reign of Henry IV', *Past and Present*, 166 (2000), 31–65.

Webb, E. A., *The Records of St Bartholomew's Priory [and] St Bartholomew the Great, West Smithfield* (Oxford University Press, 1921): BHO.

Wilkinson, B., 'The Peasants' Revolt of 1381', *Speculum*, 15 (1940) 12–35.

Wood, R. G. E., 'Essex Manorial Records and the Revolt' in L&W, 67–84.

    Wood (2): Margaret Wood, *The English Mediaeval House* (Bracken Books, 1965).

Woodhouse, A. S. P. (ed.), *Puritanism and Liberty* (2nd edn, London, 1974).

Wright, Lawrence, *Clean and Decent: The Fascinating History of the Bathroom and Water-Closet* (Penguin, 2000).

Wyclif, John, *Tractatus de Blasphemia*, ed. Michael Henry Dziewicki (London, 1893).

Young, Deborah, *The Life-Cycle in Western Europe, c. 1300–1500* (Manchester University Press, 2006).

INDEX

PICTURE CREDITS

1. Portrait of Richard II 'The Westminster Portrait', 1390s (oil on panel), English School (14th century) / Westminster Abbey, London, UK / Bridgeman Images
2. Edward III: © Dean and Chapter of Westminster
3. John of Gaunt, Duke of Lancaster (1340–99) (tempera on panel), Cornelisz, Lucas (1495–1552) (attributed to) / Private Collection / Bridgeman Images
4. Old London Bridge, detail from 'Visscher's London', 17th century (engraving), Visscher, Nicolaes (Claes) Jansz (1586–1652) / Private Collection / Bridgeman Images
5. Ms 65/1284 f.2v February: farmyard scene with peasants, from the 'Très Riches Heures du Duc de Berry' (vellum) (for facsimile copy see 65824), Limbourg Brothers (fl.1400–1416) / Musée Condé, Chantilly, France / Giraudon / Bridgeman Images
6. Balneum, from *Omne Bonum* by James le Palmer: British Library
7. Add 42130 f.166v Woman throwing corn to hens and chickens, from the 'Luttrell Psalter', c. 1325–35 (vellum), English School (14th century) / British Library, London, UK / © British Library Board. All Rights Reserved / Bridgeman Images
8. Ploughing with oxen / British Library, London, UK / © British Library Board. All Rights Reserved / Bridgeman Images

9. Add. 42130 f. 171 Harrowing, from the 'Luttrell Psalter', c. 1325–35 (vellum), English School (14th century) / British Library, London, UK / © British Library Board. All Rights Reserved / Bridgeman Images

10. Add. 42130 f. 170v Sower at Work, from the 'Luttrell Psalter', c. 1325–35 (vellum), English School (14th century) / British Library, London, UK / © British Library Board. All Rights Reserved / Bridgeman Images

11. Add. 42130 f.172v, Peasants harvesting, begun prior to 1340 for Sir Geoffrey Luttrell (1276–1345), Latin (vellum), English School (14th century) / British Library, London, UK / © British Library Board. All Rights Reserved / Bridgeman Images

12. Add. 42130 f.173 Stacking sheaves of corn, from the 'Luttrell Psalter', c. 1325–35 (vellum), English School (14th century) / British Library, London, UK / © British Library Board. All Rights Reserved / Bridgeman Images

13. Windmill, with miller / British Library, London, UK / © British Library Board. All Rights Reserved / Bridgeman Images

14. Ms 65/1284 f.11v November: feeding acorns to the pigs, from the 'Très Riches Heures du Duc du Berry' (vellum) (for facsimile see 65826), Limbourg Brothers (fl. 1400–1416) / Musée Condé, Chantilly, France / Bridgeman Images

15. Royal 6 E. VI, f.303v Clerics hunting rabbits, illustration from 'Omne Bonum', 1360–75 (vellum), English School (14th century) / British Library, London, UK / Bridgeman Images

16. The feretory of St Alban, from J. Charles Wall, *Shrines of British Saints* (1905)

17. St Albans Abbey in St Albans (colour photo), English Photographer (20th century) / Private Collection / © Look and Learn / Elgar Collection / Bridgeman Images

18. Abbey Gate (photo) / Bury St Edmunds, Suffolk, UK / Photo © Neil Holmes / Bridgeman Images

19. Cessio Actionis, from *Omne Bonum* by James le Palmer: British Library

20. Causa, from *Omne Bonum* by James le Palmer: British Library

21. Confessio iudicalis, from *Omne Bonum* by James le Palmer: British Library

22. The ruins of the chapel in the Savoy Palace, London: © Ashmolean Museum / Mary Evans
23. The Tower of London / British Library, London, UK / © British Library Board. All Rights Reserved / Bridgeman Images
24. The murder of Simon Sudbury, from 'Chroniques de France et d'Angleterre', by John Froissart: © The British Library Board
25. Skull of Archbishop Simon Sudbury: © St Gregory's Church, Sudbury
26. Roy. 18 E I f.165v Peasants' Revolt showing the banners of England and St George, John Ball shown leading the rebels, illustration from 'Chroniques de France et d'Angleterre', by John Froissart, c. 1460–80 (vellum), Netherlandish School (15th century) / British Library, London, UK / © British Library Board. All Rights Reserved / Bridgeman Images
27. Roy. 18 E I f.175 The death of Wat Tyler at Smithfield, London, in 1381 during the Peasants' Revolt, illustration from 'Chroniques de France et d'Angleterre', by John Froissart, c. 1460–80 (vellum), Netherlandish School (15th century) / British Library, London, UK / © British Library Board. All Rights Reserved / Bridgeman Images
28. Frontispiece from William Morris, *A Dream of John Ball* (1892 edition)

Endpapers: © The British Library Board